African American Humor

The Best Black Comedy from Slavery to Today

EDITED BY MEL WATKINS

FOREWORD BY DICK GREGORY

Lawrence Hill Books

Library of Congress Cataloging-in-Publication Data

African American humor : the best Black comedy from slavery to today /
edited by Mel Watkins ; foreword by Dick Gregory.
    p. cm.—(The Library of Black America)
Includes bibliographical references and index.
    ISBN 1–55652–430-7 (hardback : alk. paper)—ISBN 1-55652-431-5
(pbk.: alk. paper)
    1. African American wit and humor. 2. American prose literature—
African American authors. 3. African American proverbs. 4. African
Americans—Quotations. I. Watson, Mel. II. Gregory, Dick. III. Series.
  PN6231.N5 A37 2002
  817.008'0896073—dc21

                                     2002002895

Cover Art: Archibald Motley, Jr., *The Liar*, 1936. Courtesy of the Howard
University Gallery of Art
Jacket design by: Joan Sommers Design
Interior design by: Peirce Graphic Services

Published by Lawrence Hill Books
an imprint of Chicago Review Press, Incorporated
814 North Franklin Street
Chicago, Illinois 60610
1-55652-430-7 (cloth)
1-55652-431-5 (paper)

Printed in the United States of America
5 4 3 2 1

CONTENTS

PART TWO

Lay My Burden Down ... Emancipation to the Roaring Twenties

PART THREE

New Day's A-Coming . . . The Harlem Renaissance to the Fifties

PART FOUR

What You See Is What You Get . . . Civil Rights to the Millennium

FOREWORD

Mel Watkins's insightful chronicle of African American humor from slavery to the present is a work of brilliance. He explores the black experience of laughter in the same way a fine surgeon performs a successful operation. His work demonstrates an intelligent dedication to delivering and highlighting the contributions to the art of entertainment that people of color have made throughout history.

This work shows us the progress we have made as a people. In the time of slavery, we were identified as *things,* and when we stopped being things we became *objects*. Sixty years ago we were still considered a nonpeople, invisible in a white racist society. Sixty years ago, there was no outlet to market the type of material Mel Watkins has captured. But now this book proves that we have become human in a system that worked to keep us nonhuman. It represents yet another of the strides that we as a people have made in our struggle for equality.

African American Humor is a historic roadmap of the ways black folks embraced the art of comedy and the spoken word. Comedy was the original form of entertainment that black families created in order to survive. If we could go back to Africa before colonialism, we'd find that humor reflected joy; while in the early days of the American Negro, humor reflected pain. The various styles of black comedy have always reflected our experiences.

Mel Watkins's book reminds me of the wisdom of my momma. She would always say, "There is freedom in laughter." In a racist society, her wisdom never leaves my mind; I guess that's where I truly found *my* freedom. My first appearance at the Playboy Club in 1961 was my big break as a stand-up comic. Back in those days, many American nightclubs were owned by and/or heavily influenced by the mob, and they would not dare hire black comedians. Hugh Hefner, owner of the Playboy Club, is his own man. He has always been a leader when it comes to opening doors for black entertainers. He demonstrated great courage when he booked me at the Playboy Club with no restrictions on my act. No rules! He allowed me to be the first black comic to perform topical material in a white-owned club with an all-white audience. My performance landed me an appearance on the *Jack Paar Show* and a feature story in *Time* magazine. My first break became the first break for many black comedians nationwide.

During the mid-1900s, if you lived in New York, Chicago, or California, you might have had the privilege of seeing Negro comics every day; but if you lived in a small town—or even, as I did, in St. Louis—you didn't have the same opportunities. In St. Louis the Negro nightclubs consisted of blues singers and jazz artists—there were *no stand-up comics.* No celebrated black comedians influenced me—because there were none. Amos 'n' Andy, Rochester, and Mantan Moreland were the only black comics we heard, but nobody wanted to emulate them, including me. The only other comedians I heard were white ones on the radio. Bob Hope influenced me. I would listen to Bob Hope be a genius for that first three minutes, which were always topical, and then go into that Ma and Pa stuff. George Kirby or Bill Cosby couldn't have influenced me, because they came after me.

As the civil rights movement gained momentum in the mid-1950s, comics such as Timmie Rogers, Slappy White, and Nipsey Russell were working to integrate their audiences, attracting whites to black clubs. New York black comics were among the first to perform their stand-up acts in front of integrated audiences. But there was a difference between working an integrated audience and working a white nightclub. The white folks who owned the clubs and hired Negro comics in the mid-1950s should receive recognition, the same way we give credit to Branch Rickey for breaking the color line in baseball by signing Jackie Robinson to the Dodgers.

Our ancestors' expressions have brought laughter to our own neighborhoods in the midst of all the racism and injustice we've endured. We must understand that humor is like breathing—everyone partakes of it—but not everyone is a comedian. But there is a *big difference* between humor and comedy. One of the strongest examples of humor is found in the black church. Preachers are not comedians, but they use humor. Their job is sometimes harder than that of the comics, because you never hear them tell the same funny story twice. They have the same audience every Sunday, so they can't use the same material over and over again. A comedian is someone who makes a living telling jokes—regardless of how bad you feel or how sick you are, you have to be funny. As a comedian, you travel across the country and perform in front of a different audience every night, so a comic can use the same routine, performance after performance.

There are rules and regulations in every profession. The professional role of a comic is to make folks laugh. It is extremely important to understand that comics who have decided to be socially conscious, honest with their audiences, and without a hidden agenda are still obligated not to offend or disrespect individual patrons. I became a comic to ward off folks from laughing at me. I grew up poor. Sometimes my clothes were raggedy. One day I decided that instead of the kids laughing at me, I'd make them laugh at something else. When a comic is really good he can almost make folks without holes in their shoes or raggedy clothes feel bad. You can tell a lot of jokes quietly, but in public things change. A Rockefeller could never tell jokes about poor people in public, but a poor person can always tell jokes about rich or poor. A thin person can't tell a joke about a fat person in public, but a fat person can tell the same joke anywhere. The art of respect is extremely important in the comedic world.

Humor has always reflected its time when it comes to racism and sexism. You remember that old saying, "children should be seen and not heard"? Well, that rule also applied to women throughout history. This is the reason we've had so few women comedians, writers, and spoken-word artists. But in this book you'll encounter the work of Zora Neale Hurston, a woman who contributed source material for all black comedians. Mel Watkins honors the women who have contributed to comedy, as well as the men.

Every "actor," black or white, wants applause and recognition. Mel Watkins has provided that recognition for all who came before us, and in an elegant fashion, so that the world can applaud their artistic contributions. We must give a standing ovation to Mel for the work he has put into this book. He has done what great comics do, and provided us with a powerful presentation. I want to thank Mel, for while many of us were playing, he was working. His book is not only about a people and their comedy, but about how a people survived segregation and discrimination. We must share it with our children, and their children. Thank you, Mel: this is history at its best.

DICK GREGORY

ACKNOWLEDGMENTS

My special thanks to friends Terry Bunker and Hazel Symon for their indispensable help in preparing this manuscript, to my editor Yuval Taylor for his persistence, optimism, and timely prodding, to the writers and comics whose wit made the book possible, and to those friends whose support kept me going when I faltered.

INTRODUCTION

Negro humor is, perhaps, the most original, prolific, diverse, and entertaining humor produced by any ethnic group in this country.
—J. Mason Brewer

Humor remains one of the richest and most distinctive expressive treasures of the African American cultural heritage. It is as varied and multifaceted as black music and dance, and from its plantation and slave shanty beginnings through its evolution to a premiere attraction on television and in contemporary comedy clubs, concerts, and films it has functioned not only as a survival tactic and buffer to social inequality but also as an exuberant expression of the joy and humanity of the black folks who have created and continue to create it.

The roots of African American comedy can be traced back to African griots and an oral tradition that esteemed dramatic, colorful speech, imaginative storytelling, irony, and libelous verbal satire. Those expressive traits survived the diaspora and were perpetuated by captive black immigrants, who after arriving in America adapted them to the reality of a new language and adverse social conditions, and cleverly molded them into a uniquely American comic form.

The animal stories, rhymes, work songs, riddles, plantation sayings, jokes, and tall tales or lies that emerged from slave shanties formed the basis of America's black comic tradition. The satiric thrust of slave humor, which frequently denounced bondage and ridiculed slave masters, generally went unnoticed at the outset since, of necessity, it was either masked or delivered in tongue-in-cheek fashion. Moreover, from the 1840s to the turn of the century, when black impersonation in the form of minstrel shows became a national rage and emerged as America's most popular entertainment form, the critical, socially aware edge of slave comedy was nearly always distorted or excised by the white entertainers who mimicked blacks on stage. Still, as the examples offered in this collection illustrate, the kinship between black antebellum comedy and mainstream America's often aggressively critical and rebellious humor (which often targeted European colonial rule during the eighteenth-century struggle for American independence) was closer than most cared to admit.

Despite its lack of exposure and public misrepresentation, African American comedy remained a potent and dynamic expressive form within the black community. And during the late 1800s, despite the control and censorship of booking agents, theater owners, and publishers, isolated examples of authentic African American humor gradually began surfacing in slave narratives, animal tales like Joel Chandler Harris's Uncle Remus stories, and in the works of such black minstrel comics as Billy Kersands and Ernest Hogan.

That trend continued at the beginning of the twentieth century, when Bert Williams emerged as the nation's first black comic superstar and the first performer to consistently bring authentic black folk humor to the mainstream vaudeville stage. At about the same time, the black authors Charles W. Chesnutt and Paul Laurence Dunbar began weaving examples of folk tales and trickster humor into their writings. With the exception of works by Williams, Chesnutt, and Dunbar, however, uncensored black humor remained a scarce commodity in the public domain during the late nineteenth and early twentieth century.

Beyond the scrutiny of white America, however—on street corners and storefront porches, and in all-black barber shops, tent shows, chitlin circuit theaters, and back-alley dives—rural folk wit and innocuous gags and jokes thrived and flourished along with irreverent, often profane ballads or toasts and all manner of urban "bad nigger" vamps. That inside humor, initially told by blacks to other blacks, surfaced first in the growing body of African American folklore that collectors had begun amassing. The 1882 publication of *Uncle Remus, His Songs and His Sayings* was followed by such collections as *Negro Myths from the Georgia Coast* by Charles C. Jones (1888), *The Black Cat Club: Negro Humor and Folk-Lore* (1902), and *Plantation and Up-to-Date Humorous Negro Stories* (1905) and the raft of articles featuring stories and comic vignettes collected by folklorists that appeared in early twentieth-century "folk-lore" journals.

Many of the humorous tales collected after Emancipation revealed a side of slavery humor that had not been previously exposed in animal stories collected by Joel Chandler Harris and others. The slyly assertive behavior of slaves portrayed in the John and Ole Massa stories, for example, dispensed with the symbolic conflict between the weak but wily hare and the strong but gullible fox and directly engaged slave-master interactions—frequently portraying the trickster slave outwitting his foe. These tales candidly reflected an awareness of injustice and a seditious undertone that belied the happy-go-lucky, childlike attitude often attributed to slave humor.

Perhaps for that reason, the John tales were initially seldom printed and, according to folklorist Harry Oster, are among the "least discussed" but "most significant areas in American Negro folklore."

By the 1920s, African Americans had entered the folklore field. Arthur Huff Fauset and Zora Neale Hurston, among the first, were followed by such scholars as J. Mason Brewer, Sterling Brown, and, more recently, Darryl Cumber Dance. Their entry, according to folklorist Roger D. Abrahams, "marks the time when the story lore of Afro-Americans in the United States was collected in a manner that might place the lore in the context of the people's everyday lives." Moreover, since the relationship between audience and storyteller is crucial in any comic riff and folk tales were created for the entertainment of folks within the same community, the stories collected by blacks were likely to more closely represent authentic, in-group versions than those told to outsiders.

Zora Neale Hurston's *Mules and Men* is a case in point. Hurston grew up in Eatonville, Florida, the town to which she returned to collected material for her book. Accepted as a member of the community, she was able to not only record the folk tales but also to depict the living environment and actual circumstances in which they were related. The stories were related at "lying contests" (usually sponsored by Hurston) or other social gatherings where the jocular spirit and often satiric intent of the humor was obvious. The lore included rhymes, songs, legends, animal stories, and proverbs; and, not surprisingly, John and Ole Massa tales emerged among the folk favorites. Although virtually unknown in mainstream America, those tales would also prove a fruitful source of material for a list of black comedians ranging from Butterbeans and Susie, "Pigmeat" Markham, Tim Moore, and Moms Mabley to Redd Foxx, Dick Gregory, Flip Wilson, Richard Pryor, Steve Harvey, and Chris Rock.

Along with the more confrontational John tales, by the 1920s a genre of even more defiant, often profane urban ballads or toasts had made their appearance. The urban counterpart of rural work songs or ballads like "John Henry" and folk tales of superhuman feats by blacks, these exaggerated tributes to Stackolee, Shine, and, later, Dolemite and other "bad nigger" figures would flourish as a part of African American underground comedy throughout the century. They were forerunners of the macho attitude, bombast, and boastful, in-your-face verbal riffs that characterize so much of today's rap music.

In addition, the twenties' Harlem Renaissance witnessed the emergence of a group of black writers who enthusiastically drew on folk sources and, despite resistance to comic portrayals of blacks in literature by such cultural leaders as W. E. B. DuBois, embraced irony and satire in their works. James Weldon Johnson pointed the way when he wrote in a 1922 *New York Age* newspaper column that some aspects of the race question "were so absurd that they cannot be effectively treated except in a satirical manner."

Langston Hughes and Countee Cullen soon took up the challenge in their poetry. And in the late 1920s and early 1930s, George Schuyler, Wallace Thurman, and Rudolph Fisher published satirical novels that skewered the put-on and sham they saw on both sides of America's absurd racial posturing. Also during the 1930s, with her collected folk tales and in her fiction, Zora Neale Hurston made humor a central component in her work; and Langston Hughes emerged as one of America's foremost humorists with the novel *Not Without Laughter* and, later, with the creation of Jesse B. Simple, the streetwise Harlem wit introduced in a *Chicago Defender* column in 1943.

Outside of the black community, however, neither the ironic works of black writers nor the increasingly critical edge in the humor of comics who worked tent shows, black clubs, and chitlin circuit theaters made a significant dent in a national consciousness that primarily viewed African American comedians as simple-minded buffoons and black comedy as a testament to racial inferiority. That vision was mostly sustained through the insistently stereotyped roles offered comedians who portrayed servants and shuffling comic foils in films and on radio and early television during the 1930s, '40s, and '50s.

This collection includes examples of mainstream radio, film, and television comic performances by blacks during that era as well as samples of literary humor, classic comic routines seen in all-black venues, and the anecdotes, gibes, and jokes created and repeated in black communities. The movie performances of "Butterfly" McQueen and Stepin Fetchit, like the comedy seen in the *Amos 'n' Andy* TV show where Kingfish and Sapphire held court, were often not far removed from some genuine African American humor, which may surprise some and embarrass others. But we should remember that, as the folklorist J. Mason Brewer suggested, diversity is a cornerstone of all ethnic comedy. Black humor is principally entertainment. It varies from the innocent or pious to the boorish and profane, from caustic, socially conscious satire to buffoonish, personal defamation, and may display uplifting race pride as well as derogatory self-mockery.

McQueen's shrill histrionics, Fetchit's slack-jawed mumbling and shuffling, Kingfish's conniving, and Sapphire's over-the-top belligerence were movie and television exaggerations but, from Harlem to Watts, close approximations might have also been seen on street corners as well as in beauty parlors and barber shops where real life black folks still amused or embarrassed their friends by practicing the venerable art of "playing the fool." The problem with the period's mass media representation of black comedy was context, lack of diversity, and the near exclusive focus on that comedy's most frivolous and self-deprecatory guise.

As the civil rights movement gathered momentum in the mid-1950s, however, previously ignored, critical, and satirical aspects of African American humor became more difficult to suppress. All but the most jaded TV and film producers found it inappropriate to insist on obsequious, "Yassah, boss" caricatures while headlines depicted Southern boycotts and protests or frightened black children facing down rabid mobs in an attempt to integrate all-white schools. More than a few black comedians responded to the changing times by burying fawning, accommodationist routines and, even in integrated venues, airing edgy political and social satire that had been reserved for all-black audiences.

During the 1950s, Timmie Rogers, Slappy White, George Kirby, and Nipsey Russell were among the first black comedians to perform in primarily white clubs with a stand-up comedy act. In fact, White, who was once teamed with Redd Foxx as a comic duo, was credited as being "the father of the integrated joke" by some of his peers. And although each of these comics pioneered the use of topical humor in their acts, it was Nipsey Russell's stint at the Baby Grand in Harlem that initially drew media attention to the new breed of black social satirists. By the late 1950s, Russell was attracting a steady stream of downtown New Yorkers to Harlem with clever intellectual patter and sardonic quips like "A seat on the top deck don't mean a thing if the ship is sinking."

During that same period, the veterans Moms Mabley and Redd Foxx, whose comedy had always combined risqué sexual innuendo with political and racial gibes, were still toiling in all-black theaters and cabarets or backwater toilets—barred from most mainstream venues because of the insistently blue tone of their work. Also waiting in the wings was a group of ambitious and talented young comics that included Bill Cosby, Godfrey Cambridge, Flip Wilson, and Richard Pryor.

Surprisingly, it was the breakthrough of the lesser-known Dick Gregory that radically changed mainstream America's perception of black comedy. After a sensational debut at the Chicago Playboy Club in January 1961, Gregory quickly became a national celebrity. His cool, seemingly detached delivery and a monologue that combined street lore, topical wit, and candid observations about the escalating rights movement were perfectly suited for the times. Blacks were delighted that someone had stepped up to publicly tell it like it *was,* and whites were mesmerized by a performer who both entertained and unflinchingly articulated the grievances of a black populace which was suddenly demanding equality. The media pounced on him. A feature article in *Time* magazine was followed by appearances on the Jack Parr and David Susskind TV shows, a record contract, and bookings into the best clubs. By December 1962, a *Newsweek* story would assert: "From the moment he was booked into the Playboy Club . . . Jim Crow was dead in the joke world." Gregory had become the first African American comic superstar since Bert Williams and Stepin Fetchit.

"What a country," Gregory quipped. "Where else could I have to ride in the back of the bus, live in the worst neighborhoods, go to the worst schools, eat in the worst restaurants—and average $5,000 a week just talking about it." Perhaps more important than his own success, Gregory's ascent opened the door for many other black comedians, and, during the 1960s, veterans like Foxx and Mabley, and a group of brash young performers would take center stage. By the 1970s, in addition to records, films, and stage appearances, Foxx, Cosby, Wilson, and Pryor had each starred in their own television series—bringing their work to a national audience on a regular basis and establishing genuine black comic voices as a permanent fixture in mainstream popular culture.

African American humor had come a long way since slavery, when tricksterism, servile pretense, and playing the fool had been its only acceptable form of expression. In addition to its acceptance in mass media performance, black satire, and folklore also proliferated in literature from the 1950s to the present. Beginning with the 1952 publication of Ralph Ellison's highly acclaimed *Invisible Man,* it surfaced in serious works by such writers as Charles Wright, Chester Himes, Albert Murray, John Oliver Killens, Nikki Giovanni, Ishmael Reed, and Alice Walker as well as in the more commercial "booty call" novels that emerged in the 1990s and early twenty-first century. And with publication of the urban toasts and ballads inspired by black hustlers in the 1960s and '70s, a more scandalous, insistently antisocial vein of "bad nigger" folk humor was aired. The violence, profanity, and explicit sexuality expressed in many of these tales made the original "Shine" and "Stackolee" ballads seem benign.

By the end of the twentieth century, nearly the entire scope of African

American comedy had been explored, re-dressed, and made available to the general public in one form or another. Examples ranged from the joyous frivolity of Flip Wilson to the blasphemous mockery of urban toasts and many contemporary snaps; from the respectful wit of Bill Cosby to the ribald, hip-hop oriented burlesque of the popular cable show, *Def Comedy Jam*; and from the playful and guileless foolery of the popular "Wuzzz up" commercials to the confrontational, pointedly acerbic satire of Richard Pryor and Chris Rock.

The folk tales, poems, stories, anecdotes, routines, snaps, jokes, and celebrity quips that appear in this collection were selected on the basis of their individual merit as well as with concern for reflecting the overall diversity of African American humor. The collection therefore includes material that some prominent critics would regard as either self-derogatory "coonery" or overly explicit obscenity. While selections of this type have been restricted, it was felt that eliminating them completely would detract from the authenticity of the anthology. African American humor ridicules both those outside and those inside the ethnic group, and frequently embraces the profane. The aim of this collection is to represent all aspects of black comedy, presenting examples of both low and sophisticated humor that over the years have proven funny to all classes of black folk. To do otherwise, it was felt, would be to whitewash and distort.

The book is arranged chronologically and divided into four parts: 1– Slavery; 2–Emancipation to the early twentieth century; 3–The Harlem Renaissance to the 1950s; and 4–The civil rights movement to the present. Those divisions not only outline major historical eras in the black American experience but also set off important landmarks in the gradual mainstream emergence of black comedy.

The bulk of selections in Parts One and Two are taken from folklore and literary sources, since free expression of black humor was severely limited by prevailing social taboos during slavery, and later by the restrictions of blackface minstrel shows and black performers' second-class status in mainstream vaudeville. Much of the material from this period was written or delivered in dialect and intended to replicate the speech of ordinary black folk or, in some instances, to ridicule it. The attempt to phonetically reflect the tone and timbre of black speech in print led to some odd constructions and gratuitously skewed spellings, which are sometimes difficult to decipher. To maintain the authenticity of the humor and the period in which it originated, these selections, except where indicated, have been reprinted as they initially appeared.

The Williams and Walker and Miller and Lyles comedy teams were among the few professional performers to overcome those early restrictions and provide a glimpse of authentic African American comedy. Still, as stated earlier, the folk humor created by slaves and freed blacks before the 1920s remains one of African America's richest and most memorable comedy resources. Browsing through that material, the astute reader will quickly realize that the trickster motif which dominated that humor has frequently resurfaced (often verbatim) in the work of the best black comedians. This is particularly evident in the works of Redd Foxx, Flip Wilson, and Richard Pryor.

Part Three, which surveys the period between the 1920s and the beginning of the civil rights movement, is represented by a more diverse selection of comedy. The image of African American humor was revitalized when many Harlem Renaissance writers embraced and celebrated the black comic spirit in their works. And the upsurge of urban folk tales, with their irreverent, militantly aggressive heroes, not only foreshadowed the attitude that fueled the 1970s Black Power movement but also directly influenced the macho stance and attitude heralded in today's rap music.

During those same years, the mainstream media flooded the silver screen and the airways with highly skewed versions of comic black folks. They included characters like Rastus, Sambo, Amos 'n' Andy, Birmingham, and the irrepressible Sapphire, portrayed on radio by whites and in movies by black stars like Stepin Fetchit, Willie Best, Hattie McDaniel, and Mantan Moreland. In all-black clubs, tent shows, and theaters like the Apollo that catered to mostly black audiences, however, it was a golden age for generally frivolous but more authentic, classic comedy skits fashioned for blacks and created by notables like Stump and Stumpy, Tim Moore, "Pigmeat" Markham, Dusty Fletcher, and Moms Mabley.

Part Four focuses on the comedy that emerged from the onset of the civil rights movement to the present. This period, of course, represents the freest expression of black humor. In literature and movies as well as on radio, television, and stage, African American humor was unleashed with virtually no restraints. And from the clever stand-up comic pioneers who revamped the traditional stereotyped role that black comedians had played in integrated settings to today's boundless outpouring of black humor, African Americans have produced a galaxy of humorous work equaling or surpassing that of any other group.

As this collection demonstrates, the modern era of African American humor is studded with the works of brilliant, innovative comedians and writers. They range from the contributions of Dick Gregory, Ishmael Reed, Bill

Cosby, and Chester Himes to those of present-day superstars like Martin Lawrence and Chris Rock. Still, the accomplishments of Richard Pryor loom so large that his ultimate influence overshadows all others'. His diverse comic repertoire reflected nearly every aspect of the black humor tradition—from rural and urban folklore to mime, burlesque, and cutting edge social and political satire—and his work in films, concerts, and television had an indelible effect on the face of comedy in each of those mediums. More than any other comedian, Pryor displayed the wit, depth, irreverence, and humanity of African American comedy in all of its diversity.

Comedy is always a reflection of the time in which it was created, so readers should be mindful of the social circumstances that prevailed when individual selections in this volume first appeared. A slave or sharecropper's language and view of the world is obviously totally different than that of a twenty-first century urban apartment dweller. In that regard, taken as a whole, this collection indirectly documents the mindset and social condition of the African American community at various stages of its long struggle for freedom and social equality.

Finally, however, each of the comic tales, quips, anecdotes, and routines assembled was selected on its own comic merit within the context of the particular category of humor that it represents. It has, of course, also been shaped by the editor's taste and, to some degree, by the accessibility of certain material. The absence of humorous modern poetry and examples of comic rap lyrics, for instance, is primarily a consequence of cost. And regrettably, we were unable to obtain permission to reprint routines by some major comedians.

African American Humor: The Best Black Comedy is intended as a compendium or treasure chest that includes the funniest and most memorable examples of African American comic expression. And it is hoped that looking back—either browsing through or following the trail of black comedy from its plantation roots to the present—will both illuminate and amuse. Laughter, after all, is said to be a safety device that allows us to persevere, survive, and, even in the most stressful moments, express both our humanity and love of life. With that in mind, this collection is offered as a joyful celebration of the comic spirit that has sustained African Americans since their arrival in the Americas.

PART ONE

PLAYIN' THE FOOL . . . SLAVERY

*Got one mind for white folks to see
'Nother for what I know is me.*
                                        —Folk

A cheerful smile, humble demeanor, and the ability to make slave owners laugh were highly esteemed traits among the Africans brought to
America as slaves. The former slave and abolitionist leader Frederick Douglass suggested as much and the sociologist Charles S. Johnson supported
the claim when he wrote: "A master, unless he was utterly humorless, could
not overwork or brutally treat a jolly fellow, one who could make him laugh."
It is not surprising, then, that in order to ease the rigors of plantation life
many slaves displayed a seemingly happy-go-lucky attitude. But, as another
observer pointed out, "calculated cunning and deceit" are "the first line of
defense for any vanquished" people. To a great extent, those observations
explain the form and indirect nature of most black humor during slavery.

The common theme found in the animal and trickster tales, proverbs,
rhymes, riddles, and songs of black slaves was irony—the subtle use of language to express the opposite of its usual meaning. Even though they
spoke in broken English, a new language which they were forbidden to
read, irony was not foreign to those forced African immigrants since they
had come from oral cultures where clever speech was highly regarded.
And since rebellion was nearly always futile or fatal, "playin' the fool" or
"puttin' on massa" became staple techniques for surviving and even maintaining some semblance of self-respect.

Since few Americans were interested in recording or collecting slave folk
tales before Emancipation, and even fewer slaves would have risked relating those tales to outsiders, nearly all examples of the period's humor were

1

assembled after slaves had been freed. The animal tales collected by Joel
Chandler Harris, a white journalist, are exceptions. As a teenager, Harris had
lived on a Georgia plantation and had overheard and noted stories related
by slaves. The publication of *Uncle Remus, His Songs and His Sayings* in
1880–although somewhat distorted by the fictitious "faithful darky" nar-
rator, Uncle Remus–remains a crucial development in the preservation of
black folk humor. Many of those tales portrayed slaves in the symbolic
guise of the mischievous and cunning Brer Rabbit and cast slave owners in
the role of the gullible and villainous Brer Fox who, although stronger, was
nearly always outwitted. These animal stories, however, were only the tip
of a much larger body of trickster tales.

In the late nineteenth and early twentieth centuries, a more substantial
body of this work was discovered; those later tales included the John and
Ole Massa or Ole Marster stories, which, discarding the animal guise, depicted interactions between the cunning slave John and Ole Massa, who like
Brer Fox was continually outsmarted and bamboozled by John. The John and
Ole Massa tales have been called one of "the least discussed" and "most significant areas" in African American humor by some folklorists. There are
many reasons for the designation, one being that the stories included some
of the first examples of black humor that directly targeted and identified
whites as the butt of the joke. Unlike slave animal stories, which might have
been repeated in the presence of whites, most of these tales would have been
strictly reserved for black listeners and confined to slave quarters. Those
tales are included in Part One of this collection along with examples of playful, sometimes childlike riddles, songs, and proverbs; so-called "numskull"
tales, which portray inept or foolish blacks; and fictional accounts of slave
life written by black writers after the fact. Taken together, these examples illustrate that, while much slave folk humor had an ironic, bitter edge, its pri-
mary goal was amusement, entertainment, and a good hearty life–all the
better if it was at the expense of a cruel or boneheaded master.

◎◎

PROVERBS

PLANTATION PROVERBS

From *Uncle Remus, His Songs and His Sayings*
By Joel Chandler Harris

- Big possum climb little tree.
- Dem what eats can say grace.

- Old man Know-All died last year.
- Better the gravy dan no 'tall.
- Lazy folks' stomachs don't git tired.
- Rheumatizm don't hep at de log-rollin'.
- Mole don't see what his neighbor doin'.
- Save de pacin' march fer Sunday.
- It don't rain eve'y time de pig squeal.
- Crow an' corn can't grow in de same fiel'.
- Tattlin' woman can't make de bread rise.
- Rails split 'fo' breakfast'll season de dinner.
- Ef you want ter see yo' own sins, clean up a new groun'.
- Hog don't know w'ich part a 'im'll season de turnip salad.
- It's a blessin' de white sow don't shake de plum tree.
- Mighty po' bee dat don't make mo' honey dan he want.
- Pigs don know what a pen's fo'.
- Possum's tail good as a paw.
- Dogs don't bite at de front gate.
- Colt in de barley patch kick high.
- Jaybird don't rob his own nest.
- Pullet can't roost too high for de owl.
- Meat fried 'fo' day won't last till night.
- De howlin' dog know what he sees.
- Blind hoss don't fall w'en he follers de bit.
- Hongry nigger won't w'ar his maul out.
- Don't fling away de empty wallet.
- Blacksnake know de way ter de hen's nest.
- Looks won't do ter split rails wid.
- Settin' hens don't hanker after fresh eggs.
- Tater-vine growin' while you sleep.
- Hit take two birds fer to make a nest.
- Tarrypin walk fast 'nuff fer to go visitin'.
- Empty smokehouse makes de pullet holler.
- W'en coon take water he fixin' fer ter fight.
- Corn make mo' at de mill dan it does in de crib.
- Good luck say: "Open yo' mouf en shet you' eyes."
- Nigger dat gets hurt wukkin' oughter show de skyars.
- Fiddlin' nigger say hit's long ways ter de dance.
- Rooster makes mo' racket dan de hen w'at lays de egg.
- Meller mushmelon hollers at you fum over de fence.
- Nigger wid a pocket-han'kcher better be looked after.

- Rain crow don't sing no tune, but you can 'pend on 'im.
- One-eyed mule can't be handled on de blin' side.
- Moon may shine, but a lightered knot's mighty handy.
- Licker talks mighty loud w'en it git loose fum de jug.
- De proudness of a man don't count w'en his head's cold.
- Hongry rooster don't cackle w'en he fine a woman.
- Some niggers mighty smart, but dey can't drive de pidgins ter roost.
- You may know de way, but better keep yo' eyes on de seven stairs.
- All de buzzards in de settlement'll come to de gray mule's funeral.
- You can hide de fire, but w'at you gwine do wid de smoke?
- T'morrow may be de carridge-driver's day fer ploughin'.
- Hit's a mighty deaf nigger dat don't 'ear de dinner-ho'n.
- Hit takes a bee fer ter git de sweetness out'n de hoar-houn' blossom.
- Ha'nts don't bodder longer honest folks, but you better go 'roun' de graveyard.
- De pig dat runs off wid de year er corn gits little mo' dan de cob.
- Sleepin' in de fence-corner don't fetch Christmas in de kitchen.
- De springhouse may freeze, but de niggers'll keep de shuck-pen warm.
- Don't 'spute wid de squinch-owl. Jam de shovel in de fire.
- You'd see mo'er de mink ef he know'd whar de yard dog sleeps.
- Troubles is seasonin'. 'Simmons ain't good till dey'er fros'-bit.
- Watch out w'en yo'er gittin' all you want. Fattenin' hogs ain't in luck.

SOME NEW PROVERBS

From *Brother Gardner's Lime-Kiln Club*
By M. Quad

- Don' drop fifty cents reachin' for a dollar.
- When you can't dig froo a wall climb over it.
- You can't swim a ribber by settin' on a bank.
- If de road am up-hill, stiffen yer backbone a little mo'.
- Hoe co'n wid yer han's an' arms 'stead of yer mouf.
- Take a job at fust sight, but don' trade hosses till yer think it ober.

ANIMAL TALES AND RHYMES

Selections from *Uncle Remus, His Songs and His Sayings*
By Joel Chandler Harris

UNCLE REMUS INITIATES THE LITTLE BOY

One evening recently, the lady whom Uncle Remus calls "Miss Sally" missed her little seven-year-old. Making search for him through the house and through the yard, she heard the sound of voices in the old man's cabin, and, looking through the window, saw the child sitting by Uncle Remus. His head rested against the old man's arm, and he was gazing with an expression of the most intense interest into the rough, weather-beaten face, that beamed so kindly upon him. This is what "Miss Sally" heard:

"Bimeby, one day, arter Brer Fox bin doin' all dat he could for ter ketch Brer Rabbit, en Brer Rabbit bin doin' all he could fer ter keep 'im fum it, Brer Fox say to hisse'f dat he'd put up a game on Brer Rabbit, en he ain't mo'n got de wuds out'n his mouf twel Brer Rabbit come a lopin' up de big road, lookin' des ez plump, en ez fat, en ez sassy ez a Moggin hoss in a barley-patch.

"'Hol' on dar, Brer Rabbit,' sez Brer Fox, sezee.

"'I ain't got time, Brer Fox,' sez Brer Rabbit, sezee, sorter mendin' his licks.

"'I wanter have some confab wid you, Brer Rabbit, sez Brer Fox, sezee.

"'All right, Brer Fox, but you better holler fum whar you stan'. I'm monstus full er fleas dis mawnin',' sez Brer Rabbit, sezee.

"'I seed Brer B'ar yistiddy,' sez Brer Fox, sezee, 'en he sorter rake me over de coals kaze you en me ain't make frens en live naberly, en I tole 'im dat I'd see you.'

"Den Brer Rabbit scratch one year wid his off hinefoot sorter jub'usly, en den he ups en sez, sezee:

"'All a setting', Brer Fox. Spose'n you drap roun' termorrer en take dinner wid me. We ain't got no great doin's at our house, but I speck de ole 'oman en de chilluns kin sorter scramble roun' en git up sump'n fer ter stay yo' stummuck.' "'I'm 'gree'ble, Brer Rabbit,' sez Brer Fox, sezee.

"'Den I'll 'pen' on you,' sez Brer Rabbit, sezee.

"Next day, Mr. Rabbit an' Miss Rabbit got up soon, 'fo' day, en got some cabbiges, en some roas'n years, en some sparrer-grass, en dey fix up a smashin' dinner. Bimeby one er de litel Rabbits, playin' out in de back-yard, come runnin' in hollerin', 'Oh, ma! oh, ma! I seed Mr. Fox a comin'!' En den Brer Rabbit he tuck de chilluns by der years en make um set down, en den him en Miss Rabbit sorter dally roun' waitin' for Brer Fox. En dey keep on waitin', but no Brer Fox ain't come. Atter 'while Brer Rabbit goes to de do', easy like, en peep out, en dar, stickin' out fum behime de cornder, wuz de tip-een' er Brer Fox tail. Den Brer Rabbit shot de do' en sot down, en put his paws behime his years en begin for ter sing:

"'De place wharbouts you spill de grease,
Right dar youer boun' ter slide,
An' whar you fine a bunch er ha'r,
You sholy fine de hide.'

"Nex' day, Brer Fox sont word by Mr. Mink, en skuze hisse'f kaze he wuz too sick fer ter come, en he ax Brer Rabbit fer ter come en take dinner wid him, en Brer Rabbit say he wuz 'gree'ble.

"Bimeby, w'en de shadders wuz at der shortes', Brer Rabbit he sorter brush up en santer down ter Brer Fox's house, en w'en he got dar, he yer somebody groanin', en he look in de do' en dar he see Brer Fox settin' up in a rockin' cheer all wrop up wid flannil, en he look mighty weak. Brer Rabbit look all 'roun, he did, but he ain't see no dinner. De dish-pan wuz settin' on de table, en close by wuz a kyarvin' knife.

"'Look like you gwinder have a chicken fer dinner, Brer Fox,' sez Brer Rabbit, sezee.

"'Yes, Brer Rabbit, deyer nice, en fresh, en tender,' sez Brer Fox, sezee.

"Den Brer Rabbit sorter pull his mustarsh, en say: 'You ain't got no calamus root, is you, Brer Fox? I done got so now dat I can't eat no chicken 'ceptin' she's seasoned up wid calamus root.' En wid dat Brer Rabbit lipt out er de do' and dodge 'mong de bushes, en sot dar watchin' fer Brer Fox; en he ain't watch long, nudder, kaze Brer Fox flung off de flannil en crope out er de house en got whar he could cloze in on Brer Rabbit, en bimeby Brer Rabbit holler out: 'Oh, Brer Fox! I'll des put yo' calamus root out yer on dish yer stump. Better come git it while hit's fresh,' and wid dat Brer Rabbit gallop off home. En Brer Fox ain't never kotch 'im yit, en w'at's mo', honey, he ain't gwineter."

THE WONDERFUL TAR-BABY STORY

"Didn't the fox *never* catch the rabbit, Uncle Remus?" asked the little boy the next evening.

"He come mighty nigh it, honey, sho's you bawn—Brer Fox did. One day after Brer Rabbit fool 'im wid dat calamus root, Brer Fox went ter wuk en got 'im some tar, en mix it wid some turkentime, en fix up a contrapshun wat he call a Tar-Baby, en he tuck dis yer Tar-Baby en he sot 'er in de big road, en den he lay off in de bushes fer ter see wat de news wuz gwineter be. En he didn't hatter wait long, nudder, kaze bimeby here come Brer Rabbit pacin' down de road—lippity-clippity, clippity-lippity—dez ez sassy ez a jay-bird. Brer Fox, he lay low. Brer Rabbit come prancin' 'long twel he spy de Tar-Baby, en den he fotch up on behime legs like he wuz 'stonished. De Tar-baby, she sot dar, she did, en Brer Fox, he lay low.

"'Mawnin'!' sez Brer Rabbit, sezee—'Nice wedder dis mawnin',' sezee.

"Tar-Baby ain't sayin' nuthin', en Brer Fox, he lay low.

"'How does yo' sym'tums seem ter segashuate?' sez Brer Rabbit, sezee.

"Brer Fox, he wink his eye slow, en lay low, en de Tar-Baby, she ain't sayin' nuthin'.

"'How you come on, den? Is you deaf?' sez Brer Rabbit, sezee. 'Kaze if you is, I kin holler louder,' sezee.

"Tar-Baby stay still, en Brer Fox, he lay low.

"'Youer stuck up, dat's w'at you is,' says Brer Rabbit, sezee, 'en I'm gwineter kyore you, dat's w'at I'm gwineter do,' sezee.

"Brer Fox, he sorter chuckle in his stummuck, he did, but Tar Baby ain't sayin' nuthin'.

"'I'm gwineter larn you howter talk ter 'specttubble fokes ef hit's de las' ack,' sez Brer Rabbit, sezee. "Ef you don't take off dat hat en tell me howdy, I'm gwineter bus' you wide open,' sezee.

"Tar-Baby stay still, en Brer Fox, he lay low.

"Brer Rabbit keep on axin' 'im, en de Tar-Baby, she keep on sayin' nuthin', twel presently Brer Rabbit draw back wid his fis', he did, en blip he tuck 'er side er de head. Right dar's whar he broke his merlasses jug. His fis' stuck, en can't pull loose. De tar hilt 'im. But Tar-Baby, she stay still, en Brer Fox, he lay low.

"'Ef you don't lemme loose, I'll knock you agin,' sez Brer Rabbit, sezee, en wid dat he fotch 'er a wipe wid de udder han', en dat stuck. Tar-Baby, she ain't sayin' nuthin', en Brer Fox, he lay low.

"'Tu'n me loose, fo' I kick de natal stuffin' outen you,' sez Brer Rabbit, sezee, but de Tar-Baby, she ain't sayin' nuthin'. She des hilt on, en den Brer Rabbit lose de use er his feet in de same way. Brer Fox, he lay low. Den Brer Rabbit squall out dat ef de Tar-Baby don't tu'n 'im loose he butt 'er cranksided. En den he butted, en his head got stuck. Den Brer Fox, he sa'ntered fort', lookin' des ez innercent ez wunner yo' mammy's mockin'-birds.

"'Howdy, Brer Rabbit,' sez Brer Fox, sezee. 'You look sorter stuck up dis mawnin',' sezee, en den he rolled on de groun', en laft en laft twel he could-n't laff no mo'. 'I speck you'll take a dinner wid me dis time, Brer Rabbit. I done laid in some calamus root, en I ain't gwineter take no skuse,' sez Brer Fox, sezee."

Here Uncle Remus paused, and drew a two-pound yam out of the ashes.

"Did the fox eat the rabbit?" asked the little boy to whom the story had been told.

"Dat's all de fur de tale goes," replied the old man. "He mout, en den agin he moutent. Some say Jedge B'ar come 'long en loosed 'im—some say he didn't. I hear Miss Sally callin'. You better run 'long."

WHY MR. POSSUM LOVES PEACE

"One night," said Uncle Remus—taking Miss Sally's little boy on his knee, and stroking the child's hair thoughtfully and caressingly—"one night Brer Possum call by fer Brer Coon, 'cordin' ter 'greement, en atter gobblin' up a dish er fried greens en smokin' a seegyar, dey rambled fort' fer ter see how de ballunce er de settlement wuz gittin' 'long. Brer Coon, he wuz wunner deze yer natchul pacers, en he racked 'long same ez Mars John's bay pony, en Brer Possum he went in a han'-gallup; en dey got over heap er groun', mon. Brer Possum, he got his belly full er 'simmons, en Brer Coon, he scoop up a 'bunnunce er frogs en tadpoles. Dey amble 'long, dey did, des ez soshubble ez a baskit er kittens, twel bimeby dey hear Mr. Dog talkin' ter hisse'f way off in de woods.

"'Spozen he runs up on us, Brer Possum, w'at you gwineter do?' sezee. Brer Possum sorter laff 'round de cornders un his mouf.

"'Oh, ef he come, Brer Coon, I'm gwineter stan' by you,' sez Brer Possum. 'What you gwineter do?' sezee.

"'Who? me?' sez Brer Coon, 'Ef he run up onter me, I lay I give 'im one twis',' sezee."

"Did the dog come?" asked the little boy.

"Go 'way, honey!" responded the old man, in an impressive tone. "Go way! Mr. Dog, he come en he come a zoonin'. En he ain't wait fer ter say howdy, nudder. He des sail inter de two un um. De ve'y fus pas he make Brer Possum fetch a grin fum year ter year, en keel over like he wuz dead. Den Mr. Dog, he sail inter Brer Coon, en right dar's whar he drap his munnypus, kaze Brer Coon was cut out fer dat kinder bizness, en he fa'rly wipe up de face er de earf wid 'im. You better b'leeve dat w'en Mr. Dog got a chance to make hisse'f skase he tuck it, en w'at der wuz lef' un him went skaddlin' thoo de woods like hit wuz shot outen a muskit. En Brer Coon, he sorter lick his cloze inter shape en rack off, en Brer Possum, he lay dar like he wuz dead, twel bimeby he raise up sotter keerful like, en w'en he fine de coas' cle'r he scramble up en scamper off like sumpin was atter 'im."

Here Uncle Remus paused long enough to pick up a live coal of fire in his fingers, transfer it to the palm of his hand, and thence to his clay pipe, which he had been filling—a proceeding that was viewed by the little boy with undisguised admiration. The old man then proceeded:

"Nex' time Brer Possum meet Brer Coon, Brer Coon 'fuse ter 'spon' ter his howdy, en dis make Brer Possum feel mighty bad, seein' ez dey user make so many 'scurshuns tergedder.

"'W'at make you hol' yo' head so high, Brer Coon?' sez Brer Possum, sezee.

"'I ain't runnin' wid cowerds deze days,' sez Brer Coon. 'W'en I wants you I'll sen' fer you,' sezee.

"Den Brer Possum git mighty mad.

"'Who's enny cowerd,' sezee.

"'You is,' sez Brer Coon, 'dat's who. I ain't soshatin' wid dem w'at lies down on de groun' en plays dead w'en dar's a free fight gwine on,' sezee.

"Den Brer Possum grin en laff fit to kill hisse'f.

"'Lor', Brer Coon, you don't speck I done dat kaze I wuz 'feared, duz you?' sezee. 'Why I want no mo' skeered dan you is dis minnit. W'at wuz dey fer ter be skeered un?' sezee. 'I know'd you'd git away wid Mr. Dog ef I didn't, en I des lay dar watchin' you shake him, waitin' fer ter put in w'en de time come,' sezee.

"Brer Coon tu'n up his nose.

"'Dat's a mighty likely tale,' sezee, 'w'en Mr. Dog ain't mo'n tech you 'fo' you keel over, en lay dar stiff,' sezee.

"'Dat's des w'at I wuz gwineter tell you 'bout,' sez Brer Possum, sezee. 'I want no mo' skeer'd dan you is right now, en I wuz fixin' fer ter give Mr. Dog a sample er my jaw,' sezee, 'but I'm de most ticklish chap w'at you ever laid eyes on, en no sooner did Mr. Dog put his nose down yer 'mong my ribs dan I got ter laffin, en I laft twel I ain't had no use er my lim's,' sezee, 'en it's a mussy unto Mr. Dog dat I wuz ticklish, kaze a little mo' en I'd e't 'im up,' sezee. 'I don't mine fightin', Brer Coon, no mo' dan you duz,' sezee, 'but I declar' ter grashus ef I kin stan' ticklin'. Git me in a row whar dey ain't no ticklin' 'lowed, en I'm your man,' sezee.

"En down ter dis day"—continued Uncle Remus, watching the smoke from his pipe curl upward over the little boy's head—"down ter dis day, Brer

Possum's bound ter s'render w'en you tech him in de short ribs, en he'll laff ef he knows he's gwineter be smashed for it."

HOW MR. RABBIT WAS TOO SHARP FOR MR. FOX

"Uncle Remus," said the little boy one evening, when he had found the old man with little or nothing to do, "did the fox kill and eat the rabbit when he caught him with the Tar-Baby?"

"Law, honey, ain't I tell you 'bout dat?" replied the old darky, chuckling slyly. "I 'clar ter grashus I ought er tole you dat, but ole man Nod wuz ridin' on my eyeleds 'twel a leetle mo'n I'd a dis'member'd my own name, en den on to dat here come yo' mammy hollerin' atter you.

"W'at I tell you w'en I fus' begin? I tole you Brer Rabbit wuz a monstus soon beas'; leas'ways dat's w'at I laid out fer to ter tell you. Well, den, honey, don't you go en make no udder kalkalashuns, kaze in dem days Brer Rabbit en his fambly wuz at de head er de gang w'en enny racket wuz on han', en dar dey stayed. 'Fo' you begins fer ter wipe yo' eyes 'bout Brer Rabbit, you wait en see whar'bouts Brer Rabbit gwineter fetch up at. But dat's needer yer ner dar.

"W'en Brer Fox fine Brer Rabbit mixt up wid de Tar-Baby, he feel mighty good, en he roll on de groun' en laff. Bimeby he up'n say, sezee:

"'Well, I speck I got you dis time, Brer Rabbit,' sezee; 'Maybe I ain't, but I speck I is. You been runnin' roun' here sassin' atter me a mighty long time, but I speck you done come ter de een' er de row. You bin cuttin' up yo' capers en bouncin' 'roun' in dis naberhood ontwel you come ter b'leeve yo'se'f de boss er de whole gang. En den youer allers some'rs whar you got no bizness,' sez Brer Fox, sezee. 'Who ax you fer ter come en strike up a 'quaintence wid dish yer Tar-Baby? En who stuck you up dar whar you is? Nobody in de roun' worril. You des tuck en jam yo'se'f on dat Tar-Baby widout waitin' fer enny invite,' sez Brer Fox, sezee, 'en dar you is, en dar you'll stay twel I fixes up a bresh-pile and fires her up, kaze I'm gwineter bobby-cue you dis day, sho,' sez Brer Fox, sezee.

"Den Brer Rabbit talk mighty 'umble.

"'I don't keer w'at you do wid me, Brer Fox,' sez Brer Rabbit, sezee, 'so you don't fling me in dat brier-patch. Roas' me, Brer Fox,' sezee, 'but don't fling me in dat brier-patch,' sezee.

"'Hit's so much trouble fer ter kindle a fier,' sez Brer Fox, sezee, 'dat I speck I'll hatter hang you,' sezee.

"'Hang me des ez high as you please, Brer Fox,' sez Brer Rabbit, sezee, 'but do fer de Lord's sake don't fling me in dat brier-patch,' sezee.

"'I ain't got no string,' sez Brer Fox, sezee, 'en now I speck I'll hatter drown you,' sezee.

"'Drown me des ez deep ez you please, Brer Fox,' sez Brer Rabbit, sezee, 'but do don't fling me in dat brier-patch,' sezee.

"'Dey ain't no water nigh,' sez Brer Fox, sezee, 'en now I speck I'll hatter skin you,' sezee.

"'Skin me, Brer Fox,' sez Brer Rabbit, sezee, 'snatch out my eyeballs, t'ar out my years by de roots, en cut off my legs,' sezee, 'but do please, Brer Fox, don't fling me in dat brier-patch,' sezee.

"Co'se Brer Fox wanter hurt Brer Rabbit bad ez he kin, so he cotch 'im by de behime legs en slung 'im right in de middle er de brier-patch. Dar wuz a considerbul flutter whar Brer Rabbit struck de bushes, en Brer Fox sorter hang 'roun' fer ter see w'at wuz gwineter happen. Bimeby he hear somebody call 'im, en way up de hill he see Brer Rabbit settin' cross-legged on a chinkapin log koamin' de pitch outen his har wid a chip. Den Brer Fox know dat he bin swop off mighty bad. Brer Rabbit wuz bleedzed fer ter fling back some er his sass, en he holler out:

"'Bred en bawn in a brier-patch, Brer Fox—bred en bawn in a brier-patch!' en wid dat he slip out des ez lively ez a cricket in de embers."

MR. RABBIT GROSSLY DECEIVES MR. FOX

One evening when the little boy, whose nights with Uncle Remus are as entertaining as those Arabian ones of blessed memory, had finished supper and hurried out to sit with his venerable patron, he found the old man in great glee. Indeed, Uncle Remus was talking and laughing to himself at such a rate the little boy was afraid he had company. The truth is, Uncle Remus had heard the child coming, and, when the rosy-cheeked chap put his head in at the door, was engaged in a monologue, the burden of which seemed to be—

> "Ole Molly Har',
> W'at you doin' dar,
> Settin' in de cornder
> Smokin' yo' seegyar?"

As a matter of course this vague allusion reminded the little boy of the fact that the wicked Fox was still in pursuit of the Rabbit, and he immediately put his curiosity in the shape of a question.

"Uncle Remus, did the Rabbit have to go clean away when he got loose from the Tar-Baby?"

"Bless grashus, honey, dat he didn't. Who? Him? You dunno nuthin' 'tall 'bout Brer Rabbit ef dat's de way you puttin' 'im down. W'at he gwine 'way fer? He mouter stayed sorter close twel de pitch rub off'n his ha'r, but twern't menny days 'fo he wuz lopin' up en down de naberhood same ez ever, en I dunno ef he wern't mo' sassier dan befo'.

"Seem like dat de tale 'bout how he got mix up wid de Tar-Baby got 'roun' 'mongst de nabers. Leas'ways, Miss Meadows en de gals got win' un' it, en de nex' time Brer Rabbit paid um a visit Miss Meadows tackled 'im 'bout it, en de gals sot up a monstus gigglement. Brer Rabbit, he sot up des ez cool ez a cowcumber, he did, en let 'em run on."

"Who was Miss Meadows, Uncle Remus?" inquired the little boy.

"Don't ax me, honey. She wuz in de tale, Miss Meadows en de gals wuz, en de tale I give you like hi't wer' gun ter me. Brer Rabbit, he sot dar, he did, sorter lam' like, en den bimeby he cross his legs, he did, and wink his eye slow, en up en say, sezee:

"'Ladies, Brer Fox wuz my daddy's ridin'-hoss fer thirty year, maybe mo', but thirty year dat I knows un,' sezee; en den he paid um his 'specks, en tip his beaver, en march off, he did, des ez stiff en ez stuck up ez a fire-stick.

"Nex' day, Brer Fox cum a callin', and w'en he gun ter laff 'bout Brer Rabbit, Miss Meadows en de gals, dey ups en tells 'im 'bout w'at Brer Rabbit say. Den Brer Fox grit his toof sho' nuff, he did, en he look mighty dumpy, but w'en he riz fer ter go he up en say, sezee:

"'Ladies, I ain't 'sputin' w'at you say, but I'll make Brer Rabbit chaw up his words en spit um out right yer whar you kin see 'im,' sezee, en wid dat off Brer Fox marcht.

"En w'en he got in de big road, he shuck de dew off'n his tail, en made a straight shoot fer Brer Rabbit's house. W'en he got dar, Brer Rabbit wuz spectin' un 'im, en de do' wuz shet fas'. Brer Fox knock. Nobody ain't ans'er. Brer Fox knock. Nobody ans'er. Den he knock agin—blam! blam! Den Brer Rabbit holler out mighty weak:

"'Is dat you, Brer Fox? I want you ter run en fetch de doctor. Dat bait er pusly w'at I e't dis mawnin' is gittin' 'way wid me. Do, please, Brer Fox, run quick,' sez Brer Rabbit, sezee.

"'I come atter you, Brer Rabbit,' sez Brer Fox, sezee. 'Dere's gwineter be a party up at Miss Meadow's,' sezee. 'All de gals 'll be dere, en I promus' dat I'd fetch you. De gals, dey 'lowed dat hit wouldn't be no party 'ceppin' I fotch you,' sez Brer Fox, sezee.

"Den Brer Rabbit say he wuz too sick, en Brer Fox say he wuzzent, en dar dey had it up and down, 'sputin' en contendin'. Brer Rabbit say he can't walk. Brer Fox say he tote 'im. Brer Rabbit say how? Brer Fox say in his arms. Brer Rabbit say he drap 'im. Brer Fox 'low he won't. Bimeby Brer Rabbit say he can't ride widout a saddle. Brer Fox say he git de saddle. Brer Rabbit say he can't set in saddle less he have a bridle fer ter hol' by. Brer Fox say he git bridle. Brer Rabbit say he can't ride widout bline bridle, kaze Brer Fox be shyin' at stumps 'long de road, en fling 'im off. Brer Fox say he git bline bridle. Den Brer Rabbit say he go. Den Brer Fox say he ride Brer Rabbit mos' up ter Miss Meadow's, en den he could git down en walk de balance er de way. Brer Rabbit's 'greed, en den Brer Fox lipt out atter de saddle en de bridle.

"Co'se Brer Rabbit know de game dat Brer Fox wuz fixin' fer ter play, en he 'termin' fer ter outdo 'im, en by de time he koam his ha'r en twis' his mustarsh, en sorter rig up, yer come Brer Fox, saddle en bridle on, en lookin' ez peart ez a circus pony. He trot up ter de do' en stan' dar pawin' de ground en chompin' de bit same like sho 'nuff hoss, en Brer Rabbit he mount, he did, en dey amble off. Brer Fox can't see behime wid bline bridle on, but bimeby he feel Brer Rabbit raise one er his foots.

" 'W'at you doin' now, Brer Rabbit?' sezee.

" 'Short'nin' de lef stir'p, Brer Fox,' sezee.

"Bimeby Brer Rabbit raise up de udder foot.

" 'W'at you doin' now, Brer Rabbit?' sezee.

" 'Pullin' down my pants, Brer Fox,' sezee.

"All de time, bless grashus, honey, Brer Rabbit wer puttin' on his spurrers, en w'en dey got close to Miss Meadows's, whar Brer Rabbit wuz to git off, en Brer Fox made a motion fer ter stan' still, Brer Rabbit slap de spurrers inter Brer Fox's flanks, en you better b'leeve he got over groun'. W'en dey got ter de house, Miss Meadows en all de gals wuz settin' on de peazzer, en stidder stoppin' at de gate, Brer Rabbit rid on by, he did, en den come gallopin' down de road en up ter de hoss-rack, w'ich he hitch Brer Fox at, en den he santer inter de house, he did, en shake han's wid de gals, en set dar, smokin' his seegyar same ez a town man. Bimeby he draw in long puff, en den let hit out in a cloud, en squar hisse'f back en holler out, he did:

" 'Ladies, ain't I done tell you Brer Fox wuz de ridin'-hoss fer our fambly? He sorter losin' his gait' now, but I speck I kin fetch 'im all right in a mont' er so,' sezee.

"En den Brer Rabbit sorter grin, he did, en de gals giggle, en Miss Meadows, she praise up de pony, en dar wuz Brer Fox hitch fas' ter de rack, en couldn't he'p hisse'f."

"Is that all, Uncle Remus?" asked the little boy as the old man paused.

"Dat ain't all, honey, but 'twon't do fer ter give out too much cloff fer ter cut one pa'r pants," replied the old man sententiously.

MR. FOX IS AGAIN VICTIMIZED

When "Miss Sally's" little boy went to Uncle Remus the next night to hear the conclusion of the adventure in which the Rabbit made a riding-horse of the Fox to the great enjoyment and gratification of Miss Meadows and the girls, he found the old man in a bad humor.

"I ain't tellin' no tales ter bad chilluns," said Uncle Remus curtly.

"But, Uncle Remus, I ain't bad," said the little boy plaintively.

"Who dat chunkin' dem chickens dis mawnin'? Who dat knockin' out foke's eyes wid dat Yallerbammer sling des 'fo' dinner? Who dat sickin' dat pinter puppy atter my pig? Who dat scatterin' my ingun sets? Who dat flingin' rocks on top er my house, w'ich a little mo' en one un em would er drap spang on my head?"

"Well, now, Uncle Remus, I didn't go to do it. I won't do so any more. Please, Uncle Remus, if you will tell me, I'll run to the house and bring you some teacakes."

"Seein' um's better'n hearin' tell un um," replied the old man, the severity of his countenance relaxing somewhat; but the little boy darted out, and in a few minutes came running back with his pockets full and his hands full.

"I lay yo' mammy 'll 'spishun dat de rats' stummucks is widenin' in dis naberhood w'en she come fer ter count up 'er cakes," said Uncle Remus, with a chuckle. "Deze," he continued, dividing the cakes into two equal parts—"deze I'll tackle now, en deze I'll lay by fer Sunday.

"Lemme see. I mos' dis'member wharbouts Brer Fox en Brer Rabbit wuz."

"The rabbit rode the fox to Miss Meadow's, and hitched him to the horse-rack," said the little boy.

"W'y co'se he did," said Uncle Remus. "Co'se he did. Well, Brer Rabbit rid Brer Fox up, he did, en tied 'im to de rack, en den sot out in de peazzer wid de gals a smokin' er his seegyar wid mo' proudness dan w'at you mos' ever see. Dey talk, en dey sing, en dey play on de peanner, de gals did, twel bimeby hit come time fer Brer Rabbit fer to be gwine, en he tell um all goodby, en strut out to de hoss-rack same's ef he wuz de king er de patter-rollers [Patrols], en den he mount Brer Fox en ride off.

"Brer Fox ain't sayin' nuthin' 'tall. He des rack off, he did, en keep his mouf shet, en Brer Rabbit know'd der wuz bizness cookin' up fer him, en he feel monstus skittish. Brer Fox amble on twel he git in de long lane, outer sight er Miss Meadows's house, en den he tu'n loose, he did. He rip en he r'ar, en he cuss, en he swar; he snort en he cavort."

"What was he doing that for, Uncle Remus?" the little boy inquired.

"He wuz tryin' fer ter fling Brer Rabbit off'n his back, bless yo' soul! But he des might ez well er rastle wid his own shadder. Every time he hump hisse'f Brer Rabbit slap de spurrers in 'im, en dar dey had it, up en down. Brer Fox fa'rly to' up de groun', he did, en he jump so high en he jump so quick dat he mighty nigh snatch his own tail off. Dey kep' on gwine on dis way twel bimeby Brer Fox lay down en roll over, he did, en dis sorter on-settle Brer Rabbit, but by de time Brer Fox got back on his footses agin, Brer Rabbit wuz thoo de underbresh mo' samer dan a race-hoss. Brer Fox he lit out atter 'im, he did, en he push Brer Rabbit so close dat it wuz 'bout all he could do fer ter git in a holler tree. Hole too little fer Brer Fox fer ter git in, en he hatter lay down en res' en gedder his mine tergedder.

"While he wuz layin' dar, Mr. Buzzard come floppin' long, en seein' Brer Fox stretch out on de groun', he lit en view de premusses. Den Mr. Buzzard sorter shake his wing, en put his head on one side, en say to hisse'f like, sezee:

"'Brer Fox dead, en I so sorry,' sezee

"'No I ain't dead, nudder,' sez Brer Fox, sezee. 'I got ole man Rabbit pent up in yer,' sezee, 'en I'm a gwineter git 'im dis time ef it take twel Chris'-mus,' sezee.

"Den, atter some mo' palaver, Brer Fox make a bargain dat Mr. Buzzard wuz ter watch de hole, en keep Brer Rabbit dar wiles Brer Fox went atter his axe. Den Brer Fox, he lope off, he did, en Mr. Buzzard, he tuck up his stan' at de hole. Bimeby, w'en all git still, Brer Rabbit sorter scramble down close ter de hole, he did, en holler out:

"'Brer Fox! Oh! Brer Fox!'

"Brer Fox done gone, en nobody say nuthin'. Den Brer Rabbit squall out like he wuz mad; sezee:

"'You needn't talk less you wanter,' sezee. 'I knows youer dar, en I ain't keerin',' sezee. 'I des wanter tell you dat I wish mighty bad Brer Tukkey Buz-zard wuz here,' sezee.

"Den Mr. Buzzard try ter talk like Brer Fox:

"'W'at you want wid Mr. Buzzard?' sezee.

"'Oh, nuthin' in 'tickler, 'cep' dere's de fattes' gray squir'l in yer dat ever I see,' sezee, 'en ef Brer Tukkey Buzzard wuz 'roun' he'd be mighty glad fer ter git 'im,' sezee.

"'How Mr. Buzzard gwine ter git 'im?' sez de Buzzard, sezee.

"'Well, dars a little hole roun' on de udder side er de tree,' sez Brer Rabbit, sezee, 'en ef Brer Tukkey Buzzard wuz here so he could take up his stan' dar,' sezee, 'I'd drive dat squir'l out,' sezee.

"'Drive 'im out, den,' sez Mr. Buzzard, sezee, 'en I'll see dat Brer Tukkey Buzzard gits 'im,' sezee.

"Den Brer Rabbit kick up a racket, like he wer' drivin' sumpin' out, en Mr. Buzzard he rush 'roun' fer ter ketch de squir'l, en Brer Rabbit, he dash out, he did, en he des fly fer home."

At this point Uncle Remus took one of the tea-cakes, held his head back, opened his mouth, dropped the cake in with a sudden motion, looked at the little boy with an expression of astonishment, and then closed his eyes, and begun to chew, mumbling as an accompaniment the plaintive tune of "Don't You Grieve After Me."

The *séance* was over; but, before the little boy went into the "big house," Uncle Remus laid his rough hand tenderly on the child's shoulder, and remarked, in a confidential tone:

"Honey, you mus' git up soon Chris'mus mawnin' en open de do'; kase I'm gwineter bounce in on Marse John en Miss Sally, en holler Chris'mus gif' des like I useter endurin' the fahmin' days fo' de war, w'en ole Miss wuz 'live. I boun' dey don't fergit de ole nigger, nudder. W'en you hear me callin' de pigs, honey, you des hop up en onfassen de do'. I lay I'll give Marse John wunner deze yer 'sprize parties."

◎◎

THE APE

The hairy ape, now, chillun see,
He's lookin' fo' a li'l ole flea.
If he should tuhn aroun' we'd fine
He has no hair on his behine.

—Folk

BAD BIRDS

Jaybird settin' on hick'ry limb;
He wink at me, I wink at him.
I pick up a rock an' hit him on de chin;
Jaybird yell, "Dammit, nigguh! Don't you do dat ag'in."

Hawkie is schemin' bird
He schemes all 'roun' de sky;

He schemes into my chicken house
An' makes my chickens fly.

Ol' King Buzzazd floatin' high,
Say "Sho do wish dat cow would die."
Ol' cow died an' li'l calf cried,
"Oh mou'mah, you shall be free."

—Folk

CATCHING THE SNAKE AND THE YELLOWJACKETS *

From *Negro Myths from the Georgia Coast*
By Charles C. Jones

Buh Rabbit greedy fuh hab mo sense den all de tarruh animel. Eh yent lub fuh wuk, and eh try heap er scheme fuh git eh libbin outer edder people by fool um.

One time eh gone ter one wise Cunjur Man fuh larne um him way, and fuh git him knowledge, so him kin stonish tarruh people and mck dcm bliebe say him bin wise mo ner ebrybody. De Cunjur Man larne um heap er curous ting. At las Buh Rabbit ax um fuh gen um eh full knowledge. De Cunjur Man say: "Buh Rabbit, you hab sense nough aready." Buh Rabbit keep on bague um, and den de Cunjur Man mek answer: "Ef you kit ketch one big rattlesnake an fetch um ter me live, me guine do wuh you ax me fuh do."

Buh Rabbit git ehself one long stick and eh gone der wood. Eh hunt tel eh fine one whalin ob er rattlesnake duh quile up on one log. Eh pass de time er day berry perlite wid um, and arterwards eh bet de snake say him yent bin es long as de stick wuh him hab een him han. Buh Rattlesnake laugh at um, and eh mek answer dat eh know eh yiz long mo na de stick. Fuh settle de bet Buh Rattlesnake tretch ehself out ter eh berry lenk on de log, and Buh Rabbit pit de pole long side er um fuh medjuh um. Man sir! befo Buh Rattlesnake fine out, Buh Rabbit slip one noose roun eh neck and fasten um tight ter de en der de pole. Buh Rattlesnake twis ehself, and wrop ehself roun and roun de pole, and try fuh git eh head loose, but all eh twis and tun yent do um no good. An so Buh Rabbit ketch um, and cahr um ter de Cunjur Man.

De Cunjur Man rale surprise, and eh say: "Buh Rabbit, me always bin yeddy say you bin hab heap er sense, but now me know dat you got um. Ef you can fool Rattlesnake, you hab all de sense you want."

Wen Buh Rabbit keep on bague de Cunjur Man fuh gie um mo sense, de Cunjur Man answer: "You go fetch me er swarm er Yaller Jacket, and wen you bring um ter me, me prommus you teh gie you all de sense you want."

Ebrybody know say Yaller Jacket was den warse, an bee, an hornet. Eh sting so bad, and eh berry lub fuh drap topper ebryting wuh come close eh nes, and dout gie um any warnin. So wuh Buh Rabbit do? Eh gone an eh git one big calabash, and eh crape um out clean, and eh cut one hole een um, and e pit honey een um, and eh tie um on de een er one long pole. Den eh hunt tel eh fine er Yaller Jacket nes, an eh set de calabash close by um dout worry de Yaller Jacket, an eh leff um day, and eh tan off and watch um. Bimby de Yaller Jacket scent de honey, and dem come out de nes and gone een de calabash fuh eat de honey. Wen de calabash full er Yaller Jacket, Buh Rabbit slip up and stop de hole, and cahr um ter de Cunjur Man. De Cunjur Man mek er great miration ober wuh Buh Rabbit bin done, and eh say: "Buh Rabbit, you is suttenly de smartest of all de animal, an you sense shill git mo and mo ebry day. Mo na dat, me gwine pit white spot on you forrud, so ebrybody kin see you hab de bes sense en you head." And dat de way Buh Rabbit come fuh hab er leely tuff er white hair between eh yez.

* Some exaggerated dialect in this tale has been slightly modified for clarity.

THE FLEA

I got to thinkin' 'bout the flea,
An' how you can't figger he from she.
The boys an' girls look the same to me,
But she tell, an' so can he.

—Folk

THE WOODPECKER

Peckerwood, peckerwood,
Whut makes yo' head so red?
You peck out in de sun all day,
It's a wonder you ain't dead.

—Folk

A ROOST ON THE RIM OF THE MOON

From *Nigger to Nigger*
By E. C. L. Adams

I seen a owl settin'
On de rim er de moon.
He draw in he neck

An' rumple he feather,
An' look below at de world.

He shook de horn on he head,
Wall he big eye
An' laugh at de things
Above an' below
From he roost
On de rim er de moon.

He woke de fowls
In de barnyard,
An' de dead stirred
In dey grave,
When he laugh
From he roost
On de rim er de moon.

An' de ole folks say
He were a dead man;
Dat evil did float
Wid de sound er he voice,
When he laugh
From he roost
On de rim er de moon.

An' de dead
In de graveyard
Raise up dey voice an' moan;
Dey laugh an' dey cry
At de sound er de owl,
When he laugh
From he roost
On de rim er de moon.

He stir up de fever an' chill
Wid he shadow,
When de sound er he voice
Pass over de swamp,
When he laugh
From he roost
On de rim er de moon.

THE ROOSTER AND THE CHICKEN

The rooster and the chicken had a fight,
The chicken knocked the rooster out of sight,
The rooster told the chicken, that's all right,
I'll meet you in the gumbo tomorrow night.

—Folk

NUMSKULL TALES

TALKING TURTLE

From *American Negro Folktales*
By Richard M. Dorson

Every day John had to tote water from the bayou, and every time he'd go to the bayou he would start fussin'. "I'm tired of toting water every day." The next day he went to the bayou and he repeated the same thing (you know just like you repeat the same thing). So last one day John went to the bayou, the turtle was sitting on a log.

Turtle raised up and looked at him, and told John, "Black man, you talk too much."

So John didn't want to think the turtle was talking. He went back to the bayou, got another bucketful of water. The turtle told him the same thing. John throwed the buckets down, took and run to the house, and called Old Marster, and told him the turtle was down there talking. And so Old Marster didn't want to go because he didn't believe it. But John kept telling him the turtle was talking. So finally Old Boss 'cided he could go. But he told John if the turtle didn't talk he was going to give him a good beating. So they all went on down to the bayou, and when they got down to the bayou the turtle was sitting on a log with his head back halfway in his shell.

And so John told the turtle, "Tell Old Marster what you told me." So John begged the turtle to talk. So the turtle still didn't say anything. So Old Marster taken him back to the house, and give him a good beating, and made him git his buckets, and keep totin' water.

When John got back down to the bayou, the turtle had his head sticking up. John dipped up his water, and the turtle raised up and told him, says, "Black man, didn't I tell you you talked too much?"

THE MOJO

Folk

There was always the time when the white man been ahead of the colored man. In slavery times John had done got to a place where the Marster whipped him all the time. Someone told him, "Get you a mojo, it'll get you out of that whipping, won't nobody whip you then."

John went down to the corner of the Boss-man's farm, where the mojo-man stayed, and asked him what he had. The mojo-man said, "I got a pretty good one and a very good one and a damn good one." The colored fellow asked him, "What can the pretty good one do?" "I'll tell you what it can do. It can turn you to a rabbit, and it can turn you to a quail, and after that it can turn you to a snake." So John said he'd take it.

Next morning John sleeps late. About nine o'clock the white man comes after him, calls him: "John, come on, get up there and go to work. Plow the taters and milk the cow and then you can go back home—it's Sunday morning." John says to him, "Get on out from my door, don't say nothing to me. Ain't gonna do nothing." Boss-man says, "Don't you know who this is? It's your Boss." "Yes, I know—I'm not working for you anymore." "All right, John, just wait till I go home; I'm coming back and whip you."

White man went back and got his pistol, and told his wife, "John is sassy, he won't do nothing I tell him, I'm gonna whip him." He goes back to John, and calls, "John, get up there." John yells out, "Go on away from that door and quit worrying me. I told you once, I ain't going to work."

Well, then the white man he falls against the door and broke it open. And John said to his mojo, "Skip-skip-skip-skip." He turned to a rabbit, and ran slap out the door by Old Marster. And he's a running son of a gun, that rabbit was. Boss-man says to his mojo, "I'll turn to a greyhound." You know that greyhound got running so fast his paws were just reaching the grass under the rabbit's feet.

Then John thinks, "I got to get away from here." He turns to a quail. And he begins sailing fast through the air—he really thought he was going. But the Boss-man says, "I will turn to a chicken hawk." That chicken hawk sails through the sky like a bullet, and catches right up to that quail.

Then John says, "Well, I'm going to turn to a snake." He hit the ground and begin to crawl; that old snake was natchally getting on his way. Boss-man says, "I'll turn to a stick and beat your ass."

AMOS AND THE UNION OFFICER

Soon after Emancipation a Union Army officer encountered Amos,
a slave who had reservations about his freedom. Surprised at his
reaction, the officer scolded Amos. "Amos, I don't believe you realize you
are a free man. You can go where you please, do as you please, eat
what you please." "I awready bin eatin' ez I please," grumbled Amos.
The officer was taken aback. "I wager, Amos, you never
even tasted chicken before," he said.
"I eats chicken ev'ry Sund'y," maintained Amos doggedly.
"An' whut's mo', Massa save me de tenderes' paht."
"What part is that?"
"De gravy, uv co'se!" said Amos.

—Folk

JOHN IN JAIL

From *A Treasury of Afro-American Folklore*
By Harold Courlander

One time Old Boss get a call from the sheriff, say that John was in jail and
did Old Boss want him out on bail. Old Boss, he was mad that John give
him so much trouble, but he got to get John out cause they was work to
be done. So he went down to the sheriff's place and put ten dollars on the
line, sign some papers and take John home with him.

"How come they put you in jail?" the Boss say.

"'Spect it was 'count of Miss Elizabeth's petunias," John say.

"Old Miss Elizabeth Grant? What's her petunias got to do with it?" Old
Boss say.

"I hear tell Miss Elizabeth want a man to trim up her petunia garden,"
John say. "I got a little time now and then between workin' in the field, so
I went up there to Miss Elizabeth's place to see could she use me. I knock
on the back door and Miss Elizabeth come and ask me what I want. I tell
her I'm the man to work in her petunia garden. She ask to see my testi-
monials, and that's when I make my mistake."

JOHN AND THE BLACKSNAKE

Folk

One time John went down to the pond to catch him a few catfish. He put
his line in the water, and cause the sun was warm John began to doze off

a little. Soon as his head went down a little, he heard someone callin' his name, "John, John," like that. John jerked up his head and looked around, but he didn't see no one. Two-three minutes after that he heard it again, "John, John." He looked to one side and the other. He looked down at the water and he looked up in the air. And after that he looked behind him and saw a big old blacksnake settin' on a stone pile.

"Who been callin' my name?" says John.

"Me," the blacksnake tell him. "It's me that called you."

John don't feel too comfortable talkin' to a blacksnake, and he feel might uneasy about a blacksnake talkin' to him. He say, "What you want?"

"Just called your name to be sociable," blacksnake tell him.

John look all around to see was anyone else there. "How come you pick *me* to socialize with?"

"Well," blacksnake say, "you is the only one here, and besides that, John, ain't we both black?"

"Let's get it straight," says John, "they's two kinds of black, yours and mine, and they ain't the same thing."

"Black is black," blacksnake say, "and I been thinkin' on it quite a while. You might say as we is kin."

That was too much for John. He jumped up and sold out, went down the road like the Cannonball Express. And comin' down the road they was a wagon with Old Boss in it. Old Boss stop and wait till John get there. He say, "John, I thought you was down to the pond fishin' for catfish?"

John looked back over his shoulder, said, "I was, but I ain't."

Old Boss say, "John, you look mighty scared. What's your hurry?"

John say, "Old Boss, when blacksnakes get to talkin', that's when I get to movin'."

"Now, John," Old Boss say, "you know that blacksnakes don't talk."

"Indeed I know it," John say, "and that's why, in particular, I'm agoin', cause this here blacksnake is doin' what you say he don't."

" 'Pears to me as you been into that liquid corn again," Old Boss say. "I'm disappointed in you, John. You let me down."

"It ain't no liquid corn," John say, "It's worse than liquid corn. It's a big old blacksnake settin' on a rock pile down by the pond."

"Well," Old Boss say, "let's go take a look."

So Old Boss went with John back to the pond, and the blacksnake was still settin' on the stones.

"Tell him," John said to the blacksnake. "Tell Old Boss what you told me."

But the blacksnake just set there and didn't say a word.

"Just speak up," John say, "tell him what I hear before."

Blacksnake didn't have a word to say, and Old Boss tell John, "John, you got to stay off that corn. I'm mighty disappointed in you. You sure let me down." After that Old Boss got in his wagon and took off.

John looked mean at the blacksnake. He say, "Blacksnake, how come you make me a liar?"

Blacksnake say, "John, you sure let me down too. I spoke with you and nobody else. And the first thing you do is go off and tell everything you know to a white man."

☯☯

TRICKSTER TALES

THE LAUGH THAT MEANT FREEDOM

Folk

Nehemiah, a clever slave who had a reputation for avoiding work with his wit and humor, had been transferred from one master to another because of his ability to outwit his owners. Then David Wharton, known as the most cruel slave master in Southwest Texas, heard about Nehemiah. He bought him and vowed to "make that rascal work." The morning after Nehemiah was purchased, David Wharton approached him and said, "Now you are going to work, you understand. You are going to pick four hundred pounds of cotton today."

"Wal, Massa, dat's aw right," answered Nehemiah, "but ef Ah meks you laff, won' yuh lemme off fo' terday?"

"Well," said David Wharton, who had never been known to laugh, "if you make me laugh, I won't only let you off for today, but I'll give you your freedom."

"Ah decla', Boss," said Nehemiah, "yuh sho' is uh good lookin' man."

"I am sorry I can't say the same thing about you," retorted David Wharton.

"Oh, yes, Boss, yuh could," Nehemiah laughed out, "yuh could if yuh tole ez big uh lie ez Ah did."

David Wharton could not help laughing at this; he laughed before he thought. Nehemiah got his freedom.

MO' NIGGER

"You scoundrel, you ate my turkey," the master
said to the slave.

"Yes, suh, Massa," the slave replied, "You got less turkey
but you sho nuff got mo' Nigger."

—Folk

THE CHAMPION

Folk

The way it was, Old Master went out and bought him five hundred Negroes
on this place. And the other captain over here bought *him* five hundred Negroes. And buying the five hundred Negroes, this master has a big Negro in
there he said was stouter than any Negro that ever he bought, and he's the
champion of that bunch. This master right across the fence on the next plantation told him he had one there, listen, was stouter than the one the first
Master had there. "Well," he says, "the one I got will whip that one you got."

"Well," the first master says, "I'll bet you one thousand dollars that mine,
listen, will whip that one you got, or else take his nerve so he won't fight."
Said, "I'll bet you, understand, this hand of mine will fight this one of yours
and whip him, or else I'll bet you five hundred dollars that when your hand
gets there he won't fight mine."

Other one says, "When we goin' to meet?"

Says, "Well, Friday, let's meet 'em and let 'em fight." Say, "You have all
your peoples on the place to meet 'em to fight, and I'm goin' to have all of
mine to see to fight, and me and you goin' to be there."

Just before that Friday, next day, this first master's Negro said, "I don't
believe I can whip this other champion over yonder, but I can fix it so you'll
win the five hundred dollars if not the thousand. Just let me know where
we goin' to fight at." He said, "Give me your shovel and give me your ax."

He went down in the woods and dug up a water oak, a common tree. He
took a mule and drug it to a hole up there, and set it out in the hole. And
when he set it in the ground he put some leaves around to make it look
like the tree growed there. It wasn't goin' to wilt because it wasn't more
than twenty-four hours before they going to fight. That tree looked alive.
Then he taken all his wife's white clothes and put them around there and
set out a wash tub.

The next day when the master from the other plantation came for the
fight, the first master came with his champion with a grass line tied on him.
There was a little place in the grass line where it was weak. The master
walked his champion up to the tree and tied him to it. The other champion
from the next plantation was walkin' loose.

His master supplied to the first one, "Is this the one goin' to fight my champion?"

Said, "Yeah."

Said, "Why you got him tied up that way?"

Said, "I'm scared he'll get frustrated and mad. He's ambitious and want to fight. I'm scared he'll get loose and jump on your champion and hurt him. He's so stout I have to tie him so I can talk to him."

This other champion that come from the other plantation, he tell his master, "Death ain't but death. I ain't goin' to fight no man they got to tie a tree, else he'll kill me, so you might just as well shoot me down where I am."

The first master say, "You want to see how stout my champion is before they fight?"

Other one say, "Yeah."

He say, "Well, then, I'll make him try out that rope a little." Says to his champion, "Bill, pull against that tree a little so's this other champion can see what you are."

Bill braced his feet and pulled, and the tree start to lean. All them Negroes from the other plantation backed up when they see that. Bill pulled some more, and the roots start to pop out of the ground.

The other champion got behind his master. Says, "Shoot me down, Master, cause that man goin' to kill me anyway. I ain't goin' to fight no man that pulls trees down by the roots."

His master say to the other one, "Your champion's scared mine 'bout to death. Don't let him pull no more."

But Bill gave another tug and that tree started to come down, and the rope broke at the thin place. He came runnin' at where the masters were standing.

The other master said, "And now I'm getting' scared too. Hold him off. My champion ain't goin' to fight, so here's the five hundred dollars."

The first master tell all his hands to take Bill and hold him, and whilst they doin' that the Negroes from the other plantation just lit out for home.

Bill didn't think he could whip the other champion, but he worked it out so the other one was scared to fight him, and that's how his master won five hundred dollars in the bet.

OLD MASTER AND OKRA

Folk

Old Master had to go down to New Orleans on business, and he left his number-one slave named Okra in charge of things. Okra declared to himself he goin' to have a good time whilst Old Master was away, and the thing he did the very first mornin' was to go out and tell the other slaves, "Now you get on with your affairs. Old Master gone to New Orleans and we got to keep things goin'."

Then Okra went in the kitchen to cook himself up some food, and in the process of doin' so he got ruffled and spilled the bacon grease on top of the stove. It burst up into a big fire, and next thing you know that house was goin' up in flame and smoke. Okra he went out the window and stood off a ways, lookin' real sorry. By the time the other hands got there, wasn't nothin' else to do *but* look sorry. They was so busy with lookin' that they never noticed that the sparks lit in the wood lot and set it afire too. Well, Okra ordered everybody out to the wood lot to save it, but by then the grass was sizzlin' and poppin', a regular old prairie fire roarin' across the fields, burnin' up the cotton and everything else. They run over there with wet bags to beat it out, but next thing they knowed, the pasture was afire and all Old Master's cattle was a-goin', throttle out and racin' for the Texas Badlands.

Okra went to the barn for the horses, but soon's he opened the door they bolted and was gone. "If'n I can get that ox team hitched," Okra said, "I'll go on down to Colonel Thatcher's place and get some help." Well, minute he started to put the yoke on them oxen, the left-hand ox lit out and was gone. The right-hand ox went after him, and the both of 'em just left Okra holdin' the ox yoke up in the air. When Old Master's huntin' dog see them oxen go off that way, he figured something was wrong, and he sold out, barkin' and snappin' at their heels.

'Bout that time Okra looked around and found all the slaves had took off, too, headin' North and leavin' no tracks. He was all alone, and he had to digest all that misery by himself.

Week or two went by, and Okra went down to meet the boat Old Master comin' back on. Old Master got off feelin' pretty good. Told Okra to carry his stuff and say, "Well, Okra, how'd things go while I was away?"

"Fine, just fine," Okra say. "I notice they're fixin' the bridge over Black Creek. Ain't that good?"

"Yeah," Old Master say, "that's fine, Okra, just fine. Soon's we get home I'm goin' to change my clothes and do some quail shootin'."

"Captain," Okra say, hangin' his head, "I got a little bad news for you."

"What's that?" Old Master say.

"You ain't neither goin' quail huntin'," Okra say, "Your huntin' dog run away."

Old Master took it pretty good. He say, "Well, don't worry about it none, he'll come back. How'd he happen to run away?"

"Chasin' after the right-hand ox," Okra say. "He was tryin' to catch up with the left-hand ox."

Old Master began to frown now, and he say to Okra, "You mean the whole ox team is gone? How come?"

"I was yokin' 'em up to go after Colonel Thatcher, after the horses bolted," Okra say.

"How come the horses bolted?" Old Boss say.

"Smoke from the pasture grass. That's what scared all your livestock and made 'em break down the fence and run for the swamp."

"You mean all my livestock is gone? Okra, I goin' to skin you. How'd that pasture get on fire?"

Okra he just stood there lookin' foolish, scratchin' his head. "Reckon the fire just came across from the cotton field, Captain," he say.

"You mean my cotton's burned!" Old Master holler. "How'd that happen?"

"Couldn't put it out, Captain. Soon as we see it come over there from the wood lot, we went down with wet bags but we couldn't handle it. Man, that was sure a pretty cotton field before the fire got there."

Right now Old Master was lookin' pretty sick. He talk kind of weak. "Okra, you tryin' to tell me the wood lot's gone too?"

"I hate to tell you, Captain, but you guessed it," Okra say, kind of sad. "Imagine, all them trees gone, just 'cause of one lonesome spark."

Old Master couldn't hardly talk at all now. He just whisperin'. "Okra," he say, "Okra, where'd that spark come from?"

"Wind blew it right from the house," Okra say, "it was when the big timbers gave and came down. Man, sparks flew in the air a mile or more."

"You mean the house burned up?" Old Master say.

"Oh, yeah, didn't I tell you?" Okra reply. "Didn't burn *up*, though, so much as it burned *down*."

By now Old Master was a miserable sight, pale as a ghost and shakin' all over.

"Okra, Okra," Old Master say, "let's go get the field hands together and do somethin'!"

"Can't do that," Okra say, "I forget to tell you, they's all sold out for Michigan."

Old Master just set there shakin' his head back and forth. "Okra," he say, "why didn't you come right out with it? Why you tell me everything was fine?"

"Captain, I'm sorry if I didn't tell it right," Okra say. "Just wanted to break it to you easy."

STRONG MAN JACK

Folk

Jack was a very wise nigger. Cap'n brag on Jack. Cap'n say, "Jack can beat all swimmin'!"

Then he come tell Jack, "Jack, tomorrow a man coming here to swim with you. Want you to swim two three miles. Want you to beat him. I bet money on you. You must best him so's we can get all the money."

Now Jack can't swim nary a lick. He go get him a stove, grits meal, meat, and lard and ALL and put 'em on his back. Man come to swim with Jack he say, "What you got them bundle for and goin' swimmin'?"

Jack tell him, "You think I goin' swim three four miles 'thout any sumptin' t' eat? You must think I a big fool!"

And the man what come think if Jack goin' swim so far he have to stop and cook rations long the way he better back down. Jack's Cap'n got all THAT MONEY.

SWAPPING DREAMS

Folk

One morning, when Ike entered the master's room to clean it, he found the master just preparing to get out of bed. "Ike," he said, "I certainly did have a strange dream last night."

"Sez yuh did, Massa, sez yuh did?" answered Ike. "Lemme hyeah it."

"All right," replied the master. "It was like this: I dreamed I went to Nigger Heaven last night, and saw there a lot of garbage, some old torn-down houses, a few old broken-down, rotten fences, the muddiest, sloppiest streets I ever saw, and a big bunch of ragged, dirty Negroes walking around."

"Umph, umph, Massa," said Ike. "Yuh sho' musta et de same t'ing Ah did las' night, 'cause Ah dreamed Ah went up ter de white man's paradise, an' de streets wuz all ob gol' an' silvah, and dey wuz lots o' milk an' honey dere an' putty pearly gates, but dey wuzn't uh soul in de whole place."

THE PASSING OF GRANDISON

From *The Wife of His Youth*
By Charles W. Chesnutt

I

When it is said that it was done to please a woman, there ought perhaps to be enough said to explain anything; for what a man will not do to please a woman is yet to be discovered. Nevertheless, it might be well to state a few preliminary facts to make it clear why young Dick Owens tried to run one of his father's negro men off to Canada.

In the early fifties, when the growth of anti-slavery sentiment and the constant drain of fugitive slaves into the North had so alarmed the slave-holders of the border States as to lead to the passage of the Fugitive Slave Law, a young white man from Ohio, moved by compassion for the suffering of a certain bondman who happened to have a "hard master," essayed to help the slave to freedom. The attempt was discovered and frustrated; the abductor was tried and convicted for slave-stealing, and sentenced to a term of imprisonment in the penitentiary. His death, after the expiration of only a small part of the sentence, from cholera contracted while nursing stricken fellow prisoners, lent to the case a melancholy interest that made it famous in anti-slavery annals.

Dick Owens had attended the trial. He was a youth of about twenty-two, intelligent, handsome, and amiable, but extremely indolent, in a graceful and gentlemanly way; or, as old Judge Fenderson put it more than once, he was lazy as the Devil—a mere figure of speech, of course, and not one that did justice to the Enemy of Mankind. When asked why he never did anything serious, Dick would good-naturedly reply, with a well-modulated drawl, that he didn't have to. His father was rich; there was but one other child, an unmarried daughter, who because of poor health would probably never marry, and Dick was therefore heir presumptive to a large estate. Wealth or social position he did not need to seek, for he was born to both. Charity Lomax had shamed him into studying law, but notwithstanding an hour or so a day spent at old Judge Fenderson's office, he did not make remarkable headway in his legal studies.

"What Dick needs," said the judge, who was fond of tropes, as became a scholar, and of horses, as was befitting a Kentuckian, "is the whip of necessity, or the spur of ambition. If he had either, he would soon need the snaffle to hold him back."

But all Dick required, in fact, to prompt him to the most remarkable thing he accomplished before he was twenty-five, was a mere suggestion from Charity Lomax. The story was never really known to but two persons until after the war, when it came out because it was a good story and there was no particular reason for its concealment.

Young Owens had attended the trial of this slave-stealer, or martyr—either or both—and, when it was over, had gone to call on Charity Lomax, and, while they sat on the veranda after sundown, had told her all about the trial. He was a good talker, as his career in later years disclosed, and described the proceedings very graphically.

"I confess," he admitted, "that while my principles were against the prisoner, my sympathies were on his side. It appeared that he was of good family, and that he had an old father and mother, respectable people, dependent upon him for support and comfort in their declining years. He had been led into the matter by pity for a negro whose master ought to have been run out the country long ago for abusing his slaves. If it had been merely a question of old Sam Briggs's negro, nobody would have cared anything about it. But father and the rest of them stood on the principle of the thing, and told the judge so, and the fellow was sentenced to three years in the penitentiary."

Miss Lomax had listened with lively interest.

"I've always hated old Sam Briggs," she said emphatically, "ever since the time he broke a negro's leg with a piece of cordwood. When I hear of a cruel deed it makes the Quaker blood that came from my grandmother assert itself. Personally I wish that all Sam Briggs's negroes would run away. As for the young man, I regard him as a hero. He dared something for humanity. I could love a man who would take such chances for the sake of others."

"Could you love me, Charity, if I did something heroic?"

"You never will, Dick. You're too lazy for any use. You'll never do anything harder than playing cards or fox-hunting."

"Oh, come now, sweetheart! I've been courting you for a year, and it's the hardest work imaginable. Are you never going to love me?" he pleaded.

His hand sought hers, but she drew it back beyond his reach.

"I'll never love you, Dick Owens, until you have done something. When that time comes, I'll think about it."

"But it takes so long to do anything worth mentioning, and I don't want to wait. One must read two years to become a lawyer, and work five more to make a reputation. We shall both be gray by then."

"Oh, I don't know," she rejoined. "It doesn't require a lifetime for a man to prove that he is a man. This one did something, or at least tried to."

"Well, I'm willing to attempt as much as any other man. What do you want me to do, sweetheart? Give me a test."

"Oh, dear me!" said Charity, "I don't care what you *do,* so you do *something.* Really, come to think of it, why should I care whether you do anything or not?"

"I'm sure I don't know why you should, Charity," rejoined Dick humbly, "for I'm aware that I'm not worthy of it."

"Except that I do hate," she added, relenting slightly, "to see a really clever man so utterly lazy and good for nothing."

"Thank you, my dear: a word of praise from you has sharpened my wits already. I have an idea! Will you love me if *I* run a negro off to Canada?"

"What nonsense!" said Charity scornfully. "You must be losing your wits. Steal another man's slave, indeed, while your father owns a hundred!"

"Oh, there'll be no trouble about that," responded Dick lightly. "I'll run off one of the old man's; we've got too many anyway. It may not be quite as difficult as the other man found it, but it will be just as unlawful, and will demonstrate what I am capable of."

"Seeing's believing," replied Charity. "Of course, what you are talking about now is merely absurd. I'm going away for three weeks, to visit my aunt in Tennessee. If you're able to tell me, when I return, that you've done something to prove your quality, I'll—well, you may come and tell me about it."

II

Young Owens got up about nine o'clock next morning, and while making his toilet put some questions to his personal attendant, a rather bright looking young mulatto of about his own age.

"Tom," said Dick.

"Yas, Mars Dick," responded the servant.

"I'm going on a trip North. Would you like to go with me?"

Now, if there was anything that Tom would have liked to make, it was a trip North. It was something he had long contemplated in the abstract, but had never been able to muster up sufficient courage to attempt in the concrete. He was prudent enough, however, to dissemble his feelings.

"I wouldn't min' it, Mars Dick, ez long ez you'd take keer er me an' fetch me home all right."

Tom's eyes belied his words, however, and his young master felt well assured that Tom needed only a good opportunity to make him run away. Having a comfortable home, and a dismal prospect in case of failure, Tom was not likely to take any desperate chances; but young Owens was satisfied that in a free State but little persuasion would be required to lead Tom astray. With a very logical and characteristic desire to gain his end with the least necessary expenditure of effort, he decided to take Tom with him, if his father did not object.

Colonel Owens had left the house when Dick went to breakfast, so Dick did not see his father till luncheon.

"Father," he remarked casually to the colonel, over the fried chicken, "I'm feeling a trifle run down. I imagine my health would be improved somewhat by a little travel and change of scene."

"Why don't you take a trip North?" suggested his father. The colonel added to paternal affection a considerable respect for his son as the heir of a large estate. He himself had been "raised" in comparative poverty, and had laid the foundations of his fortune by hard work; and while he despised the ladder by which he had climbed, he could not entirely forget it, and unconsciously manifested, in his intercourse with his son, some of the poor man's deference toward the wealthy and well-born.

"I think I'll adopt your suggestion, sir," replied the son, "and run up to New York; and after I've been there awhile I may go on to Boston for a week or so. I've never been there, you know."

"There are some matters you can talk over with my factor in New York," rejoined the colonel, "and while you are up there among the Yankees, I hope you'll keep your eyes and ears open to find out what the rascally abolitionists are saying and doing. They're becoming altogether too active for our comfort, and entirely too many ungrateful niggers are running away. I hope the conviction of that fellow yesterday may discourage the rest of the breed. I'd just like to catch any one trying to run off one of my darkeys. He'd get short shrift; I don't think any Court would have a chance to try him."

"They are a pestiferous lot," assented Dick, "and dangerous to our institutions. But say, father, if I go North I shall want to take Tom with me."

Now, the colonel, while a very indulgent father, had pronounced views on the subject of negroes, having studied them, as he often said, for a great many years, and, as he asserted oftener still, understanding them perfectly. It is scarcely worth while to say, either, that he valued more highly than if he had inherited them the slaves he had toiled and schemed for.

"I don't think it safe to take Tom up North," he declared, with promptness and decision. "He's a good enough boy, but too smart to trust among those low-down abolitionists. I strongly suspect him of having learned to read, though I can't imagine how. I saw him with a newspaper the other day, and while he pretended to be looking at a woodcut, I'm almost sure he was reading the paper. I think it by no means safe to take him."

Dick did not insist, because he knew it was useless. The colonel would have obliged his son in any other manner, but his negroes were the outward and visible sign of his wealth and station, and therefore sacred to him.

"Whom do you think it safe to take?" asked Dick. "I suppose I'll have to have a body-servant."

"What's the matter with Grandison?" suggested the colonel. "He's handy enough, and I reckon we can trust him. He's too fond of good eating to risk losing his regular meals; besides, he's sweet on your mother's maid, Betty, and I've promised to let 'em get married before long. I'll have Grandison up, and we'll talk to him. Here, you boy Jack," called the colonel to a yellow youth in the next room who was catching flies and pulling their wings off to pass the time, "Go down to the barn and tell Grandison to come here."

"Grandison," said the colonel, when the negro stood before him, hat in hand.

"Yas, marster."

"Haven't you always got all you wanted to eat?"

"Yas, marster."

"And as much whiskey and tobacco as was good for you, Grandison?"

"Y-a-s, marster."

"I should like to know, Grandison, whether you don't think yourself a great deal better off than those poor free negroes down by the plank road, with no kind master to look after them and no mistress to give them medicine when they're sick and—and—"

"Well, I sh'd jes' reckon I is better off, suh, den dem low-down free niggers, suh! Ef anybody ax 'em who dey b'long ter, dey has ter say nobody, er e'se lie erbout it. Anybody ax me who I b'long ter, I ain' got no 'casion ter be shame' ter tell 'em, no, suh, 'deed I ain', suh!"

The colonel was beaming. This was true gratitude, and his feudal heart thrilled at such appreciative homage. What cold-blooded, heartless monsters they were who would break up this blissful relationship of kindly protection on the one hand, of wise subordination and loyal dependence on the other! The colonel always became indignant at the mere thought of such wickedness.

"Grandison," the colonel continued, "your young master Dick is going North for a few weeks, and I am thinking of letting him take you along. I shall send you on this trip, Grandison, in order that you may take care of your young master. He will need someone to wait on him, and no one can ever do it so well as one of the boys brought up with him on the old plantation. I am going to trust him in your hands, and I'm sure you'll do your duty faithfully, and bring him back home safe and sound—to old Kentucky."

Grandison grinned. "Oh yas, marster, I'll take keer er young Mars Dick."

"I want to warn you, though, Grandison," continued the colonel impressively, "against these cussed abolitionists, who try to entice servants from their comfortable homes and their indulgent masters, from the blue skies, the green fields, and the warm sunlight of their southern home, and send them away off yonder to Canada, a dreary country, where the woods are full of wildcats and wolves and bears, where the snow lies up to the eaves of the houses for six months of the year, and the cold is so severe that it freezes your breath and curdles your blood; and where, when runaway niggers get sick and can't work, they are turned out to starve and die, unloved and uncared for. I reckon, Grandison, that you have too much sense to permit yourself to be led astray by any such foolish and wicked people."

"'Deed, suh, I would n' low none er dem cussed, low-down abolitionists ter come nigh me, suh. I'd—I'd—would I be 'lowed ter hit 'em, suh?"

"Certainly, Grandison," replied the colonel, chuckling, "hit 'em as hard as you can. I reckon they'd rather like it. Begad, I believe they would! It would serve 'em right to be hit by a nigger!"

"Er ef I didn't hit 'em, suh," continued Grandison reflectively, "I'd tell Mars Dick, en *he'd* fix 'em. He'd smash de face off'n 'em, suh, I jes' knows he would."

"Oh yes, Grandison, your young master will protect you. You need fear no harm while he is near."

"Dey won't try ter steal me, will dey, marster?" asked the negro, with sudden alarm.

"I don't know, Grandison," replied the colonel, lighting a fresh cigar. "They're a desperate set of lunatics, and there's no telling what they may resort to. But if you stick close to your young master, and remember always that he is your best friend, and understands your real needs, and has your true interests at heart, and if you will be careful to avoid strangers who try to talk to you, you'll stand a fair chance of getting back to your home and your friends. And if you please your master Dick, he'll buy you a present, and a string of beads for Betty to wear when you and she get married in the fall."

"Thanky, marster, thanky, suh," replied Grandison, oozing gratitude at every pore; "you is a good marster, to be sho', suh; yas, 'deed you is. You kin jes' bet me and Mars Dick gwine git 'long jes' lack I wuz own boy ter Mars Dick. En it won't be my fault ef he don' want me fer his boy all de time, w'en we come back home ag'in."

"All right, Grandison, you may go now. You needn't work any more today, and here's a piece of tobacco for you off my own plug."

"Thanky, marster, thanky, marster! You is de bes' marster any nigger ever had in dis worl'." And Grandison bowed and scraped and disappeared round the corner, his jaws closing around a large section of the colonel's best tobacco.

"You may take Grandison," said the colonel to his son. "I allow he's abolitionist-proof."

III

Richard Owens, Esq., and servant, from Kentucky, registered at the fashionable New York hostelry for Southerners in those days, a hotel where an atmosphere congenial to Southern institutions was sedulously maintained. But there were negro waiters in the dining-room, and mulatto bell-boys, and Dick had no doubt that Grandison, with the native gregariousness and garrulousness of his race, would foregather and palaver with them sooner or later, and Dick hoped that they would speedily inoculate him with the virus of freedom. For it was not Dick's intention to say anything to his servant about his plan to free him, for obvious reasons. To mention one of them, if Grandison should go away, and by legal process be recaptured, his young master's part in the matter would doubtless become known, which would be embarrassing to Dick, to say the least. If, on the other hand, he should merely give Grandison sufficient latitude, he had no doubt he would eventually lose him. For while not exactly skeptical about Grandison's perfervid loyalty, Dick had been a somewhat keen observer of human nature, in his own indolent way, and based his expectations upon the force of the example and argument that his servant could scarcely fail to encounter. Grandison should have a fair chance to become free by his own initiative; if it should become necessary to adopt other measures to get rid of him, it would be time enough to act when the necessity arose; and Dick Owens was not the youth to take needless trouble.

The young master renewed some acquaintances and made others, and spent a week or two very pleasantly in the best society of the metropolis, easily accessible to a wealthy, well-bred young Southerner, with proper introductions. Young women smiled on him, and young men of convivial habits pressed their hospitalities; but the memory of Charity's sweet, strong face and clear eyes made him proof against the blandishments of the one sex and the persuasions of the other. Meanwhile he kept Grandison supplied with pocket-money, and left him mainly to his own devices. Every night when Dick came in he hoped he might have to wait upon himself, and every morning he looked forward with pleasure to the prospect of making his toilet unaided. His hopes, however, were doomed to disappointment, for every night when he came in Grandison was on hand with a bootjack, and a nightcap mixed for his young master as the colonel had taught him to mix it, and every morning Grandison appeared with his master's boots blacked and his clothes brushed, and laid his linen out for the day.

"Grandison," said young Dick one morning, after finishing his toilet, "this is the chance of your life to go around among your own people and see how they live. Have you met any of them?"

"Yas, suh, I's seen some of 'em. But I don' keer nuffin fer 'em, suh. Dey're diffe'nt f'm de niggers down ou' way. Dey 'lows dey're free, but dey ain' got sense 'nuff ter know dey ain' half as well off as dey would be down Souf, whar dey'd be 'preciated."

When two weeks had passed without any apparent effect of evil example upon Grandison, Dick resolved to go on to Boston, where he thought the atmosphere might prove more favorable to his ends. After he had been at the Revere House for a day or two without losing Grandison, he decided upon slightly different tactics.

Having ascertained from a city directory the addresses of several well-known abolitionists, he wrote them each a letter something like this:

> Dear Friends and Brothers—
> A wicked slaveholder from Kentucky, stopping at the Revere House, has dared to insult the liberty-loving people of Boston by bringing his slave into their midst. Shall this be tolerated? Or shall steps be taken in the name of liberty to rescue a fellow-man from bondage? For obvious reasons I can only sign myself,
> A Friend of Humanity

That this letter might have an opportunity to prove effective, Dick made it a point to send Grandison away from the hotel on various errands. On one of these occasions Dick watched him for quite a distance down the street. Grandison had scarcely left the hotel when a long-haired, sharp-featured man came out behind him, followed him, soon overtook him, and kept along beside him until they turned the next corner. Dick's hopes were roused by this spectacle, but sank correspondingly when Grandison returned to the hotel. As Grandison said nothing about the encounter, Dick hoped there might be some self-consciousness behind this unexpected reticence, the results of which might develop later on.

But Grandison was on hand again when his master came back to the hotel at night, and was in attendance again in the morning, with hot water, to assist at his master's toilet. Dick sent him on further errands from day to day, and upon one occasion came squarely up to him—inadvertently, of course—while Grandison was engaged in conversation with a young white man in clerical garb. When Grandison saw Dick approaching, he edged away from the preacher and hastened toward his master, with a very evident expression of relief upon his countenance.

"Mars Dick," he said, "dese yer abolitioner is jes' pesterin' de life out er me tryin' ter git me ter run away. I don't pay no 'tention ter 'em, but dey riles me so sometimes dat I'm feared I'll hit some of 'em some er dese days, an' dat mought git me inter trouble. I ain' said nuffin' ter you 'bout it, Mars Dick, fer I did n' wanter 'sturb yo' min'; but I don' like it, suh; no, suh, I don't! Is we gwine back home 'fo' long, Mars Dick?"

"We'll be going back soon enough," replied Dick somewhat shortly, while he inwardly cursed the stupidity of a slave who could be free and would not, and registered a secret vow that if he were unable to get rid of Grandison without assassinating him, and were therefore compelled to take him back to Kentucky, he would see that Grandison got a taste of an article of slavery that would make him regret his wasted opportunities. Meanwhile he determined to tempt his servant yet more strongly.

"Grandison," he said next morning, "I'm going away for a day or two, but I shall leave you here. I shall lock up a hundred dollars in this drawer and give you the key. If you need any of it, use it and enjoy yourself—spend it all if you like—for this is probably the last chance you'll have for some time to be in a free State, and you'd better enjoy your liberty while you may."

When he came back a couple of days later and found the faithful Grandison at his post, and the hundred dollars intact, Dick felt seriously annoyed. His vexation was increased by the fact that he could not express his feelings adequately. He did not even scold Grandison; how could he, indeed, find fault with one who so sensibly recognized his true place in the economy of civilization, and kept it with such touching fidelity?

"I can't say a thing to him," groaned Dick. "He deserves a leather medal, made out of his own hide tanned. I reckon I'll write to father and let him know what a model servant he has given me."

He wrote his father a letter which made the colonel swell with pride and pleasure. "I really think," the colonel observed to one of his friends, "that Dick ought to have the nigger interviewed by the Boston papers, so that they may see how contented and happy our darkeys really are."

Dick also wrote a long letter to Charity Lomax, in which he said, among other things, that if she knew how hard he was working, and under what difficulties, to accomplish something serious for her sake, she would no longer keep him in suspense, but overwhelm him with love and admiration.

Having thus exhausted without result the more obvious methods of getting rid of Grandison, and diplomacy having also proved a failure, Dick was forced to consider more radical measures. Of course he might run away himself, and abandon Grandison, but this would be merely to leave him in the United States, where he was still a slave, and where, with his notions of loyalty, he would speedily be reclaimed. It was necessary, in order to accomplish the purpose of his trip to the North, to leave Grandison permanently in Canada, where he would be legally free.

"I might extend my trip to Canada," he reflected, "but that would be too palpable. I have it! I'll visit Niagara Falls on the way home, and lose him on the Canada side. When he once realizes that he is actually free, I'll warrant that he'll stay."

So the next day saw them westward bound, and in due course of time, by the somewhat slow conveyances of the period, they found themselves at Niagara. Dick walked and drove about the Falls for several days, taking Grandison along with him on the Canadian side, watching the wild whirl of the waters below them.

"Grandison," Dick said, raising his voice above the roar of the cataract, "do you know where you are now?"

"I's wid you, Mars Dick; dat's all I keers."

"You are now in Canada, Grandison, where your people go when they run away from their masters. If you wished, Grandison, you might walk away from me this very minute, and I could not lay my hand upon you to take you back."

Grandison looked around uneasily.

"Let's go back ober de ribber, Mars Dick. I's feared I'll lose you ovuh heah, an' den I won' hab no marster, an' won't nebber be able to git back home no mo'."

Discouraged, but not yet hopeless, Dick said, a few minutes later—

"Grandison, I'm going up the road a bit, to the inn over yonder. You stay here until I return. I'll not be gone a great while."

"Is dey any er dem dadblasted abolitioners roun' heah, Mars Dick?"

"I don't imagine that there are," replied his master, hoping there might be. "But I'm not afraid of *your* running away, Grandison. I only wish I were," he added to himself.

Dick walked leisurely down the road to where the whitewashed inn, built on stone, with true British solidity, loomed up through the trees by the roadside. Arrived there he ordered a glass of the ale and a sandwich, and took a seat at a table by a window, from which he could see Grandison in the distance. For a while he hoped that the seed he had sown might have fallen on fertile ground, and that Grandison, relieved from the restraining power of a master's eye, and finding himself in a free country, might get up and walk away; but the hope was vain, for Grandison remained faithfully at his post, awaiting his master's return. He had seated himself on a broad flat stone, and, turning his eyes away from the grand and awe-inspiring spectacle that lay close at hand was looking anxiously toward the inn where his master sat cursing his ill-timed fidelity.

By and by a girl came into the room to serve his order, and Dick very naturally glanced at her; and as she was young and pretty and remained in attendance, it was some minutes before he looked for Grandison. When he did so his faithful servant had disappeared.

To pay his reckoning and go away without the change was a matter quickly accomplished. Retracing his footsteps toward the Falls, he was, to his great disgust, as he approached the spot where he had left Grandison, the familiar form of his servant stretched out on the ground, his face to the sun, his mouth open, sleeping the time away, oblivious alike to the grandeur of the scenery, the thunderous roar of the cataract, or the insidious voice of sentiment.

"Grandison," soliloquized his master, as he stood gazing down at his ebony encumbrance, "I do not deserve to be an American citizen; I ought not to have the advantages I possess over you; and I certainly am not worthy of Charity Lomax, if I am not smart enough to get rid of you. I have an idea! You shall yet be free, and I will be the instrument of your deliverance. Sleep on, faithful and affectionate servitor, and dream of the blue grass and the bright skies of old Kentucky, for it is only in your dreams that you will ever see them again!"

Dick retraced his footsteps towards the inn. The young woman chanced to look out of the window and saw the handsome young gentleman she had waited on a few minutes before, standing in the road a short distance away, apparently engaged in earnest conversation with a colored man employed as hostler for the inn. She thought she saw something pass from the white man to the other, but at that moment her duties called her away from the window, and when she looked out again the young gentleman had disappeared, and the hostler, with two other young men of the neighborhood, one white and one colored, were walking rapidly towards the Falls.

IV

Dick made the journey homeward alone, and as rapidly as the conveyance of the day would permit. As he drew near home his conduct in going back without Grandison took on a more serious aspect than it had borne at any previous time, and although he had prepared the colonel by a letter sent several days ahead, there was still the prospect of a bad quarter of an hour with him; not, indeed, that his father would upbraid him, but he was likely to make searching inquiries. And notwithstanding the vein of quiet recklessness that had carried Dick through his preposterous scheme, he was a very poor liar, having rarely had occasion or inclination to tell anything but the truth. Any reluctance to meet his father was more than offset, however, by a stronger force drawing him homeward, for Charity Lomax must long since have returned from her visit to her aunt in Tennessee.

Dick got off easier than he expected. He told a straight story, and a truthful one, so far as it went.

The colonel raged at first, but rage soon subsided into anger, and anger moderated into annoyance, and annoyance into a sort of garrulous sense of injury. The colonel thought he had been hardly used; he had trusted this negro, and he had broken faith. Yet, after all, he did not blame Grandison so much as he did the abolitionists, who were undoubtedly at the bottom of it.

As for Charity Lomax, Dick told her, privately of course, that he had run his father's man, Grandison, off to Canada, and left him there.

"Oh, Dick," she had said with shuddering alarm, "what have you done? If they knew they'd send you to the penitentiary, like they did that Yankee."

"But they don't know it," he had replied seriously, adding, with an injured tone, "You don't seem to appreciate my heroism like you did that of the Yankee; perhaps it's because I wasn't caught and sent to the penitentiary. I thought you wanted me to do it."

"Why Dick Owens!" she exclaimed. "You know I never dreamed of any such outrageous proceeding.

"But I presume I'll have to marry you," she concluded, after some insistence on Dick's part, "if only to take care of you. You are too reckless for anything; and a man who goes chasing all over the North, being entertained by New York and Boston society and having negroes to throw away, needs some one to look after him."

"It's a most remarkable thing," replied Dick fervently, "that your views correspond exactly with my profoundest convictions. It proves beyond question that we were made for one another."

*

They were married three weeks later. As each of them had just returned from a journey, they spent their honeymoon at home.

A week after the wedding they were seated, one afternoon, on the piazza of the colonel's house, where Dick had taken his bride, when a negro from the yard ran down the lane and threw open the big gate for the colonel's buggy to enter. The colonel was not alone. Beside him, ragged and travel-stained, bowed with weariness, and upon his face a haggard look that told of hardship and privation, sat the lost Grandison.

The colonel alighted at the steps.

"Take the lines, Tom," he said to the man who had opened the gate, "and drive round to the barn. Help Grandison down—poor devil, he's so stiff he can hardly move!—and get a tub of water and wash him and rub him down, and feed him, and give him a big drink of whiskey, and then let him come round and see his young master and his new mistress."

The colonel's face wore an expression compounded of joy and indignation—joy at the restoration of a valuable piece of property; indignation for reasons he proceeded to state.

"It's astounding, the depths of depravity the human heart is capable of! I was coming along the road three miles away, when I heard some one call me from the roadside. I pulled up the mare, and who should come out of the woods but Grandison. The poor nigger could hardly crawl along, with the help of a broken limb. I was never more astonished in my life. You could have knocked me down with a feather. He seemed pretty far gone—and I had to give him a mouthful of whiskey to brace him up so he could tell his story. It's just as I thought from the beginning, Dick; Grandison had no notion of running away; he knew when he was well off, and where his friends were. All the persuasions of abolition liars and runaway niggers did not move him. But the desperation of those fanatics knew no bounds; their guilty consciences gave them no rest. They got the notion somehow that Grandison belonged to a nigger-catcher, and had been brought North as a spy to help capture ungrateful runaway servants. They actually kidnapped him—just think of it!—and gagged him and bound him and threw him rudely into a wagon, and carried him into the gloomy depths of a Canadian forest, and locked him in a lonely hut, and fed him on bread and water for three weeks. One of the scoundrels wanted to kill him, and persuaded the others that it ought to be done; but they got to quarreling about how they should do it, Grandison escaped, and, keeping his back steadily to the North Star, made his way, after suffering incredible hardships, back to the old plantation, back to his master, his friends, and his home. Why, it's as good as one of Scott's novels! Mr. Simms or some other one of our Southern authors ought to write it up."

"Don't you think, sir," suggested Dick, who had calmly smoked his cigar throughout the colonel's animated recital, "that that kidnapping yarn sounds a little improbable? Isn't there some more likely explanation?"

"Nonsense, Dick; it's the gospel truth! Those infernal abolitionists are capable of anything—everything! Just think of their locking the poor, faithful nigger up, beating him, kicking him, depriving him of his liberty, keeping him on bread and water for three long, lonesome weeks, and he all the time pining for the old plantation!"

There were almost tears in the colonel's eyes at the picture of Grandison's sufferings that he conjured up. Dick still professed to be slightly skeptical, and met Charity's severely questioning eye with bland unconsciousness.

The colonel killed the fatted calf for Grandison, and for two or three weeks the returned wanderer's life was a slave's dream of pleasure. His fame spread throughout the county, and the colonel gave him a permanent place among the house servants, where he could always have him conveniently at hand to relate his adventures to admiring visitors.

*

About three weeks after Grandison's return the colonel's faith in sable humanity was rudely shaken, and its foundations almost broken up. He came near losing his belief in the fidelity of the negro to his master—the servile virtue most highly prized and most sedulously cultivated by the colonel and his kind. One Monday morning Grandison was missing. And not only Grandison, but his wife, Betty the maid; his mother, aunt Eunice; his father, uncle Ike; his brothers, Tom and John, and his little sister Elsie, were likewise absent from the plantation and a hurried search and inquiry in the neighborhood resulted in no information as to their whereabouts. So much valuable property could not be lost without an effort to recover it, and the wholesale nature of the transaction carried consternation to the hearts of those whose ledgers were chiefly bound in black. Extremely energetic measures were taken by the colonel and his friends. The fugitives were traced, and followed from point to point, on their northward run through Ohio. Several times the hunters were close upon their heels, but the magnitude of the escaping party begot unusual vigilance on the part of those who sympathized with the fugitives, and strangely enough, the underground railroad seemed to have had its tracks cleared and signals set for this particular train. Once, twice, the colonel thought he had them, but they slipped through his fingers.

One last glimpse he caught of his vanishing property, as he stood, accompanied by a United States marshal, on a wharf at a port on the south shore of Lake Erie. On the stern of a small steamboat which was receding rapidly from the wharf, with her nose pointing toward Canada, there stood a group of familiar dark faces, and the look they cast backward was not one of longing for the fleshpots of Egypt. The colonel saw Grandison point him out to one of the crew of the vessel, who waved his hand derisively toward the colonel. The latter shook his fist impotently—and the incident was closed.

POMPEY AND THE JACKASS

From the 1855 slave narrative, *From Slave Cabin to Pulpit*
By Peter Randolph

> "Pompey, how do I look?" the master asked.
> "O, massa, mighty. You looks mighty."
> "What do you mean 'mighty,' Pompey?"
> "Why, massa, you looks noble."
> "What do you mean by noble?"
> "Why, suh, you looks just like a lion."
> "Why, Pompey, where have you ever seen a lion?"
> "I saw one down in yonder field the other day, massa."
> "Pompey, you foolish fellow, that was a jackass."
> "Was it, massa? Well, suh, you looks just like him."

◎◎

RHYMES, RIDDLES, AND SONGS

WE RAISE DE WHEAT

From *My Bondage and My Freedom*
By Frederick Douglass

We raise de wheat, dey gib us de corn;
We bake de bread, dey gib us de crust;

We sif de meal, dey gib us de huss;
We peal de meat, dey gib us de skin;
And dat's de way dey takes us in.
We skims de pot, dey gib us de liquor,
An' say, "Dat's good enough fer a nigger."

RUN, NIGGER, RUN

Folk

Run, nigger, run; de patter-roller catch you;
Run, nigger, run; it's almost day.
Run, nigger, run; de patter-roller catch you;
Run, nigger, run, and try to get away.

Run, nigger, run, he run his best,
Stuck his head in a hornet's nest,
Jumped de fence and run fr'm de paster,
White man run, but nigger run faster.

alternate stanzas:
Run, nigger, run; de patter-roller'll catch you;
Run, nigger, run; it's almost day.
Dat nigger run, dat nigger flew,
Dat nigger lost his Sunday shoe.

Run, nigger, run; de patter-roller'll catch you;
Run, nigger, run, and try to get away.
Dat nigger run, dat nigger flew,
Dat nigger tore his shirt in two.

MASSA HAD A YALLER GAL

Folk

Massa had a yaller gal, he brought her from de Souf;
Her hair it curled so very tight she couldn't shut her mouf.

Chorus
Oh I ain't got time to tarry, Oh I ain't got time to tarry,
An' I ain't got time to tarry, boys, for I's gwine away.

He took her to de tailor, to have her mouf made small;
She swallowed up de tailor, tailorshop an' all.

Chorus
Massa had no hooks or nails, or anything like that;
So on this darky's nose he used to hang his hat.

COMIC LYRICS FROM SLAVE FOLK AND WORK SONGS

From *I Went to Atlanta*
Folk

Missus in the big house, Mammy in the yard,
Missus holdin' her white hands, Mammy workin' hard.
Old Marse ridin' all time, Niggers workin' round,
Marse sleepin' all day, Niggers diggin' in the ground.
John Morgan came to Danville and cut a mighty dash,
Last time I saw him he was under whip and lash.
I went to Atlanta, Never been dere a fo'.
White folks eat de apple, Nigger wait fo' de co'.
I went to Charleston, Never been dere a fo'.
White folks sleep on feather bed, Nigger on de flo'.

*

Our Fader which art in heaben,
White man owe me eleben and pay me seben.
D'y kingdom come, d'y will be done,
If I hadn't tuck dat I wouldn't git none.
—Anonymous

JOHN AND OLE MASSA TALES

Zora Neale Hurston added to the allure of these tales when she suggested that the trickster hero John was closely associated with the magic and mystery of the conjuring root John de Conquer. "High John de Conquer came to be a man, and a mighty man at that," Hurston wrote in 1943. "Old Massa didn't know, of course, but High John de Conquer was there walking his plantation like a natural man. . . . Old John, High John could beat the unbeatable. He was top-superior to the whole mess of sorrow. He could beat it all, and what made it so cool, finish it off with a laugh." While Ole Massa was laughing at Brer Rabbit, Hurston submits that unbeknownst to whites, Old John or High John de Con-

quer was "playing his tricks of making a way out of no-way. Hitting a straight
lick with a crooked stick. Winning the jackpot with no other stake than a laugh."

Although most of these tales portrayed John outwitting the master, some fell
into the trickster being tricked category. Two of the latter tales are included
in the following selections.

THE HORSEFLY

Folk

John and Old Boss was taking a load of cotton to the auction, and whilst
riding along, a horsefly came down on Old Boss and bit him in the back of
the neck. Old Boss gave out a holler, saying, "What was that?"

John say, "Nothin' but a common horsefly, Boss."

Boss say, "John, that weren't no horsefly. Horseflies go after mules and
jackasses."

"True, true," John say. "Howsoever, that one was a horsefly."

"Now listen, John, I say it weren't no horsefly," Old Boss say.

"Seem to me like it were," says John.

"John," Old Boss say, "you aren't calling me some kind of a mule or jackass, are you?"

"No, sir, Old Boss. You don't 'pear to be neither a mule or a jackass. Ain't
nobody round here ever say anything like that. All I knows . . . ," John say.
"All I knows . . . "

"All you knows is what?" Old Boss say.

John scratched his head. "All I knows," he say, "is I never hear tell that a
horsefly can be fooled 'bout such things."

THE DUCKS GET THE COTTON

Folk

The way it was, this man named John sharecropped cotton for Old Boss, but
whenever he sold his cotton it seemed like he owed Old Boss more than he
got for it. If John made a hundred dollars on his cotton, well, then, Old Boss
looked at his papers and made black marks all over 'em with his pencil. He'd
say, "John, 'pears to me you got a balance to me of one hundred sixty-seven
dollars and fourteen cents." And John'd say, "Old Boss, that seem a mite more'n
I get for the cotton." Old Boss tell him, "Don't worry on it too long, John. Just
give me the hundred and we'll let the rest on it ride over till next year."

Now, one time John was getting' the wagon ready to take in some cotton and Old Boss come by. "That's a nice load of cotton you got there, John," he say. "How much you reckon it'll bring?" But John was tired of that balance he always got on Old Boss's bookkeepin' books. He say, "Well, now, the way things is this year it's hard to tell." And Old Boss say, "John, what you mean it's hard to tell?" John scratch his head and look mournful. "They tell me," says John, "that they's a epidemic of ducks this year." Old Boss say, "That don't make no sense, John. What you mean about a epidemic of ducks?" "I can't rightly tell you 'bout that," John say, "but I just hear tell that the ducks is hell on cotton prices." "That's just nonsense, John," says Old Boss. "You just come on past my place on your way home and we'll settle up."

John went in to town, spent the day there and sold his cotton. He bought a few victuals at the town store and then come on back. When Old Boss saw him comin' along the road he went out to meet him. He said, "John, 'spect you did real good with your cotton. How much you make on it?" John say, "Old Boss, like I tell you, they's a duck epidemic goin' on over there, and I didn't come out good at all." "I heard you say about a duck epidemic before," says Old Boss, "and it don't make no more sense now than then. What you talkin' 'bout, John?"

"Well, to be particular short about it, Old Boss, I sold the cotton all right, and I had the money in my hand, but before I knowed it the ducks got it all. They deducks for the rotten bolls, they deducks for puttin' my wagon in the wrong place, they deducks for the commission, they deducks for the taxes, they deducks for this sugar and flour I bought, they deducks for this thing and that thing till by the time it's all over the ducks get it all. So I reckon we got to settle up some other time."

John said giddap and left Old Boss standin' side of the road. And when he get home he take his cotton money out of his shirt and put it in the jar. "All Old Boss want is to settle up," he say. "But what I need a little bit of is to settle down."

BABY IN THE CRIB

Folk

John stole a pig from Old Marsa. He was on his way home with him and his Old Marsa seen him. After John got home he looked out and seen his Old Marsa coming down to the house. So he put this pig in a cradle they used to rock the babies in in them days (some people called them cribs), and he covered him up. When his Old Marster come in John was sitting there rocking him.

Old Marster says, "What's the matter with the baby, John?" "The baby got the measles." "I want to see him," John said. "Well you can't; the doctor said if you uncover him the measles will go back in on him and kill him." So his Old Marster said, "It doesn't matter; I want to see him, John." He reached down to uncover him.

John said, "If that baby is turned to a pig now, don't blame me."

THE FIGHT

Folk

You take in the South, they always have one strong colored guy on all the plantations. He's given a lot of consideration by the boss—usually he be foreman. Can put two or three of the others in his back pocket.

So one plantation owner said to the other, "My colored guy can whip your guy." The other boss said, "I'll be damned if he can." So they signed up for a fight, them two farm owners. And so each man went and told the tough colored guy on his place that he got a fight coming up. Each tough guy went off to himself thinking, "I can't whip that bastard." Jim said, "I can't whip John," and John said, "I can't whip Jim." But back in slavery times you can't back out. So they set a date for the fight.

So the boss said to each colored guy, "What do you want for the fight? What are you going to wear?" Jim he thought he'd make a display to frighten John. He asks his boss to make a link chain, about four feet long, with an iron stake at the end of it, to drive into the ground, and to put an iron ring in his nose. And he'll be scratching and kicking up dirt when John comes, like a bull, and running back and forward on the chain. And his boss would be trying to keep him quiet. "Steady, steady there, Jim, whoa, just a few minutes."

When John's boss asked him what he wanted, he said, "Just give me Old Puss to ride down to the battling ground." He was quiet-like, tough but quiet. He was slow riding down—he almost like to be late, and forfeit the bet. That was a great big day, a holiday, people from twenty miles around was there in their horses and buggy and ox teams. So when he was late, his Missus got worried, and as soon as he came riding down she went over to him. John saw Jim on the chain and he was studying how to scare him, he was already scared himself. He's thinking fast, working his brain. When his Missus come over, he knew she would say something pretty flip. So he thinks: the minute she opens her mouth, I'll slap her. Missus said, "What kept you? Why you so late?" (*Very rough*) John he slapped her face. Jim pulled up the stake and ran, sold out, forfeited the fight.

So the loser, Jim's master, had to pay off John's boss the three or four thousand dollars they'd put in a bag. Still, John's boss got mad about his wife being slapped. He asked John, "What was the idea slapping my wife?"

"Well, Jim knowed if I slapped a white woman I'd a killed him, so he ran."

THE YEARLING

Folk

In the old days the only things the slaves got good to eat is what they stole. Old Marster lost a yea'ling, and some of the preacher's members knowed its whereabouts. So Old Marster told him to preach the hell out of the congregation that Sunday, so that whomsoever stole the yea'ling would confess having it.

The preacher got up and pernounced to the crowd: "Some of you have stole Old Marster's yea'ling. So the best thing to do is to go to Old Marster and confess that you stole the yea'ling. And get it off right now. Because if you don't, Judgment Day, the man that stole the Master's yea'ling will be there. Old Marster will be there too, the yea'ling will be there too—the yea'ling will be *staring* you in the face."

John gets up and says to the preacher, "Mr. Preacher, I understand you to say, Judgment Day, the man that stole Old Marster's yea'ling will be there, Old Marster will be there, the yea'ling will be there, yea'ling will be *staring* you in the face."

Preacher says, "That's right."

John replied then, "Let Old Marster git his yea'ling on Judgment Day— that'll be time enough."

OLD MARSTER EATS CROW

Folk

John was hunting on Old Marster's place, shooting squirrels, and Old Marster caught him, and told him not to shoot there any more. "You can keep the two squirrels you got but don't be caught down here no more." John goes out the next morning and shoots a crow. Old Marster went down that morning and caught him, and asked John to let him see the gun. John gave him the gun, and then Marster told him to let him see the shell. And Old Marster put the shell in the gun. Then he backed off from John, pointing the gun, and told John to pick the feathers off the crow, halfway down. "Now start at his head, John, and eat the crow up to where you stopped picking the feathers at."

When John finished eating, Marster gave him the gun back and throwed him the crow. Then he told John to go on and not let him be caught there no more.

John turned around and started off, and got a little piece away. Then he stopped and turned and called Old Marster. Old Marster said, "What you want, John?" John pointed the gun and says, "Lookee here, Old Marster," and throwed Old Marster the half a crow. "I want you to start at his ass and eat all the way, and don't let a feather fly from your mouth."

JOHN PRAYING

Folk

This old Boss-man said he was going to whip John within an inch of his life on Wednesday night. John started praying every day from Sunday to Wednesday. On Wednesday evening that was his last prayer. He told him, "Lord, I been praying every day since Sunday and you've never failed me. I want you to take me away this evening." The boys heard the prayer and they went down and climbed the tree with a ladder rope. So when John made his final prayer that night he said, "Lord I got to go, because I've only got fifteen minutes before my execution."

So they said, "Okay John, you'll have to come by way of the rope because my chariot is broke."

He said, "All right, Lord, let it down, I'm willing to go any way you carry me."

Little boys up in the tree put down the rope, said, "John, put your head in this loop." So they commenced tightening on the rope, and he commenced praying fast.

"O Lord, didn't you say you know everything? Well, don't you know damn well you choking me?"

OLD BOSS AND JOHN AT THE PRAYING TREE

Folk

This also happened back in the old days too. It was one year on a plantation when crops were bad. There wasn't enough food for all the slave hands, no flour at all; all they had to eat was fatback and cornbread. John and his buddy was the only slickers on the farm. They would have two kinds of meat in the house, all the lard they could use, plenty flour and plenty sugar, biscuits every morning for breakfast. (They was rogues.) The boss kept a-missing meat, but they was too slick for him to catch 'em at it.

Every morning, he'd ask John, "How you getting along over there with your family?" John said, "Well, I'm doing all right, Old Marster. (*High-pitched, whiny*) I'm fair's a middling and spick as a ham, coffee in the kittle, bread on the fire, if that ain't living I hope I die."

The Old Boss checked on John. And he saw his hams and lard and biscuits all laid up in John's place. (In those days people branded their hams with their own name.) He said, "John, I can see why you're living so high. You got all my hams and things up there." "Oh, no," John told him, "those ain't none of your ham, Boss. God give me them ham. God is good, just like you, and God been looking out for me, because I pray every night."

Boss said, "I'm still going to kill you John, because I know that's my meat."

Old John was real slick. He asked his Marster, "Tonight meet me at the old 'simmon tree. I'm going to show you God is good to me. I'm going to have some of your same ham, some of your same lard, and some of your same flour."

So that night about eight o'clock (it was dark by then in the winter), John went for his partner. They get everything all set up in the tree before John goes for Old Boss. They get out to the tree. Old Boss brings along his double-barreled shotgun, and he tells John, "Now if you don't get my flour and stuff, just like you said you would, you will never leave this tree."

So John gets down on knees and begins to pray. "Now, Lord, I never axed you for nothing that I didn't get. You know Old Marster here is about to kill me, thinking I'm stealing. Not a child of yours would steal, would he, Lord?" He says, "Now I'm going to pat on this tree three times. And I want you to rain down persimmons." John patted on the tree three times and his partner shook down all the persimmons all over Old Boss. Boss shakes himself and says, "John, Old Boss is so good to you, why don't you have God send my meat down?"

John said, "Don't get impatient; I'm going to talk to him a little while longer for you." So John prayed, "Now Lord, you know me and I know you. Throw me down one of Old Boss's hams with his same brand on it."

Just at that time the ham hit down on top of Old Boss's head. Old Boss grabbed the ham, and said, "John, I spec you better not pray no more." (Old Boss done got scared.) But John kept on praying and the flour fell. Old Boss told John, "Come on John, don't pray no more." "I just want to show you I'm a child of God," John tells him, and he prays again. "Send me down a sack of Old Boss's sugar, the same weight and the same name like on all his sacks."

"John, if you pray any more no telling what might happen to us," Boss said. "I'll give you a forty-acre farm and a team of mules if you don't pray no more." John didn't pay no attention; he prayed some more. "Now, God, I want you to do me a personal favor. That's to hop down out of the tree and horsewhip the hell out of Old Boss." So his buddy jumped out with a white sheet and laid it on Old Boss.

Boss said, "You see what you gone and done, John; you got God down on me. From now on you can go free."

PART TWO

LAY MY BURDEN DOWN ...
EMANCIPATION TO THE ROARING TWENTIES

Slave Owner:
Ah, dear, faithful, loyal Uncle Tom!
Lincoln has forced you to accept freedom—against
my wishes, and, I am sure, against yours.
Dear old friend and servant, you
need not leave this plantation. Stay here with us;
kindly, gentle, self-sacrificing Uncle Tom!
Uncle Tom:
Thank you, deah, kine, lovin', gen'rous Massa.
I reckon I'll leave. But befo' I go I wants
you ter know I will allus 'membuh you
ez de son uv a bitch you is an' allus wuz!

—Anonymous

Emancipation brought new hope and expectations to the former slaves. That hope was heightened by the federal government's attempt to assist freed Southern blacks during Reconstruction, but the effort lasted only a decade (1867–77). Afterward, the enactment of Black Codes and Jim Crow laws (which the Supreme Court upheld in the *Plessy v. Ferguson* decision of 1896) established a segregated society that was nearly as oppressive as bondage. Still, while not entirely free, African Americans were more independent, and during the late nineteenth and early twentieth centuries, their humor began to mirror the new reality. Black comedy of this period began more openly reflecting sentiments and attitudes that had been carefully masked in the plantation setting.

The more assertive tone of that comedy is reflected in the interchange between the slave owner and freedman which begins this section. In general, while traditional folk stories, self-mocking tales, and playful, freewheeling "lies" remained popular, comedy within the black community began to openly express the simmering resentment built up during the past two centuries. Disclosure of the John and Ole Massa tales, the folk idolization of the first black heavyweight champion, Jack Johnson (who refused to kowtow to whites and defied Jim Crow laws), and the surfacing of irreverent "Bad Nigger" tales and even more scandalous and profane urban ballads like "The Signifying Monkey" and "Shine, or the Sinking of the *Titanic,*" reflected the black community's discontent, anger, and estrangement. These contentious aspects of African American comedy, however, were seldom depicted in the mass media.

On the mainstream stage, in print, and—by the turn of the century—silent films, more frivolous, servile examples of black comedy prevailed. There were breakthroughs, however, in the fiction and poetry of writers Paul Lawrence Dunbar and Charles W. Chesnutt and the works of the Bert Williams and George Walker and Flournoy Miller and Aubrey Lyles comedy teams. As a featured solo performer in Ziegfeld Follies, Bert Williams emerged as the first black superstar comic and, despite blackface makeup, significantly humanized the mainstream image of black comedy. Overall, from Emancipation through World War I and the beginning of the Jazz Age, black humor took a roller coaster ride that paralleled the events of the times. It reflected the exultation of freedom, the dismay derived from the institution of legalized segregation, and the new militancy that began to emerge with urban migration and the return of black WWI veterans.

◎◎

LIES AND HOW COME TALES

GIT BACK!

Folk

I know y'all don't wanna hear it, 'cause it's a mite personal for some folks. But I'm goin' tell you why our people is black. See, God didn't create folks all at once. You know, He give 'em this part, then He call 'em back and give 'em another one. Well, when He was near through shapin' 'em up, he started callin' 'em in to give 'em color. Now our folks was layin' out under the tree of life restin' and sleepin', and they didn't hear when they was called. Finally, God sent Gabriel out to find 'em. When he told 'em God wanted 'em, they got real excited and they all run up to the throne pushin' and shovin' each other. God seed what was hap'nin', so he hollered "Git back!" They all thought He say, "Git black!" And that's why we been black to this very day.

APPLE PEELIN'

A black man and a white man was bragging
on their huntin' skills, talkin' about how good they was.
So the white man took out his pistol.
He pulled out a dime, threw it up in the air and shot a
hole clean through the middle of the coin.
Then the black man threw up an apple and
pulled out his knife; before that apple hit
the ground, he peeled it, cored it, and diced it.

—Folk

HEARD THE BULLET TWICE

Folk

Young man name Hank had pressed charges against this fellow who shot at him after they had an argument outside the barber shop. At the trial, the other fellow's lawyer was questioning Hank about some conflicts in his testimony. The lawyer say, "You testified that when the defendant pulled his gun you took off and ran. Well, how did you know that he was shooting at you?"

Hank say, "I heard de gun fire furst, den I heard de bullet when it pass by me."

"Are you absolutely sure that you heard the bullet pass you?"

"Yes suh, I'm sho' I heard de bullet pass me, fact, I heard it twice."

"You sure you heard the bullet twice—that's hard to believe. Could you please explain that to the court?"

"Well, suh, it was like this. Furst, I heard that bullet when it pass me—den I heard it again when I pass it."

THE STORY OF THE DELUGE AND HOW IT CAME ABOUT

From *Uncle Remus, His Songs and His Sayings*
By Joel Chandler Harris

"One time," said Uncle Remus—adjusting his spectacles so as to be able to see how to thread a large darning-needle with which he was patching his coat—"one time, way back yander, 'fo' you wuz borned, honey, en 'fo' Mars John er Miss Sally wuz borned—way back yander 'fo' enny un us wuz borned, de anemils en de beasteses sorter 'lecshuneer roun' 'mong deyselves, twel at las' dey 'greed fer ter have a 'sembly. In dem days," continued the old man, observing a look of incredulity on the little boy's face, "in dem days creeturs had lots mo' sense dan dey got now; let 'lone dat, dey had sense same like folks. Hit was tech en go wid um, too, mon, en w'en dey make up dere mines w'at hatter be done, 'twant mo'n menshun'd 'fo' hit wuz done. Well, dey 'lected dat dey hatter hole de complaints, en w'en de day come dey was wuz on han'. De Lion, he wuz dere, kaze he wuz de king, en he hatter be dere. De Rhynossyhoss, he wuz dere, en de Elephent, he wuz dere, en de Cammils, en de Cows, en plum down ter de Crawfishes, dey wuz dere. Dey wuz all dere. En w'en de Lion shuck his mane, en tuck his seat in de big cheer, den de sesshun begun fer ter commence."

"What did they do, Uncle Remus?" asked the little boy.

"I kin skacely call to mine 'zackly w'at dey did do, but dey spoke speeches, en hollered, en cusst, en flung der langwidge 'roun' des like w'en yo' daddy gwineter run fer de legislater en got lef'. Howsomever, dey 'ranged der 'fairs, en splained der bizness. Bimeby, w'ile dey wuz 'sputin' 'longer wunner nudder, de Elephent tromped on wunner de Crawfishes. Co'se w'en dat creetur put his foot down, w'atsumever's under dere's bound fer ter be squashed, en dey wuzn't nuff er dat Crawfish lef' fer ter tell dat he'd bin dar.

"Dis make de udder Crawfishes mighty mad, en dey sorter swawmed tergedder en draw'd up a kinder peramble wid some wharfo'es in it, en read her out in de 'sembly. But, bless grashus! sech a racket wuz a gwine on dat nobody ain't hear it, 'ceppin' may be de Mud Turkle en de Spring Lizzud, en dere enfloons wuz pow'ful lackin'.

"Bimeby, w'iles de Nunicorn wuz 'sputin' wid de Lion, en w'ile de Hyener wuz a laffin ter hisse'f, de Elephent squshed anudder one er de Crawfishes, en a little mo'n he'd er ruint de Mud Turkle. Den de Crawfishes, w'at dey wuz lef' un um, swawmed tergedder en draw'd up anudder peramble wid sum mo' wharfo'es: but dey might ez well er sung Ole Dan Tucker ter a harrycane. De udder creeturs wuz too bizzy wid der fussin' fer ter 'spon' unto de Crawfishes. So dar dey wuz, de Crawfishes, en dey kep' on gittin madder en madder en skeerder en skeerder, twel bimeby dey gun de wink ter de Mud Turkle en de Spring Lizzud, en den dey bo'd little holes in de groun' en went down outer sight."

"Who did, Uncle Remus?" asked the little boy.

"De Crawfishes, honey. Dey bo'd inter de groun' en kep' on bo'in twel dey onloost de fountains er de earf; en de waters squirt out, en riz higher en higher twel de hills wuz kivvered, en de creeturs wuz all drownded; en all bekaze dey let on 'mong deyselves dat dey wuz bigger dan de Craw-fishes."

Then the old man blew the ashes from a smoking yam, and proceeded to remove the peeling.

"Where was the ark, Uncle Remus?" the little boy inquired, presently.

"W'ich ark's dat?" asked the old man, in a tone of well-feigned curiosity.

"Noah's ark," replied the child.

"Don't you pester wid ole man Noah, honey. I boun' he tuck keer er dat ark. Dat's w'at he wuz dere fer, en dat's w'at he done. Leas'ways, dat's w'at dey tells me. But don't you bodder longer dat ark, 'ceppin' your mammy fetches it up. Dey mout er bin two deloojes, en den agin dey moutent. Ef dey wuz enny ark in dish yer w'at de Crawfishes brung on, I ain't heern tell un it, en w'en dey ain't no arks 'roun', I ain't got no time fer ter make um en put um in dere. Hit's gittin' yo' bedtime, honey."

Why the Negro Is Black

From *Uncle Remus, His Songs and His Sayings*
By Joel Chandler Harris

One night, while the little boy was watching Uncle Remus twisting and waxing some shoe-thread, he made what appeared to him to be a very curious discovery. He discovered that the palms of the old man's hands were as white as his own, and the fact was such a source of wonder that he at last made it the subject of remark. The response of Uncle Remus led to the earnest recital of a piece of unwritten history that must prove interesting to ethnologists.

"Tooby sho de pa'm er my han's w'ite, honey," he quietly remarked; "en, w'en it come ter dat, dey wuz a time w'en all de w'ite folks 'uz black—blacker dan me, kaze I done bin yer so long dat I bin sorter bleach out."

The little boy laughed. He thought Uncle Remus was making him the victim of one of his jokes; but the youngster was never more mistaken. The old man was serious. Nevertheless, he failed to rebuke the ill-timed mirth of the child, appearing to be altogether engrossed in his work. After a while he resumed:

"Yasser. Fokes dunner w'at bin yit, let 'lone w'at gwinter be. Niggers is niggers now, but de time wuz w'en we 'uz all niggers tergedder."

"When was that, Uncle Remus?"

"Way back yander. In dem times we 'uz all un us black; we 'uz all niggers tergedder, en 'cordin' ter all de 'counts w'at I years fokes 'uz gittin' 'long 'bout ez well in dem days ez dey is now. But atter 'w'ile de news come dat dere wuz a pon' er water some'rs in de naberhood, w'ich ef dey'd git inter dey'd be wash off nice en w'ite, en den one un um, he fine de place en make er splunge inter de pon', en come out w'ite ez a town gal. En den, bless grashus! w'en de fokes seed it, dey make a break fer de pon', en dem w'at

wuz de soopless, dey got in fus en dey come w'ite; en dem w'at wuz de nex'
soopless, dey got in nex', en dey come out merlaters; en dey wuz sech a
crowd un um dat dey mighty nigh use de water up, w'ich w'en dem yuthers
come 'long, de morest dey could do wuz ter paddle about wid der foots en
dabble in it wid der han's. Dem wuz de niggers, en down ter dis day dey
ain't no w'ite 'bout a nigger 'ceppin de pa'ms er der han's en de soles er der
foot."

The little boy seemed to be very much interested in this new account of
the origin of races, and he made some further inquiries, which elicited
from Uncle Remus the following additional particulars:

"De Injun en de Chinee got er be 'counted 'long er de merlatter. I ain't
seed no Chinee dat I knows un, but dey tells me dey er sorter 'twix' a brown
en a brindle. Dey er all merlatters."

"But mamma says the Chinese have straight hair," the little boy suggested.

"Co'se, honey," the old man unhesitatingly responded, "dem w'at git ter
de pon' time nuff fer ter git der head in de water, de water hit onkink der
h'ar. Hit bleedzd ter be dat away."

THE FIRST WHITE MAN

"Cain wuz an evil black man who wuz allus
fightin' 'n gamblin'," the preacher told his congegation.
"He killed his own brudda Abel in a fight
ova a watermelon. De Lawd come behin' 'n ask Cain wheah
his brudda wuz. Dat sassy nigger answer,
'Am I my brudda's keeper? I don't know wheah he at!'
But den de Lawd speak up real loud and mad,
'Wheah is yo' brudda?'
Dis time Cain turn aroun', he sees it de Lawd speakin'.
He got so scared his stand right straight an' his face turn pale.
An' dat wheah de first white man come from."

—Folk

THE WATER'S DEEP

Two fellows was walkin' over this long bridge and,
'bout the time they got to the middle, they had to piss.
So one fellow walk over to rail, pull out his dick

and commence to relievin' hisself.
"Damn, the water cold," he say to his friend.
Then his friend pull out his thing and start to take a leak.
When he finished up, he turned and say,
"Yeah, and it's deep, too!"

—Folk

⊚⁄⊚

DE OLE 'OMAN AN' ME

By A. C. Gordon

We doesn't live as wunst we did—
    De grub's done struck a change;
An' when I mentions ash-cake now,
    My wife she thinks it strange.

She's got sot-up dese las' few years,
    An' wheat-bread's all de go;
But, somehow, seems I'd like ter tas'e
    Some ash-cake pone wunst mo'.

De buttermilk has done give way
    Ter tea an' coffee now;
"An' possum-fat," she always says,
    "Ain't fit to eat nohow."

She doesn't ever foot it now,
    Like how she used ter do;
But drives my yaller mule ter town,
    An' wushes he was two!

She hasn't had a homespun coat
    For many a long day,
But w'ars de fines' sort o' clo'es,
    Made jes' de white folks way.

She doesn't call me "Ichabod,"
    Or "Ich," or "Old Fool" now;
An' ef I mention "my old crowd,"
    'Tud sartin raise a row.

"Tis "Mister Brown" an' "Mistis Brown,"
    Ontwel it seems to me
We've done gone changed our nat'rel selves
    F'om what we used ter be.

I know, beca'se as how I's tried
    An' never seed it gee;
It's awful hard ter teach new tricks
    Ter ole dogs sich as me.

Dat broad-clof coat she made me buy,
    It don't feel half so good
As dat ole jeans I used ter w'ar
    A-cuttin' marster's wood.

An' beefsteak ain't fer sich as me,
    Instid o' possum-fat;
An' "Mister Brown" ain't "Ichabod"—
    I can't git over dat!

So Mistis Brown may go ter town
    A-drivin' o' dat mule
Jes' when she likes; but, sartin sho'
    I ain't gwi' play de fool!

An' as fer her insistin' how
    Dat I should try ter learn
Dem A B C's de chillun reads—
    'Tis no consarn o' her'n.

I doesn't keer what grub she eats,
    Or what she calls herself,
Or ef she has a bo'fy now
    'Stid o' a cubbud-shelf.

I doesn't keer how fine her clo'es
    May be, or what de style—
I'm able fur ter pay fer dat,
    An' has been so some while.

Dar's only one o' all her ways
    Gits over me fer sho'—
I p'int'ly hones fer possum-fat
    An' ash-cake-pone wunst mo'!

UNCLE REMUS'S CHURCH EXPERIENCE

From *Uncle Remus, His Songs and His Sayings*
By Joel Chandler Harris

The deacon of a colored church met Uncle Remus recently, and, after some uninteresting remarks about the weather, asked:

"How dis you don't come down ter chu'ch no mo', Brer Remus? We er bin er havin' some mighty 'freshen' times lately."

"Hit's bin a long time sence I bin down dar, Brer Rastus, an' hit'll be longer. I done got my dose."

"You ain't done gone an' unjined, is you, Brer Remus?"

"Not zackly, Brer Rastus. I des tuck'n draw'd out. De members 'uz a blame sight too mutuel fer ter suit my doctrines."

"How wuz dat, Brer Remus?"

"Well, I tell you, Brer Rastus. W'en I went ter dat chu'ch, I went des ez umbill ez de nex' one. I went dar fer ter sing, an' fer ter pray, an' fer ter wushup, an' I mos' giner'lly allers had a stray shinplarster w'ich de ole 'oman say she want sont out dar ter dem cullud fokes 'cross de water. Hit went on dis way twel bimeby, one day, de fus news I know'd der was a row got up in de amen cornder. Brer Dick, he 'nounced dat dey wern't nuff money in de box; an' Brer Sim said if dey wern't he speck Brer Dick know'd whar it disappeared ter; an' den Brer Dick 'low'd dat he won't stan' no 'probusness, an' wid dat he haul off an' tuck Brer Sim under de jaw—*ker blap!*—an' den dey clinched an' drapped on de flo' an' fout under de benches an' 'mong de wimmen.

" 'Bout dat time Sis Tempy, she lipt up in de a'r, an' sing out dat she done gone an' tromple on de Ole Boy, an' she kep' on lippin' up an' slingin' out 'er han's twel bimeby—*blip!*—she tuck Sis Becky in de mouf, an' den Sis Becky riz an' fetch a grab at Sis Tempy, an' I clar' ter grashus ef hit didn't 'pear ter me like she got a poun' er wool. Atter dat de revivin' sorter het up like. Bofe un um had kin 'mong de mo'ners, an' ef you ever see skufflin' an' scramblin' hit wuz den an' dar. Brer Jeems Henry, he mounted Brer Plato an' rid 'im over de railin', an' den de preacher he start down fum de pulpit, an' des ez he wuz skippin' onter de flatform a hyme-book kotch 'im in de bur er de year, an' I be bless 'ef it didn't soun' like a bungshell'd busted. Des den, Brer Jesse, he riz up in his seat, sorter keer-less like, an' went down inter his britches atter his razer, an' right den I know'd sho' nuff trubble wuz begun. Sis Dilsey, she seed it herse'f, an' she tuck'n let off wunner dem hallyluyah hollers, an' den I disremember w'at come ter pass.

"I'm gittin' sorter ole, Brer Rastus, an' it seem like de dus' sorter shet out de pannyrammer. Fuddermo', my lim's got ter akin, mo' speshully w'en I year Brer Sim an' Brer Dick a snortin' and a skufflin' under de benches like ez dey wuz sorter makin' der way ter my pew. So I kinder hump myse'f an' scramble out, and de fus man w'at I seed was a p'leeceman, an' he had a nigger 'rested, an' de fergiven name er dat nigger wuz Remus."

"He didn't 'res' you, did he, Brer Remus?"

"Hit's des like I tell you, Brer Rastus, an' I hatter git Mars John fer to go inter my bon's fer me. Hit ain't no use fer ter sing out chu'ch ter me, Brer Rastus. I done bin an' got my dose. W'en I goes ter war, I wanter know w'at I'm doin'. I don't wanter git hemmed up 'mong no wimmen and preachers. I wants elbow-room, an' I'm bleedzd ter have it. Des gimme elbow-room."

"But Brer Remus, you ain't—"

"I mout drap in, Brer Rastus, an' den agin I moutn't, but w'en you duz see me santer in de do', wid my specs on, youk'n des say to de conger-gashun, sorter familious like, 'Yer come ole man Remus wid his hoss-pistol, an' ef dar's much uv a skuffle 'roun' yer dis evenin' youer gwineter year fum 'im.' Dat's me, an' dat's what you kin tell um. So long! 'Member me to Sis Abby."

◉◉

THE CONJURER'S REVENGE

From The Conjure Woman
By Charles W. Chesnutt

Sunday was sometimes a rather dull day at our place. In the morning, when the weather was pleasant, my wife and I would drive to town, a distance of about five miles, to attend the church of our choice. The afternoons we spent at home, for the most part, occupying ourselves with the newspapers and magazines, and the contents of a fairly good library. We had a piano in the house, on which my wife played with skill and feeling. I possessed a passable baritone voice, and could accompany myself indifferently well when my wife was not by to assist me. When these resources failed us, we were apt to find it a little dull.

One Sunday afternoon in early spring,—the balmy spring of North Car-olina, when the air is in that ideal balance between heat and cold where one wishes it could always remain,—my wife and I were seated on the front piazza, she wearily but conscientiously ploughing through a missionary report, while I followed the impossible career of the blonde heroine of a rudimentary novel. I had thrown the book aside in disgust, when I saw Julius coming through the yard, under the spreading elms, which were already in full leaf. He wore his Sunday clothes, and advanced with a dignity of movement quite different from his week-day slouch.

"Have a seat, Julius," I said, pointing to an empty rocking-chair.

"No, thanky, boss, I'll des set here on de top step."

"Oh, no, Uncle Julius," exclaimed Annie, "take this chair. You will find it much more comfortable." The old man grinned in appreciation of her solicitude, and seated himself somewhat awkwardly.

"Julius," I remarked, "I am thinking of setting out scuppernong vines on that sand-hill where the three persimmon-trees are; and while I'm working there, I think I'll plant watermelons between the vines, and get a little something to pay for my first year's work. The new railroad will be finished by the middle of summer, and I can ship the melons North, and get a good price for them."

"Ef you er gwine ter hab any mo' ploughin' ter do," replied Julius, "I 'spec' you'll ha' ter buy ernudder creetur, 'ca'se hit's much ez dem hosses kin do ter 'ten' ter de wuk dey got now."

"Yes, I thought of that. I think I'll get a mule; a mule can do more work, and doesn't require as much attention as a horse."

"I would n' 'vise you ter buy no mule," remarked Julius, with a shake of his head.

"Why not?"

"Well, you may 'low hit's all foolis'ness, but ef I wuz in yo' place, I would n' buy no mule."

"But that isn't a reason; what objection have you to a mule?"

"Fac' is," continued the old man, in a serious tone, "I doan lack ter dribe a mule. I's alluz afeared I mought be imposin' on some human creetur; eve'y time I cuts a mule wid a hick'ry, 'pears ter me mos' lackly I's cuttin' some er my own relations, er somebody e'se w'at can't he'p dey-se'ves."

"What put such an absurd idea into your head?" I asked.

My question was followed by a short silence, during which Julius seemed engaged in a mental struggle.

"I dunno ez hit's wuf w'ile ter tell you dis," he said, at length. "I doan ha'dly 'spec' fer you ter b'lieve it. Does you 'member dat club-footed man w'at hilt de hoss fer you de yuther day w'en you was gittin' out'n de rock-away down ter Mars Archie McMillan's sto'?"

"Yes, I believe I do remember seeing a club-footed man there."

"Did you eber see a club-footed nigger befo' er sence?"

"No, I can't remember that I ever saw a club-footed colored man," I replied, after a moment's reflection.

"You en Mis' Annie would n'wanter b'lieve me, ef I wuz ter 'low dat dat man was oncet a mule?"

"No," I replied, "I don't think it very likely that you could make us believe it."

"Why, Uncle Julius!" said Annie severely, "What ridiculous nonsense!"

This reception of the old man's statement reduced him to silence, and it required some diplomacy on my part to induce him to vouchsafe an explanation. The prospect of a long, dull afternoon was not alluring, and I was glad to have the monotony of Sabbath quiet relieved by a plantation legend.

"W'en I wuz a young man," began Julius, when I finally prevailed upon him to tell us the story, "dat club-footed nigger—his name is Primus—use' ter b'long ter ole Mars Jim McGee ober on de Lumbe'ton plank-road. I use' ter go ober dere ter see a 'oman w'at libbed on de plantation; dat's how I come ter know all erbout it. Dis yer Primus wuz de livelies' han' on de place, alluz a-dancin', en drinkin', en runnin' roun', en singin', en pickin' de banjo; 'cep'n' once in a w'ile, w'en he'd 'low he wa'n't treated right 'bout sump'n ernudder, he'd git so sulky en stubborn dat de w'ite folks could n' ha'dly do nuffin wid 'im.

"It wuz 'gin' de rules fer any er de han's ter go 'way fum de plantation at night; but Primus did n' min' de rules, en went w'en he felt lack it; en de w'ite folks purten' lack dey did n' know it, fer Primus was dange'ous w'en he got in dem stubborn spells, en dey'd ruther not fool wid 'im.

"One night in de spring er de year, Primus slip' off fum de plantation, en went down on de Wim'l'ton Road ter a dance gun by some er de free niggers down dere. Dey wuz a fiddle, en a banjo, en a jug gwine roun' on de outside, en Primus sung en dance' 'tel 'long 'bout two o'clock in de mawnin', w'en he start' fer home. Ez he come erlong back, he tuk a nigh-cut 'cross de cottonfiel's en 'long by de aidge er de Min'al Spring Swamp, so ez ter git shet er de patteroles w'at rid up en down de big road fer ter keep de darkies fum runnin' roun' nights. Primus was sa'nt'rin' 'long, studyin' 'bout de good time he'd had wid de gals, w'en, ez he wuz gwine by a fence co'nder, w'at sh'd he heah but sump'n grunt. He stopped a minute ter listen, en he heared sump'n grunt ag'in. Den he went ober ter de fence whar he heard de fuss, en dere, layin' in de fence co'nder, on a pile er pine straw, he seed a fine, fat shote.

"Primus look' ha'd at de shote, en den sta'ted home. But somehow er 'nudder he couldn' git away fum dat shote; w'en he tuk one step for'ards wid one foot, de yuther foot 'peared ter take two steps back'ards, en so he kep' nachly getting' closeter en closeter ter de shote. It was de beatin'es' thing! De shote des'peared ter cha'm Primus, en fus' thing you know Primus foun' hisse'f 'way up de road wid de shote on his back.

"Ef Primus had 'a' knowed whose shote dat wuz, he'd 'a' manage' ter git pas' it somehow er 'nudder. Ez it happen', de shote b'long ter a cunjuh man w'at libbed down in de free-nigger sett'ement. Co'se de cunjuh man did n' hab ter wuk his roots but a little w'ile 'fo' he foun' out who took his shote, en den de trouble begun. One mawnin', a day er so later, en befo' he got de shote eat up, Primus did n' go ter wuk w'en de hawn blow, en w'en de oberseah wen' ter look fer him, dey wa' no trace er Primus ter be 'skivered nowhar. W'en he did n' come back in a day er so mo', eve'ybody on de plantation 'lowed he had runned erway. His marster a'vertise' him in de papers, en offered a big reward fer 'im. De nigger-ketchers fotch out dey dogs, en track' 'im down ter de aidge er de swamp, en den de scent gun out; en dat was de las' anybody seed er Primus fer a long, long time.

"Two er th'ee weeks atter Primus disappear', his marster went ter town one Sad'day. Mars Jim was stan'in' in front er Sandy Campbell's bar-room, up by de ole wagon-ya'd, w'en a po' w'ite man fum down on de Wim'l'ton Road come up ter 'im en ax' 'im, kinder keerless lack, ef he did n' wanter buy a mule.

"'I dunno,' says Mars Jim; 'it 'pens on de mule, en on de price. Whar is de mule?'

"'Des 'roun' heah back er ole Tom McAllister's sto',' says de po' w'ite man.

"So de po' w'ite man tuk Mars Jim 'roun' back er de sto', en dere stood a monst'us fine mule. W'en de mule see Mars Jim, he gun a whinny, des lack he knowed him befo'. Mars Jim look' at de mule, en de mule 'peared ter be soun' en strong. Mars Jim 'lowed dey 'peared ter be sump'n fermilyus 'bout de mule's face, 'spesh'ly his eyes; but he had n' los' naer mule, en did n' hab no recommemb'ance er habin' seed de mule befo'. He ax' de po' buckrah whar he got de mule, en de po' buckrah say his brer raise' de mule down on Rockfish Creek. Mars Jim was a little s'picious er seein' a po' w'ite man wid sech a fine creetur, but he fin'lly 'greed ter gib de man fifty dollars fer de mule,—'bout ha'f w'at a good mule was wuf dem days.

"He tied de mule behin' de buggy w'en he went home, en put 'im ter ploughin' cotton de nex' day. De mule done mighty well fer th'ee er fo' days, en den de niggers 'mence' ter notice some quare things erbout him. Dey wuz a medder on de plantation whar dey use' ter put de hosses en mules ter pastur'. Hit was fence' off fum de cornfiel' on one side, but on de yuther side'n de pastur' was a terbacker-patch w'at wa'n't fence' off, 'ca'se de beastisses doan none un 'em eat terbacker. Dey doan know w'at's good! Terbacker is lack religion, de good Lawd made it fer people, en dey ain' no yuther creetur w'at kin 'preciate it. De darkies notice' dat de fus' thing de new mule done, w'en he was turnt inter de pastur', wuz ter make fer de ter-backer-patch. Co'se de did n' think nuffin un it, but nex' mawnin', w'en dey went ter ketch 'im, dey 'skivered dat he had eat up two whole rows er ter-backer plants. Atter dat dey had ter put a halter on 'im, en tie 'im ter a stake, er e'se dey would n' 'a' been naer leaf er terbacker lef' in de patch.

"Ernudder day one er de han's, name' 'Dolphus, hitch' de mule up, en dribe up here ter dis yer vimya'd,—dat wuz w'en ole Mars Dugal' own' dis place. Mars Dugal' had kilt a yearlin', en de naber w'ite folks all sont ober fer ter git some fraish beef, en Mars Jim had sont 'Dolphus fer some too. Dey wuz a wine-press in de ya'd whar 'Dolphus lef' de mule a-stan'in', en right in front er de press dey wuz a tub er grape-juice, des pressed out, en a little ter one side a bairl erbout half full er wine w'at had be'n stan'in' two er th'ee days, en had begun ter git sorter sha'p ter de tas'e. Dey wuz a cou-ple er bo'ds on top er dis yer bairl, wid a rock laid on 'em ter hol' 'em down. Ez I wuz a-sayin', 'Dolphus lef' de mule stan'in' in de ya'd, en went inter de smoke-house fer ter git de beef. Bimeby, w'en he come out, he seed de mule a-stagg'rin' 'bout de ya'd; en 'fo' 'Dolphus could git dere ter fin' out w'at wuz de matter, de mule fell right ober on his side, en laid dere des' lack he was dead.

"All de niggers 'bout de house run out dere fer ter see w'at wuz de mat-ter. Some say de mule had de colic; some say one thing en some say enud-der; 'tel bimeby one er de han's seed de top wuz off'n de bairl, en run en looked in.

"'Fo' de Lawd!' he say, 'dat mule drunk! He be drinkin' de wine.' En sho' 'nuff, de mule had pas' right by de tub er fraish grape-juice en push' de kiver off'n de bairl, en drunk two er th'ee gallon er de wine w'at had been stan'in' long ernough fer ter begin ter git sha'p.

"De darkies all made a great 'miration 'bout de mule gittin' drunk. Dey never had n' seed nuffin lack it in dey bawn days. Dey po'd water ober de mule, en tried ter sober 'im up; but it wa'n't no use, en 'Dolphus had ter take de beef home on his back, en leabe de mule dere, 'tel he slep' off 'is spree.

"I doan 'member whe'r I tol' you er no, but w'en Primus disappear' fum de plantation, he lef' a wife behin' 'im,—a monst'us good-lookin' yaller gal, name' Sally. W'en Primus had be'n gone a mont' er so, Sally 'mence' fer git lonesome, en tuk up wid ernudder young man name' Dan, w'at b'long' on de same plantation. One day dis yer Dan tuk de noo mule out in de cotton-fiel' fer ter plough, en w'en dey wuz gwine 'long de tu'n-row, who sh'd he meet but dis yer Sally. Dan look' 'roun' en he did n' see de oberseah nowhar, so he stop' a minute fer ter run on wid Sally.

"'Hoddy, honey,' sezee. 'How you feelin' dis mawnin'?'

"'Fus' rate,' 'spon' Sally. "Dey wuz lookin' at one ernudder, en dey did n' naer one un 'em pay no 'tention ter de mule, who had turnt 'is head 'roun' en wuz lookin' at Sally ez ha'd ez he could, en stretchin' 'is neck en raisin' 'is years, en whinnyin' kinder sof' ter hisse'f.

"'Yas, honey,' 'lows Dan, 'en you gwine ter feel fus' rate long ez you sticks ter me. Fer I's a better man dan dat low-down runaway nigger Primus dat you be'n wastin' yo' time wid.'

"Dan had let go de plough-handle, en had put his arm 'roun' Sally, en wuz des gwine ter kiss her, w'en sumpin ketch' 'im by the scruff er de neck en flung 'im 'way ober in de cotton-patch. W'en he pick 'isse'f up, Sally had gone kitin' down de tu'n-row, en de mule wuz stan'in' dere lookin' ez ca'm en peaceful ez a Sunday mawnin'.

"Fus' Dan had 'lowed it wuz de oberseah w'at had cotch' 'im wastin' 'is time. But dey wa'n't no oberseah in sight, so he 'cluded it must 'a' be'n de mule. So he pitch' inter de mule en lammed 'im ez ha'd ez he could. De mule tuk it all, en 'peared ter be ez 'umble ez a mule could be; but w'en dey wuz makin' de turn at de een' er de row, one er de plough-lines got under de mule's hin' leg. Dan retch' down ter git de line out, sorter keer-less like, w'en de mule haul' off en kick 'im clean ober de fence inter a brier-patch on de yuther side.

"Dan wuz mighty so' fum 'is woun's en scratches, en wuz laid up fer two er th'ee days. One night de noo mule got out'n de pastur', en went down to de quarters. Dan wuz layin' dere on his pallet, w'en he heard sump'n ban-gin' erway at de side er his cabin. He raise' up on one shoulder en look' roun', w'en w'at should he see but de noo mule's head stickin' in de winder, wid his lips drawed back over his toofs, grinnin' en snappin' at Dan des' lack he wanter eat 'im up. Den de mule went roun' ter de do', en kick' er-way lack he wanter break de do' down, 'tel bimeby somebody come 'long en driv him back ter de pastur'. W'en Sally come in a little later fum de big house, whar she'd be'n waitin' on de w'ite folks, she foun' po' Dan nigh 'bout dead, he wuz so skeered. She 'lowed Dan had had de nightmare; but w'en dey look' at de do', dey seed de marks er de mule's huffs, so dey could n' be no mistake 'bout w'at had happen'.

"Co'se de niggers tol' dey marster 'bout de mule's gwines-on. Fust he did n' pay no 'tention ter it, but atter a w'ile he tol' 'em ef dey did n' stop dey foolis'ness, he gwine tie some un 'em up. So atter dat dey did n' say nuffin mo' ter dey marster, but dey kep' on noticin' de mule's quare ways des de same.

"Long 'bout de middle er de summer dey wuz a big camp-meetin' broke out down on de Wim'l'ton Road, en nigh 'bout all de po' w'ite folks en free niggers in de settlement got 'ligion, en lo en behol'! 'mongs 'em wuz de cunjuh man w'at own' de shote w'at cha'med Primus.

"Dis cunjuh man wuz a Guinea nigger, en befo' he wuz sot free had use' ter b'long ter a gent'eman down in Sampson County. De cunjuh man say his daddy wuz a king, er a guv'ner, er some sorter w'at-you-may-call-'em 'way ober yander in Affiky whar de niggers come fum, befo' he was stoled erway en sol' ter de spekilaters. De cunjuh man had he'ped his marster out'n some trouble ernudder wid his goopher, en his marster had sot him free, en bought him a tra' er land down on de Wim'l'ton Road. He purten' ter be a cow-doctor, but eve'ybody knowed w'at he r'al'y wuz.

"De cunjuh man had n' mo' d'n come th'oo good, befo' he wuz tuk sick wid a col' w'at he kotch kneelin' on de groun' so long at de mou'ners' bench. He kep' gittin' wusser en wusser, en bimeby de rheumatiz tuk holt er 'im, en drawed him all up, 'tel one day he sont word up ter Mars Jim McGee's plantation, en ax' Pete, de nigger w'at tuk keer er de mules, fer ter come down dere dat night en fetch dat mule w'at his marster had bought fum de po' w'ite man dyoin' er de summer.

"Pete did n' know w'at de cunjuh man wuz dribin' at, but he did n' daster stay way; en so dat night, w'en he'd done eat his bacon en his hoe-cake, en drunk his 'lasses-en-water, he put a bridle on de mule, en rid 'im down ter de cunjuh man's cabin. W'en he got ter de do', he lit en hitch' de mule, en den knock' at de do'. He felt mighty jubous 'bout gwine in, but he was bleedst ter do it; he kowed he could n' he'p 'isse'f.

"'Pull de string,' sez a weak voice, en w'en Pete lif' de latch en went in, de cunjuh man was layin' on de bed, lookin' pale en weak, lack he did n' hab much longer fer ter lib.

"'Is you fotch' de mule?' sezee.

"Pete say yes, en de cunjuh man kep' on.

"'Brer Pete,' sezee, I's be'n a monst'us sinner man, en I's done a power er wickedness endyoin' er my days; but de good Lawd is wash' my sins erway, en I feels now dat I's boun' fer de kingdom. En I feels, too, dat I ain' gwine ter git up fum dis bed no mo' in dis worl', en I wants ter ondo some er de harm I done. En dat's de reason, Brer Pete, I sont fer you ter fetch dat mule down here. You 'member dat shote I was up ter yo' plantation inquirin' 'bout las' June?'

"'Yas,' says Pete, 'I 'member yo axin' 'bout a shote you had los'.'

"'I dunno whe'r you eber l'arnt it er no,' says de cunjuh man, 'but I done knowed yo' marster's Primus had tuk de shote, en I wuz boun' ter git eben wid 'im. So one night I cotch' 'im down by de swamp on his way ter a candy-pullin', en I th'owed a goopher mixtry on 'im, en turnt 'im ter a mule, en got a po' w'ite man ter sell de mule, en we 'vided de money. But I doan want ter die 'tel I turn Brer Primus back ag'in.'

"Den de cunjuh man ax' Pete ter take down one er two go'ds off'n a she'f in de corner, en one er two bottles wid some kin' er mixtry in 'em, en set 'em on a stool by de bed; en den he ax' 'im ter fetch de mule in.

"W'en de mule come in de do', he gin a snort, en started fer de bed, des lack he was gwine ter jump on it.

"'Hol' on dere, Brer Primus!' de cunjuh man hollered. 'I's monst'us weak, en ef you 'mence on me, you won't nebber hab no chance fer ter git turn' back no mo'.'

"De mule seed de sense er dat, en stood still. Den de cunjuh man tuk de go'ds en bottles, en 'mence' ter wuk de roots en yarbs, en de mule 'mence' er turn back ter a man,—fust his years, den de res' er his head, den his shoulders en arms. All de time de cunjuh man kep' on wukkin' his roots; en Pete en Primus could see he wuz gittin' weaker en weaker all de time.

"'Brer Pete,' sezee, bimeby, 'gimme a drink er dem bitters out'n dat green bottle on de she'f yander. I's gwine fas', en it'll gimme strenk fer ter finish dis wuk.'

"Brer Pete look' up on de mantelpiece, en he seed a bottle in de corner. It was so da'k in de cabn he could n' tell whe'r it wuz a green bottle er no. But he hilt de bottle ter de cunjuh man's mouf, en he tuk a big mouff'l. He had n' mo' d'n swallowed it befo' he 'mence' ter holler.

"'You gimme de wrong bottle, Brer Pete; dis yer bottle's got pizen in it, en I's done fer dis time, sho'. Hol' me up, fer de Lawd's sake! 'tel I git th'oo turnin' Brer Primus back.'

"So Pete hilt him up, en he kep' on wukkin' de roots, 'tel he got de goopher all tuk off'n Brer Primus 'cep'n' one foot. He had n' got his foot mo' d'n half turnt back befo' his strenk gun out enti'ely, en he drap' de roots en fell back on de bed.

"'I can't do no mo' fer you, Brer Primus,' sezee, 'but I hopes you will fergib me fer w'at harm I done you. I knows de good Lawd done fergib me, en I hope ter meet you bofe in glory. I sees de good angels waitin' fer me up yander, wid a long w'ite robe en a starry crown, en I'm on my way ter jine 'em.' En so de cunjuh man died, en Pete en Primus went back ter de plantation.

"De darkies all made a great 'miration w'en Primus come back. Mars Jim let on lack he did n' b'lieve de tale de two niggers tol'; he sez Primus had runned erway, en stay' 'tel he got ti'ed er de swamps, en den come back on him ter be fed. He tried ter 'count fer de shape er Primus' foot by sayin' Primus got his foot smash', er snake-bit, er sump'n, w'iles he wuz eerway, en den stayed out in de woods whar he could n' git it kyoed up straight, 'stidder comin' long home whar a doctor could 'a' 'tended ter it. But de niggers all notice' dey marster did n' tie Primus up, ner take on much 'ca'se de mule wuz gone. So dey 'lowed dey marster must'a had his s'picions 'bout dat conjuh man."

My wife had listened to Julius's recital with only mild interest. When the old man had finished it she remarked:—

"That story does not appeal to me, Uncle Julius, and is not up to your usual mark. It isn't pathetic, it has no moral that I can discover, and I can't see why you should tell it. In fact, it seems to me like nonsense."

The old man looked puzzled as well as pained. He had not pleased the lady, and he did not seem to understand why.

"I'm sorry, ma'm," he said reproachfully, "ef you doan lack dat tale. I can't make out w'at you means be some er dem wo'ds you uses, but I'm tellin' nuffin' but de truf. Co'se I did n' see de cunjuh man tu'n 'im back, fer I wuz n' dere; but I be'n hearin' de tale fer twenty-five yeahs, en I ain' got no 'casion fer ter 'spute it. Dey's so many things a body knows is lies, dat dey ain' no use gwine roun' findin' fault wid tales dat mought des ez well be so ez not. F'instance, dey's a young nigger gwine ter school in town, en he come out heah de yuther day en 'lowed dat de sun stood still en de yeath turnt roun' eve'y day on a kinder axletree. I tol' dat young nigger ef he did n' take hisse'f 'way wid dem lies, I'd take a buggy-trace ter 'im; fer I sees de yeath stan'in' still all de time, en I sees de sun gwine roun' it, en ef a man can't b'lieve w'at 'e sees, I can't see no use in libbin'—mought's well die en be whar we can't see nuffin. En ernudder thing w'at proves de tale 'bout dis ole Primus is de way he goes on ef anybody ax' him how he come by dat club-foot. I axed 'im one day. mighty perlite en civil, en he call' me a' ole fool, en got so mad he ain' spoke ter me sence. Hit's monst'us quare. But dis is a quare worl', anyway yer kin fix it," concluded the old man, with a weary sigh.

"Ef you makes up yo' min' not ter buy dat mule, suh," he added, as he rose to go, "I knows a man w'at's got a good hoss he wants ter sell,— leas'ways dat's w'at I heared. I'm gwine ter pra'rmeetin' ternight, en I'm gwine right by de man's house, en ef you'd lack ter look at de hoss, I'll ax 'im ter fetch him roun'."

"Oh, yes," I said, "you can ask him to stop in, if he is passing. There will be no harm in looking at the horse, though I rather think I shall buy a mule."

Early next morning the man brought the horse up to the vineyard. At that time I was not a very good judge of horse-flesh. The horse appeared sound and gentle, and, as the owner assured me, had no bad habits. The man wanted a large price for the horse, but finally agreed to accept a much smaller sum, upon payment of which I became possessed of a very fine-looking animal. But alas for the deceitfulness of appearances! I soon ascertained that the horse was blind in one eye, and that the sight of the other was very defective; and not a month elapsed before my purchase developed most of the diseases that horse-flesh is heir to, and a more worthless, broken-winded, spavined quadruped never disgraced the noble name of horse. After worrying through two or three months of life, he expired one night in a fit of the colic. I replaced him with a mule, and Julius henceforth had to take his chances of driving some metamorphosed unfortunate.

Circumstances that afterward came to my knowledge created in my mind a strong suspicion that Julius may have played a more than unconscious part in this transaction. Among other significant facts was his appearance, the Sunday following the purchase of the horse, in a new suit of store clothes, which I had seen displayed in the window of Mr. Solomon Cohen's store on my last visit to town, and had remarked on account of their striking originality of cut and pattern. As I had not recently paid Julius any money, and as he had no property to mortgage, I was driven to conjecture to account for his possession of the means to buy the clothes. Of course I would not charge him with duplicity unless I could prove it, at least to a moral certainty, but for a long time afterwards I took his advice only in small doses and with great discrimination.

@/@

JOHN SHARECROPS FOR OLD BOSS

Folk

John, he heard they was an Old Boss up the river had twenty good acres to let out to a reliable man, and he went up there and told him he was as good a man as he could find to farm that land.

"You got credentials?" Boss ask him.

John say, "You mean something to tell how good I can work?"

"That's it," Boss tell him. "And I don't want no shiftless, stupid black man settin' on my place."

John show him the calluses on his hands, say, "Boss, these calluses is my credentials, and as to bein' stupid, anyone can tell you I'm a sharp man to come and sharecrop for you."

"Well, now," the Boss say, "we goin' to give it a try." He take John with him and they go down to the twenty acres. Now Old Boss can't think nothin' 'cept cotton, and he tell John this way: "We got to speak of the arrangements. You ready?"

John say, "Yes, Captain, I'm ready."

Boss say, "John, the arrangements is that we go half and half. That suit you?"

"Yes, sure suits me," John say.

"The way it is," Boss say, "I get the tops and you get the bottoms."

John ponder on it a while.

Boss say, thinkin' about all that cotton, "What's the matter, John, don't it suit you?"

John tell him, "Why, yes, sir, Captain, it suits me fine. We can shake hands on that."

They shake hands on it and Boss went home.

John, he went to work on that land, plowed it all up and harried it. Then he plant. But he don't plant cotton like Boss has in his mind, he plant 'taters. And 'bout the time the 'taters has good green vines on 'em, John stop by Boss's house, say, "Captain, the crop is growin' mighty fine. You want to see how it looks?"

Boss say, "Yes, I'm comin' to look. Been meanin' to get down there long before this." When he get there he see John workin' in that great big 'tater patch.

"Captain," John tell him, "count of you ask for the tops and you give me the bottoms, you sure got you'self a mighty fine crop of greens. I goin' to bring them over in the wagon soon as I dig out the 'taters."

Boss, he got a real sad look on him. He say, "Well, John, you sure fix me that time. But I got one thing to tell you. Next year you better look out, cause I goin' to take the bottoms and you can take the tops."

John shake his head up and down. "That's sure a fair arrangement," he say, "and I'm ready to shake hands on it."

So they shake hands 'bout the next year's crop, and Boss went home.

Well the next year John don't plant 'taters, he plant the field with oats. This time the Boss don't stay away so long, and on the way down he meet John on the road.

John say, "Captain, you come just at the right time. I sure want you to look at the crop. It's comin' along just fine."

When they was gettin' close to the field, John tell him, "Guess this year goin' to make you feel pretty happy, Captain, cause you takes the bottoms and leaves me the tops."

"Yes, John, this year I take the bottoms, but what you goin' to do with the tops sure mystifies me plenty."

Then they come to the field and Old Boss just stand there lookin'.

"That crop sure is pretty, ain't it?" John say. "Never did see a better stand of oats long as I been farmin'. You goin' to get a sizable lot of stalks, Captain. Reckon it goin' to make good straw to bed down the horses."

Old Boss shake his head, say, "John you outsmart me. You never said you was plantin' oats. But it goin' to be different next year. It goin' to be so different you ain't goin' to like it one bit. The way it goin' to be, John, is that I am goin' to take the tops and the bottoms and you get what is left. All you get is the middle. And if you ain't ready to shake hands on it right now you can pack up and get in your wagon and find you'self a home elsewhere."

John, he pondered some on that one.

"Well," Old Boss say, "what's it goin' to be?"

"Look like they isn't too much in it for me," John say, "but you been good to me on this place, Captain, and I goin' to take that proposition and shake on it."

Next year John plowed up all his twenty acres and harried the ground good, and after that he planted his crop. Old Boss was pretty busy with things, but round the middle of July he consider he better go over and see how John's field is doin'. He met John on the road again.

John say, "Old Boss, I was just on the way to get you. It's a real nice crop I got and I want you to see it."

And when they got to John's field, what you think Old Boss found? All John had planted was corn, twenty acres of it.

"You sure got a mighty fine stand of tassels above and stalks at the bottom," John say. "But me and my family prefers the ears in the middle. What kind of arrangement you want to make for next year?"

Old Boss say, "John, next year they ain't goin' to be no top, bottom or middle arrangement. I'll take same as you, just half and half."

JOHN ON TRIAL

Folk

One day the sheriff came out to the plantation and arrested John, one of the Negro workers. They took John down to the jailhouse with two white workers who were arrested that same day on a nearby plantation. John and the two white fellows were all charged with stealing, and came to trial on the same day.

John was known for lyin' and coming up with good excuses for whatever he did but he was scared when they brought him into court. He tried hard as he could and still couldn't think of an excuse for what he did. The white men were being tried first, so John decided to listen and copy whatever they say when his turn came.

The first white man was accused of stealing a horse.

"Guilty or not guilty?" the judge asked.

"Not guilty," the man said. "I've owned that horse ever since he was a colt." The case was dismissed.

The next white man was accused of stealing a cow. When he was called up to the stand the judge asked, "Guilty or not guilty?"

"Not guilty," the defendant said. "I've owned that cow ever since she was a calf." The Judge dismissed the case.

Then John was called up to the stand. He was accused of stealing a wagon.

"Guilty or not guilty?" the judge asked.

"Not guilty, yo' honor, suh," John said. "Ah been ownin' dat wagon ever since it was a wheelbarrow."

UNCLE REMUS AND THE SAVANNAH DARKEY

From *Uncle Remus, His Songs and His Sayings*
By Joel Chandler Harris

The notable difference existing between the negroes in the interior of the cotton states and those on the seaboard—a difference that extends to habits and opinions as well as to dialect—has given rise to certain ineradicable prejudices which are quick to display themselves whenever an opportunity offers. These prejudices were forcibly, as well as ludicrously, illustrated in Atlanta recently. A gentleman from Savannah had been spending the summer in the mountains of north Georgia, and found it convenient to take along a body-servant. The body-servant was a very fine specimen of the average coast negro—sleek, well-conditioned, and consequential—disposed to regard with undisguised contempt everything and everybody not indigenous to the rice-growing region—and he paraded around the streets with quite a curious and critical air. Espying Uncle Remus languidly sunning himself on a corner, the Savannah darkey approached.

"Mornin', sah."

"I'm sorter up an' about," responded Uncle Remus, carelessly and calmly. "How is you stannin' it?"

"Tanky you, my helt mos' so-so. He mo' hot dun in de mountain. Seen so lak man mus' git neeth de shade. I enty fer see no rice-bud in dis pa'ts."

"In dis w'ich?" inquired Uncle Remus, with a sudden affectation of interest.

"In dis pa'ts. In dis country. Da plenty in Sawanny."

"Plenty whar?"

"Da plenty in Sawanny. I enty fer see no crab an' no oscher; en swimp, he no stay 'roun'. I lak some rice-bud now."

"Youer talkin' 'bout deze yer sparrers, w'ich dey er all head, en 'lev'm un makes one moufful, I speck," suggested Uncle Remus. "Well, dey er yer," he continued, "but dis ain't no climate whar de rice-birds flies inter yo' pockets en gits out de money an' makes de change derse'f; an' de isters don't shuck off der shells en run over ter you on de street, an' no mo' duz de s'imp hull derse'f an' drap in yo' mouf. But dey er yer, dough. De scads 'll fetch um."

"Him po' country fer true," commented the Savannah negro; "he no like Sawanny. Down da, we set need de shade an' eaty de rice-bud, an' de buckra man drinky him wine, an' smoky him seegyar all troo de night. Plenty fer eat an' not much fer wuk."

"Hit's mighty nice, I speck," responded Uncle Remus, gravely. "De nigger dat ain't hope up 'longer high feedin' ain't got no grip. But up yer whar fokes is gotter scramble 'roun' an' make der own livin', de vittles wat's kumerlated widout enny sweatin' mos' allers gener'lly b'longs ter some yuther man by rights. One hoe-cake an' a rasher er middlin' meat las's me fum Sunday ter Sunday, an' I'm in a mighty big streak er luck w'en I gits dat."

The Savannah negro here gave utterance to a loud, contemptuous laugh, and began to fumble somewhat ostentatiously with a big brass watch-chain.

"But I speck I struck up wid a payin' job las' Chuseday," continued Uncle Remus, in a hopeful tone.

"Wey you gwan do?"

"Oh, I'm waitin' on a cullud gemmun fum Savannah—wunner deze yer high livers you bin tellin' 'bout."

"How dat?"

"I loant 'im two dollars," responded Uncle Remus, grimly, "an' I'm waitin' on 'im fer de money. Hit's wunner deze yer jobs w'at las's a long time."

The Savannah negro went off after his rice-birds, while Uncle Remus leaned up against the wall and laughed until he was in imminent danger of falling down from sheer exhaustion.

JESSE JAMES AND THE GRAVEYARD

Folk

After Jesse James, the famous bank robber, robbed a bank out there in Kansas, a posse was hot on his trail. So he was looking for a place to hide his money. One of his gang members told him to put it in the Negro graveyard because all the colored folks was scared of dead folks and they wouldn't bother with it.

Jesse didn't know it, but there was an escaped Negro convict hiding out in the graveyard the night they come to hide the money. That nigger wasn't scared a nothin', not even the sheriff. When he saw Jesse and his gang, he quick climbed up a tree so they wouldn't know he was there.

After Jesse buried the money, he put a sign over it. Sign say, "Dead and Buried." The Negro watched the whole thing, and just soon as Jesse and Frank left, he climb down from that tree, dug up the money, and hightailed it.

'Bout two weeks later, when Jesse and the gang returned to get their money, the sign they left was gone. There was a new sign, and it said: "Risen and Gone!"

POST-SLAVERY APHORISMS

Folk

- De crawfish in a hurry look like he tryin' to git dar yesterday.
- Path wid de deepest footprints ain't de only road to heben.
- Ugly nigger don't fool much wid de lookin' glass.
- De rich git richer and de po' git children.

- Some smart folks show dey ignunce mistakin' fact for truth.
- Souls like cotton, de cleaner de cotton de quicker de dirt shows.
- It don't make much diffunce whar the rain come fum, jes' so it hits de groun' in de right place.
- De price of your hat ain't de measure of your brain.
- If you want ter fine a lost pin, look fer de sharp end.
- When it take half a hoecake to ketch a catfish, you better let 'em lone.
- Muzzle on de yard dog unlocks de smokehouse.
- You wins some and you loses some, but most times you jes' get rained out.
- Heap o' people rickerlec' favors by markin' 'em in de snow.
- Quicksand don't advertize by hangin' out stop signs.
- Don't trus' a gittar-playin' man wid de strings o' yo gal's heart.
- Cain't always harvest no grapes when you struggles in folks' moral vineyard.

WHEN MALINDY SINGS

By Paul Laurence Dunbar

G'way an' quit dat noise, Miss Lucy—
  Put dat music book away;
What's de use to keep on tryin'?
  Ef you practise twell you're gray,
You cain't sta't no notes a-flyin'
  Lak de ones dat rants and rings
F'om de kitchen to de big woods
  When Malindy sings.

You ain't got de nachel o'gans
  Fu' to make de soun' come right,
You ain't got de tu'ns an' twistin's
  Fu' to make it sweet an' light.
Tell you one thing now, Miss Lucy,
  An' I'm tellin' you fu' true,
When hit comes to raal right singin',
  'T ain't no easy thing to do.

Easy 'nough fu' folks to hollah,
  Lookin' at de lines an' dots,

When dey ain't no one kin sence it,
   An' de chune comes in, in spots;
But fu' real melojous music,
   Dat jes' strikes yo' hea't and clings,
Jes' you stan' an' listen wif me
   When Malindy sings.

Ain't you nevah hyeahd Malindy?
   Blessed soul, rek up de cross!
Look hyeah, ain't you jokin', honey?
   Well, you don't know whut you los'.
Y' ought to hyeah dat gal a-wablin',
   Robins, la'ks, an' all dem things,
Heish dey moufs an' hides dey faces
   When Malindy sings.

Fiddlin' man jes' stop his fiddlin',
   Lay his fiddle on de she'f;
Mockin'-bird quit tryin' to whistle,
   'Cause he jes' so shamed hisse'f.
Folks a-playin' on de banjo
   Draps dey fingahs on de strings—
Bless yo' soul—fu'gits to move 'em,
   When Malindy sings.

She jes' spreads huh mouf and hollahs,
   "Come to Jesus," twell you hyeah
Sinnahs' tremblin' steps and voices,
   Timid-lak a-drawin' neah;
Den she tu'ns to "Rock of Ages,"
   Simply to de cross she clings,
An' you fin' yo' teahs a-drappin'
   When Malindy sings.

Who dat says dat humble praises
   Wif de Master nevah counts?
Heish yo' mouf, I hyeah dat music,
   Ez hit rises up an' mounts—
Floatin' by de hills an' valleys,
   Way above dis buryin' sod,
Ez hit makes its way in glory
   To de very gates of God!

Oh, hit's sweetah dan de music
  Of an edicated band;
An' hit's dearah dan de battle's
  Song o' triumph in de lan'.
It seems holier dan evenin'
  When de solemn chu'ch bell rings,
Ez I sit an' ca'mly listen
  While Malindy sings.

Towsah, stop dat ba'kin, hyeah me!
  Mandy, mek dat chile keep still;
Don't you hyeah de echoes callin'
  F'om de valley to de hill?
Let me listen, I can hyeah it,
  Th'oo de bresh of angel's wings,
Sof' an' sweet, "Swing Low, Sweet Chariot,"
  Ez Malindy sings.

PRACTICAL PREACHER

They used to baptize people by immersion in the river,
and in some rural areas they still do. In one of those backwoods
    communities a preacher put a sister under.
When she came up, instead of praising the Lord
    she shouted, "I seen Jesus! I seen Jesus!"
"No you didn't," said the preacher. "Jus' say 'Blessed
        be the Lawd, I'm saved.'"
"But I seen Jesus!" she yelled again.
"Oh hesh up, Sistah," the preacher snapped impatiently,
  "I seen that too. It wasn't nothin' but a turtle!"

—Folk

THE PREACHER AND THE BOARD MEETING

Folk

A country preacher in Tunica, Mississippi finished his sermon and then told the congregation that he wanted the members of the board to stay for a few minutes. A stranger who had been passing through town and stopped in the church that morning remained in his seat after everybody else but the elders and deacons left the church.

The minister approached him and said, "Sir, maybe you misuderstood, but I only asked that the board stay for the meeting."

"Well, that sho nuff include me," the stranger said, "cause I ain't never been mo' bored in my life."

COLORED IN AMERICA

Queried about his thoughts on being a Negro
in America, the laconic, ever tactful
Ziegfeld Follies star **Bert Williams** replied,
"It's no disgrace to be colored,
but it is very inconvenient."

◎◎

THE FRUITFUL SLEEPING OF THE REV. ELISHA EDWARDS

From *The Strength of Gideon and Other Stories*
By Paul Laurence Dunbar

There was great commotion in Zion Church, a body of Christian worshippers, usually noted for their harmony. But for the last six months, trouble had been brewing between the congregation and the pastor. The Rev. Elisha Edwards had come to them two years before, and he had given them good satisfaction as to preaching and pastoral work. Only one thing had displeased his congregation in him, and that was his tendency to moments of meditative abstraction in the pulpit. However much fire he might have displayed before a brother minister arose to speak, and however much he might display in the exhortation after the brother was done with the labors of hurling philippics against the devil, he sat between in the same way, with head bowed and eyes closed.

There were some who held that it was a sign in him of deep thoughtfulness, and that he was using these moments for silent prayer and meditation. But others, less generous, said that he was either jealous of or indifferent to other speakers. So the discussion rolled on about the Rev. Elisha, but it did not reach him and he went on in the same way until one hapless day, one tragic, one never-to-be-forgotten day. While Uncle Isham Dyer was exhorting the people to repent of their sins, the disclosure came. The old man had arisen on the wings of his eloquence and was painting hell for the sinners in the most terrible colors, when to the utter surprise of the whole congregation, a loud and penetrating snore broke form the throat of the pastor of the church. It rumbled down the silence and startled the congregation into sudden and indignant life like the surprising cannon of an invading host. Horror-stricken eyes looked into each other, hands were thrown into the air, and heavy lips made round O's of surprise and anger. This was his meditation. The Rev. Elisha Edwards was asleep!

Uncle Isham Dyer turned around and looked down on his pastor in disgust, and then turned again to his exhortations, but he was disconcerted, and soon ended lamely.

As for the Rev. Elisha himself, his snore rumbled on the through the church, his head drooped lower, until with a jerk, he awakened himself. He sighed religiously, patted his foot upon the floor, rubbed his hands together, and looked complacently over the aggrieved congregation. Old ladies moaned and old men shivered, but the pastor did not know what they had discovered, and shouted Amen, because he thought something Uncle Isham had said was affecting them. Then, when he arose to put the cap sheaf on his local brother's exhortations, he was strong, fiery, eloquent, but it was of no use. Not a cry, not a moan, not an Amen could he gain from his congregation. Only the local preacher himself, thinking over the scene which had just been enacted, raised his voice, placed his hands before his eyes, and murmured, "Lord he'p we po' sinnahs!"

Brother Edwards could not understand this unresponsiveness on the part of the people. They had been wont to weave and moan and shout and sigh when he spoke to them, and when, in the midst of his sermon, he paused to break into spirited song, they would join with him until the church rang again. But this day, he sang alone, and ominous glances were flashed from pew to pew and from aisle to pulpit. The collection that morning was especially small. No one asked the minister home to dinner, an unusual thing, and so he went his way, puzzled and wondering.

Before church that night, the congregation met together for conference. The exhorter of the morning himself opened proceedings by saying, "Brothahs an' sistahs, de Lawd has opened ouah eyes to wickedness in high places."

"Oom—oom—oom, he have opened ouah eyes," moaned an old sister.

"We have been puhmitted to see de man who was intrusted wid de guidance of dis flock a-sleepin' in de houah of duty, an' we feels grieved ternight."

"He sholy were asleep," sister Hannah Johnson broke in, "dey ain't no way to 'spute dat, dat man sholy were asleep."

"I kin testify to it," said another sister, "I p'intly did hyeah him sno', an' I hyeahed him sno't w'en he waked up."

"An' we been givin' him praise fu' meditation," pursued Brother Isham Dyer, who was only a local preacher, in fact, but who had designs on ordination, and the pastoring of Zion Church himself.

"It ain't de sleepin' itse'f," he went on, "ef you 'member in de Gyarden of Gethsemane, endurin' de agony of ouah Lawd, dem what he tuk wid him fu' to watch while he prayed, went to sleep on his han's. But he fu'give 'em, fu' he said, 'De spirit is willin' but de flesh is weak.' We know dat dey is times w'en de eyes grow sandy, an' de haid grow heavy, an' we ain't accusin' ouah brothah, nor a-blamin' him fu' noddin'. But what we do blame him fu' is fu' 'ceivin' us, an' mekin' us believe he was prayin' an' meditatin', w'en he wasn't doin' a blessed thing but snoozin'."

"Dat's it, dat's it," broke in a chorus of voices. "He 'ceived us, dat's what he did."

The meeting went stormily on, the accusation and the anger of the people against the minister growing more and more. One or two were for dismissing him then and there, but calmer counsel prevailed and it was decided to give him another trial. He was a good preacher they had to admit. He had visited them when they were sick, and brought sympathy to their afflictions, and a genial presence when they were well. They would not throw him over, without one more chance, at least, of vindicating himself.

This was well for the Rev. Elisha, for with the knowledge that he was to be given another chance, one trembling little woman, who had listened in silence and fear to the tirades against him, crept out of the church, and hastened over in the direction of the parsonage. She met the preacher coming toward the church, hymn-book in hand, and his Bible under his arm. With a gasp, she caught him by the arm, and turned him back.

"Come hyeah," she said, "come hyeah, dey been talkin' 'bout you, an' I want to tell you."

"Why, Sis' Dicey," said the minister complacently, "what is the mattah? Is you troubled in sperit?"

"I's troubled in sperit now," she answered, "but you'll be troubled in a minute. Dey done had a church meetin' befo' services. Dey foun' out you was sleepin' dis mornin' in de pulpit. You ain't only sno'ed, but you sno'ted, and dey 'lowin' to give you one mo' trial, an' ef you falls f'om grace agin, dey gwine ax you fu' to 'sign f'om de pastorship."

The minister staggered under the blow, and his brow wrinkled. To leave there in disgrace; where would he go? His career would be ruined. The story would go to every church of the connection in the country, and he would be an outcast from his cloth and his kind. He felt that it was all a mistake after all. He loved his work, and he loved his people. He wanted to do the right thing, but oh, sometimes, the chapel was hot and the hours were long. Then his head would grow heavy, and his eyes would close, but it had been only for a minute or two. Then, this morning, he remembered how he had tried to shake himself awake, how gradually, the feeling had overcome him. Then—then—he had snored. He had not tried wantonly to deceive them, but the Book said, "Let not thy right hand know what thy left hand doeth." He did not think it necessary to tell them that he dropped into an occasional nap in church. Now, however, they knew it all.

He turned and looked down at the little woman, who waited to hear what he had to say.

"Thankye, ma'am, Sis' Dicey," he said. "Thankye, ma'am. I believe I'll go back an' pray ovah this subject." And he turned and went back into the parsonage.

Whether he had prayed over it or whether he merely thought over it, and made his plans accordingly, when the Rev. Elisha came into church that night, he walked with a new spirit. There was a smile on his lips, and the light of triumph in his eyes. Throughout the Deacon's long prayer, his loud and insistent Amens precluded the possibility of any sleep on his part. His sermon was a masterpiece of fiery eloquence, and as Sister Green stepped out of the church door that night, she said, "Well, ef Brothah Edwards slep' dis mornin', he sholy prached a wakenin' up sermon ter-night." The congregation hardly remembered that their pastor had ever been asleep. But the pastor knew when the first flush of enthusiasm was over that their minds would revert to the crime of the morning, and he made plans accordingly for the next Sunday which should again vindicate him in the eyes of his congregation.

The Sunday came round, and as he ascended to the pulpit, their eyes were fastened upon him with suspicious glances. Uncle Isham Dyer had a smile of triumph on his face, because the day was a particularly hot and drowsy one. It was on this account, the old man thought, that Rev. Elisha asked him to say a few words at the opening of the meeting. "I reckon he wants to go to sleep again, but ef he don't sleep dis day to his own confusion, I ain't hyeah." So he arose, and burst into a wonderful exhortation on the merits of a Christian life.

He had scarcely been talking for five minutes, when the ever watchful congregation saw the pastor's head droop, and his eyes close. For the next fifteen minutes, little or no attention was paid to Brother Dyer's exhortation. The angry people were nudging each other, whispering, and casting indignant glances at the sleeping pastor. He awoke and sat up, just as the exhorter was finishing in a fiery period. If those who watched him, were expecting to see any embarrassed look on his face, or show of timidity in his eyes, they were mistaken. Instead, his appearance was one of sudden alertness, and his gaze that of a man in extreme exaltation. One would have said that it had been given to him as to the inspired prophets of old to see and to hear things far and beyond the ken of ordinary mortals. As Brother Dyer sat down, he arose quickly and went forward to the front of the pulpit with a firm step. Still, with the look of exaltation on his face, he announced his text, "Ef he sleep he shell do well."

The congregation, which a moment before had been all indignation, suddenly sprang into the most alert attention. There was a visible pricking up of ears as the preacher entered into his subject. He spoke first of the benefits of sleep, what it did for the worn human body and the weary human soul, then turning off into a half-humorous, half-quizzical strain, which was often in his sermons, he spoke of how many times he had to forgive some of those who sat before him to-day for nodding in their pews; then raising his voice, like a good preacher, he came back to his text, exclaiming, "but ef he sleep, he shell do well."

He went on then, and told of Jacob's sleep, and how at night, in the midst of his slumbers the visions of angels had come to him, and he had left a testimony behind him that was still a solace to their hearts. Then he lowered his voice and said:

"You all condemns a man when you sees him asleep, not knowin' what visions is a-goin' thoo his mind, nor what feelin's is a-goin' thoo his heart. You ain't conside'in' that mebbe he's a-doin' mo' in the soul wo'k when he's asleep then when he's awake. Mebbe he sleep, w'en you think he ought to be up a-wo'kin'. Mebbe he slumber w'en you think he ought to be up an' erbout. Mebbe he sno' an' mebbe sno't, but I'm a-hyeah to tell you, in de wo'ds of the Book, that they ain't no 'sputin' 'Ef he sleep, he shell do well!'"

"Yes, Lawd!" "Amen!" "Sleep on Ed'ards!" some one shouted. The church was in smiles of joy. They were rocking to and from with the ecstasy of the sermon, but the Rev. Elisha had not yet put on the cap sheaf.

"Hol' on," he said, "befo' you shouts er befo' you sanctions. Fu' you may yet have to tu'n yo' backs erpon me, an' say, 'Lawd he'p the man!' I's a-hyeah to tell you that many's the time in this very pulpit, right under yo' very eyes, I has gone f'om meditation into slumber. But what was the reason? Was I a-shirkin' er was I lazy?"

"Shouts of "No! No!" from the congregation.

"No, no," pursued the preacher, "I wasn't a-shirkin' ner I wasn't a-lazy, but the soul within me was a wo'kin' wid the min', an' as we all gwine ter do some day befo' long, early in de mornin', I done fu'git this ol' body. My haid fall on my breas', my eyes close, an' I see visions of anothah day to come. I see visions of a new Heaven an' a new earth, when we shell all be clothed in white raimen', an' we shell play ha'ps of gol', an' walk de golden streets of the New Jerusalem! That's what been a runnin' thoo my min', w'en I set up in the pulpit an' sleep under the Wo'd; but I want to ax you, was I wrong? I want to ax you, was I sinnin'? I want to p'int you right hyeah to the Wo'd, as it are read out in yo' hyeahin' ter-day. 'Ef he sleep, he shell do well.'"

The Rev. Elisha ended his sermon amid the smiles and nods and tears of his congregation. No one had a harsh word for him now, and even Brother Dyer wiped his eyes and whispered to his next neighbor, "Dat man sholy did sleep to some pu'pose," although he knew that the dictum was a death-blow to his own pastoral hopes. The people thronged around the pastor as he descended from the pulpit, and held his hand as they had done of yore. One old woman went out, still mumbling under her breath, "Sleep on, Ed'ards, sleep on."

There were no church meetings after that, and no tendency to dismiss the pastor. On the contrary, they gave him a donation party next week, at which Sister Dicey helped him to receive his guests.

◎/◎

MOVE MY EARS

Billy Kersands, the popular black vaudeville and
minstrel performer who could sing *Swanee River* with two
billiard balls in his mouth, once told the Queen of England,
"If God ever wanted my mouth any bigger,
he would have to move my ears."

◎/◎

BANK ROBBERS

By Williams and Walker

Bert Williams and George Walker met and performed together as a team from 1893, when they met in San Francisco, until 1911, when Walker died. Typically, in their stage act Williams assumed the role of the shiftless darky and Walker, who was a remarkable dancer, played the fast-talking trickster or dandy. They were among the early twentieth century's most influential comedy/dance teams. The following is a representative example of their stage patter.

Walker: I tells you I'm lettin' you in on this 'cause you're a friend of mine. I could do this alone . . . but I wants you to share in it 'cause we's friends. Now after you gets into the bank you fill the satchel with money.

Williams: Whose money?

Walker: That ain't the point. We don't know who put the money in there, and we don't know why they got it. And they won't know why we got it. All you have to do is put the money in the satchel. I'll get you the satchel—ain't nothin' to bother 'bout—that's 'cause you're a friend of mine, see.

Williams: And what do I do with dis satchel?

Walker: All you got to do is bring it to me at the place where I tells you.

Williams: When they come to count up the cash and finds it short, then what?

Walker: By that time we'll be far, far away—where the birds is singin' and the flowers is in bloom.

Williams: And if they catch us they'll put us so far, far away we never will hear no birds singin'. Everybody knows you can't smell no flowers through a stone wall.

BERT WILLIAMS

After the death of his partner George Walker, Williams worked as a single act but maintained the stage guise of the shiftless darky. He became the nation's first black superstar performer and was recognized as one of America's foremost comedians.

STORIES AND JOKES

An old colored lady was injured in a railway accident, and someone urged her to sue for damages.

"Lord knows, I done got nuff damages," she said. "What I'm gwine sue fuh is repairs."

*

The wooden-legged preacher was admiring Spruce's hogs from outside the fence. "Ah Brother Rigby, dem hogs a yourn is in fine condition."

And Spruce answered, "They sho is. If all of us was as fit to die as dem hogs is, dare wouldn't be a thing for you to preach about."

*

When Spruce Bigby became the father of twins, the wooden-legged preacher stopped by to congratulate him.

"Well, Bruthuh Bigby, I heah dat de Lord has smiled on you."

"You's heared wrong," Spruce said, "de Lord's done laughed out loud!"

*

Spruce Bigby put on his Sunday best with his near-gold-headed cane. He met the wooden-legged preacher, who said to Spruce, "Ah, Brother Bigby, dare ain't go gold-head canes in Heben."

"Naw," answered Spruce, "An' dare ain't no wooden-legged preachers dare neither."

*

Spruce Bigby said to his wife one night, rather suspicious like, "Look heah, honey, did you wash dis heah fish 'fo you baked it?"

His wife answered, "Whut's de matter wid you, man? You crazy? Who ever hered tell a washin' a fish. Ain't he done lived all his lifetime in de water?"

*

After looking up and down the bill of fare without enthusiasm, a customer at a restaurant finally decided on a dozen fried oysters.

The colored waiter seemed confused by the order and finally stammered out an apology.

"I'se ve'y sorry, suh, ve'y sorry, but we's all out uv all shellfish—'ceptin' aigs."

*

One time when I was trampin' out in the country a old farmer come along the road with one a them old-time country horses and wagons and he let me ride on in to town with him.

Ev'ry now and then the horse would stop and kind of prick up his ears and he kept on doing it so much that finally I asked the old man if his horse was balky.

He said, "Naw sir, taint nothin' the matter wid him. He's alright. He jes stops dat way to listen."

I say, "To listen!"

He say, "Yas suh. He's skeered somebody might say 'whoa' an' he wouldn't hear it."

*

Dey was tryin' a very dear friend of ours the other day fuh murder an' right in front a me was settin' two mo' colored fellers. When de trial was nearly over, one of 'em says to the other, "Looks like dey goin' to convick him sho'."

The other one say, "Not only convick him, looks like dey goin' hang him."

Then the first one say, "Aw, man, dey don't hang no murd'rers in de state a New York."

The other one say, "Well, whut do dey do wid 'em den?"

"Why, dey kills 'em wid elocution."

*

The family Susie cooked for moved out to the West Coast to live. They took Susie with them. After they had been there some months, she said to her madam, "I don't spec' I'm goin' to be able to stay out here, Miss Em'ly. You see, de colored folks out here ain't de same. They's mo' like de Hawaiians or de Indians an', you see, I'se always been used to de pu'e Angle Saxon type."

*

"So, you say yo' name is Goodbar. Is you any relation to Cornelius Good-bar?"

"Very distunt, very distunt, suh. I wuz my mammy's fus' chile an' Cornelius wuz de sebenteenth. Dat's de way uv it."

*

Simmons the barber say to a gent'man he wuz shavin' the other day, "Is I ever shaved you befo'?"

De gent'man say, "Yea, once."

Simmons say, "Yea, I thought I 'membered yo' face."

De gent'man say, "Yea, it's all healed up now."

When Simmons got thru shavin' de man dis time, de man went to de washstand and took an' put some water in his mouth an' commence rollin' it roun' in dare and kinder garglin' it up an' down an' puffin' his jaws out wid de water still in his mouth.

Simmons look at 'em and say, "Why, whut's de matter?"

De man say, "Nuthin', only I jes want tuh see ef my face will hold water—dat's all."

*

De man ask his friend, "Did you git down on yo' knees when you purposed to Miss Emmaline de yuther night?"

De friend say, "I couldn't, man—she was settin' on 'em."

*

He had been very cranky on the trip to New York and as the train was pulling into Grand Central Station he asked the porter, "Shall I get off at this end of the car?"

"Why, uh, you kin suit yo'self, suh," the porter said. "Bofe ends stops."

Songs and Rhymes

When It's All Goin' Out and Nothin' Comin' In

Money is the root of all evil,
No matter where you happen to go.
But nobody has any objections to de root,
Now ain't that so?

You know how it is with money;
How it makes you feel at ease.
De world puts on a big broad smile,
An' yo' friends am as thick as bees.

But oh, when yo' money is runnin' low,
An' you'se clingin' to a solitary dime,
Yo' creditors are numerous an' yo' friends is few,
Oh dat am the awful time!

Chorus

Dat am the time, oh dat am the time,
When it's all goin' out and nothin' comin' in,
Dat am the time when the troubles begin.
Money is gettin' low, people say: "I told you so."
And you can't borrow a penny from any of your kin,
An' it's all goin' out and nothin' comin' in.

BELIEVE ME

Believe me, I'm gettin' tired of always bein' the "dub,"
Dey's worked on me so faithful till I'se worn down to a nub.
You all hab heard about the straw that broke the camel's back,
Well, a bubble added to my load, would surely make mine crack.

But believe me;
Woe be to he or she
Who tries to ease me that bubble.
Believe you me!

DAT'S HARMONY

Mister Schubert's serenade is grand,
I certainly love to hear a big brass band
Play Sousa's marches by the score.
And I likes good opera, and what is more,
That pleasing melody in F
Is sho' some music—well, I guess.
But folks makes a mistake you see
When they say that's all to harmony.

Chorus

'Cause when your wife says, "Come to your dinner, John,"
Dat's harmony.
When you just gits a whiff of what she's bringin' in,
Dat's harmony.
Wid all due credit to a big brass band,
De sweetest sweet music in de land
Is when you hear de sizzle of de fryin' pan.
Boy, dat's harmony!

JONAH MAN

My luck started when I was born
Leastwise so the old folks say
That same hard luck's been my best friend
To this very day.
When I was young, mamma's friends—
    to find a name they tried.
They named me after pappa,
    and the same day pappa died.

Chorus
I'm a Jonah. I'm a Jonah man.
My family for many for many years
Would look at me, then shed some tears.
Why I am dis Jonah, I don't understand.
But I'm a good substantial, full-fledged, real, first-class
    Jonah man.

THE PIG AND THE PORCUPINE

A pig once met a porcupine, 'twas on a summer day,
And said to her, "Will you be mine? I like your stylish way."
With that the porcupine got mad and raised an awful stir,
She filled that pig so full of quills he looked just like a burr.
I'm stuck on you, he cried in pain.
I see your point is plain.
But you have pierced my tender heart,
'Cause I just felt that cupid's dart.

Although I'm pork, I pine for you,
Miss Porcupine, Miss Pork-I-pine.
Please take those toothpicks off your back,
Please don't decline, don't decline.

DOUGHNUTS ROUND

Doughnuts round
Weight more'n a pound
Drop'em on the floor
And they shake the ground.

The Medicine Man

Oh the medicine man with the grip in his hand,
He's in every land.
When he explains about your pains
Your hand will on end stand.
If you feelin' kinder sick
Why you better run quick.
Run as quick as you can
'Cause nobody knows but the medicine man.

Nervermo'

Of co'se I is not Mister Poe
Cryin' to git to Leano'
Wid her done died long, long ago:
Now my wife's name ain't Leano'
Her name is Flo', dat's all, plain Flo'
An' she ain't dead an' whut is mo'
To where she lives is jes' a block or so—
But do you hear me cryin'
To get to Flo'?
Ah, "Nevermo'," an' den some mo'.

Sayings and Observations

- The only thing we know about death is dat it's always fatal.
- De only way tuh keep a lie frum gittin' foun' out is tuh stop tellin' it.
- Don't loaf 'round de corners an' 'pend on de Lord fuh yo' daily bread. De Lord ain't runnin' no bakery.
- In dis big worl', if all de rascals whut's 'sposed tuh be gent'mens had a halter 'roun' dare neck, rope would be wuth a whole lot mo'n whut it is.
- It's alright tuh stick tuh facts but some folks sticks tuh'um so close dat dey makes fools out a dey sef'. I knows a man, ef you wuz tuh talk tuh him 'bout Jacob's Ladder he'd wanter know how many steps twuz in it.
- Ole man Shotesberry lived eighty years wid one foot in de grave. I knows lots of dem kind. Jes' like cranes—rests better on one foot.
- A man ought not never to git drunk 'bove de neck.

- We all oughter live so, dat when a knock comes at yo' do', widout yo' con'shuns hurtin' one bit, you kin throw yo' head back an' holler, "Come in."
- Who wuz it said dat one half de mis'ry in de worl' wuz caused by men whut drinks an' women whut can't cook? Yea, verily.
- Some men never learns whut a good name dey had 'til dey loses it.
- Heah's another "Yea, verily." Ef slander is a snake, den it's got wings, 'cause it flys heap mo'n it creeps.
- Don't stan' 'roun' waitin' fuh somethin' tuh turn up—git out an' turn up somethin'.
- Dar's a lot of people goin' thru life carryin' grouches dat makes 'em look like dey got de bilious fever, ever' time dey smile dey look like de shamed uv it.
- I has noticed dat de unfortunit men's frens lives a long ways off.
- I never seed a woman give folks a piece uv her mind as often as Tempy Drake an' still have plenty lef'.
- A twenty-dollar suit won't cover up a thirty-cent man.
- All men is born free an' equal, but some men is born equal to 'bout six others.
- It sho is a fac' dat endurin' de las' few years a whole lot a truf is been wifdrawn frum circulation.
- I seed in de papers dis mornin' whare a man dropped dead while he was washin' his face an' han's. Why is it dat folks will pu'sist in foolin' wid water?
- I always did think a whole lot uv ole Noah an' I'm willin' tuh give him de benefit uv de doubt an' say dat *maybe* dey slipped in, but if dey didn't slip den ole Noah either didn't have as much sense as he needed or else he wuz drunk at de time when he passed a male an' female mosquito into de Ark long wid de rest a de pairs a varmints.
- Not long ago in some state out west de courts decided dat snorin' wuz good grounds fuh a divorce; dey claim dat now dat state is run over wid schools dat guarantee tuh teach you how tuh snore.
- Too much likker pu'duces a largeness uv de liver an' a smallness uv de pocketbook.
- Dat thing called "fame" is like a fo'-leaf clover; it is foun' much mo' oftener by dem whut ain't lookin' fuh it dan by dem whut is.
- Somebody made a great mistake when dey gived de cat nine lives an' de chicken jes one.

- Dare ain't no pleasure in havin' nothin' tuh do; de fun uv it is in havin' a whole lot tuh do an' not doin' it.
- De po'house is mostly crowded wid good intentions an' lost oppurtunities an' uv co'se you'll also find quite a few hard lucks, misfortunes, an' bad managements scattered aroun'.
- Who wuz it said dat, "True religion is like true wisdom," de mo' uv it you got de less you tries tuh show it.
- To whoever it twuz dat said, "A tombstone is de only thing dat kin stan' upright an' lie on it's face at de same time," I says, yea verily.
- Dis worl' is full a people dat talks so much 'bout whut dey *kin* do an' whut dey *goin'* tuh do, dat dey nevuh gits time tuh commence.
- Nevuh try tuh make like dat you is whut you ain't. It don't fool nobody dat's wo'th bein' fooled, an' anuther thing, it's gen'ly expensive.
- Treat ev'ybody wid kindness. Taint no tellin' who's goin' git hol'ta money nex'.
- Befo' marriage a young man will kiss his sweetheart anywhares. Aftuh dey's married three a fo' years, he don't seem tuh care much 'bout kissin' her nowhares.
- Dey say dat long life 'pends on peace an' quietness. If dat is so, I knows some fam'lies dat oughter been extinct long ago.
- When a man commences talkin' 'bout su'cide an' wushin' fuh death, it's putty good bettin' dat he's done give up all hopes uv findin' a wife. Either dat ur he's been married a long time.
- Lots a folks who wouldn't lend you a quatuh will spen' valu'ble time givin' you advice dat you don't want.
- Some gals whut's been thru school an' knows all 'bout 'rithmetic, still b'lieves when dey goes to a shoe sto' dat six go into two.
- A home widout chillun is no doubt peaceful an' quiet; but so is a graveyard.
- Ole man procras-t-nation is one a de worst crim'nuls in de worl'. He's a thief uv time, an' time once lost is gone fo' good. Yea, verily.
- Ole man death is one caller dat you can't tell dat lie to 'bout not bein' at home. Amen.
- In de olden times daddies use to say to dey sons, "Pay as you go; if you can't pay, don't go." Now days it's, "Go as you please an' don't pay 'less you has to."

- Good fur nothin' parunts ain't got no right to quarrul wid dare chillun 'bout bein' lazy. You can't make a race hoss out'uv a jack ass.
- In our town dey use to have a system uv hangin' out a yaller flag when dare wuz small-pox in a house, but dey had to do 'way wid it. So many folks took to hangin' 'em out on de days dat collectors wuz due to come aroun'.
- Some woman in some a dem outlandish states somewhares out wes' claims dat she is possessed wid de devul. De only diffunce 'tween her an' other women is dat she ain't shame to own up to it.
- Folks don't care much 'bout de pedigree uv a hoss 'til he wins a race, an' de same thing 'plies to men.
- A friend a mine says dat his idea uv happiness is "nothin' to do, plenty to do it wid, an' lots a time to do it in."
- De animal dat kin git long wid de leas' 'mount uv nourishment is de moth. He don't eat nuthin' but holes.
- Men is like fiddles; dey don't git real good 'til dey's ole—neither do women.
- Man ain't nevuh too ole to yearn.
- De Lord created fools so dat wise men would have somethin' to be thankful fuh.
- Some folks shows de mos' liberal'ty when dey ain't got nothin'.
- Mankind ain't neither as good as he says he is nur as bad as dey makes out he is.
- Anytime you commences to git de big head, you oughter stop an' think 'bout all de great men whut's died an' how well de worl' got along widout 'em.
- Oppertunities is things dat some folks makes, some folks uses, an' other folks looks at widout seeing.
- De jealous man is always lookin' fuh somethin' an' hopin' dat he won't find it.
- Who wuz it said dat a ignoramus wuz somebody dat didn't know nothin' ur somebody dat jes' half knowed somethin' ur somebody dat knowed somethin' dey didn't have no bizness knowin'.
- Lots a folks lights dare lamp at noontime; dat's de reason dey ain't got no oil when night comes.
- Watch de man whut sees wrong in eve'ything, 'cause it's a good bet dat he's full uv it.

- De man dat ain't never mistaken 'bout other folks is always mistaken 'bout hisself.
- When you'se got a ailment, it's good to think uv all de ailments you ain't got.
- Folks wid de big head swears dat nothin' ain't good dat dey can't understan'.
- When it is black dark, you can't tell white frum black, much less any color line.
- If you has two wives, dat's bigamy; if you has many wives, dat's polygamy; if you has jes one wife, dat's monotony.

OBJECTIONS

A Baptist preacher suggested to his flock that they
could upgrade their property by erecting a fence
around the burial plot behind the church.
"I protests!" shouted one of the deacons.
"State your objections," the preacher said.
"I got two objections, suh," the deacon said. "In de furst place,
Nobody in dat cemetary kin git out if dey tries. In de
second place, ain't nobody on de outside studyin' to git
in dere anyhow."

—Folk

CHILDREN'S RHYME

I had a little dog, his name was Dash;
I'd rather be a nigger than poor white trash.

—Folk

LORD, WILL I EVER

A black man and a white working on a road crew
both stop to look when an attractive white woman walks past.
"Oh, Lord, will I ever," the black man sighed.
"Nah nigger, never," the white man said.
"As long as there's life, there's hope," the black said.
"Yeah," the white man snapped.
"And as long as there's a nigger there's a rope."

—Folk

AN INDIGNATION DINNER

By James David Corrothers

Dey was hard times jes fo' Christmas round our neighborhood one year;
So we held a secret meetin', whah de white folks couldn't hear,
To 'scuss de situation, an' to see what could be done
Towa'd a fust-class Christmas dinneh an' a little Christmas fun.

Rufus Green, who called de meetin', ris an' said: "In dis here town,
An' throughout de land, de white folks is a'tryin' to keep us down."
S' 'e: "Dey bought us, sold us, beat us; now dey 'buse us 'ca'se we's free;
But when dey tetch my stomach, dey's done gone too fur foh me!

"Is I right?" "You sho is, Rufus!" roared a dozen hungry throats.
"Ef you'd keep a mule a-wo'kin', don't you tamper wid his oats.
Dat's sense," continued Rufus. "But dese white folks nowadays
Has done got so close and stingy you can't live on what dey pays.

"Here 'tis Christmas-time, an', folkses, I's indignant 'nough to choke.
Whah's our Christmas dinneh comin' when we's mos' completely broke?
I can't hahdly 'fo'd a toothpick an' a glass o' water. Mad?
Say, I'm desp'ret! Dey jes better treat me nice, dese white folks had!"

Well, dey 'bused de white folks scan'lous, till old Pappy Simmons ris,
Leanin' on his cane to s'pote him, on account his rheumatis',
An' s' 'e: "Chillun, whut's dat wintry wind a-sighin' th'ough de street
'Bout yo' wasted summeh wages? But, no matter, we mus' eat.

"Now, I seed a beau'ful tuhkey on a certain gemmun's fahm.
He's a-growin' fat an' sassy, an' a-struttin' to a chahm.
Chickens, sheeps, hogs, sweet pertaters—all de craps is fine dis year;
All we needs is a committee foh to tote de goodies here."

Well, we lit right in an' voted dat it was a gran' idee,
An' de dinneh we had Christmas was worth trabblin' miles to see;
An' we eat a full an' plenty, big an' little, great an' small,
Not beca'se we was dishonest, but indignant, sah. Dat's all.

SAME OLD QUESTION

The renowned scholar and rights leader **W. E. B. DuBois**
recalled that, after a speech on the problems
faced by black Americans before a group of
prominent whites, a white woman approached

him and asked, "Do you know where
I can get a good colored cook?"

@/@

INDEFINITE TALK ROUTINE

By Miller and Lyles

Along with Williams and Walker, the comedy team of (Flournoy) Miller and (Aubrey) Lyles was among the influential black comic acts in early twentieth century America. The team's Indefinite Talk *bit remained a staple on the black theater circuit until the 1960s.*

First Comic: Who he goin marry?

Second Comic: He goin marry the daughter of Mr.—

First Comic   That's a nice girl. Lemme tell you, I heard once—

Second Comic: Naw, that was her sister. I'm keepin' company with her.

First Comic: You are?

Second Comic: Oh yeah, I been with her now ever since—

First Comic: I didn't know you knew her that long.

Second Comic: Sure!

First Comic: And I thought all the time she was—

Second Comic: She was! But she cut him out.

First Comic: Well, you know, I was talkin' to her father the other day and the first thing—

Second Comic: That was yo' fault. What you should'a done was—

First Comic: I did!

Or, in a different version:

First Comic: How come you can't pay me now?

Second Comic: Horse races.

First Comic: What track you play at?

Second Comic: I play over there at—

First Comic: That track's crooked. Why don't you play over here around—

Second Comic: That's where I lost my money!

First Comic: Yeah! How much did you lose?

Second Comic: I lost about—

First Comic: You didn't have that much!

Second Comic: Naw?

First Comic: No. All you had was about—

Second Comic: I had more than that.

First Comic: Really?

Second Comic: Yeah, and you know what, I bet on a horse and that rascal didn't come in until—

First Comic: Was he that far behind?

Second Comic: Yeah!

First Comic: What jockey was ridin' him?

Second Comic: A jockey by the name of—

First Comic: He can't ride! I thought he went out there to ride for—

Second Comic: He did! But they fired him. He came on back—

First Comic: No he didn't!

Second Comic: Oh yeah.

@/@

BAD NIGGER TALES

JACK JOHNSON* AND THE HOTEL CLERK

Folk

Jack Johnson went to a Jim Crow hotel and asked the desk clerk for a room. When the clerk raised up and saw that Johnson was black, he angrily responded, "We don't serve your kind here." Johnson asked again, and the clerk repeated himself. The champion laughed, pulled out a roll of money and politely said, "Oh, you misunderstand me. I don't want it for myself, I want it for my wife—she's your kind!"

* Jack Johnson became the first black heavyweight boxing champion in 1908. In addition to exploits in the ring, he was known for his exorbitant lifestyle, his public fraternizing with white women at a time when such behavior was reason for lynching, and his flagrant disrespect for white authority. His way of life inspired a number of folk tales and rhymes, and, according to some, was the inspiration for the slang term for black male genitalia.

CHAMPION'S STILL A NIGGER

The Yankees hold the play,
The white man pull the trigger:
But it makes no difference what the white man say,
The World Champion's still a nigger.

—Folk

JACK JOHNSON IN GEORGIA

Folk

It was on a hot day in Georgia when Jack Johnson drove into town. He was really flying: zoom! Behind his fine car was a cloud of red Georgia dust as far as the eye could see. The sheriff flagged him down and said, "Where do you think you're going, boy, speeding like that? That'll cost you $50."

Johnson never looked up, he just reached in his pocket, handed the sheriff a $100 bill and started to gun the motor: ruuummmmm, ruuummmmm! Just before Johnson pulled off, the sheriff shouted, "Don't you want your change?

Johnson replied, "Keep it, 'cause I'm coming back the same way I'm going!" ZOOOOOOOM!

LOOKING FOR CHANGE

A wealthy real estate tycoon from Memphis checked
into a swank New York hotel and loudly called
for "a colored boy" to carry his bags to his room.
The bell hop, a Negro student working his way through
college, rushed over and carried the luggage to the
man's room, then waited at the door for his tip.
Finally, the tycoon approached him and asked,
"Boy, do you have change for a dollar?"
"Sir," the bell hop said, "in this hotel a dollar is change!"

—Folk

WHO GOES THERE?

Folk

A soldier was trying to sneak off a Southern military base to visit his girlfriend in town after curfew. But when he tried to slip past the sentry, he heard a voice yell, "Who goes there?"

"Me," the soldier replied.

"Don't you know no one's allowed off the base tonight, boy," the sentry said.

"Listen here," the soldier said, "I got a mother in heaven, a father in hell, and a gal in town. Damned if I ain't gonna see one a them tonight!"

MIND YO' BUSINESS

"Sam, what makes your nose so flat?" the man
asked a busy cotton picker.
"I ain't sure, boss," the cotton picker replied,
"but I figger it's to keep me from stickin'
it into other people's business."

—Folk

KILL ME IF YOU CAN

Folk

These three men was all on death row—a Jew, an Irishman, and a nigger—and the authorities told them they could choose any which way they want to die. The Jew say, "I wanna eat myself to death." So they brought him a hundred-course meal, and the fellow ate and ate and ate 'til he couldn't eat no mo'. He finally died with a great big smile on his face.

The Irishman say, "I wanna drink myself to death." So they brought him a gallon of every kind a liquor under the sun. He sat there and drink every drop a that hooch. When he died, he didn't even know his name, but he was smilin' like all get out.

The nigger say, "I wanna screw myself to death." So they brought in a hundred womens. When they come back two weeks later, the hundred womens was all laying on the floor dead, and the nigger was sitting there smilin' and playing with his Johnson.

JOHN AND THE JUDGE

Folk

Judge:	John, what is this about you kicking someone?
John:	Captum, what would you do if someone called you a black son of bitch?
Judge:	John, you know nobody will ever call me that.

John: Well, Captum, spose they call you the kind of son of bitch you is?

Judge: Give him 30 days!

⚚

CAN'T WIN FOR LOSING

Folk

A colored man died and wandered up to the gates of Heaven.

"Write yo' name down in dis heah book," ordered St. Peter.

The colored man signed his name, and St. Peter looked around and asked, "Wheah's yo' mule?"

"I ain't ridin'," said the man.

"Dat's too bad, 'cause we ain't takin' walkin' people in dis week. You gotta be ridin'."

Sad and dejected, the colored man walked down the road toward the spot where the bus stops for people going the Other Way. He was near 'bout there when he met a white man. "Wheah you goin'?" asked the colored man.

"To Heaven," the white man say.

The colored man shook his head. "You ain't goin' git in," he said. "I jes' came from up there an' St. Peter ain't takin' walk-ins, only ride-ins."

They sat down on a rock to think about it, and all of a sudden the colored man come up with an idea. "Hey, I knows how both us kin git in," he said. "You git on my back an' I'll pertend I'm the mule." The white man's face lit up with excitement, and he climbed up on top the colored man's shoulders. Then they headed on back toward the Pearly Gates and knocked as loud as they could.

"Who dat?" St. Peter called.

"It's me, a honest, right-doin' man," the white man said.

"You walkin'?" asked St. Peter.

"No, I'm riding."

"All right, you can come in," said St. Peter, "but you have tuh leave yo' mule outside."

GUILTY AS CHARGED

"It is this court's opinion,"
a white Mississippi judge announced,

"that this here innocent colored
boy . . . uh, the defendant,
is guilty as charged!
—Folk

BOTTOM BOUND

By Stringbeans and Sweetie

Black male and female comedy teams were extremely popular acts during the early 1900s. Usually they performed on the black theater circuit before exclusively black audiences, and their material often reflected the loud-talking, signifying, and frontin' (posturing) that typified some of the period's urban street humor. Stringbeans and Sweetie was one of the top teams on the circuit by 1915. Their act included dance, suggestive comic interchanges, and topical songs like the following.

Listen no-good womens
Stop kickin' us men aroun'.
'Cause us men gonna be your iceberg
And send you sinkin' down.

Sinkin' like *Titanic*
Sinkin' sinkin' down.
Oh you no good womens listen
You sure is bottom bound.

White folks got all the money
Colored folks got all the signs.
Signs won't buy you nothin'
Folks, you better change yo' mind.

Sinkin' like *Titanic*
Sinkin' sinkin' down.
If you don't change yo' way of livin'
You sure is bottom bound.

SHINE, OR THE SINKING OF THE *TITANIC*

Folk

It was 1912 when the awful news got around
That the great *Titanic* was sinking down.

Shine came running up on deck, told the Captain, "Please,
The water in the boiler room is up to my knees."
Captain said, "Take your black self on back down there!
I got a hundred-fifty pumps to keep the boiler room clear."
Shine went back in the hole, started shoveling coal,
Singing, "Lord, have mercy, Lord, have mercy on my soul!"

and continue with Shine's escape:

The old *Titanic* was beginning to sink.
Shine pulled off his clothes and jumped in the brink.
He said, "Little fish, big fish, and shark fishes, too,
Get out of my way because I'm coming through."

Captain on bridge hollered, "Shine, Shine, save poor me,
And I'll make you rich as any man can be."
Shine said, "There's more gold on land than there is on sea."
And he swam on.

In the street versions that I heard as a teenager, Shine was a more hostile, bit-ter hero and the tale was more profane and sardonic.

It was a cold day in May when the news went 'round,
That's when they heard the *Titanic* went down.
Say, Shine come runnin' to the deck to see.
Say, "Damn, Captain, the water is up to my knee."
Captain say, "Get your black ass on back down there,
I got a hundred-fifty pumps to keep the boiler room clear."

Shine say, "That may be true but you carryin' a load."
Say, "I might take my chances jumping overboard."
Shine went on back down to the hole,
Picked up his shovel and started shovelin' coal.
But the ship was rollin' and sinkin' fast,
Shine say, "I'm leavin' if it get to my ass."

Then the water rushed in clean up to Shine's neck,
And that's when Shine rushed back to deck.
Captain say, "Shine, don't have no worry don't have no doubt,
I got a hundred more pumps to keep the water out."
Shine say, "I don't like chitlin's and I don't eat ham,
And I don't believe them pumps is worth a damn."

Captain say, "Shine, oh, Shine, don't be no fool and don't be no clown."
Say, "Anybody go overboard is bound to drown."
Shine say, "Now, Captain, that could be true.
But I'm taking my chances out there in the blue."
Shine dropped his clothes and jumped off the ship.
The passengers and crew was bitin' they lip.

Say, Shine hit the water with a hell of a splash.
Everybody wondered if the nigga would last.
He rose from the depths and began to swim,
With a thousand millionaires lookin' at him.
Say, "Whales, snails and tortoises, too,
Git out my way, 'cause I'm comin' through."
    And Shine swam on.

Captain rushed to the bridge, say, "Shine, save poor me,
And I'll make you as rich as any rich man can be,"
Shine say, "There's more gold on land than there is on sea,
I'm swimmin' back home to git what's comin' to me.
You hate my people and you hate my face,
Now jump overboard and give these sharks a chase."
    And Shine swam on.

Captain's daughter came rushing up to the rail
With her bag in her hand and dress 'round her tail.
She say, "Shine, oh Shine, save poor me!
I'll give you all the tail your eyes can see."
Shine say, "There's more tail on land than there is on sea,
I got thirty *fine* momma's waitin' at home for me."
    And Shine swam on.

Shine come up on a baby floatin' alone,
His eyes was half closed and he started to moan.
Shine say, "Baby, baby, please don't cry.
All God's children got a time to die.
You young and innocent and that's just fine,
But you gotta hit this water just like old Shine."
    And Shine swam on.

The men folks moan and the ladies cry,
Everybody on board knew they had to die.

But Shine could swim and Shine could float.
Throwed his ass like a motorboat.
Say the Devil looked up from hell and grin,
Say, "He's a black, swimming motherfucker.
I think he's gon' make it on in."
    And Shine swam on.

* The date of origin for this urban folk ballad, according to folklorist Alan Dundes, is somewhere between 1912 (the year the *Titanic* sank) and 1920. During the 1970s, Shine's superhuman feats prompted writer Ishmael Reed to call him the "Black American Ulysses."

☯☯

THE SIGNIFYING MONKEY *

Folk

Said the Monkey to Lion, one bright, sunny day,
"There's a bad motherfucker livin' down yo' way.
You take that sucker to be yo' friend,
But the way he talks about yo' mamma is a goddamn sin.
Talks about yo' daddy and yo' sister, too,
Matter of fact, he don't show too much respect fo' you."

Now, the Lion took off like a bat outta hell,
Bananas split open and coconuts fell.
Lion found the Elephant sittin' under a tree,
Say, "Now, motherfucker, you belong to me."
Elephant looked outta the corner of his eyes,
Say, "Go on, motherfucker, play with somebody yo' size."
But the Lion wouldn't listen, and he made a pass.
The Elephant kicked him dead in the ass.

Now they fought all night and they fought all day.
Don't know how the Lion ever got away.
He crawled back through the jungle, more dead than alive,
And that's when the Monkey started the signifying jive.
Say, "Hey Mr. Lion, you didn't fare too well,
Seem to me, you caught all the hell.
You look like a ho' with the seven-year-itch,
And you s'pose to be King of the Jungle, ain't that a bitch.
Now, motherfucker, don't you dare roar,
'Cause I'll jump down and kick yo' ass some more."

But the Monkey got frantic, started jumpin' up and down.
His foot missed the limb, he fell dead on the ground.
Like a bolt of lightnin' and a streak of heat,
The Lion was on with all fo' feet.
Monkey looked up with tears in his eyes,
Say, "Please, Mr. Lion, I apologize.
But, if you let me get my balls out the sand
I'll fight yo' ass like a natural man."

Say, "If you jump back like a good man should,
I'll bounce yo' ass all over these woods."
Lion stepped back and was ready to fight,
But the Monkey jumped up and was clean outta sight.
And I heard him shout as he hauled out of view,
"Tell yo' momma and yo' daddy, too,
Signifying Monkey made a fool outta you."

* Like "Shine," this urban ballad has remained extremely popular throughout most of the
twentieth century. Here again, the trickster theme emerges as the weaker creature outwits
the stronger—in this instance, the lion, who is "supposed" to be the king of the jungle, is
tricked. A polite version was recorded by the jazz vocalist Oscar Brown, Jr., and more scat-
ological versions have appeared as toasts and in routines by some 1990s comics.

PART THREE

NEW DAY'S A-COMIN' ...
THE HARLEM RENAISSANCE TO THE FIFTIES

Don't get me wrong, it ain't no
disgrace to come from the South.
But it's a disgrace to go back down there.
　　　　　　　　　　　　　　—Moms Mabley

For fifteen years Miss Camp
had been devoting her life to the service of mankind.
Not until now had the startling possibility occurred to her
that Negroes might be mankind, too.
　　　　　　　　　—Rudolph Fisher, *The Walls of Jericho*

In a 1925 essay, professor Alain Locke asserted that the "New Negro" had emerged, explaining that mass migration to large cities in the North and Midwest had transformed blacks from devoted semi-slaves to a race of proud aspiring individuals. Old notions of toadying black mammies, Sambos, and Uncle Toms were outdated, he maintained. Not all of white America, of course, agreed with Locke or the young black writers and artists who gathered in Harlem, "the Mecca of the New Negro," to join the cultural movement that came to be known as the Harlem Renaissance.

So, even as whites flocked to Harlem and other black urban centers to revel, dance to black music, and brush shoulders with the New Negro, in Hollywood films of the period the old stereotypical Negro reigned and was nearly always depicted as a Tom, mammy, coon, or servant. Radio, the era's new media, also echoed that distorted vision as it reprised slavery caricatures of blacks, unleashing a rash of minstrel-style shows in which whites portrayed dimwitted black characters with outlandish names like Sugarfoot and Sassafrass, Moonshine and Sawdust, Watermelon and Cantaloupe,

111

Buck and Wheat, and Anesthetic and Cerebellum. The much maligned *Amos 'n' Andy Show*—radio's most popular program—seemed positively uplifting in comparison to most of its competitors.

Those popular, mass-media comic stereotypes influenced all Americans—even the African American performers who worked the black theater circuit. For one thing, most club and theater owners on the TOBA circuit were white, and they often demanded comedy that reflected their own expectations. And, as the old numskull folk tales illustrate, black audiences were certainly not above laughing at themselves or, at least, at other inept Negroes—unlike many whites they didn't assume that *all* black folks looked or acted alike. As a result, from the 1920s to the 1940s, black circuit humor was a mixed bag. Some skits (see "Great Men" below) dredged the bottom of the black laughing barrel and mirrored mainstream caricature. Most focused exclusively on black-on-black situations, poking fun at henpecked husbands, unfaithful wives, and rural or "country" attitudes. Some, like "Here Come de Judge," Pigmeat Markham's sly parody of the judicial system, deftly added a touch of social satire to the homespun burlesque and became classics.

On the streets, common black folks laughed at the antics of black circuit performers as well as at popular media-molded comic figures played by Stepin Fetchit, Willie Best, "Butterfly" McQueen, and Eddie "Rochester" Anderson. But, as in the past, they also amused themselves with jokes and stories that were either too risqué or too critical of white America to be repeated on the mainstream or black circuit stage. Despite the buffoonish image of blacks projected by the mass media and generally playful tone of black circuit comedy, this was a period of growing agitation in black communities. Marcus Garvey's "Back to Africa" movement, increased legal pressure by the NAACP to eliminate Jim Crow laws, and the return of black soldiers from World War II inspired a raft of ironic folk stories that were pointedly critical of American racism. By the late 1940s, some of this material was creeping into the stage humor of pioneer comics like Redd Foxx and Moms Mabley.

The most sophisticated black humor from the late 1920s to the 1940s was provided by Harlem Renaissance writers, and this section includes samples of the best of their writing. Generally, those works were not as popular as the era's stage and film comedy; Langston Hughes's tales of Jesse B. Simple, a down-to-earth Harlem resident, was the exception to the rule. Simple's keen observations of racial, social, and domestic matters made him one of the period's most popular as well as funniest and most endearing characters.

This was a period of rapid transition, however, and by the early 1950s Simple's subtle racial protestations and homely wit seemed too tame for many African Americans. The southern boycotts and protests that led to an all-out rights movement had begun, and there was an increased demand for more outspoken voices. In stage comedy, Foxx and Mabley led the way and bright new comedians like Nipsey Russell began making waves. Selections from film, radio, television, the stage, and the street are represented in this section.

BUTTERBEANS AND SUSIE

By the 1920s, Butterbeans and Susie had become the most beloved husband and wife team on the black theatrical circuit. Examples of their early songs and patter appear below.

GET YOURSELF A MONKEY-MAN *

Susie: The man I got, he's a hard-workin' man, he works all the time, and on Saturday night when he brings me his pay, he better not be short one dime.

Butterbeans: He's a brand new fool and a monkey-man. I'd whip you every time you breathe; rough treatment, Susie, is 'zactly what you need.

* A monkey-man is a servile or whipped husband who is completely controlled by his woman.

TOO MANY UPS

Susie: I'm ready to go down South.

Butterbeans: I ain't goin' with you, Sue.

Susie: Why ain't you goin' with me, Butter?

Butterbeans: 'Cause there's too many ups down South.

Susie: What you mean "ups," Butter?

Butterbeans: Well, early in the mornin' you got to wake up. Then you got to get up. Then you got to go out and on the farm, and if you didn't do the work like the boss said, the boss would beat you up.

I WANT A HOT DOG IN MY ROLL

Susie: I want it hot, I don't want it cold. I want it so it fit my roll.

Butterbeans: My dog's never cold! Here's a dog that long and lean.

Susie: I sure will be disgusted, if I don't get my mustard. . . . Don't want no excuse, it's got to have a lot of juice.

I AIN'T SCARED OF YOU

Susie: Yassir, Butter, I'm through with you, that's right.

Butterbeans: Through with who?

Susie: Through with you.

Butterbeans: What's wrong?

Susie: What's wrong? After all I've done for you, you don't appreciate me.

Butterbeans: What have you done so much that I didn't appreciate?

Susie: You know what I done.

Butterbeans: What you do?

Susie: Didn't I give you those shoes you got on?

Butterbeans: Yes, you give 'em to me.

Susie: Aw right, then. And what happened after I give 'em to you?

Butterbeans: Yeah, what happened after you give 'em to me?

Susie: That's just what I wanna know. What did happen?

Butterbeans: I like to run my fool self to death tryin' to get away from the man you stole the shoes from.

Susie: Butter, you know I ain't stole no shoes. And again, Butter, you know when I first got you, what was you doin' for a livin'?

Butterbeans: Yeah, what *was* I doin' when you first got me?

Susie: You know what you was doin'.

Butterbeans: What was I doin'?

Susie: Sittin' on a old, dirty fish wagon, sellin' fish for a livin'.

Butterbeans: And where was you?

Susie: That's just what I wanna know. Where was I?

Butterbeans: Sittin' right on the front seat, blowin' a fish horn for advertisement.

Susie: Say listen, Butter, you ain't been doin' a thing but panning me every since I left the sunny South.

Butterbeans: I only been speakin' the truth.

Susie: You goin' make me mad one of these days, and I'm goin' bust you right square in the mouth.

Butterbeans: Now look here, sister, you might hit me in the mouth, but I want you to understand—

Susie: Understand what?

Butterbeans: I'm goin' run you so fast 'round these doggone corners until your waist is gonna be dippin' in sand.

Susie: You know, Butter, I found you in one-two-three.

Butterbeans: In four-five-six, you flew off me, too.

Susie: Listen, Butter, you know I ain't scared a you.

Butterbeans: And you know I ain't scared a you.

Susie: Say listen, they ain't no fence between us, Butter.

Butterbeans: Now, sister, tell me what is you gonna do?

Susie: What I'm goin' do? Now if you wanna fight, cross that line.

Butterbeans: What line?

Susie: That line, and I'll show you how bad I am.

Butterbeans: Well, how bad is you?

Susie: When you hop up on this pool table, I'll show you how well I can shoot.

Butterbeans: Yeah, and I'll run fourteen straight in, and then bank out.

Susie: Butter, you know I ain't scared a you.

Butterbeans: And I ain't scared a you!

UNTIL THE REAL THING COMES ALONG

Butterbeans: I'd fight all the animals in the zoo, I'd grab a lion and tear a tiger in two. If that ain't love, it'll have to do.

Susie: Yeah, til when, Butter, til when.

Butterbeans: Until another *fool* come along.

◎◎

INDEFINITE SENTENCE

A man arrested for vagrancy was brought before
a country judge. "Guilty or not guilty," the judge asked.
"Not guilty, suh," the man answered.
"Well, what do you do?"
"Oh, this and that."
"When do you work?"
"Ah, well . . . now and then."
"Lock him up," the judge snapped.
"How long 'fore I get out, yo' honor?" the man asked.
"Sooner or later!"

—Folk

◎◎

FROM *THE WALLS OF JERICHO*

By Rudolph Fisher

*The following selection from Fisher's second novel is set at a fund-raising ben-
efit for a civil rights organization, where, among others, we meet Agatha
Cramp, a white philanthropist who has recently accepted the "startling possibility" that "Negroes might be mankind too," and Fred Merrit, one of the first
trickster mulattos to emerge in American fiction.*

X

Upstairs in the box of J. Pennington Potter, who was one of the dozen vice-
residents of the General Improvement Association, an incredibly ill-chosen
variety of personalities squirmed. It was J. Pennington Potter's conviction
that only admixture produced harmony between the races. He argued
quite logically. Prejudice and misunderstanding were due to mutual ignorance and ignorance due to silence. This silence must be broken. How
break it save by acquaintanceship—how acquaint save by admixture? Social admixture—there was the solution to all the problems of race.

And so he proceeded to admix. There was himself, proud, loud, and pompous, and his wife, round, brown, and expansile, who always seemed bursting with something to say, but had never been known to say it; a woman so inflated with her husband's bombast that one felt she'd collapse at a single thrust. There was the Hon. Buckram Byle, an ex-alderman from the twenty-ninth district, whose presence was intended to give the party some notion of the dignity of a Negro public servant. This he assuredly did, his habit being to stand apart, alone, with folded arms, motionless, silent, scowling, in the depths of meditation. But few suspected the real basis of this air: that Mr. Byle was simply very angry at his young and pretty wife, Nora, who had managed to elude his jealously watchful eye all evening; and the scowl, as usual, evidenced his resolution to take her straight home the moment she should reappear. There was Noel Dunn, the Nordic editor of an anti-Nordic journal, who missed no item of scene or conversation that he thought he could use for copy. Dunn's readers gobbled up pro-Negro pieces, not because they were pro-Negro so much as because they were anti-White, and he and Mrs. Dunn were frequent visitors to Harlem, finding the Pennington Potters convenient wedges in effecting several profitable entrances.

The Potters were very proud of this friendship, and J. Pennington never missed a chance to mention, parenthetically of course, that Mr. and Mrs. Noel Dunn were up to dinner the night before last. The Dunns were known among their friends to mention these excursions also, but not at all parenthetically. The Dunns always explained elaborately about the "wealth of material" to be found in Negro Harlem, and they punctuated their apologies with different intonations of the word "marvelous." Everything in Harlem, to the Dunns, was simply "marvelous!"

A friend of the Dunns, one Tony Nayle, who was visiting Harlem for the first time, was absent from the box at the moment. He had found the music and Nora Byle an irresistible combination; and Nora admitted later that she had continued dancing with him not merely to aggravate her jealous spouse, but also to verify what at first she could hardly believe. Nora always insisted that fays danced with a rhythm all their own, if any. She found Tony Nayle to be the first fay partner she'd ever known, so she said, to dance as though he was paying attention to the music at all.

And finally, side by side in the front of the box, sat Fred Merrit and Miss Agatha Cramp.

It would have been enough to kill the spirit of any party just to have the inarticulate Mrs. Potter as its hostess; enough to distress any company just to inject into it a chronically jealous husband like Byle, let alone bringing his pretty wife, Nora, into contact with the attractive and willing-to-learn Tony; enough to insure discomfort in any group to include guests whose purposes were so different—amusement, profit, uplift; difficult enough to bring together unacquainted, dissimilar people without attempting to mix diverse motives as well. But to have put Fred Merrit and Miss Agatha Cramp side by side—this was the master touch; only a J. Pennington Potter could have done that.

*

One view only did they all have in common, the scene on the dance floor below.

"Marvelous!" said Mr. Dunn.

"Marvelous!" echoed Mrs. Dunn.

"Wonderful!" said J. Pennington Potter with a certain air of discovery.

So dense was the crowd of dancers, so close each couple to the next, that an observer from above might easily have lost the sense that these were actually people. They seemed rather some turbulent congress of bright colored, inanimate things, propelled by a force over which they had no control. The couples were like the leaves and petals of flowers strewn thick on a stream; describing little individual figures and turns, circling capriciously in groups here and there, but all borne steadily onward in one common undertrend. Each seemed to answer with a smile the whim of every breeze; all actually obeyed unaware the steadfast pull of the current.

"Marvelous!" duoed the Dunns.

"Wonderful!" said J. Pennington Potter.

"M-m—" grunted the Hon. Buckram Byle.

"Don't you think, Penny," said Noel Dunn, "that your organization would be more specifically defined it were named The General Negro Improvement Association?"

"Why, yes. Yes, indeed. That is, perhaps. As a matter of fact we originally conceived the name as the General Negro Improvement Association. But it was I myself who contended, and without successful contradiction, that any improvement of the American Negro would inevitably improve all other Americans as well. There was therefore—ah—no point, you see, in including the word 'Negro,' and I succeeded in having it deleted."

Mr. Dunn smiled, noting that the trap-drummer was at the moment very amusing.

*

Meanwhile Miss Agatha Cramp sat quite overwhelmed at the strangeness of her situation. This was her introduction to the people she planned to uplift. True to her word she had personally investigated the G.I.A. and been welcomed with open arms. Certain members of the executive board knew her and her past works—one of two had been associated with her in other projects—and her experience, resources, and devotion to service were unanimously acclaimed assets. And nobody minded her excessively corrective attitude—all new board members started out revising things. Furthermore, the Costume Ball was at hand and that would be enough to upset anybody's ideas of revision.

Never had Miss Cramp seen so many Negroes in one place at one time. Moreover, never had she dreamed that so many of her own people would for any reason imaginable have descended to mingle with these Negroes. She had prided herself on her own liberality in joining this company tonight. And so it shocked and outraged her to see that most of these fair-skinned visitors were unmistakably enjoying themselves, instead of maintaining the aloof, kindly dignity proper to those who must sacrifice to serve. And of course little did she suspect how many of the fair-skinned ones were not visitors at all but natives.

When she met Nora Byle, for instance, she was first struck with the beauty of her "Latin type." To save her soul she could not help a momentary stiffening when Buckram Byle, who was a jaundice-brown, was presented as Nora's husband: Intermarriage! She recovered. No. The girl was one of those mulattoes, of course; a conclusion that brought but temporary relief, for the next moment the debonair Tony Nayle had gone off with the "mulatto," both of them flirting disgracefully.

It was all in all a situation which robbed Miss Cramp of words; but she smiled bravely through her distress and found no little relief in sitting beside Fred Merrit, whose perfect manner, cherubic smile and fair skin were highly comforting. She had not yet noticed the significant texture of his hair.

"Well, what do you think of it?" Merrit eventually asked.

"I don't know what to think, really. What do you think?"

"I? Why—it's all too familiar now for me to have thoughts about. I take it for granted."

"Oh—you have worked among Negroes a great deal, then?"

Merrit grinned. "All my life."

"How do you find them?"

That Merrit did not resist the temptation and admit his complete identity at this point is easier to explain than to excuse. There was first his admitted joy in discomforting members of the dominant race. Further, however, there was a special complex of reasons closer to hand.

Merrit was far more outraged by the flirtation between Nora Byle and Tony Nayle than had been even Miss Cramp herself, and with greater cause. His own race prejudice was a bitterer, more deep-seated emotion than was hers, and out of it came an attitude that caused him to look with great suspicion and distrust upon all visitors who came to Harlem "socially." He insisted that the least blameworthy motive that brought them was curiosity, and held that he, for one, was not on exhibition. As for the men who came oftener than once, he felt that they all had but one motive, the pursuit of Harlem women; that their cultivation of Harlem men was a blind and an instrument in achieving this end, and that the end itself was always illicit and therefore reprehensible.

It was with him a terribly serious matter, of which he could see but one side. When Langdon once hinted gently that maybe it was a two-way reaction, he snorted the suggestion away as nonsense. That he should allow it to disturb him so profoundly meant that it went profoundly back into his own life, as it did into the lives of most people of heredity so diverse as his. The everyday difficulty of his own adjustment engendered in him an unforgiving hatred of those past generations responsible for it. Hence every suggestion that history might repeat itself in this particular occasioned revolt. If there could be no fair exchange, said he, let there be no exchange at all.

He knew that no two ardent individuals would ever be concerned with any such formulas, but the very ineffectuality of what seemed to him so just a principle rendered its violation the more irritating. And in the particular case of Tony and Nora—well, he rather liked Nora himself.

And so beneath his pleasant manner, there was a disordered spirit which at this moment almost gleefully accepted the chance to vent itself on Miss Agatha Cramp's ignorance. To admit his identity would have wholly lost him this chance. And as for the fact that she was a woman, that only made the compensation all the more complete, gave it a quality of actual retaliation, of parallel all the more satisfying.

"How do I find Negroes? I like them very much. Ever so much better than white people."

"Oh Mr. Merrit! Really?"

"You see, they have so much more color."

"Yes. I can see that." She gazed upon the mob. "How primitive these people are," she murmured. "So primitive. So unspoiled by civilization."

"Beautiful savages," suggested Merrit.

"Exactly. Just what I was thinking. What abandonment—what unrestraint—"

"Almost as bad as a Yale–Harvard football game, isn't it?" Merrit's eyes twinkled.

"Well," Miss Cramp demurred, "that's really quite a different thing, you know."

"Of course. This unrestraint is the kind that is hostile to society, hostile to civilization. This is the sort of thing that you and I as sociologists must contend with, must wipe out."

"Yes indeed. Quite so. This sort of thing is, as you say, quite unfortunate. We must educate these people out of it. There is much to be done."

"Listen to that music. Savage too, don't you think?"

"Just what occurred to me. That music is like the beating of—what do they call 'em—dum-dums, isn't it?"

"I was just trying to think what it recalled," mused Merrit with great seriousness. "Tom-toms! That's it—of course. How stupid of me. Tom toms. And the shuffle of feet—"

"Rain," breathed Miss Cramp, who, since her new interest, had deemed it her duty to read some of Langdon's poetry. "Rain falling in a jungle."

"Rain?"

"Rain falling on banana leaves," said the lady. And the gentleman assented, "I know how it is. I once fell on a banana peel myself."

"So primitive." Miss Cramp turned to Mrs. Dunn, who sat behind and above her. "The throb of the jungle," she remarked.

"Marvelous!" exhaled Mrs. Dunn.

"These people—we can do so much for them—we must educate them out of such unrestraint."

Whereupon Tony and Nora appeared laughing and breathless at the box entrance; and Tony, descendant of Cedrics and Caesars, loudly declared:

"I'm going to get that bump-the-bump dance if it takes me the whole darn night!"

"Bump the what?" Miss Agatha wondered.

"Come on, Gloria," Tony urged Mrs. Dunn. "You ought to know it, long as you've been coming to Harlem. Mrs. Byle gives me up. You try."

Mrs. Dunn smiled and quickly rose. "I'll say I will. Come along. It's perfectly marvelous."

*

"Furthermore," expounded J. Pennington Potter, "there is a tendency among Negro organizations to incorporate too many words in a single designation with the result that what is intended as mere appellation becomes a detailed description. Take for example the N.O.U.S.E. and the I.N.I.A.W. There can be no excuse for entitlements of such prolixity. They endeavor to encompass a society's past, present, and future, embracing as well a description of motive and instrument. There is no call you will agree, no excuse, no justification for delineation, history and prophecy in a single title."

"Quite so, Penny," said Mr. Dunn. "Mrs. Byle, may I have this dance?"

"Certainly," said Nora, smiling a trifle too amusedly.

"We're going home after this one," growled her husband as passed.

*

Miss Cramp said in a low voice to Merrit:

"Isn't he a wonderful person?"

"Who?" wondered Merrit.

"Mr. Potter. He talks so beautifully and seems so intelligent."

"He is intelligent, isn't he?" said Merrit, as if the discovery surprised him.

"He must have an awfully good head."

"Unexcelled for certain purposes."

"I had no idea they were ever so cultured. How simple our task would be if they were all like that."

"Like Potter? Heaven forbid!"

"Oh, Mr. Merrit. Really you mustn't let your prejudices prevail. Negroes deserve at least a few leaders like that."

"I don't know what they've ever done to deserve them," he said.

Unable to win him over to her broader viewpoint, she changed the subject.

"Mrs. Byle is very pretty, isn't she?"

"Yes."

"She is so light in complexion for a Negress."

"A what?"

"A Negress. She *is* a Negress, isn't she?"

"Well, I suppose you'd call her that."

"It *is* hard to appreciate, isn't it? It makes one wonder, really. Mrs. Byle is almost as fair as I am, while—well, look at that girl down there. Absolutely black. Yet both—"

"Negresses."

"Exactly what I was thinking. I was just thinking—Now how long have there been Negroes in our country, Mr. Merrit?"

"Longer than most one hundred percent Americans, I believe."

"Really?"

"Since around 1500, I understand. And in numbers since 1619."

"How well informed you are, Mr. Merrit. Imagine knowing dates like that—Why that's between three and four hundred years ago, isn't it? But of course four hundred years isn't such a long time if you believe in evolution. I consider evolution very important, don't you?"

"Profoundly so."

"But I was just thinking. These people have been out of their native element only three or four hundred years, and just see what it has done to their complexions! It's hard to believe that just three hundred years in our country has brought about such a great variety in the color of the black race."

"Environment is a powerful influence, Miss Cramp," murmured Merrit.

"Yes, of course. Chiefly the climate, I should judge. Don't you think?"

Merrit blinked, then nodded gravely, "Climate undoubtedly. Climate. Changed conditions of heat and moisture and so on."

"Yes, exactly. Remarkable isn't it? Now just consider, Mr. Merrit. The northern peoples are very fair—the Scandinavians, for example. The tropic peoples, on the other hand are very dark—often black like the Negroes in their own country. Isn't that true?"

"Undeniably."

"Now if these very same people here tonight had originally gone to Scandinavia—three or four hundred years ago, you understand—some of them would by now be as fair as the Scandinavians! Why they'd even have blue eyes and yellow hair!"

"No doubt about that," Merrit agreed meditatively. "Oh yes. They'd have them without question."

"Just imagine!" marveled Miss Cramp. "A Negro with skin as fair as your own!"

"M-m. Yes. Just imagine," said he without smiling.

XI

The comments of the occupants of nearby boxes would have been illuminating to J. Pennington Potter's party, the box, for example, containing Cornelia Bond's guests. Among these were young Dr. and Mrs. Peter Long, Mrs.

Hernie Boston, Conrad White, who was a writer of stories about Negroes, and Betty Brown, his fiancée. Miss Cramp would have found their comments vulgar, unforgivable of Con and Betty, who had a way of forgetting all about the fact that they were white. J. Pennington Potter would have classed them as "Preposterous!" Dunn would have taken notes and written an editorial on the passing of Nordic supremacy. Merrit would have chuckled inwardly with glee.

"Who's the scrawny neophyte with the J. Popeyed Potters?" from the reputedly wealthy Cornelia, who was tall and regal in bearing and thoroughly, beautifully Ethiopian in appearance.

"There are two," said Hernie. "Which one?"

"Where's the two?" demanded Cornelia.

"One's off dancing with Nora Byle."

"Nothing scrawny about *him*," said Sarah Long.

"No," agreed Cornelia, "and nothing dumb. The way he's learning, it won't be long now—that Nora Byle is a dog."

"Jealous!" grinned Hernie. "After the way you extracted Jimmie Polio from her clutches?"

"Don't be a damn fool, Hernie. Wonder where Jimmy ran off to, come to think of it? Hasn't reported to headquarters for an hour—Sarah"—to Mrs. Long, "I want you and that bad-haired husband of yours over to a little stomp-down Saturday night. Consider yourselves flattered—Con and Betty'll be the only other shines present." Her eyes fell again on Miss Agatha Cramp. "That's the homeliest woman in the world, bar none," she avowed.

Peter Long, who was "tight," rose and sang in a loud voice:

"Oh her face was sharp as a butcher's cleaber,
    But dat did not seem to grieb 'er—"

*

"She's looking right at you, Cornelia," said Hernie.

"Yea," said Cornelia, "and I bet ten dollars she's saying, 'Beautiful savage' or 'So primitive.'"

Conrad said, "Potter's got a sense of humor anyhow. Hooking her up with Gloria Dunn and Nora Byle. I'll bet Gloria snubbed her."

"No, Con. You're the only fay I know that draws the color line on other fays."

"It's natural. Downtown I'm only passing. These," he waved grandiloquently, "are my people."

"Yea—so you seem to think, the way you sell 'em for cash," said Cornelia.

"They enjoy being sold," returned Con.

Betty said, "Don't you think that Nora Byle has the most beautiful hands in the world?"

"I never pay much attention to her–hands," grinned Con.

"All the girls I know in Harlem have beautiful hands," Betty complained.

"You don't know many, then," Cornelia remarked.

"Just look at mine," Betty went on. "Pudgy as a poodle's paw. This Caucasian superiority stuff is a lot of bunk."

"Don't let your liquor out-talk you, Betty."

"No danger," said Betty. Then, "Say–do you know what I'm going to do?"

"Commit suicide," suggested Cornelia.

"In a way. I'm going to write a novel much better than anything Con has done–"

"Not much of an ambition–"

"–and present it as the work of a Negro."

"Negress," corrected Hernie with irony.

"Well," said Con, "you can be sure of two things."

"What?"

"You can be sure some critic will call it the best thing ever done by a Negro."

"Yes," said Cornelia, "as if that's paying you a hell of a compliment."

"And," Con continued, "you can be sure that some fay will insist that it should have been more African."

"And the critic's name," said Cornelia, "will probably be Rabinowitch."

A tall, very blond young man with rosy cheeks, whose eyelids were ptotic with alcohol, came clambering into the box as if he had six pairs of feet.

"Where's my Ethiopian?" he cried at the top of his lungs, peering about myopically and waving his arms like antennae. "Hey!–where's my Ethiopian queen?"

"Jimmy!" called Cornelia. "Bottle that racket. Come here and sit down, you imp."

"Where?" pleaded Jimmy Polio. "Can't see you at all, really. Can't seem to get my silly eyes open–"

"Look, Con," said Betty, indicating Miss Agatha Cramp, who had heard Jimmy's cry and was now observing from a distance. "Look at the horror on that poor woman's face. She's just about ready to die."

Together they looked at the wide-eyed Miss Cramp and together they chuckled with merriment.

*

"Well," sighed Miss Cramp, "Mr. Potter told me that this would be an excellent chance to observe different types of Negroes."

"It seems to be an excellent chance to observe different types of Caucasians, also," said Merrit.

"Disgusting, isn't it? I can't understand why people of apparently our own kind, Mr. Merrit—It's humiliating, isn't it?"

"They out-Herod the Romans, don't they?"

"Unpardonable. How can we hope to help these others if we set so poor an example ourselves?"

"An excellent point. If we are not careful, instead of helping them, we will find them helping us."

"Helping us?"

"Yes. Or more. Transforming us. If things go on like this, one of these days this country's going to wake up with dark brown skin and kinky hair."

"Horrible!"

"Horrible? Why?"

"Oh, Mr. Merrit!"

"I really see nothing horrible about it. I rather think the country would enjoy it."

"Well—I for one shouldn't."

"But think, Miss Cramp," he prodded, "how much better off our country would be—"

"With dark brown skin? I can't imagine—"

"No. Figuratively of course. With a spiritual attitude—an emotional make-up like the Negro's."

"Just what do you mean?"

"This tropic nonchalance, as Locke calls it. This acceptance of circumstance not with a shrug, like the Oriental, but with a characteristic grin. Nobody laughs at the miseries of life like the Negro. He laughs at himself, at his own pains and dangers and disappointments and oppressions. He accepts things, not with resignation but with amusement. That, it seems to me, should be a most alarming thing for his enemy to see."

"I don't understand at all."

"No? Suppose you were fighting somebody, and at every blow you delivered, your antagonist simply grinned and came on. Wouldn't you soon get scared? Wouldn't you begin to lose your nerve? Would you begin wondering if maybe the other fellow wasn't grinning at the futility of your blows—if maybe he wasn't just biding his time in the certainty of his power? How could you be sure what he was laughing at? Himself? Maybe. But I know I'd begin to think he might be laughing at *me*."

"It isn't easy to follow you, Mr. Merrit. But it seems to me that the Negro would be far better off if he didn't laugh so much, no matter at whom. He doesn't take anything seriously. If he did, if he worried more, I think he'd be far better off today."

"Well—maybe today, Miss Cramp. But what about tomorrow?"

"What *can* you mean?"

"Wouldn't it be funny, Miss Cramp, if the Negro let his fair-skinned brother—or cousin, to be a trifle more exact—do all the so-called serious work? Build bridges, dig canals, capture natural forces, fly airplanes, amass wealth, evolve society—these are serious things. Wouldn't it be amusing if the Negro let others worry their brains out devising and developing the civilized luxuries of life—while he spent his time simply living, developing nothing but his capacity for enjoyment; and then when the job was finished, stepped in and took complete possession? Suppose—just suppose, for one can never know—that this irrepressible laughter, this resiliency, is caused by the confidence that he will reap what his oppressors have sown?"

"But that's impossible. Where will he ever get the power to take complete possession?"

"Power? Sheer force of numbers—the overwhelming majority of dark skins in the earth. Together with the—er—the effect of climate. If the climate keeps changing, or if people keep exposing themselves to changes in climate, the time will eventually come when there won't be but a few pure skins left—Now won't it be positively uproarious if the serious achievements reach their height about then?"

"Well," she said after a moment, "I don't think either you or I need worry over that, Mr. Merrit. It's altogether too remote. If I can't see that far, I doubt that any Negro can. It need not worry you at all."

"Quite right. Nobody needs worry over any of it—past, present, or future. Its course is unchangeable by anything so futile as people's worry. That's the joker in this very occasion, Miss Cramp. Uplift the Negro? Why, his position is the most profoundly strategic on earth."

"You really think so?"

"He that is last shall be first."

"Well, that would certainly be awful, wouldn't it?"

There was silence between them.

Presently Miss Cramp remembered that Merrit had been presented to her as an inured bachelor. She said:

"Mr. Merrit, these are serious questions. We must thresh them out some time."

"I should like nothing better," he said.

"Do you spend the summer in town?"

"I'm leaving for the country tomorrow but I'll be back the end of the summer."

"Then you must come and see me on your return. We shall have so much to discuss."

"Nothing would give greater pleasure," he said, and she saw from the present pleasure in his eyes that he must mean what he was saying.

It gave her a thrill. "Summers," she sighed, "are so long, aren't they?"

*

"My maid," said Miss Cramp, "is a Negress. The first one I have ever had, and I must say, the best. She is very pretty, too. She is so different from what one thinks of on hearing the term, Negress. Extremely pretty, really."

"And she remains a maid?"

"Why not? It's honest work and very good pay."

"The pretty ones usually prefer to go on the stage."

"Oh, Linda wouldn't think of any such thing. You see she was raised in an Episcopal Orphanage and seems to be rather religious—I was quite glad to learn how many Negroes are Episcopalian. I didn't know there were any, did you?"

"Are there?"

"A large number, from what this girl says. And what do you think Mr. Merrit? Religious as she is, she never sings spirituals!"

"No? I can't believe it. But she must have some vices?"

"Her only recreation is dancing. Her rector seems to be a very up-to-date person. There are weekly affairs at her church community center and she always goes."

"Must be an awfully dull person."

"On the contrary, extremely interesting. It was through her that I learned of the General Improvement Association. No doubt she is here tonight. In fact, I thought I saw her once just now, down there on the floor, dancing."

She looked sharply for a prolonged moment, then suddenly exclaimed,

"I did too! There she is, there. That tall one in the gypsy costume—isn't she unusual?"

"The one just starting to dance with the big chap in gray?"

"Yes."

Merrit too looked sharply. Appreciation of unfamiliar features at that distance in a crowd was difficult, but—

"I've seen that girl somewhere. You say she's your maid?"

"I'm positive that's Linda."

A moment's rumination; then he remembered. Slowly over his face came an expression of elation far more than commensurate with the recognition.

"Miss Cramp," he said, "do you by any chance live on Court Avenue?"

"Yes, I do." She was extremely well pleased. "I was about to give you my address. However did you know?"

"Why, Miss Cramp," there was no mistaking his joy, "we're neighbors!"

"Really? Why, Mr. Merrit!"

"You live at three hundred nine, don't you?"

"Yes!"

"And I live at three thirteen—that is I will when I come back to town."

"How lovely! But—how—?"

"I saw that girl go into your house one morning when I was having some things moved in. She had her own key."

"Well, isn't this nice, Mr. Merrit." She laughed. "I suppose when you saw Linda come in like that, with her own key, you thought you might even have got into a Negro neighborhood?"

"I admit, I wondered."

"That would have been tragic." She lowered her voice. "I can imagine nothing more awful. To help them is quite all right. To live beside them is quite another matter."

"It is indeed, Miss Cramp. It is indeed."

"You need never have any fear of that in Court Avenue. Frankly, we are rather exclusive, you know."

"I had that in mind when I purchased."

"And to think we are next door neighbors, Mr. Merrit."

They beamed at each other, each in the delight of his own withheld motive, his own private anticipations; a tableau that was soon interrupted by the noisy return of the two couples that had been dancing. Whereupon, rather suddenly it seemed, Merrit decided that he must leave. He rose to go.

"I shall look forward to your call," she reminded.

"If I could only be sure you were doing that," said he, "you've no idea the pleasure 'twould give me."

"You can be sure," she said.

As he left, he chuckled and chided himself:

"Damn shame to worry that poor woman like that—she'll die before the night's over. Somebody'll tell her sure."

THE FAITH HEALER

Folk

An old couple, well past retirement, sat in rocking chairs one night dozing off and listening to the radio when a revival meeting came on and they heard the voice of a faith healer. "IF YOU BELIEVE IN THE LORD," the preacher shouted, "I CAN HEAL YOU TONIGHT! DO YOU BELIEVE IN THE POWER OF THE LORD? IF YOU DO, JUST PUT ONE HAND ON THE RADIO, PRAY WITH ME, AND PUT THE OTHER HAND ON WHAT AILS YOU! AND REMEMBER, ALL THINGS ARE POSSIBLE, THE LORD CAN WORK MIRACLES!"

The old woman reached over, closed her eyes and started praying to herself. She put her other hand over her old heart and started rocking back and forth. Now the husband wasn't a believer, but when he saw his wife praying, he decided he might as well give it a try. He reached over and put his hand on the radio. He started calling on the Lord, then he slipped his other hand down to his lap. It surprised the old woman when she heard him praying, so she opened her eyes and looked over at him.

She shook her head and said, "Josh, the reverend said he could heal the sick, not raise the dead."

EARLY BLUES LYRICS

Some of these women I just can't understand,
All you women I just can't understand,
They cook cornbread for their husbands and biscuits for their man.

Cornbread Blues

I axed Mister Charlie—
What time of day;
He looked at me,
Threw his watch away.
I axed Mister Charlie—
Just give me one dime.
'Go on, old nigger,
You're a dime behind.'

—Folk

High yeller, she'll kick you, that ain't all,
When you step out at night 'nother mule in your stall.

Brownskin Woman

She's a big fat mamma,
Meat shakin' on her bones;
And every time she moves,
Some skinny gal done lost her home.

—Folk

Look heah, papa, you don't treat pigmeat the way you should,
If you don't believe that it's pigmeat ask in the neighborhood.
I ain't good-lookin', I ain't got no great long hair,
But I don't have no worry, I know it's pigmeat anywhere.

Pigmeat Blues

Jelly roll, jelly roll ain't so hard to find,
There's a baker shop in town bakes it brown like mine,
I got sweet jelly, a lovin' sweet jelly roll,
If you taste my jelly, it'll satisfy your worried soul.
I never been to church and I never been to school,
Come down to jelly, I'm a jelly-rollin' fool,
I got sweet jelly to satisfy my worried soul,
I like to have my jelly and I like to have my fun.

New Jelly Roll Blues

Your peaches look mellow hanging way up in your tree,
I like your peaches so well, they are takin' effect on me.
I'm gonna get my step-ladder, babe,
I'm gonna climb up on your limb.

Peach Tree Blues

You go down to the warehouse,
White folks say it ain't no use.
Government ain't givin' away nothin',
But that canned grapefruit juice.
                    Warehouse Man Blues

GHOST STORY

By Tim Moore and Andrew Tribel

During the first half of the twentieth century, most black comics worked in teams. This example of the ever popular ghost story featured the legendary Tim Moore—later known for his role as Kingfish in the TV version of Amos 'n' Andy*—and Andrew Tribel, a relatively unknown comic. Their stage routine appeared in its entirety in* Darktown Revue, *a 1931 film by the pioneer black filmmaker Oscar Micheaux.*

[The routine begins with a casual conversation between Moore and Tribel:]

Tribel: The Island Queen come in dis mornin', let's go down to de levee and see what she brought in.

Moore: Yeah, you can go to dah levee if you wanna. I was down dere yesterday mornin' and got insulted.

Tribel: Who insulted you?

Moore: When dat boat pulled in, outta all of dem folks standin' round on dah levee, the man had to come off the boat and walk up and insult me.

Tribel: How'd he insult you?

Moore: Ask me did I wanna work!

[The skit takes a different turn when Moore explains what happened after he stumbled into a haunted house.]

Moore: I was scared to stay in and I was scared to come out. I knowed there was ghosts in that house.

Tribel: How'd you know it?

Moore: Cause it was chilly in dere. And I thought I'd build me a fire. I looked down into the fireplace and dere was wood and shavin's all ready to be lit! I reached up on dah mantelpiece to get a match. Just as I went to light dah wood and shavin's, dah wood and shavin's disappeared. Wasn't no wood, and they wasn't no shavin's. Live coals burnin' in the grate, red hot!

Tribel: What kinda grate was dat?

Moore: Red hot and steady heatin'. And dat ain't all. I could see dem coals movin' round. All at once dis little kitty come crawlin' out dem hot coals.

Tribel: Outta dah hot coals?

Moore: A little tiny kitty come outta dem hot coals. Turned around and eat some'a dah fire and sit dere and laughed at me, "Ha-ha," like dat.

Tribel: Boy, I don't blame dat cat for laughin', 'cause dah first time I seen you I like to laugh myself to death.

Moore: And boy, dah cat had on a bathing suit and got up on the edge of dah fire and dived down into dem hot coals and when he come up he had on a tuxedo. And come here talkin' Polish to me.

Tribel: What kinda cat was dat?

Moore: A pole cat, fool!

*

Moore: Boy, dah cat got big as a mule. And turned around and told me to shut up. Then started over where I was. And dat's when it happened.

Tribel: And dat's when what happened?

Moore: Dat's when the window got broke out and dah blind got knocked off.

Tribel: You don't mean to stood up and tell me dat you come through dat window.

Moore: I didn't go around it! All I remember was I started and dah window was in my way. And boy, if I had missed dat window, dat wall woulda been ruined.

Tribel: How come you leave dat house in such a unindignified manner? Why didn't you use de doah?

Moore: The doah! You showin' yo' ignorance now.

Tribel: Is I?

Moore: Is you ever been to any school outside de reform school?

Tribel: Yeah.

Moore: Uh-huh. Well, in school did you take up any kinda manual trainin'?

Tribel: Yeah.

Moore: Did you study woodwork?

Tribel: Yeah!

Moore: Well, in yo' studies a woodwork did you take up windowry or doah-ry?

Tribel: Nah.

Moore: You didn't take dem.

Tribel: Nah.

Moore: But you knows a couple of carpenters and a architect or two.

Tribel: Yeah!

Moore: Well, the next carpenter you see, you ask him and he'll explain to you about doahs. He'll tell you dat a doah was made fo' folks what had a lot a time. But when dat cat spoke to me—

Tribel: Yeah.

Moore: . . . by me being punctual, my time dere was up! And right den dah window got well.

Tribel: What you mean, de window got well?

Moore: It got rid of its *pane!*

❦❦

WHY WOMEN GOT THE ADVANTAGE OF MEN

From *Mules and Men*

By Zora Neale Hurston

"Don't you know you can't git de best of no woman in de talkin' game? Her tongue is all de weapon a woman got," George Thomas chided Gene. "She could have had mo' sense, but she told God no, she'd ruther take it out in hips. So God give her ruthers. She got plenty hips, plenty mouf and no brains."

"Oh, yes, womens is got sense too," Mathilda Moseley jumped in. "But they got too much sense to go 'round braggin' about it like y'all do. De lady people always got de advantage of mens because God fixed it dat way."

"Whut ole black advantage is y'all got?" B. Moseley asked indignantly. "We got all de strength and all de law and all de money and you can't git a thing but whut we jes' take pity on you and give you."

"And dat's jus' de point," said Mathilda triumphantly. "You *do* give it to us, but how come you do it?" And without waiting for an answer Mathilda began to tell why women always take advantage of men.

You see in de very first days, God made a man and a woman and put 'em in a house together to live. 'Way back in them days de woman was just as strong as de man and both of 'em did de same things. They useter get to fussin' 'bout who gointer do this and that and sometime they'd fight, but they was even balanced and neither one could whip de other one.

One day de man said to hisself, "B'lieve Ah'm gointer go and see God and ast Him for a li'l mo' strength so Ah kin whip dis 'oman and make her mind. Ah'm tired of de way things is." So he went on up to see God.

"Good mawnin', Ole Father."

"Howdy man. Whut you doin' 'round my throne so soon dis mawnin'?"

"Ah'm troubled in mind, and nobody can't ease mah spirit 'ceptin' you."

God said: "Put yo' plea in de right form and Ah'll hear and answer."

"Ole Maker, wid de mawnin' stars glitterin' in yo' shinin' crown, wid de dust from yo' footsteps makin' worlds upon worlds, wid de blazin' bird we call de sun flyin' out of yo' right hand in de mawnin' and consumin' all day de flesh and blood of stump-black darkness, and comes flyin' home every evenin' to rest on yo' left hand, and never once in all yo' eternal years, mistood de left hand for de right, Ah ast you *please* to give me mo' strength than dat woman you give me, so Ah kin make her mind. Ah know you don't want to be always comin' down way past de moon and stars to be straightenin' her out and its got to be done. So give me a li'l mo' strength, Ole Maker and Ah'll do it."

"All right, Man, you got mo' strength than woman."

So de man run all de way down de stairs from Heben till he got home. He was so anxious to try his strength on de woman dat he couldn't take his time. Soon's he got in de house he hollered "Woman! Here's yo' boss. God done tole me to handle you in which ever way Ah please. Ah'm yo' boss."

De woman flew to fightin' 'im right off. She fought 'im frightenin' but he beat her. She got her wind and tried 'im agin but he whipped her agin. She got herself together and made de third try on him vigorous but he beat her every time. He was so proud he could whip 'er at last, dat he just crowed over her and made her do a lot of things she didn't like. He told her, "Long as you obey me, Ah'll be good to yuh, but every time yuh rear up Ah'm gointer put plenty wood on yo' back and plenty water in yo' eyes."

De woman was so mad she went straight up to Heben and stood befo' de Lawd. She didn't waste no words. She said, "Lawd, Ah come befo' you mighty mad t'day. Ah want back my strength and power Ah useter have."

"Woman, you got de same power you had since de beginnin'."

"Why is it then, dat de man kin beat me now and he useter couldn't do it?"

"He got mo' strength than he useter have. He come and ast me for it and Ah give it to 'im. Ah gives to them that ast, and you ain't never ast me for no mo' power."

"Please suh, God, Ah'm astin' you for it now. Jus' gimme de same as you give him."

God shook his head. "It's too late now, woman. Whut Ah give, Ah never take back. Ah give him mo' strength than you and no matter how Ah give you, he'll have mo'."

De woman was so mad she wheeled around and went on off. She went straight to de devil and told him what had happened.

He said, "Don't be dis-incouraged, woman. You listen to me and you'll come out mo' than conqueror. Take dem frowns out yo' face and turn round and go right on back to Heben and ast God to give you dat bunch of keys hangin' by de mantel-piece. Then you bring 'em to me and Ah'll show you what to do wid 'em."

So de woman climbed back up to Heben agin. She was mighty tired but she was more out-done that she was tired so she climbed all night long and got back up to Heben agin. When she got befo' de throne, butter wouldn't melt in her mouf.

"O Lawd and Master of de rainbow, Ah know yo' power. You never make two mountains without you put a valley in between. Ah know you kin hit a straight lick wid a crooked stick."

"Ast for whut you want, woman."

"God, gimme dat bunch of keys hangin' by yo' mantel-piece."

"Take 'em."

So de woman took de keys and hurried on back to de devil wid 'em. There was three keys on de bunch. Devil say, "See dese three keys? They got mo' power in 'em than all de strength de man kin ever git if you handle 'em right. Now dis first key is to de do' of de kitchen, and you know a man always favors his stomach. Dis second one is de key to de bedroom and he don't like to be shut out from dat neither and dis last key is de key to de cradle and he don't want to be cut off from his generations at all. So now you take dese keys and go lock up everything and wait till he come to you. Then don't you unlock nothin' until he use his strength for yo' benefit and yo' desires."

De woman thanked 'im and tole 'im, "If it wasn't for you, Lawd knows whut us po' women folks would do."

She started off but de devil halted her. "Jus' one mo' thing: don't go home braggin' 'bout yo' keys. Jus' lock up everything and say nothin' until you git asked. And then don't talk too much."

De woman went on home and did like de devil tole her. When de man come home from work she was settin' on de porch singin' some song 'bout "Peck on de wood make de bed go good."

When de man found de three doors fastened what useter stand wide open he swelled up like pine lumber after a rain. First thing he tried to break in cause he figgered his strength would overcome all obstacles. When he saw he couldn't do it, he ast de woman, "Who locked dis do'?"

She tole 'im, "Me."

"Where did you git de key from?"

"God give it to me."

"He run up to God and said, "God, woman got me locked 'way from my vittles, my bed and my generation, and she say you give her the keys."

God said, "I did, Man, Ah give her de keys, but de devil showed her how to use 'em."

"Well, Ole Maker, please gimme some keys jus' lak 'em so she can't git de full control."

"No, Man, what Ah give Ah give. Woman got de key."

"How can Ah know 'bout my generations?"

"Ast de woman."

So de man come on back and submitted hisself to de woman and she opened de doors.

He wasn't satisfied but he had to give in. 'Way after while he said to de woman, "Le's us divide up. Ah'll give you half of my strength if you lemme hold de keys in my hands."

De woman thought dat over so de devil popped and tol her, "Tell 'im, naw. Let 'im keep his strength and you keep yo' keys."

So de woman wouldn't trade wid 'im and de man had to mortgage his strength to her to live. And dat's why de man makes and de woman takes. You men is still braggin' 'bout yo' strength and de women is sittin' on de keys and lettin' you blow off till she git ready to put de bridle on you.

B. Moseley looked over at Mathilda and said, "You just like a hen in de barnyard. You cackle so much you give de rooster de blues."

Mathilda looked over at him archly and quoted:

Stepped on a pin, de pin bent
And dat's de way the story went.

"Y'all lady people ain't smarter than *all* men folks. You got plow lines on some of us, but some of us is too smart for you. We go past you jus' like lightnin' thru de trees," Willie Sewell boasted. "And what make it so cool, we close enough to you to have a scronchous time, but never no halter on our necks. Ah know they won't git none on dis last neck of mine."

"Oh, you kin be had," Gold retorted. "Ah mean dat abstifically."

"Yeah? But not wid de trace chains. Never no shack up. Ah want dis tip-in love and tip yo' hat and walk out. Ah don't want nobody to have dis dyin' love for me."

Richard Jones said: "Yeah, man. Love is a funny thing; love is a blossom. If you want yo' finger bit poke it at a possum."

◎⁄◎

SOUND ADVICE

During World War II, a colonel in a colored
regiment noticed that one of the enlisted men
was always nearby—never left his side.
During a lull in the action, as they huddled in a foxhole
a good distance from the front lines,
the colonel said, "My boy, you're a good soldier
you stuck by me during this whole engagement."
The enlisted man said, "Yes, suh, I'm doin' 'zactly
what my mama told me—she say,
'Stick with the officers and you always be safe.'"

—Folk

୧/୨

FROM *BLACK NO MORE*

By George Schuyler

Schuyler's first novel was a fictional account of America's reaction after the Harlem-based black scientist, Dr. Junius Crookman, discovers a chemical that changes blacks to whites. The following early chapters depict some of the social chaos caused by the doctor's startling discovery.

Chapter Three

Dr. Junius Crookman, looking tired and worn, poured himself another cup of coffee from the percolater near by and turning to Hank Johnson, asked "What about that new electrical apparatus?"

"On th' way, Doc. On th' way," replied the former Numbers baron. "Just talkin' to th' man this mornin'. He says we'll get it tomorrow, maybe."

"Well, we certainly need it," said Chuck Foster, who sat beside him on the large leather divan. "We can't handle all of the business as it is."

"How about those new places you're buying?" asked the physician.

"Well, I've bought the big private house on Edgecombe Avenue for fifteen thousand and the workmen are getting it in shape now. It ought to be ready in about a week if nothing happens," Foster informed him.

"If nuthin' happens?" echoed Johnson. "Whut's gonna happen? We're settin' on th' world, ain't we? Our racket's within th' law, ain't it? We're makin' money faster'n we can take it in, ain't we? Whut could happen? This here is the best and safest graft I've ever been in."

"Oh, you never can tell," cautioned the quondom realtor. "These white newspapers, especially in the South, are beginning to write some pretty strong editorials against us and we've only been running two weeks. You know how easy it is to stir up the fanatical element. Before we know it they're liable to get a law passed against us."

"Not if I c'n git to th' legislature first," interrupted Johnson. "Yuh know, Ah knows how tuh handle these white folks. If yuh 'Say it with Bucks' you c'n git anything yuh want."

"There is something in what Foster says, though," Dr. Crookman said. "Just look at this bunch of clippings we got in this morning. Listen to these: 'The Viper in Our Midst,' from the Richmond *Blade;* 'The Menace of Science' from the Memphis *Bugle;* 'A Challenge to Every White Man' from the

Dallas *Sun;* 'Police Battle Black Mob Seeking White Skins,' from the Atlanta *Topic;* 'Negro Doctor Admits Being Taught by Germans,' from the St. Louis *North American.* Here's a line or two from an editorial in the Oklahoma City *Hatchet:* 'There are times when the welfare of our race must take precedence over law. Opposed as we always have been to mob violence as the worst enemy of democratic government, we cannot help but feel that the intelligent white men and women of New York City who are interested in the purity and preservation of their race should not permit the challenge of Crookmanism to go unanswered, even though these black scoundrels may be within the law. There are too many criminals in this country already hiding behind the skirts of the law.'

"And lastly, one from the Tallahassee *Announcer* says: 'While it is the right of every citizen to do what he wants to do with his money, the white people of the United States cannot remain indifferent to this discovery and its horrible potentialities. Hundreds of Negroes with newly-acquired white skins have already entered white society and thousands will follow them. The black race from one end of the country to the other has in two short weeks gone completely crazy over the prospect of getting white. Day by day we see the color line which we have so laboriously established being rapidly destroyed. There would not be so much cause for alarm in this, were it not for the fact that this vitiligo is not hereditary. In other words, THE OFFSPRING OF THESE WHITENED NEGROES WILL BE NEGROES! This means that your daughter, having married a supposed white man, may find herself with a black baby! Will the proud white men of the Southland so far forget their traditions as to remain idle while this devilish work is going on?"

"No use singin' th' blues," counseled Johnson. "We ain' gonna be both'd heah, even if them crackahs down South do raise a little hell. Jus' lissen to th' sweet music of that mob out theah! Eve'y scream means fifty bucks. On'y reason we ain't makin' mo' money is 'cause we ain't got no mo' room."

"That's right," Dr. Crookman agreed. "We've turned out one hundred a day for fourteen days." He leaned back and lit a cigarette.

"At fifty bucks a th'ow," interrupted Johnson, "that means we've took in seventy thousand dollahs. Great Day in th' mornin'! Didn't know tha was so much jack in Harlem."

"Yes," continued Crookman, "we're taking in thirty-five thousand dollars a week. As soon as you and Foster get that other place fixed up we'll be making twice that much."

From the hallway came the voice of the switchboard operator monotonously droing out her instructions: "No, Dr, Crookman cannot see any-one. . . . Dr. Crookman has nothing to say. . . . Dr. Crookman will issue a statement shortly. . . . Fifty Dollars. . . . No, Dr. Crookman isn't a mulatto. . . . I'm very sorry but I cannot answer that question."

The three friends sat in silence amid the hum of activity around them. Hank Johnson smiled down at the end of his cigar as he thought back over his rather colorful and hectic career. To think that today he was one of the leading Negroes of the world, one who was taking an active and important part in solving the most vexatious problem in American life, and yet only ten years before he had been working on a Carolina chain gang. Two years he had toiled on the roads under the hard eye and ready rifle of a cruel white guard; two years of being beaten, kicked and cursed, of poor food and vermin-infested habitations; two years for participating in a little crap game. Then he had drifted to Charleston, got a job in a pool room, had a stroke of luck with the dice, come to New York and landed right in the midst of the Numbers racket. Becoming a collector or "runner," he had managed his affairs well enough to be able to start out soon as a "banker." Money had poured in from Negroes eager to chance one cent in the hope of winning six dollars. Some won but most lost and he had prospered. He had purchased an apartment house, paid off the police, dabbled in the bail bond game, given a couple of thousand dollars to advance Negro Art and been elected Grand Permanent Shogun of the Ancient and Honorable Order of the Crocodiles, Harlem's largest and most prosperous secret society. Then young Crookman had come to him with his proposition. At first he had hesitated about helping him but later was persuaded to do so when the young man bitterly complained that the dicty Negroes would not help to pay for the studies abroad. What a stroke of luck, getting in on the ground floor like this! They'd all be richer than Rockefeller inside of a year. Twelve million Negroes at fifty dollars apiece! Great Day in the morning! Hank spat regally into the brass cuspidor across the office and reared back contentedly on the soft cushion of the divan.

Chuck Foster was also seeing his career in retrospect. His life had not been as colorful as that of Hank Johnson. The son of a Birmingham barber, he had enjoyed such educational advantages as that community afforded the darker brethren; had become a schoolteacher, an insurance agent and a social worker in turn. Then, along with the tide of migration, he had drifted first to Cincinnati, then to Pittsburgh and finally to New York. There the real estate field, unusually lucrative because of the paucity of apart-ments for the increasing Negro population, had claimed him. Cautious, careful, thrifty and devoid of sentimentality, he had prospered, but not without some ugly rumors being broadcast about his sharp business methods. As he slowly worked his way up to the top of Harlem society, he had sought to live down this reputation for double-dealing and shifty practices, all too true of the bulk of his fellow realtors in the district, by giving large sums to Young Men's and Young Women's Christian Associations, by offering scholarships to young Negroes, by staging elaborate parties to which the dicty Negroes of the community were invited. He had been glad of the opportunity to help subsidize young Crookman's studies abroad when Hank Johnson pointed out the possibilities of the venture. Now, although the results so far exceeded his wildest dreams, his natural conservatism and timidity made him somewhat pessimistic about the future. He supposed a hundred dire results of their activities and only the day before he had increased the amount of his life insurance. His mind was filled with doubts. He didn't like so much publicity. He wanted a sort of genteel popularity but no notoriety.

*

Despite the coffee and cigarettes, Dr. Junius Crookman was sleepy. The responsibility, the necessity of overseeing the work of his physicians and nurse, the insistence of the newspapers and the medical profession that he reveal the secrets of his treatment and a thousand other vexatious details had kept him from getting proper rest. He had, indeed, spent most of his time in the sanitarium.

This hectic activity was new to him. Up until a month ago his thirty-five years had been peaceful and, in the main, studious ones. The son of an Episcopal clergyman, he had been born and raised in a city in central New York, his associates carefully selected in order to protect him as much as possible from the defeatist psychology so prevalent among American Negroes and given every opportunity and inducement to learn his profession and become a thoroughly cultivated and civilized man. His parents, though poor, were proud and boasted that they belonged to the Negro aristocracy. He had had to work his way through college because of the failure of his father's health but he had come very little in contact with the crudity, coarseness and cruelty of life. He had been monotonously successful but he was sensible enough to believe that a large part of it was due, like most success, to chance. He saw in his great discovery the solution to the most annoying problem in American life. Obviously, he reasoned, if there were no Negroes, there could be no Negro problem. With-out a Negro problem, Americans could concentrate their attention on something constructive. Through his efforts and the activities of Black-No-More, Incorporated, it would be possible to do what agitation, education and legislation had failed to do. He was naïvely surprised that there should be opposition to his work. Like most men with a vision, a plan, a program or a remedy, he fondly imagined people to be intelligent enough to accept a good thing when it was offered to them, which was conclusive evidence that he knew little about the human race.

Dr. Crookman prided himself above all on being a great lover of his race. He had studied its history, read of its struggles and kept up with its achievements. He subscribed to six or seven Negro weekly newspapers and two of the magazines. He was so interested in the continued pro-gress of American Negroes that he wanted to remove all obstacles in their path by depriving them of their racial characteristics. His home and office were filled with African masks and paintings of Negroes by Ne-groes. He was what was known in Negro society as a Race Man. He was wedded to everything black except the black woman—his wife was a white girl with remote Negro ancestry, of the type that Negroes were wont to describe as being "able to pass for white." While abroad he had spent his spare time ransacking the libraries for facts about the achieve-ments of Negroes and having liaisons with comely and available fraus and frauliens.

"Well, Doc," said Hank Johnson, suddenly, "you'd bettah go on home 'n git some sleep. Ain' no use killin' you'sef. Eve'thing's gonna be all right heah. You ain' gotta thing tuh worry 'bout."

"How's he gonna get out of here with that mob in front?" Chuck in-quired. "A man almost needs a tank to get through that crowd of darkies."

"Oh, Ah've got all that fixed, Calamity Jane," Johnson remarked casually. "All he' gotta do is tuh go on down staihs tuh the basem'nt, go out th' back way an' step into th' alley. My car'll be theah waitin' fo' 'im."

"That's awfully nice of you, Johnson," said the physician. "I am dead tired. I think I'll be a new man if I can get a few hours of sleep."

A black man in white uniform opened the door and announced: "Mrs. Crookman!" He held the door open for the Doctor's petite, stylishly-dressed wife to enter. The three men sprang to their feet. Johnson and Foster eyed the beautiful little octoroon appreciatively as they bowed, thinking how easily she could "pass for white," which would have been something akin to a piece of anthracite coal passing for black.

"Darling!" she exclaimed, turning to her husband. "Why don't you come home and get some rest? You'll be ill if you keep on in this way."

"Jus' whut Ah bin tellin' him, Mrs. Crookman," Johnson hastened to say. "We got eve'ything fixed tuh send 'im off."

"Well, then, Junius, we'd better be going," she said decisively.

Putting on a long overcoat over his white uniform, Dr, Crookman, wearily and meekly followed his spouse out of the door.

"Mighty nice looking girl, Mrs. Crookman," Foster observed.

"Nice lookin'!" echoed Johnson, with mock amazement. "Why, nigguh, that ooman would make uh rabbit hug uh houn'. Doc sez she's cullud, an' she sez so, but she looks mighty white tuh me."

"Everything that looks white ain't white in this man's country," Foster replied.

*

Meantime there was feverish activity in Harlem's financial institutions. At the Douglass Bank the tellers were busier than bootleggers on Christmas Eve. Moreover, they were short-handed because of the mysterious absence of Bunny Brown. A long queue of Negroes extended down one side of the bank, out of the front door and around the corner, while bank attendants struggled to keep them in line. Everybody was drawing out money; no one was depositing. In vain the bank officials pleaded with them not to withdraw their funds. The Negroes were adamant: they wanted their money and wanted it quick. Day after day this had gone on ever since Black-No-More, Incorporated, had started turning Negroes white. At first, efforts were made to bulldoze and intimidate the depositors but that didn't succeed. These people were in no mood to be trifled with. A lifetime of being Negroes in the United States had convinced them that there was great advantage in being white.

"Mon, whutcha tahlk ab't?" scoffed a big, black British West Indian woman with whom an official was remonstrating not to draw out her money. "Dis heah's mah mahney, ain't it? Yuh use mah mahney alla time, aintcha? Whutcha mean, Ah shouldn't draw't out? . . . You gimme mah mahney or Ah broke up dis place!"

"Are you closing your account, Mr. Robinson?" a soft-voiced mulatto teller inquired of a big, rusty stevedore.

"Ah ain't openin' it," was the rejoinder. "Ah wants th' whole thing, an' Ah don't mean maybe."

Similar scenes were being enacted at the Wheatley Trust Company and local Post Office station.

An observer passing up and down the streets would have noted a general exodus from the locality. Moving vans were backed up to apartment houses on nearly every block.

The "For Rent" signs were appearing in larger number in Harlem than at any time in twenty-five years. Landlords looked on helplessly as a apartment after apartment emptied and was not filled. Even the refusal to return deposits did not prevent the tenants from moving out. What, indeed, was fifty, sixty or seventy dollars when one was leaving behind insult, ostracism, segregation and discrimination? Moreover, the whitened Negroes were saving a great deal of money by being able to change localities. The mechanics of race prejudice had forced them into the congested Harlem area where, at the mercy of white and black real estate sharks, they had been compelled to pay exorbitant rentals because the demand for housing far exceeded the supply. As a general rule the Negroes were paying one hundred per cent more than white tenants in other parts of the city for a smaller number of rooms and worse service.

The installment furniture and clothing houses in the area were also beginning to feel the results of the activities of Black-No-More, Incorporated. Collectors were reporting their inability to locate certain families or the articles they had purchased on time. Many of the colored folk, it was said, had sold their furniture to second-hand stores and vanished with the proceeds into the great mass of white citizenry.

At the same time there seemed to be more white people on the streets of Harlem than at any time in the past twenty years. Many of them appeared to be on the most intimate terms with the Negroes, laughing, talking, dining and dancing in a most un-Caucasian way. This sort of association had always gone on at night but seldom in the daylight.

Strange Negroes from the West and South who had heard the good news were to be seen on the streets and in public places, patiently awaiting their turn at the Crookman Institute.

*

Madame Sisseretta Blandish sat disconsolately in an armchair near the front door of her ornate hair-straightening shop, looking blankly at the pedestrians and traffic passing to and fro. These two weeks had been hard ones for her. Everything was going out and nothing was coming in. She had been doing very well at her vocation for years and was acclaimed in the community as one of its business leaders. Because of her prominence as the proprietor of a successful enterprise engaged in making Negroes appear as much like white folks as possible, she had recently been elected for the fourth time a Vice-President of the American Race Pride League. She was also head of the Women's Committee of the New York Branch of the Social Equality League and held an important place in local Republican politics. But all of these honors brought little or no money with them. They didn't help to pay her rent or purchase the voluminous dresses she required to drape her Amazonian form. Only that day her landlord had brought her the sad news that he either wanted his money or the premises.

Where, she wondered, would she get the money? Like most New Yorkers she put up a big front with very little cash behind it, always looking hopefully forward to the morrow for a lucky break. She had two-thirds of the rent money already, by dint of much borrowing, and if she could "do" a few nappy heads she would be in the clear; but hardly a customer had crossed her threshold in a fortnight, except two or three Jewish girls from downtown who came up regularly to have their hair straightened because it wouldn't stand inspection in the Nordic world. The Negro women had seemingly deserted her. Day after day she saw her old customers pass by hurriedly without even looking in her direction. Verily a revolution was taking place in Negro society.

"Oh, Miss Simpson!" cried the hair-straightener after a passing young lady. "Ain't you going to say hello?"

The young woman halted reluctantly and approached the doorway. Her brown face looked strained. Two weeks before she would have been a rare sight in the Black Belt because her kinky hair was not straightened; it was merely combed, brushed and neatly pinned up. Miss Simpson had vowed that she wasn't going to spend any dollar a week having he hair "done" when she only lacked fifteen dollars of having money enough to quit the Negro race forever.

"Sorry, Mrs. Blandish," she apologized, "but I swear I didn't see you. I've been just that busy that I haven't had eyes for anything or anybody except my job and back home again. You know I'm all alone now. Yes, Charlie went over two weeks ago and I haven't heard a word from him. Just think of that! After all I've done for that nigger. Oh well! I'll soon be over there myself. Another week's work will fix me all right."

"Humph!" snorted Mme. Blandish. "That's all you niggers are thinking about nowadays. Why don't you come down here and give me some business? If I don't hurry up and make some more money I'll have to close up this place and go to work myself."

"Well, I'm sorry, Mrs. Blandish," the girl mumbled indifferently, moving off toward the corner to catch the approaching street car, "but I guess I can hold out with this here bad hair until Saturday night. You know I've taken too much punishment being dark these twenty-two years to miss this opportunity. . . . Well," she flung over her shoulder, "Goodbye! See you later."

Madame Blandish settled her 250 pounds back into her armchair and sighed heavily. Like all American Negroes she had desired to be white when she was young and before she entered business for herself and became a person of consequence in the community. Now she had lived long enough to have no illusions about the magic of a white skin. She liked her business and she liked her social position in Harlem. As a white woman she would have to start all over again, and she wasn't so sure of herself. Here at least she was somebody. In the great Caucasian world she would be just another white woman, and they were becoming a drug on the market, what with the simultaneous decline of chivalry, the marriage rate and professional prostitution. She had seen too many elderly, white-haired Caucasian females scrubbing floors and toiling in sculleries not to know what being just another white woman meant. Yet she admitted to herself that it would be nice to get over being the butt for jokes and petty prejudice.

The Madame was in a quandary and so also were hundreds of others in the upper stratum of Harlem life. With the Negro masses moving out from under them, what other alternative did they have except to follow. True, only a few hundred Negroes had so far vanished from their wonted haunts, but it was known that thousands, tens of thousands, yes, millions would follow them.

Chapter Four

MATTHEW FISHER, alias Max Disher, joined the Easter Sunday crowds, twirling his malacca stick and ogling the pretty flappers who passed giggling in their Spring finery. For nearly three months he had idled around the Georgia capital hoping to catch a glimpse of the beautiful girl who on New Year's Eve had told him "I never dance with niggers." He had searched diligently in almost every stratum of Atlanta society, but he had failed to find her. There were hundreds of tall, beautiful, blonde maidens in the city; to seek a particular one whose name one did not know was somewhat akin to hunting for a Russian Jew in the Bronx or a particular Italian gunman in Chicago.

For three months he had dreamed of this girl, carefully perused the society columns of the local newspapers on the chance that her picture might appear in them. He was like most men who have been repulsed by a pretty girl, his desire for her grew stronger and stronger.

He was not finding life as a white man the rosy existence he had anticipated. He was forced to conclude that it was pretty dull and that he was bored. As a boy he had been taught to look up to white folks as just a little less than gods; now he found them little different from the Negroes, except that they were uniformly less courteous and less interesting.

Often when the desire for the happy-go-lucky, jovial good-fellowship of the Negroes came upon him strongly, he would go down to Auburn Avenue and stroll around the vicinity, looking at the dark folk and listening to their conversation and banter. But no one down there wanted him around. He was a white man and thus suspect. Only the black women who ran the "Call Houses" on the hill wanted his company. There was nothing left for him except the hard, materialistic, grasping, ill-bred society of the whites. Sometimes a slight feeling of regret that he had left his people forever would cross his mind, but it fled before the painful memories of past experiences in this, his home town.

The unreasoning and illogical color prejudice of most of the people with whom he was forced to associate, infuriated him. He often laughed cynically when some coarse, ignorant white man voiced his opinion concerning the inferior mentality and morality of the Negroes. He was moving in white society now and he could compare it with the society he had known as a Negro in Atlanta and Harlem. What a let-down it was from the good breeding, sophistication, refinement and gentle cynicism to which he had become accustomed as a popular young man about town in New York's Black Belt. He was not able to articulate this feeling but he was conscious of the reaction nevertheless.

For a week now, he had been thinking seriously of going to work. His thousand dollars had dwindled to less than a hundred. He would have to find some source of income and yet the young white men with whom he talked about work all complained that it was very scarce. Being white, he finally concluded, was no Open Sesame to employment for he sought work in banks and insurance offices without success.

During this period of idleness and soft living, he had followed the news and opinion in the local daily press and confessed himself surprised at the antagonistic attitude of the newspapers toward Black-No-More, Incorporated. From the vantage point of having formerly been a Negro, he was able to see how the newspapers were fanning the color prejudice of the white people. Business men, he found were also bitterly opposed to Dr. Crookman and his efforts to bring about chromatic democracy in the nation.

The attitude of these people puzzled him. Was not Black-No-More getting rid of the Negroes upon whom all of the blame was placed for the backwardness of the South? Then he recalled what a Negro street speaker had said one night on the corner of 138th Street and Seventh Avenue in New York: that unorganized labor meant cheap labor; that the guarantee of cheap labor was an effective means of luring new industries into the South; that so long as the ignorant white masses could be kept thinking of the menace of the Negro to Caucasian race purity and political control, they would give little thought to labor organization. It suddenly dawned upon Matthew Fisher that this Black-No-More treatment was more of a menace to white business than to white labor. And not long afterward he became aware of the money-making possibilities involved in the present situation.

How could he work it? He was not known and he belonged to no organization. Here was a veritable gold mine but how could he reach the ore? He scratched his head over the problem but could think of no solution. Who would be interested in it that he could trust?

He was pondering this question the Monday after Easter while breakfasting in an armchair restaurant when he noticed an advertisement in a newspaper lying in the next chair. He read it and then re-read it:

THE KNIGHTS OF NORDICA

Want 10,000 Atlanta White Men and Women to
Join in the Fight for White Race Integrity.

Imperial Klonklave Tonight

The racial integrity of the Caucasian Race is being
threatened by the activities of a scientific
black Beelzebub in New York

Let us Unite Now Before It Is

TOO LATE!

Come to Nordica Hall Tonight
Admission Free.

Rev. Henry Givens,
Imperial Grand Wizard

Here, Matthew figured, was just what he had been looking for. Probably he could get in with this fellow Givens. He finished his cup of coffee, lit a cigar and paying his check, strolled out into the sunshine of Peachtree Street.

He took the trolley out to Nordica Hall. It was a big, unpainted barn-like edifice, with a suite of offices in front and a huge auditorium in the rear. A new oil cloth sign reading "THE KNIGHTS OF NORDICA" was stretched across the front of the building.

Matthew paused for a moment and sized up the edifice. Givens must have some money, he thought, to keep up such a large place. Might not be a bad idea to get a little dope on him before going inside.

"This fellow Givens is a pretty big guy around here, ain't he?" he asked the young man at the soda fountain across the street.

"Yessah, he's one o' th' bigges' men in this heah town. Used to be a big somethin' or other in th' old Ku Klux Klan 'fore it died. Now he's stahtin' this heah Knights o' Nordica."

"He must have pretty good jack," suggested Matthew.

"He oughtta have," answered the soda jerker. "My paw tells me he was close to th' money when he was in th' Klan."

Here, thought Matthew, was just the place for him. He paid for his soda and walked across the street to the door marked "Office." He felt a slight tremor of uneasiness as he turned the knob and entered. Despite his white skin he still possessed the fear of the Klan and kindred organizations possessed by most Negroes.

A rather pretty young stenographer asked him his business as he walked into the ante room. Better be bold, he thought. This was probably the best chance he would have to keep from working, and his funds were getting lower and lower.

"Please tell Rev. Givens, the Imperial Grand Wizard, that Mr. Matthew Fisher of the New York Anthropological Society is very anxious to have about a half-hour's conversation with him relative to his new venture." Matthew spoke in an impressive, businesslike manner, rocked back on his heels and looked profound.

"Yassah," almost whispered the awed young lady, "I'll tell him." She withdrew into an inner office and Matthew chuckled softly to himself. He wondered if he could impress the old fakir as easily as he had the girl.

Rev. Henry Givens, Imperial Grand Wizard of the Knights of Nordica, was a short, wizened, almost bald, bull-voiced, ignorant ex-evangelist, who had come originally from the hilly country north of Atlanta. He had helped in the organization of the Ku Klux Klan following the Great War and had worked with zeal only equaled by his thankfulness to God for escaping from the precarious existence of an itinerant saver of souls.

Not only had the Rev. Givens toiled diligently to increase the prestige, power and membership of the defunct Ku Klux Klan, but he had also been a very hard worker in withdrawing as much money from its treasury as possible. He convinced himself, as did the other officers, that his stealing was not stealing at all but merely appropriation of rightful reward for his valuable services. When the morons finally tired of supporting the show and the stream of ten-dollar memberships declined to a trickle, Givens had been able to retire gracefully and live on the interest of his money.

Then, when the newspapers began to recount the activities of Black-No-More, Incorporated, he saw a vision of work to be done, and founded the Knights of Nordica. So far there were only a hundred members but he had high hopes for the future. Tonight, he felt would tell the story. The prospect of a full treasury to dip into again made his little gray eyes twinkle and the palms of his skinny hands itch.

The stenographer interrupted him to announce the newcomer.

"Hum-n!" said Givens, half to himself. "New York Anthropological Society, eh? This feller must know somethin'. Might be able to use him in this business. . . . All right, show him in!"

The two men shook hands and swiftly appraised each other. Givens waved Matthew to a chair.

"How can I serve you, Mr. Fisher?" he began in sepulchral tone dripping with unction.

It is rather," countered Matthew in his best salesman's croon, "how I can serve you and your valuable organization. As an anthropologist, I have, of course, been long interested in the works with which you have been identified. It has always seemed to me that there was no question in American life more important than that of preserving the integrity of the white race. We all know what has been the fate of those nations that have permitted their blood to be polluted with that of inferior breeds." (He had read some argument like that in a Sunday supplement not long before, which was the extent of knowledge of anthropology.) "This latest menace of Black-No-More is the most formidable the white people of America have had to face since the founding of the Republic. As a resident of New York City, I am aware, of course, of the extent of the activities of this Negro Crookman and his two associates. Already thousands of blacks have passed over into the white race. Not satisfied with operating in New York City, they have opened their sanitariums in twenty other cities from Coast to Coast. They open a new one almost every day. In their literature and advertisements in the darky newspapers they boast that they are now turning four thousand Negroes white every day." He knitted his blond eyebrows. "You see how great the menace is? At this rate there will not be a Negro in the country in ten years, for you remember that the rate is increasing every day as new sanitariums are opened. Don't you see that something must be done about this immediately? Don't you see that Congress must be aroused; that these places must be closed?" The young man glared with belligerent indignation.

Rev. Givens saw. He nodded in his head as Matthew, now glorying in his newly-discovered eloquence made point after point, and concluded that this pale, dapper young fellow, with his ready tongue, his sincerity, his scientific training and knowledge of the situation ought to prove a valuable asset to the Knights of Nordica.

"I tried to interest some agencies in New York," Matthew continued, "but they are all blind to this menace and to their duty. Then someone told me of you and your valuable work, and I decided to come down here and have a talk with you. I had intended to suggest the organization of some such militant secret order as you have started, but since you've already seen the necessity for it, I want to hasten to offer my services as a scientific man and one familiar with the facts and able to present them to your members.

"I should be very glad," boomed Givens, "very happy, indeed, Brother Fisher, to have you join us. We need you. I believe you can help us a great deal. Would you, er–ah, be interested in coming out to the mass meeting this evening? It would help us tremendously to get members if you would be willing to get up and tell the audience what you have just related about the progress of this iniquitous nigger corporation in New York."

Matthew pretended to think over the matter for a moment or two and then agreed. If he made a hit at the initial meeting, he would be sure to get on the staff. Once there he could go after the larger game. Unlike Givens, he had no belief in the racial integrity nonsense nor any confidence in the white masses whom he thought were destined to flock to the Knights of Nordica. On the contrary he despised and hated them. He had the average Negro's justifiable fear of the poor whites and only planned to use them as a stepladder to the real money.

When Matthew left, Givens congratulated himself upon the fact that he had been able to attract such talent to the organization in its very infancy. His ideas must be sound, he concluded, if scientists from New York were impressed by them. He reached over, pulled the dictionary stand toward him and opened the big book at A.

"Lemme see, now," he muttered aloud. "Anthropology. Better git that word straight 'fore I go talkin' too much about it. . . . Humn! Humn! . . . That boy must know a hull lot." He read over the definition of the word twice without understanding it, closed the dictionary, pushed it away from him, and then cutting off a large chew of tobacco from his plug, he leaned back in his swivel chair to rest after the unaccustomed mental exertion.

Matthew went gaily back to his hotel. "Man alive!" he chortled to himself. "What a lucky break! Can't keep old Max down long. . . . Will I speak to 'em? Well, I won't stay quiet!" He felt so delighted over the prospect of getting close to some real money that he treated himself to an expensive dinner and a twenty-five cent cigar. Afterward he inquired further about old man Givens from the house detective, a native Atlantan.

"Oh, he's well heeled—the old crook!" remarked the detective. "Damnify could ever understand how such ignorant people get a-hold of th' money; but there y'are. Owns as pretty a home as you can find around these parts an' damn 'f he ain't stahtin' a new racket."

"Do you think he'll make anything out of it?" inquired Matthew, innocently.

"Say, Brother, you mus' be a stranger in these parts. These damn, ignorant crackers will fall fer anything fer a while. They ain't had no Klan here fer goin' on three years. Leastwise it ain't been functionin'." The old fellow chuckled and spat a stream of tobacco juice into a nearby cuspidor. Matthew sauntered away. Yes, the pickings ought to be good.

Equally enthusiastic was the Imperial Grand Wizard when he came home to dinner that night. He entered the house humming one of his favorite hymns and his wife looked up from the evening paper with surprise on her face. The Rev. Givens was usually something of a grouch but tonight he was happy as a pickpocket at a country fair.

"What's th' mattah with you?" she inquired, sniffing suspiciously.

"Oh, Honey," he gurgled, "I think this here Knights of Nordica is going over big; going over big! My fame is spreading. Only today I had a long talk with a famous anthropologist from New York and he's going to address our mass meeting tonight."

"What's an anthropologist?" asked Mrs. Givens, wrinkling her seamy brow.

"Oh-er, well, he's one of these here scientists what knows all about this here business what's going on up there in New York where them niggers is turning each other white," explained Rev. Givens hastily but firmly. "He's a mighty smaht feller and I want you and Helen to come out and hear him."

"B'lieve Ah will," declared Mrs. Givens, "if this heah rheumatism'll le' me foh a while. Doan know 'bout Helen, though. Evah since that gal went away tuh school she ain't bin int'rested in nuthin' upliftin'!"

Mrs. Givens spoke in a grieved tone and heaved her narrow chest in a deep sigh. She didn't like all this newfangled foolishness of these young folks. They were getting away from God, that's what they were, and she didn't like it. Mrs. Givens was a Christian. There was no doubt about it because she freely admitted it to everybody, with or without provocation. Of course she often took the name of the creator in vain when she got to quarreling with Henry; she had the reputation among her friends of not always stating the exact truth; she hated Negroes; her spouse had made bitter and profane comment concerning her virginity on their wedding night; and as head of the ladies' auxiliary of the defunct Klan she had copied her husband's financial methods; but that she was a devout Christian no one doubted. She believed the Bible from cover to cover, except what it said about people with money, and she read it every evening aloud, greatly to the annoyance of the Imperial Grand Wizard and his modern and comely daughter.

Mrs. Given's had probably once been beautiful but the wear and tear of a long life as the better half of an itinerant evangelist was apparent. Her once flaming red hair was turning gray and roan-like, her hatchet face was a criss-cross of wrinkles and lines, she was round-shouldered, hollow-chested, walked with a stoop and long, bony, white hands looked like claws. She alternately dipped snuff and smoked an evil-smelling clay pipe, except when there was company at the house. At such times Helen would insist her mother "act like civilized people."

Helen was twenty and quite confident that she herself was civilized. Whether she was or not, she was certainly beautiful. Indeed, she was such a beauty that many of the friends of the family insisted that she must have been adopted. Taller than either of her parents, she was stately, erect, well proportioned, slender, vivid and knew how to wear her clothes. In only one way did she resemble her parents and that was in things intellectual. Any form of mental effort, she complained, made her head ache, and so her parents had always let her have her way about studying.

At the age of eleven she had been taken from the third grade in public school and sent to an exclusive seminary for the double purpose of gaining social prestige and concealing her mental incapacity. At sixteen when her instructors had about despaired of her, they were overjoyed by the decision of her father to send the girl to a "finishing school" in the North. The "finishing school" about finished what intelligence Helen possessed; but she came forth, four years later, more beautiful, with a better knowledge of how to dress and how to act in exclusive society, enough superficialities to enable her to get by in the "best" circles and a great deal of that shallow facetiousness that passes for sophistication in American upper-class life. A winter in Manhattan had rounded out her education. Now she was back home, thoroughly ashamed of her grotesque parents, and, like the other girls of her set, anxious to get a husband who at the same time was handsome, intelligent, educated, refined and rolling in wealth. As she was ignorant of the fact that no such man existed, she looked confidently forward into the future.

"I don't care to go down there among all those gross people," she informed her father at the dinner table when he broached the subject of the meeting. "They're so crude and elemental, don't you know," she explained, arching her narrow eyebrows.

"The common people are the salt of the earth," boomed Rev. Givens. "If it hadn't been for the common people we wouldn't have been able to get this home and send you off to school. You make me sick with all your modern ideas. You'd do a lot better it you'd try to be more like your Ma."

Both Mrs. Givens and Helen looked quickly at him to see if he was smiling. He wasn't.

"Why don'cha go, Helen?" pleaded Mrs. Bivens. "Yo fathah sez this heah man f'm N'Yawk is uh—uh scientist or somethin' an' knows a whole lot about things. Yuh might l'arn somethin'. Ah'd go mys'f if 'twasn't fo mah rheumatism." She sighed in self-pity and finished gnawing a drumstick.

Helen's curiosity was aroused and although she didn't like the idea of sitting among a lot of mill hands, she was anxious to see and hear this reputedly brilliant young man from the great metropolis where not long before she had lost both her provincialism and chastity.

"Oh, all right," she assented with mock reluctance. "I'll go."

*

The Knights of Nordica's flag-draped auditorium slowly filled. It was a bare, cavernous structure, with sawdust on the floor, a big platform at one end, row after row of folding wooden chairs and illuminated by large, white lights hanging from the rafters. On the platform was a row of five chairs, the center one being high-backed and gilded. On the lectern down-stage was a bulky bible. A huge American flag was stretched across the rear wall.

The audience was composed of the lower stratum of white working peo-ple: hard-faced, lantern-jawed, dull-eyed adult children, seeking like all humanity for something permanent in the eternal flux of life. The young girls in their cheap finery with circus makeup on their faces; the young men, aged before their time by child labor and a violent environment; the middle-aged folk with their shiny, shabby garb and beaten countenances; all ready and eager to be organized for any purpose except improvement of their intellects and standard of living.

Rev. Givens opened the meeting with a prayer "for the success, O God, of this thy work, to protect the sisters and wives and daughters of these, thy people, from the filthy pollution of an alien race."

A choir of assorted types of individuals sang "Onward Christian Soldiers" earnestly, vociferously and badly.

They were about to file off the platform when the song leader, a big, beefy, jovial mountain of a man, leaped upon the stage and restrained them.

"Wait a minute, folks, wait a minute," he commanded. Then turning to the assemblage: "Now people let's put some pep into this. We wanna all be happy and get in th' right spirit for this heah meetin'. Ah'm gonna ask the choir to sing th' first and last verses ovah ag'in, and when they come to th' chorus, Ah wantcha to all join in. Doan be 'fraid. Jesus wouldn't be 'fraid to sing 'Onward Christian Soldiers,' now would he? Come on, then. All right, choir, you staht; an' when Ah wave mah han' you'all join in on that theah chorus."

They obediently followed his directions while he marched up and down the platform, red-faced and roaring and waving his arms in time. When the last note had died away, he dismissed the choir and stepping to the edge of the stage he leaned far out over the audience and barked at them again.

"Come on, now, folks! Yuh caint slow up on Jesus now. He won't be sat-isfied with jus' one ole measly song. Yuh gotta let 'im know that yuh love 'im; that y're happy an' contented; that yuh ain't got no troubles an' ain't gonna have any. Come on, now. Le's sing that ole favorite what yo'all like so well: 'Pack Up Your Troubles in Your Old Kit Bag and Smile, Smile, Smile.'

"He bellowed and they followed him. Again the vast hall shook with sound. He made them rise and grasp each other by the hand until the song ended.

Matthew, who sat on the platform alongside old man Givens viewed the spectacle with amusement mingled with amazement. He was amused because of the similarity of this meeting to the religious orgies of the more ignorant Negroes and amazed that earlier in the evening he should have felt any qualms about lecturing to these folks on anthropology, a subject with which neither he not his hearers were acquainted. He quickly saw that these people would believe anything that was shouted at them loudly and convincingly enough. He knew what would fetch their applause and bring in their memberships and he intended to repeat it over and over.

The Imperial Grand Wizard spent a half-hour introducing the speaker of the evening, dwelt upon his supposed scholastic attainments, but took pains to inform them that, despite Matthew's vast knowledge, he still believed in the Word of God, the sanctity of womanhood and the purity of the white race.

For an hour Matthew told them at the top of his voice what they believed: i.e., that white skin was a sure indication of the possession of superior intellect and moral qualities; that all Negroes were inferior to them; that God had intended for the United States to be a white man's country and that with His help they could keep it so; that their sons and brothers might inadvertently marry Negresses or, worse, their sisters and daughters might marry Negroes, if Black-No-More, Incorporated, was permitted to continue its dangerous activities.

For an hour he spoke, interrupted at intervals by enthusiastic gales of applause, and as he spoke his eye wandered over the females in the audience, noting the comeliest ones. As he wound up with a spirited appeal for eager soldiers to join the Knights of Nordica at five dollars per head and half-dozen "planted" emissaries led the march of suckers to the platform, he noted for the first time a girl who sat in the front row and gazed up at him rapidly.

She was titian blonde, well-dressed, beautiful and strangely familiar. As he retired amid thunderous applause to make way for Rev. Givens and the money collectors, he wondered where he had seen her before. He studied her from his seat.

Suddenly he knew. It was she! The girl who had spurned him; the girl he had sought so long; the girl he wanted more than anything in the world! Strange that she should be here. He had always thought of her as a refined, educated and wealthy lady, far above associating with such people as these. He was in a fever to meet her, some way, before she got out of his sight again, and yet he felt just a little disappointed to find her here.

He could hardly wait until Givens seated himself again before questioning him as to the girl's identity. As the beefy song leader led the roaring of the popular closing hymn, he leaned toward the Imperial Grand Wizard and shouted: "Who is that tall golden-haired girl sitting in the front row? Do you know her?'

Rev. Givens looked out over the audience, craning his skinny neck and blinking his eyes. Then he saw the girl, sitting within twenty feet of him.

"You mean that girl sitting right in front, there?" he asked, pointing.

"Yes, that one," said Matthew, impatiently.

"Heh! Heh! Heh!" chuckled the Wizard, rubbing his stubbly chin. "Why that there's my daughter, Helen. Like to meet her?"

Matthew could hardly believe his ears. Givens's daughter! Incredible! What a coincidence! What luck! Would he like to meet her? He leaned over and shouted "Yes."

◎╱◎

HANGING OUT

A young Negro from Chicago was
on his way to Mississippi to see his folks.
The bus stopped in one of them little
back water Southern towns, and he didn't see
no colored folks. He was lookin' for
somethin' to do, so ask this old white man
where do Negroes hang out.
The white man look at him real hard,
then pointed to a big tree in front of the court house
and say, "See that limb over yonder, boy?"

— Folk

GREAT MEN

From *Ten Minutes to Live*
By Oscar Micheaux

The unidentified blackface comedy team in this cabaret scene excerpted from Oscar Micheaux's 1932 film depicts a typical example of the low or numskull humor of the 1920s and '30s. It was standard fare on radio and in films and Broadway musicals. Micheaux often inserted this type of comedy into his movies to broaden their appeal and attract white audiences.

Comic 1:   What you wanna do is stop talkin' 'bout goin' to jail. Uplift yo'-self, elevate, be somebody. Follow in the footsteps a great men.

Comic 2:   Now what the use of me bein' somebody and elevatin'. What good it's goin' do me, I wanna go somewhere I can eat.

Comic 1:   Well, that's all right. If you elevate, then you can eat.

Comic 2:   I cain' even join the Fresh Air Camp, but dat don't mean nothin' to me now. Gimme less liberty and more food. Got a whole lotta freedom and starvin' to death.

Comic 1:   You oughta be satisfied.

Comic 2:   I never will forget the words my grandmother use' to tell me when I was a little boy. She use to hold me on her lap and look into my big blue eyes . . . She push my goldilocks back from my forehead and said, "Son, my darlin' son, where dere's a will dere's a way."

Comic 1:   She was right!

Comic 2:   I got a will to eat, but I cain' find the way.

Comic 1:   Keep on lookin', you'll find it.

Comic 2:   But now since you said dat, ah, elevation . . . you know, dat's sumpthin' good. We ought to do that. Get outta the gutter and step on the sidewalk . . .

Comic 1:   Now you talkin'.

Comic 2:   Follow in the footsteps of great men . . .

Comic 1:   Yeah!

Comic 2:   Men like Booker T. Washington.

Comic 1:   That's a great man.

Comic 2:   That's a man whose name is known everywhere.

Comic 1:   Yeah!

Comic 2:   The chillun knows him, his picture is in de books and papers. Why? Because he was a man that done sumpthin'.

Comic 1:   Yeah! Ah, what did he do?

Comic 2:   I don't know. But whatever it was, he done it.

Comic 1:   Yeah.

Comic 2:   And look at dat other great man.

Comic 1:	Who was that?
Comic 2:	Dat great soldier—
Comic 1:	Who?
Comic 2:	Frederick Douglass . . . put his gun on his shoulder, walked out onto de battlefield, and said, "Gimme liberty or shoot me."
Comic 1:	Uh-huh.
Comic 2:	And dey shot him.
Comic 1:	What?
Comic 2:	But there's a man—
Comic 1:	Who?
Comic 2:	Abraham Lincoln.
Comic 1:	Dat's a great boy!
Comic 2:	Now dat's a man that's known everywhere too.
Comic 1:	Sure dat's—
Comic 2:	He was a man that done sumpthin'.
Comic 1:	Yeah, dat's the boy that cut down his papa's cherry tree!

[The second comic stops, shakes his head and stares at his partner in disbelief.]

◎◎

CHITLIN' CIRCUIT ROUTINES

Many memorable comic routines were developed on the black theater circuit (also called the chitlin' circuit and TOBA—Theater Owners' Booking Association or "tough on black asses"). And while they are usually attributed to individual comics, most drew heavily on contemporary folk humor and evolved over time with various contributors adding subtle changes. Generally, it was the comedian who popularized the routine on stage who received credit for creating it. So, although Pigmeat Markham is commonly accepted as the originator of the "Here Come de Judge" bit, the emcee and actor Ralph Cooper insisted that he initially wrote it. Similarly, both John "Spider Bruce" Mason and Dusty Fletcher claimed credit for "Open the Door, Richard," but by virtue of his stage act Fletcher's name is usually associated with it. Originators aside, the following routines were popular classics on the chitlin' circuit, and, as in the case of the first bit, "Go Ahead and Sing," close approximations often sur-

faced in the acts of well-known mainstream comedians like Abbott and Costello without reference to their source.

GO AHEAD AND SING

By Rastus Murray and Henry Drake

[Two guys standing on a street corner decide that they can make some money by singing and passing the hat among the crowd. One begins soliciting pedestrians trying to attract a crowd, and the other starts belting out an old blues tune. As soon as he starts, a policeman approaches.]

Policeman: Hey, you can't sing around here!

First Man: Who you talkin' to, me?

Policeman: Yeah, you and him too. You can't sing on this corner.

First Man: You better talk to him. I ain't doin' nothin' but standin' here.

Policeman: I wanna explain something to you. There's a hospital down the street. It has a lot of sick people in there and you're disturbing them. If you want to sing, go to another corner, but you can't sing around here.

Singer: Yes, sir, I'll stop singing here.

Policeman: You understand, then?

Singer: Oh, yes, sir—yes sir!

[The policeman leaves, and the singer turns to his friend.]

Singer: Come on, let's go.

First Man: Go where? Why should we move? We're citizens. We got a right to stand here and sing. Ain't no flatfoot gonna tell us what to do. You go ahead and sing. When he comes back, I'll talk to him.

Singer: You sure it's all right?

First Man: Sure, ain't nothin' wrong. Go ahead and sing.

[The singer begins again, and the policeman rushes back.]

Policeman: Wait a minute, didn't I just tell you not to sing on this corner?

Singer: Yeah, I know, officer, but my partner said it was all right.

Policeman: I don't care what your partner told you. I said you can't sing here. This is the last time I'm gonna tell you. If I have to come again, I'm gonna take this billy club and put it upside your head. Then I'm gonna take you to jail!

[The policeman turns to walk away.]

First Man: You ain't gonna hit me in my head.

Policeman: What?

[He starts beating the singer over the head with his billy club.]

Policeman: Now let that be a lesson to you!

Singer: [holding his head] Yes sir, cap'tum, Yes, sir!

[Again, the policeman starts to leave.]

First Man: You gotta lot of nerve, beatin' on a citizen. You ain't gonna hit me no more.

[The policeman comes back and starts beating the singer on his feet, and, as the first man continues to agitate, the policeman beats the singer off the stage. Blackout.]

AIN'T NOBODY HERE!

By Willie Too Sweet

[The skit opens in a bedroom with a jealous husband talking to his wife as she sits on their bed.]

Husband: I'm leaving now, and I don't want nobody in this house while I'm gone. If the mailman comes with a letter, tell him to shove it under the door. If the milkman comes, tell him to take it back and bring it back later. If the iceman comes, tell him it's too hot, we don't need any.

Wife: But we need ice, it's gonna be very hot.

Husband: I don't care how hot it gets. Tell him to come back when I'm here, you understand?

Wife: Yes, darling, but you know I never have a man in the house when you're away.

Husband: I ain't sure about that, I heard rumors.

Wife: That's not true. No man has ever been here when you're not home.

Husband: Well, make sure you keep it that way. I've got to get the fertilizer and put it on strong, and I don't want nobody here.

[As soon as the husband leaves, another man slips into the bedroom.]

2nd Man: Did he leave? I'm so glad he's gone.

[They begin hugging, and immediately somebody knocks on the door.]

Wife: It's my husband coming back! He's so jealous. If he finds you here, I don't know what will happen.

2nd Man: Oh my God, let me out of here.

[The man runs into the closet as the husband burst into the room and starts accusing his wife.]

Husband: There's a man in here, I know it.

Wife: No, darling, there's no one here, I swear.

[The husband races around the room looking behind the dresser, under the bed and the table; after each search, he turns to his wife and says:]

Husband: I guess you're right, ain't nobody here.

Wife: See, I told you nobody was here.

[Finally, the husband walks over to the closet door and yanks it open. The second man is standing there with two pistols aimed directly at the husband.]

Husband: Yeah, I knew you was right, ain't nobody here either!

[Husband slams the door shut. Blackout.]

OPEN THE DOOR, RICHARD

By Dusty Fletcher

A slightly altered musical adaptation of this routine was recorded in 1946. It became an immediate hit, making it one of the first black comedy bits to cross over and become popular in white America. During the late 1940s and '50s, over two dozen versions were recorded, including one by Fletcher, who had been performing the bit on stage since the twenties. Fletcher's stage rendition depended as much on pantomime and his acrobatic performance on a sole prop, a ladder, as it did on verbal jokes. The following version is based on an Apollo Theater performance by Fletcher in the fifties.

[The scene unfolds as a drunken Fletcher, who has been thrown out of a bar, returns home to his apartment, mumbling, "I wonder what did Richard do with that key? Wonder did he go to sleep with the key? Well that's alright. I'll just wake him up and make him open the door." The monologue continues with Fletcher alternately speaking to the audience and shouting at Richard.]

"OPEN THE DOOR, RICHARD! That's the boy I rooms with. I know he ain't goin out no where cause I got on the clothes. OPEN THE DOOR, RICHARD. Now that's the reason I don't like to room with nobody. He don't want to open the door for me. And I owes just as much rent up there as he do.

"I don't care, I'm gonna move Saturday anyhow. Dis old woman, she chargin' too much rent, three dollars a month. And got the nerve to be mad because we eleven months in the rear. Why she come askin' me this mornin', said, 'When you boys want to give me some of my back rent?' So I told her she lucky if she gettin the front rent out of me.

"RICHARD, OPEN THAT DOOR.

"Then she come askin' me when is I'm gwinin' to work. I ain't thinkin' bout no work. I don't want no job. I'm goin back on relief Monday. I was on relief last summer but I don't know, they got short of help and they couldn't send your checks out and you had to go git em, so I give it up.

"Now here come the police . . . aw, it's alright. I'll git in. I'll go around through the back and I'll come around through the alley. I don't want no police. I'll git in—I betta man I git in. Hey Richard! Ain't this a shame, the police is looking for me. I done got myself locked out and now I'm goin' git myself locked up.

"Now, let's see here, now. It used to be an old step ladder layin around here somewhere. Oh, here it is. I know what I'll do. I'll take this ladder and climb up on the transom, that's what I'll do.

[Fletcher stands the ladder upright and climbs a few rungs before slipping, stumbling, and nearly falling. He climbs back up the ladder and balances himself. Then a policeman appears on stage.]

"Say, boy, what are you doing up on that ladder?"
"OPEN THE DOOR, RICHARD—the man out here."

"What are you doing up on that ladder?"

"I live up here."

"You live up there?"

"Yes sir."

"Well, why don't you come down and go in the door?"

"I don't live in the door. I live on the second floor."

"Come on down off that ladder."

"Ah, this is my ladder officer."

"I don't care whose ladder it is. You come down!"

"You mean to tell me a man can't stood on his own ladder?"

"No, a man can't stood on his own ladder."

"Oh, OPEN THE DOOR RICHARD. Well I guess that must be a new law just come out. S'pose I don't come down. Then what's gonna happen?"

"I'm gonna whoop you until you get sober."

"Whoop who?"

"I'm gonna whoop *you*."

[The officer approaches and starts hitting Fletcher's feet with his billy club.]

"Wait a minute officer, what you doin'? Don't do that man, you hittin' my bunion. Don't do that! HEY RICHARD, OPEN THAT DOOR!"

[The policeman continues swinging at Fletcher.]

"Don't do that, man, that hurt my bunion. Ain't this a shame, let me come on down. You act like one of them police ain't never arrest nobody befo'."

[Fletcher drops the ladder and falls to the stage with the policeman standing over him.]

"Ah . . . er, what you say you goin' do now?"

"I said, I'm gonna whoop you until you get sober."

[The policeman resumes whipping Fletcher with the billy club.]

"Wait a minute. Let's get some understanding here. You're gonna whoop who?"

"I'm gonna whoop *you*."

"Oh, no you ain't."

"I won't do what?"

"Whoop me? Nah you won't!'

[Policeman continues beating.]

"Wait a minute, wait a minute, officer. I, er . . . I was jes' playin'. Ha, ha, ha. Ah, what the hell . . . OPEN THE DOOR UP THERE, RICHARD! Wait, officer, wait a minute. Let's git some understandin'. The judge told me not to come down there no mo'. You goin' mess me up. OPEN THE DOOR, RICHARD!"

[Policeman starts to drag Fletcher off the stage.]

"Tell ma and them they got me, Richard. I'll be seein' you. RICHARD, WHY DIDN'T YOU OPEN THAT DOOR?"

[Blackout.]

WHERE'S THE MONEY

By Spo-Dee-O-Dee

This short routine—like some Butterbeans and Susie material—is an example of the monkey-man versus dominant male theme that was extremely popular in black comedy from the twenties to the forties. Moms Mabley often played the washerwoman on stage.

[Flashily dressed man approaches a bedraggled washerwoman.]

Spo-Dee-O-Dee: Hey woman, where's the money?

[Woman reaches into her pocket, searching for cash.]

Spo-Dee-O-Dee: Bring it over here, woman—right now!
Washerwoman: But I need the money for food.
Spo-Dee-O-Dee: You ate yesterday. You want to eat everyday?

[He counts the money, then hands her some loose change.]

Spo-Dee-O-Dee: Here, woman, get yourself some Saltine Crackers and save some of them for me!

[Blackout.]

HERE COME DE JUDGE

By Dewey "Pigmeat" Markham

This routine evolved during the early 1920s, and by the end of the decade Dewey "Pigmeat" Markham had made it the cornerstone of his act. It was revived and brought to national attention again in the 1960s when Sammy Davis, Jr., and, later, Flip Wilson reprised it on Rowan and Martin's Laugh-In.

[The skit usually began with an introduction by the emcee.]

Hear ye, hear ye, the Court of Swing
Is now about ready to do its thing.
Don't want no tears, don't want no jive,
Above all things, don't want no lies.
Our judge is hip, his boots are tall,
He'll judge you jack, big or small.
So fall in line, his stuff is sweet,
Peace, brothers, here's Judge Pigmeat.

[With the emcee chanting, "Here come de judge, here come de judge," Markham, in blackface makeup and a black robe, would come onto the stage and take his place at the lectern. He opened with lines like:]

"The judge is higher'n a Gawgia pine! Everybody's gonna do some time this mawnin'."

Or, when he was truly ornery:

"The judge is mean dis mawnin', I'm goin' start by givin' myself thirty days—next case!"

[This lead-in was followed by several short blackout bits featuring different comedians brought before the judge. After Markham announced that everybody would do some time, for instance, the skit might continue as follows:]

Lawyer: Your honor, that's not fair! I object!

Judge: Object! You object! You all the time comin' in here and objectin' me outa decisions. Why man, I got all these years in my book and somebody's gotta do 'em! Ain't gonna be me! Where's your first client . . . he's *guilty!*

Client: Judge, please, don't you remember me? I'm the man who introduced you to your wife!

Judge: Introduced me to my wife? Life . . . you sonofagun!

HALF MINE

By John "Spider Bruce" Mason

[Mason, wearing blackface makeup, plays an expectant father pacing up and down the corridor outside the maternity ward. The sound of

a crying child is heard and, moments afterward, a nurse and an extremely light-skinned doctor come out with two bundles.]

Nurse:　　Twins! Sir, your wife has given birth to twins.

[Anxiously, Mason rushes over and looks at the babies, then steps
back as he sees something that disturbs him.]

Mason:　　How come one of them is so black and the other is so light?

Doctor:　　That's just the way they was born. Must come from the father.

Mason:　　Yeah, well I don't think I'm gonna pay that bill for $200 I just
got.

Doctor:　　Here, let me pay my half!

[Blackout.]

෴

THE CONJURE-MAN DIES

By Rudolph Fisher

*The characters Jinx and Bubber provided broad comic relief in Rudolph
Fisher's novels. This excerpt from* Conjure-Man *occurs just after Jinx discovers a corpse in a Harlem tenement.*

Meanwhile Jinx and Bubber, in Frimbo's waiting-room on the second floor,
were indulging in one of their characteristic arguments. This one had
started with Bubber's chivalrous endeavors to ease the disturbing situation
for the two women, both of whom were bewildered and distraught and one
of whom was young and pretty. Bubber had not only announced and described in detail just what he had seen, but, heedless of the fact that the
younger woman had almost fainted, had proceeded to explain how he had
known, long before it occurred, that he had been about to "see death." To
dispel any remaining vestiges of tranquillity, he had added that the death
of Frimbo was but one of three. Two more were at hand.

"Soon as Jinx here called me," he said, "I knowed somebody's time had
come. I busted on in that room yonder with him—y'all seen me go—and sho'
'nough, there was the man, limp as a rag and stiff as a board. Y'see, the
moon don't lie. 'Cose most signs ain't no 'count. As for me, you won't find
nobody black as me that's less suprastitious."

"Jes' say we won't find nobody black as you and stop. That'll be the truth," growled Jinx.

"But a moonsign is different. Moonsign is the one sign you can take for sho'. Moonsign—"

"Moonshine is what you took for sho' tonight," Jinx said.

"Red moon mean bloodshed, new moon over your right shoulder mean good luck, new moon over your left shoulder mean bad luck, and so on. Well, they's one moonsign my grandmammy taught me befo' I was knee high and that's the worst sign of 'em all. And that's the sign I seen tonight. I was walkin' down the Avenue feelin' fine and breathin' the air—"

"What do you breathe when you don't feel so good?"

"—smokin' the gals over, watchin' the cars roll by—feelin' good, you know what I mean. And then all of a sudden I stopped. I store."

"You whiched?"

"Store. I stopped and I store."

"What language you talkin'?"

"I store at the sky. And as I stood there starin', sump'm didn't seem right. Then I seen what it was. "Y'see, they was a full moon in the sky—"

"Funny place for a full moon, wasn't it?"

"—and as I store at it, they come up a cloud—wasn't but one cloud in the whole sky—and that cloud come and crossed over the face o' the moon and blotted it out—jes' like that."

"You sho' 'twasn't yo' shadow?"

"Well there was the black cloud in front o' the moon and the white moonlight all around it and behind it. All of a sudden I seen what was wrong. That cloud had done took the shape of a human skull!"

"Sweet Jesus!" The older woman's whisper betokened the proper awe. She was an elongated, incredibly thin creature, ill-favored in countenance and apparel; her loose, limp, angular figure was grotesquely disposed over a stiff-backed arm-chair, and dark, nondescript clothing draped her too long limbs. Her squarish, fashionless hat was a little awry, her scrawny visage, already disquieted, was now inordinately startled, the eyes almost comically wide above the high cheek bones, the mouth closed tight over her teeth whose forward slant made the lips protrude as if they were puckering to whistle.

The younger woman, however, seemed not to hear. Those dark eyes surely could sparkle brightly, those small lips smile, that clear honey skin glow with animation; but just now the eyes stared unseeingly, the lips were a short, hard, straight line, the skin of her round pretty face al-

most colorless. She was obviously dazed by the suddenness of this unexpected tragedy. Unlike the other woman, however, she had not lost her
poise, though it was costing something to retain it. The trim, black, high-
heeled shoes, the light sheer stockings, the black seal coat which fell
open to reveal a white-bordered pimiento dress, even the small close-
fitting black hat, all were quite as they should be. Only her isolating de-
tachment betrayed the effect upon her of the presence of death and the
law.

"A human skull!" repeated Bubber. "Yes, ma'am. Blottin' out the moon.
You know what that is?"

"What?" said the older woman.

"That's death on the moon. It's a moonsign and it's never been known
to fail."

"And it means death?"

"Worse 'n that, ma'am. It means three deaths. Whoever see death on the
moon"—he paused, drew breath, and went on in an impressive lower tone—
"gonna see death three times!"

"My soul and body!" said the lady.

But Jinx saw fit to summon logic. "Mean you go'n' see two more folks
dead?"

"Gonna stare 'em in the face."

"The somebody ought to poke yo' eyes out in self-defense."

Having with characteristic singleness of purpose discharged his duty as
a gentleman and done all within his power to set the ladies' minds at rest,
Bubber could now turn his attention to the due and proper quashing of his
unappreciative commentator.

"Whyn't you try it?" he suggested.

"Try what?"

"Pokin' my eyes out."

"Huh. If I thought that was the onliest way to keep from dyin', you could
get yo'self a tin cup and a cane tonight."

"Try it then."

"'Tain't necessary. That moonshine you had'll take care o' everything.
Jes' give it another hour to work and you'll be blind as Baltimo' alley."

"Trouble with you," said Bubber, "is, you' ignorant. You' dumb. The inside o' yo' head is all black."

"Like the outside o' yourn."

"Is you by any chance alludin' to me?"

"I ain't alludin' to that policeman over yonder."

"Lucky for you he is over yonder, else you wouldn't be alludin' at all."

"Now you gettin' bad, ain't you? Jus' 'cause you know you got the advantage over me."

"What advantage?"

"How could I hit you when I can't even see you?"

"Well if I was ugly as you is, I wouldn't want nobody to see me."

"Don't worry, son. Nobody'll ever know how ugly you is. Yo' ugliness is shrouded in mystery."

"Well yo' dumbness ain't. It's right there for all the world to see. You ought to be back in Africa with the other dumb boogies."

"African boogies ain't dumb," explained Jinx. "They' jes' dark. You ain't been away from there long, is you?"

"My folks," returned Bubber crushingly, "left Africa ten generations ago."

"Yo' folks? Shuh. Ten generations ago, you-all wasn't folks. You-all hadn't qualified as apes."

Thus as always, their exchange of compliments flowed toward the level of family history, among other Harlemites a dangerous explosive which a single word might strike into instantaneous violence. It was only because the hostility of these two was actually an elaborate masquerade, whereunder they concealed the most genuine affection for each other, that they could come so close to blows that were never offered.

Yet to the observer this mock antagonism would have appeared alarmingly real. Bubber's squat figure sidled belligerently up to the long and lanky Jinx; solid as a fire-plug he stood, set to grapple; and he said with unusual distinctness:

"Yea? Well—yo' granddaddy was a hair on a baboon's tail. What does that make you?"

The policeman's grin of amusement faded. The older woman stifled a cry of apprehension.

The younger woman still sat motionless and staring, wholly unaware of what was going on.

☉☉

NO'LASSES

"Liza," the mother said to her daughter, who was on her
way to school, "you want some 'lasses on
your hoe cakes?" "Momma, you say molasses, not lasses."

"Chile, don't talk foolishness to me. How you
goin' have mo'lasses when you ain't had no'lasses yet?"
— Folk

     ℰ/ℰ

QUIPS AND CRACKS FROM
HOLLYWOOD FILM CLOWNS

*During the 1930s and '40s, black roles in Hollywood films were limited al-
most exclusively to grotesquely stereotyped comic servants. The characters portrayed—primarily timid, whining, slow-witted, and lazy but fleet-footed
types—were scripted to mouth some of the most ludicrous lines ever delivered
by black comedians. It is a tribute to their talent that they often overcame the
material to generate outstanding comic performances.*

STEPIN FETCHIT

A drowsy Fetchit is wakened
by the telephone and mumbles to the female caller,
"I was laying here dreamin' everybody
was trying to wake me up. . . .
Why I have a dream like that?
I ain't botherin' nobody, just tendin'
to my business, doin' nothin', restin' up."
Then he asks, "What size hair is you got?
I sorta recognize yo' voice but yo'
breath sound like you eatin' a onion."
Before hanging up, he tells her,
"Right now, I'm goin' finish
a little nap I started week befo' last."
—From *Richard's Answer*

*In the following exchange, Fetchit is being questioned by a police officer about
an unsolved murder. The comic's meandering reply, which leads to a risqué
pun, is an example of his oblique humor in films.*

Detective: What do you know about handling a knife?

Fetchit: I knows lots about a knife but I ain't goin' tell you. But I know
     I cain't eat my mash potatoes without no fork—

Detective: Stop the foolishness!

Fetchit: I ain't foolin' mister, cause I have to have a fork for everything
             I eat. If I cain't fork it, I cain't . . . well, uh, I just don't bother
             with it myself.

—From *Miracle in Harlem*

MATTHEW "STYMIE" BEARD

"Uh-uh, my daddy
ain't no chauffeur . . . My daddy
is just a crap-shootin' fool!"
—From the *Our Gang* series

WILLIE BEST

"When folks stop breathin' and walkin',
I'm through wit' 'em," Best tells his boss
when asked to enter a darkened cemetery.
"Don't worry, there's
six feet between you and them,"
the boss assures him.
"Yessuh," he replies, "and it's goin' be
six miles between us any minute now."

*

"I ain't afraid but
my feets ain't goin' stand around
and see my body get abused."
—From *The Smiling Ghost*

"BUTTERFLY" McQUEEN

"Gee, Miss Scarlett, I don't
know nothin' 'bout birthin' no babies."

*

"Miss Scarlett, my mammy
always said to put a knife under the bed,
'cause it cuts the pain."
—From *Gone with the Wind*

*

"Who dat say who dat when you say who dat?"
—From *Affectionately Yours*

MANTAN MORELAND

Moreland was best known for his role as Birmingham, the chauffeur in the Charlie Chan detective series—the source of the following quips.

"Feets, don't fail me now!"
or:
"Feets, do yo' stuff!"

*

#1 Son:	Confucius remind us, Birmingham, that he who fights and runs away—
Mantan:	I know . . . will live to run another day!
#1 Son:	If you're scared Birmingham, just keep saying to yourself, "I'm not afraid, I'm not afraid."
Mantan:	I'm not afraid, *I'm* not afraid. I'm *not* afraid.
#1 Son:	How do you feel now?
Mantan:	I feel like a liar!

*

"No sir, I ain't 'fraid of
no dead folks . . . not as long
as they still livin'."

@/@

RADIO REPARTEE

By Eddie "Rochester" Anderson

Anderson gained national recognition in the role of Rochester, Jack Benny's valet, on radio and television and went on to become one of the most successful black comic actors of the mid-twentieth century. The following exchanges are from early radio shows with Benny.

Benny: Where is the suit I gave you the money for?

Rochester: Well, I'll tell ya boss. I was on my way to the store and got mixed up in a game of African badminton.

Benny: Oh, so you lost your suit in a crap game, huh?

Rochester: Yes, sir. I rolled myself right out of the Easter parade.

—The Jell-O Program (1938)

*

Rochester: I thought I'se back in Harlem.

Benny: Harlem? I told you before, all those people at the station were Indians.

Rochester: Indians?

Benny: Yes.

Rochester: Well, just the same, I saw a papoose eatin' a pork chop.

Benny: Well, what of it? He can be an Indian and still eat a pork chop.

Rochester: I know, but he had it between two slices of watermelon.

—The Jack Benny Show (1938)

*

Benny: Wait a minute, wait a minute. Do you mean to say you lost my bicycle shooting *craps?*

Rochester: Well, I was lucky for the first three passes.

Benny: Lucky? . . . And then what happened?

Rochester: My dice went into a minuet . . . and my opponent became suspicious.

Benny: Oooh. . . . Well, I don't care what happened. . . . I want you to go to that garage, and tell your friend to give back my bicycle.

Rochester: Without payin' for it?

Benny: Yes, without payin' for it. . . . Just *grab* it.

Rochester: Now wait a minute, boss. . . . That boy's got a razor that does everything but run out and get the mail.

Benny: Well Rochester, what are you scared of? . . . You carry a razor yourself.

Rochester: Yeah, but it's only a *Gillette* and I'm out of blades.

—*The Jell-O Program* (1942)

*

Benny: Hey, Rochester, have you got my shoes?

Rochester: Here they are, Boss.

Benny: Those are my sports shoes. Where did you ever see sports shoes with a full dress suit?

Rochester: In the Harlem Esquire.

Benny: Well, run over to my dressing room and get my plain black ones and hurry.

Rochester: Black coat, black shoes, black pants . . . you is de most *monotonous* man I ever worked for.

—*The Jell-O Program* (1937)

THE LAZIEST MAN IN THE WORLD

By Stepin Fetchit

I'm so lazy, even when I walked in my sleep I used to hitchhike. My head was so bald I used to comb it with a spoon. People say, "How'd you get in pictures?" I say, "Well . . . when I was a kid I always wanted to be somethin, course I didn't want to do nothing to be it. I used to go 'round trying to get a job doing nothin, but everywhere I went they either wanted me to do somethin or else they didn't wanna give you nothin for it. So I kept tryin til I growed up, then I seen this man in California makin a picture, and I say, 'Mr., you want somebody to do nothin,' and they say, 'Yeah.' So I been busy working every since. Yeah, and I work up to the place where the less I have to do, the mo' I make. Tryin to make as much as I can, so when I get old I can rest."

HOW OLD?

Fed up with sportswriters' repeated
questions about his age, the venerable baseball legend
Satchel Paige developed a standard reply:
"How old would you be if
you didn't know how old you are?"

⊚⁄⊚

MEXICANA ROSE

Folk *

Way down in old Sonora where the pot grows tall,
Vultures fly the skies, and the rattlesnakes crawl.

Scorpions creep over dead men's bones,
And coyotes yelp in blood curdling tones.

It was hot, dry desert waste
That I first came face to face

With the queen of all the whores,
Señorita Bonita, the Mexican Rose.

I was traveling with my partner, Cocaine Smitty,
On our way to pull some whores in Mexico City.

Now we were big-time pimps from the New York scene,
And believe me, Jim, we were both clean.

I had a sharkskin vine in a powder blue,
Black wingtips from Bendette's, sparkling new,

My shirts were from Brook's; my socks cost a pound;
I wore solid gold cufflinks—I knew I was down.

I wore a hat from Disney with fifty-dollar tag,
And my snakeskin billfold was loaded with swag.

My man Smitty was also pressed,
And looked real tough, I must confess.

He had on a three-hundred-dollar vine
Straight from the Phil Kronfield line.

His shirt and tie were Edmond Clapp,
And he sported a P. Santini cap.

Now his cufflinks looked like they cost a grand,
But I peeped on the back; they said "Made in Japan."

Well, pulling some whores was our pimping motto,
As we pushed toward the border in my black Eldorado.

When we reached the border, we had to give our name,
Long-Shoe Sam and Smitty Cocaine.

When we reached Sonora we needed some gas,
So I pulled into a station and said, "Fill 'er up fast."

The we stepped into Pancho's for a bite to eat,
But when we dug the waitress, our knees got weak.

She was dressed like a native in sombrero and jeans
And said, "Qué pasa, señores? Tamales or beans?"

"There's just one thing I want," said Smitty, "and I'll give you a clue.
It's the best dish in the house, and it seems to be you."

She had eyes like diamonds; big, black, and bold,
And her soft smooth skin was the color of gold.

Her lips ran like a cool mountain well
That showed all the fire and brimstone of hell.

Her hair was long and shiny with a glare.
And she had a body that would make Jane Russell stop and stare.

Her lips, hips, and kiester were so shapely and fine
Smitty went berserk and screamed, "She's got to be mine!"

He said, "Come here, baby, and tell me your name.
My name is Smitty, they call me Cocaine."

Then he pulled her aside and showed her his dough
And said, "I'm taking you back to be my whore."

For a minute I thought the bitch was going for his spiel,
Till she shot back, "Creep, are you for real?

"Cocaine Smitty from New York City,
For a half-ass pimp you sure talk shitty.

"What makes you think I want to be your whore?
You'd take me to New York, and then where would I go?

"All you pimps come down here talking that shit;
Last time it was a horn-blowing chump named Stitt.

"He was drug-using cat who didn't have a dime,
But I'd go back with him before I'd fall for your line.

"Sure you'll take me to New York, buy me rings and fancy clothes;
But I don't need your shit, lame, I'm the Mexicana Rose!

"I want to *own* New York, and you're not that slick."
"Here, take my money," cried Smitty, "and let me be your trick."

"Be my trick? Why you insult my pride.
Go hit on one of them Indian bitches selling blankets outside."

By this time I'd moved in to give this bitch a closer observation,
So I told Smitty, "Beat it, you must be beat for conversation.

"I thought you were a thoroughbred, my ace man,
But I find you're a comical stud, funnier than Charlie Chan.

"I thought you were a mackman, a master at the Game;
But I peeped your hole card, you're a funny-time lame.

"You wait till I get back to the Big Apple and tell all the crowd
How you come down to Mexico sounding all loud,

"Hit on a bitch to be your whore,
And turned stone-cold trick when she said no!"

"Ha!" said Smitty, coming up from behind.
"Do you think your game is stronger than mine?"

"Not only do I think it's stronger," I said with a jerk,
"But step aside, creep, and watch a master at work."

I sat at the table, crossed my knees,
And said, "Waitress, two tequilas, please."

When I pulled out some pot and Rose said, "Yeah!"
I dug right away that she was no square.

As we sat there gaily blowing on our hemp,
I whispered, "Rose, darling, let me be your pimp.

"I've had queens, stallions, all kinds of a whore,
But I've never had a whore like you before.

"I won't treat you like no lady, or any fancy queen;
I'll take all your money and treat you real mean.

"There's not going to be a whole lot of rings and fancy clothes,
But you better make me more money than all them other whores.

"'Cause if you come up weak, I'm going for your knot and gut
And throw you in the gutter like an ordinary slut.

"But if you follow the rules according to the Game
We'll soon be on Easy Street with much money and cocaine."

"Damn," said Rose, "I thought I was a way-out bitch,
And here you shoot me a prop like I was a witch!

"I go for you, Sam, I think you're boss,
But don't think you can ever put me in a cross.

"Before I say yes or before I say no,
Let's go in the game room and see what you know."

First she engaged me in a nine-ball game,
But that sharp-shooting bitch won every frame.

Next cards, which wasn't my stick;
Not that my game was weak, but hers was so goddamn slick.

But when we came to craps, that was a different story;
That's when I came out of my slump and went into my glory.

I shot five-two for seven and five-six for eleven,
And from there on in I was really in heaven.

Now I shook the dice and threw them on the floor.
They turned up ten—a six and a four.

Rose said, "Let's play for higher stakes—my body and soul
Against your black Eldorado trimmed in pure gold."

Rose picked up the dice and shot them one-two;
She shrugged and sat, 'cause she knew she had blew.

Now I shivered and trembled, more dead than alive,
Till I made my point the hard way, five and five.

"I have lost," said Rose, "and now I'm yours,
But I'm not going to be like the rest of your whores.

"I'll make a whole lot money for you, 'cause hustling's in my blood,
And because I go for you and think you're a way-out stud.

"I'll take numbers, cop stuff, steal booze or anything of value from

three-cent stamps to rockets,
I'll play the Murphy to the point of death, and I'll even pick pockets.

"I'll rob trains and banks and lots of other things,
And take the weight for narcotics rings."

"Damn!" I said. "Now this is *it*.
This broad is mine, and she talks a whole lot of shit.

"She'll keep me in kilos of C and in the champagne
By turning tricks and beating lames.

"Never again will I have to pawn my clothes
As long as I have a bitch like the Mexicana Rose.

"She'll be the best of the hustlers, the queen of the whores,
The pride of New York, the Mexicana Rose."

Now we'd forgotten Smitty, who was digging all the while,
Or else we'd have dug his madman smile.

Cocaine's mind had snapped with hate,
And he reached in his pocket for his .38.

He said, "If I can't have this bitch for my very own,
I'll kill both of you chumps and head back home.

"Say your prayers, Long-Shoe. You're the first to go."
But Rose jumped in and said, "Hell, no!"

"Kill me, creep, but not Long-Shoe Sam,
For I love him madly, he's my motherfucking man.

"He's a thoroughbred, my kind of guy,
And just to prove it, I'm ready to die."

"Quiet," said Smitty, "or I'll draw you on a bead."
"Faggot," said Rose, "your heart's a mustard seed."

Now what Rose said was true, Smitty didn't want to fight,
But his finger pulled the trigger just out of pure fright.

The bullet struck Rose high on her head,
And she toppled over backwards, damn near dead.

Cocaine Smitty stood there stunned,
Then he dropped his pistol and started to run.

But before he got within ten feet of the door
I dropped him with a cap from my Colt .44.

I shot him in the ass, and I shot him in the teeth,
And I said, "Now, creep, you ain't got no beef."

Now Rose was in her death throb and started to twitch.
She said, "I'm sorry, pretty papa, I could have made you rich."

Well, I took her body back to New York City
With the cigar-box remains of Cocaine Smitty.

I gave her a way-out funeral and didn't spare no cash,
I buried her in satin lace and an ermine sable sash.

I gave her the Queen Victoria crown and the Cinderella shoes
And hired Count Basie to play the "St. Louis Blues."

That's the end of my toast, there's no more to be said
Except that on her tombstone it simply read:

"Here lies the body of Mexicana Rose,
Destined to be the queen of the whores.

"She died young, much before her time.
Before she had a chance to make her man a dime.

"She was shot in the head by Smitty Cocaine,
A notorious shortstop and a practical lame.

"But she died brave, protecting her man,
Dean of all mackmen, Long-Shoe Sam."

* This toast, although set in a Mexican border town, has been popular among black hustlers
since at least the 1930s. This version was related in 1954 by a prison inmate who grew up
in Brooklyn.

◉◎◉

FASTBALL

"Trying to sneak a fastball past [Buck Leonard,
the Negro League baseball great]," said
Hall of Famer **Monte Irvin,**
"was like trying to sneak a sunrise past a rooster."

CARTOON

By Oliver W. Harrington
From *Dark Laughter: The Satiric Art of Oliver W. Harrington*

"Say boy, I just wanted to say that I don't mind sittin' next to the coloreds at
any old lunch-bar. Want'a try me out buddy?"

MOMS MABLEY

My slogan is if it don't fit
don't force it. In other words,
if you can't make it, don't fake it.
Let somebody else take it.

OLD MEN

No honey, I don't like no old men, uh-uh. No, no old men. I'd rather pay a young man's way from here to California than to tell an old man the distance. Some old man sittin' out there in the audience last night, had the nerve to wink at me. Got his eye closed, and he so weak he couldn't get it to open. It stayed like that all night. Older than that old husband I used to have. And he was so weak that he got out of breath picking his tooth.

And another thing, see, 'cause Mom is here, 'cause Mom know, you know. I'm going to be nice to anybody I go with, you know. But I ain't goin' to let no young man look at me and tell me, "Oh baby you look good to me." You know, I don't like that. "You glamorous baby and you look good to me. I don't care if you ain't got no teeth. You send me."

Send him where? I can look in the mirror. I know what's happenin'. I do it everyday. But some women listen to that jive, see. And give a man all her money. And then soon as he got all the money he done the paper doll—cut out.

COUNTING ON HIS FINGERS

Love my young children though honey, yeah. Love my children. Yesterday I was over to the school, one of them old church schools. Got some very smart children over there in Dunbar, you know. I teach school to all my children, gettin' awful smart. I went over there and the teacher told the little boy, say, "Show Moms how smart you are." Say, "How much is two and two?"

He said, "Four."

She said, "Uh-uh, uh-uh, you're countin' on you fingers." Say, "How much is four and four?" She say, "You're counting on your fingers. Take your hands from behind your back. I can see you counting on your fingers."

He said, "Eight."

She said, "That's right but stop counting on your fingers." Little boy got mad, he tucked his hands in his pockets, and commenced to pout. The teacher said, "Now don't get mad son. How much is five and five?"

He said, "Eleven."

$25 A QUESTION

Man walked into a psychiatrist's office. He say, "Mister, I know you're an expensive man but I just got to find out something." He says, "How much would it cost for two questions?"

He said, "Fifty dollars, twenty five dollars a question." Says, "And hurry up. I'm in a big hurry." Said, "First question."

He said, "Well the first question is, ah, do you think it's possible that I could be in love with an elephant?"

The doctor says, "Why of course not. Impossible, I never heard of . . . it's impossible for you to be in love with an elephant. Next question."

He said, "The next question is, do you know anybody that would like to buy a very large engagement ring?"

CAB CALLOWAY

I got a telephone call this morning from one of my ex-boyfriends, Cab Calloway—yeah, he's one of Mom's ex-boyfriends. Well we never exactly married but we did some heavy roomin', you know. That is when we were younger. When it made sense. Now we just friends. Oh, I used to love Cab. Wake up every morning, his hair'd be layin' all over the pillow, mine be layin' on the dresser.

But he was mean to Mom though. Oh I think that was the meanest boyfriend I ever went with. Cab Calloway. Oh, he treated Mom like a dog. In fact he called me a dog. And sometime I wished I'd a been a dog and he'd a been a tree.

LOVE IS LIKE A GAME OF CHECKERS

I saw a little girl standin' up there cryin' her eyes out. Just cryin'.

I said, "What's the matter honey."

She say, "I'm in love."

I say, "You in what!"

She say, "I'm in love."

I say, "Honey, do you know what love is?"

She say, "Yeah, I think so." She say, "'Cause I can't eat and I can't sleep."

I say, "Darlin', you got indigestion." I say, "Baby, you listen to Moms. Love is just like a game of checkers, children. You sure got to know what man to move. Cause if you move the wrong man, and he jump you—TEAR YOUR MASON AND DIXON LINE UP."

MIAMI—RED LIGHTS FOR US

But let me tell you, I was on my way down to Miami, I mean They'ami. I'm riding along in my Cadillac you know, going through one of them little towns in Carolina. Passed through a red light. One of them big cops come runnin' over to me, "Hey, hey woman! Don't you know you went through a red light?"

I say, "Yeah, I know I went through a red light."

"Well what'd you do that for?"

I said, "'Cause I saw all you white folks goin' on the green light, I thought the red light was for us. I didn't know."

And after I got down there honey, guess who they had me entertaining—the Ku Klux Klan. You talk about scared. But honey, I made those people laugh so much they forgot what they come for.

Oh, I'm telling you the truth. Now they want me to go to New Orleans. It'll be Old Orleans before I get down there. Greyhound ain't gonna take me down there and the bloodhounds run me back. I'll tell you that.

Have you heard the new Greyhound bus slogan? "Ride an integrated bus and leave the fightin' to us." Don't get Mom wrong, now. It ain't no disgrace to come from the South. It's a disgrace to go back down there.

OLD MAN IN THE HOSPITAL

Talking about an old man. Oh, honey, I seen a poor old man, he was so sick. I went over to the hospital to visit him. Oh, he was pitiful, he was so sick. He so sick and his throat was all swelled and bandaged up. Couldn't eat nothin', no food. They had to feed him through his hip you know. But they was good to him. They give him all kinda fine nice things to eat you know. The doctor was doin' all he could you know. But yet and still he looked so sad.

So the doctor said, "Why do you look so sad?" Said, "Don't we give you anything that you want, all them nice steaks and ice cream, and everything else that you want?"

He said, "Yes, but you don't' give me the main thing that I like."

Doctor say, "Well, what do you want?"

He says, "I want some coffee." Say, "I want some coffee so bad. I love coffee."

The doctor say, "Well you don't have to worry about that. I'll give you some coffee." So he went and got a funnel and turned him over and gave him some coffee.

He said, "Ahhhhhhh!"

The doctor says, "What's the matter? Too hot?"

He says, "No, too sweeeeeeet."

OLD MEN LEFT BEHIND

But getting down to seriousness, as much as we've talked, as much as we've pleaded with that man, as much as we've pleaded look like this is it. Look like they're goin to fight above everything. They done called the preserves in. When they start to usin' up the preserves look out young men you're goin' to have to go.

And if they do let me tell you, you women something. If they have war, I'm goin'. I'm goin' with the young men. I'm not goin' stay back here like I did before with them wrecks. I'm not goin' do it. Because what Uncle Sam left back here I wouldn't a given to a dog. Them 4-F's wasn't nothin'. And them old men died like flies. Them old men went down at the station pattin' them young boys on the back, talkin' about go ahead son, we'll keep up the morale. They couldn't keep up nothin'.

ACCIDENTS

But darlin' you know everybody have so many accidents, so many accidents. My brother had an accident, but he married her. And she was so ugly. Oh, that woman was so ugly. He used to take her to work with him, keep from kissing her good-bye.

Yeah, you know. And talking about accidents, I seen a terrible one on my way here. Walkin' down Broad Street and a man dropped a lit cigarette down in a manhole, open manhole, and tried to step on it.

Walkin' on down Broad Street, you know, minding my own business, you know. And so I met a friend of mine that just got married. I say, "I certainly am surprised at you, son."

He say, "What?"

I say, "What's the matter with you and your father, you're not getting along?"

He say, "My father mad at me 'cause I didn't give him a piece of my weddin' cake."

I say, "Well your father's right. You should a give him a piece of your weddin' cake."

He say, "He didn't give me none of his."

I say, "Why you wasn't even born when your father got married."

He say, "Well, he knew I was due here, he should have put me up a piece."

ROBBERS

It's so much crime! Oh I never heard of so much. Three men walked into an apartment this morning. Wasn't nobody there but an old woman around eighty-five years old and her two young daughters. Pretty girls around eighteen, nineteen. Walked into the room, said, "Throw up your hands." Say, "All right, give me your money, your jewelry, everything you got. And then I'm gonna attack each one of you."

One girl fell down on her knees, say, "Oh please, do anything you want to me but don't bother my dear old grandmother."

Grandma say, "Shut up gal. You heard what the man said."

THOUGHT I WAS HAVING A GOOD TIME

A woman went into a bar, and her husband was settin' up at the bar. She said, "There you are. Settin' up here at the bar drinkin', enjoyin' yourself, havin' fun, havin' a good time. Bartender, give me a drink. I want you to give me the same thing he's drinkin', and I want you to give me a double of it."

The bartender give her some of that hundred proof Grand Dad, and she drank it down. The top of her head almost flew off. She looked at him, says, "Oh, goodness. How can you drink that terrible stuff? Oh, my goodness."

He said, "And you thought I was having a good time."

She went on home. After she got home in about an hour he walks in. She met at the door. She says, "Well, I guess you found out that home is the best place after all."

He say, "I don't know. It's the only place open."

YOU AIN'T SO SMART

This man say, "You can't fool me, I've been to school."

I say, "Ah, you ain't so smart." I say, "If you so smart, I want you to answer one question." I say, "How many sides does a house got?"

He say, "Four."

I say, "That shows you how much sense you got. A house has got eight sides."

He say, "Got four!"

I say, "I said it got eight!"

He say, "I said it got four!"

I say, "Name them four sides you talkin' about."

He say, "North side, south side, east side, and west side."

I say, "Inside, outside, topside, and bottom side, fool.

Dog on the Bus

I was fixin' to get the bus, you know to come and work. And an old lady was standing with her little dog, you know. Some rich old lady was standing there with her dog waiting for the bus. The bus came, she started on the bus. The man say, "I'm very sorry but you can't bring no dog on the bus. They don't allow dogs on the bus."

She said, "Well, my little Fee Fee must go where I go. He's a very nervous dog, and I'm going to take my dog . . ."

He say, "No, no lady. You can't bring no dog on no bus."

Oh, she raised Cain! She say, "You know what you can do with your old bus, don't you?"

He say, "Yeah, you do the same, the same thing with the dog and you can ride."

Trouble with Old Men

Some of the hometown people been talkin' about me. Yeah, they even said that I was prejudiced. I'm not prejudiced. I'm not. But I don't like no old men, I don't give a damn what color he is. If I want to go with Brook Benton, that's my business.

I married an old man and I was nothin but a child, and he was dead as a doornail. Don't be like my old man was. I told him one day, I said, "You're sick, why don't you take out some insurance?"

He say, "I ain't gonna take out a damn bit." Say, "When I die I want it to be a sad day for everybody."

His suspenders were bigger than he was. That's the truth. And weak. He was so weak, one day he went to pop his finger and broke his wrist. One day he bit down on a pancake and got lockjaw.

I said to him one day, I say, "We invited up in the country for the weekend, I'm goin'." I say, "You know anything about the country?"

He say, "Sure. I know all about the country. In fact I used to live in the country when I was a boy."

I say, "When you was a boy everybody lived in the country."

◎◎

JESSE B. SIMPLE TALES

By Langston Hughes

TEMPTATION

"When the Lord said, 'Let there be light,' and there was light, what I want to know is where was us colored people?"

"What do you mean, 'Where were we colored people?'" I said.

"*We must not* of been there," said Simple, "because we are still dark. Either He did not include me or else I were not there."

"The Lord was *not* referring to people when He said, 'Let there be light.' He was referring to the elements, the atmosphere, the air."

"He must have included some people," said Simple, "because white people are light, in fact, *white*, whilst I am dark. How come? I say, we were not there."

"Then where do you think we were?"

"Late as usual," said Simple, "old C. P. Time. We must have been down the road a piece and did not get back on time."

"There was no C. P. Time in those days," I said. "In fact, no people were created—so there couldn't be any Colored People's Time. The Lord God had not yet breathed the breath of life into anyone."

"No?" said Simple.

"No," said I, "because it wasn't until Genesis 2 and 7 that God 'formed man of the dust of the earth and breathed into his nostrils the breath of life and man became a living soul.' His name was Adam. Then He took one of Adam's ribs and made a woman."

"Then trouble began," said Simple. "Thank God, they was both white."

"How do you know Adam and Eve were white?" I asked.

"When I was a kid I seen them on the Sunday school cards," said Simple. "Ever since I been seeing a Sunday school card, they was white. That is why I want to know where was us Negroes when the Lord said, 'Let there be light'?"

"Oh, man, you have a color complex so bad you want to trace it back to the Bible."

"No, I don't. I just want to know how come Adam and Eve was white. If they had started out black, this world might not be in the fix it is today. Eve might not of paid that serpent no attention. I never did know a Negro yet that liked a snake."

"That snake is a symbol," I said, "a symbol of temptation and sin. And that symbol would be the same, no matter what the race."

"I am not talking about no symbol," said Simple. "I am talking about the day when Eve took that apple and Adam et. From then on the human race has been in trouble. There ain't a colored woman living what would take no apple from a snake—and she better not give no snake-apples to her husband!"

"Adam and Eve are symbols, too," I said.

"You are simple yourself," said Simple. "But I just wish we colored folks had been somewhere around at the start. I do not know where we was when Eden was a garden, but we sure didn't get in on none of the crops. If we had, we would not be so poor today. White folks started out ahead and they are still ahead. Look at me!"

"I am looking," I said.

"Made in the image of God," said Simple, "but I never did see anybody like me on a Sunday school card."

"Probably nobody looked like you in Biblical days," I said. "The American Negro did not exist in B.C. You're a product of Caucasia and Africa, Harlem and Dixie. You've been conditioned entirely by our environment, our modern times."

"Times have been hard," said Simple, "but still I am a child of God."

"In the cosmic sense, we are all children of God."

"I have been baptized," said Simple, "also anointed with oil. When I were a child I come through at the mourners' bench. I was converted. I have listened to Daddy Grace and et with Father Divine, moaned with Elder Lawson and prayed with Adam Powell. Also I have been to the Episcopalians with Joyce. But if a snake were to come up to me and offer *me* an apple, I would say, 'Varmint, be on your way! No fruit today! Bud, you got the wrong stud now, so get along somehow, be off down the road because you're lower than a toad!' Then that serpent would respect me as a wise man—and this world would not be where it is—all on account of an apple. That apple has turned into an atom now."

"To hear you talk, if you had been in the Garden of Eden, the world would still be a Paradise," I said. "Man would not have fallen into sin."

"Not *this* man," said Simple. "I would have stayed in that garden making grape wine, singing like Crosby, and feeling fine! I would not be scuffling out in this rough world, neither would I be in Harlem. If I was Adam I would just stay in Eden in that garden with no rent to pay, no landladies to dodge, no time clock to punch—and *my* picture on a Sunday school card. I'd be a *real gone guy* even if I didn't have but one name—Adam—and no initials."

"You would be *real gone* all right. But you were not there. So my dear fellow, I trust you will not let your rather late arrival on our contemporary stage distort your perspective."

"No," said Simple.

THERE OUGHT TO BE A LAW

"Look here at these headlines, man, where Congress is busy passing laws. While they're making all these laws, it looks like to me they ought to make one setting up a few Game Preserves for Negroes."

"What ever gave you that fantastic idea?" I asked.

"A movie short I saw the other night,"said Simple, "about how the government is protecting wild life, preserving fish and game, and setting aside big tracts of land where nobody can fish, shoot, hunt, nor harm a single living creature with furs, fins, or feathers. But it did not show a thing about Negroes."

"I thought you said the picture was about 'wild life.' Negroes are not wild."

"No," said Simple, "but we need protection. This film showed how they put aside a thousand acres out West where the buffaloes roam and nobody can shoot a single one of them. If they do, they get in jail. It also showed some big National Park with government airplanes dropping food down to the deers when they got snowed under and had nothing to eat. The government protects and takes care of buffaloes and deers—which is more than the government does for me or my kinfolks down South. Last month they lynched a man in Georgia and just today I see where the Klan has whipped a Negro within a inch of his life in Alabama. And right up North here in New York a actor is suing a apartment house that won't even let a Negro go up on the elevator to see his producer. That is what I mean by Game Preserves for Negroes—Congress ought to set aside some place where we can go and nobody can jump on us and beat us, neither lynch us nor Jim Crow us every day. Colored folks rate as much protection as a buffalo, or a deer."

"You have a point there," I said.

"This here movie showed great big beautiful lakes with signs up all around:

NO FISHING—STATE GAME PRESERVE

But it did not show a single place with a sign up:

NO LYNCHING

It also showed flocks of wild ducks settling down in a nice green meadow behind a government sign that said:

NO HUNTING

It were nice and peaceful for them fish and ducks. There ought to be some place where it is nice and peaceful for me, too, even if I am not a fish or a duck.

"They showed one scene with two great big old longhorn elks locking horns on a Game Preserve somewhere out in Wyoming, fighting like mad. Nobody bothered them elks or tried to stop them from fighting. But just let me get in a little old fist fight here in this bar, they will lock me up and the Desk Sergeant will say, 'What are you colored boys doing, disturbing the peace?' Then they will give me thirty days and fine me twice as much as they would a white man for doing the same thing. There ought to be some place where I can fight in peace and not get fined them high fines."

"You disgust me," I said. "I thought you were talking about a place where you could be quiet and compose your mind. Instead, you are talking about fighting."

"I would like a place where I could do both," said Simple. "If the government can set aside some spot for a elk *to be a elk* without being bothered, or a fish *to be a fish* without getting hooked, or a buffalo *to be a buffalo* without being shot down, there ought to be some place in this American country where a Negro can be a Negro without being Jim Crowed. There ought to be a law. The next time I see my congressman, I am going to tell him to introduce a bill for Game Preserves for Negroes."

"The Southerners would filibuster it to death," I said.

"If we are such a problem to them Southerners," said Simple, "I should think they would want some place to preserve us out of their sight. But then, of course, you have to take into consideration that if the Negroes was taken out of the South, who would they lynch? What would they do for sport? A Game Preserve is for to keep people from bothering anything that is living.

"When that movie finished, it were sunset in Virginia and it showed a little deer and its mama lying down to sleep. Didn't nobody say, 'Get up, deer, you can't sleep here,' like they would to me if I was to go to the White Sulphur Springs Hotel."

"'The foxes have holes, and the birds of the air have nests; but the Son of a man hath not where to lay his head.'"

"That is why I want Game Preserves for Negroes," said Simple.

RACE RELATIONS

"Don't let's talk about it," he said when I asked him about Joyce. "Don't ever mention her name. I can't stand it. I have tried every way I know to make up with that woman. But she must have a heart like a rock cast in the sea. I have also tried every way I know to forget her. But no dice. I cannot wear her off my mind. I've even taken up reading. This week I bought all the colored papers from the *Black Dispatch* to the *Afro-American,* trying to get a race-mad on, reading about lynchings, head-whippings, barrings-out, sharecroppers, cheatings, discriminations, and such. No dice. I have drunk five bottles of beer tonight and I'm still sober. Nothing has no effect. So let's just not talk about Joyce.

"There is a question, anyhow, I want to ask you because I wish to change the subject," Simple said.

"Them colored papers are full of stuff about Race Relations Committees functioning all over the country, and how they are working to get rid of the poll tax and to keep what few Negroes still have jobs from losing them, and such. But in so far as I can tell, none of them committees is taking up the real problems of race relations because I always thought *relations* meant being related. Don't it? And to be related you have to have relations, don't you? But I don't hear nobody speaking about us being kinfolks. All they are talking about in the papers is poll taxes and jobs."

"By relations, I take it that you mean intermarriage? If that is what you mean, nobody wants to talk about that. That is a touchy subject. It is also beside the point. Equal rights and fair employment have nothing to do with intermarriage."

"Getting married," said Simple, "is also a equal right."

"You do not want to marry a white woman, do you?" I asked.

"I do not," said Simple, "but I figure some white woman might want to marry me."

"You'd better not let Joyce hear you talking like that," I said. "You know colored women do not like the idea of intermarriage at all."

"I know they don't," said Simple. "Neither do white men. But if the races are ever going to relate, they must also mate, then you will have race relations."

"Race relations do not necessarily have to be on so racy a basis," I said.

"At any rate, speaking about them in such a manner only infuriates the South. It makes Southerners fighting mad."

"I do not see why it should infuriate the South," said Simple, "because the South has always done more relating than anybody else. There are more light-skinned Negroes in the South whose pappy was a white man than there is in all the rest of this whole American country."

"True," I said, "many colored people are related to white people down South. But *some* relationships are private matters, whereas things like equal job opportunities, an unsegregated army, the poll tax, and no more Jim Crow cars affect everybody, in bed or out. These are the things Race Relations Committees are trying to deal with all over the country. It would only complicate the issues if they brought up intermarriage."

"Issues are complicated already," said Simple. "Why, I even got white blood in me myself, dark as I am. And in some colored families I know personally down South, you can hardly tell high yellows from white."

"My dear fellow," I said, "the basic social issues which I am talking about are not to be dealt with on a family basis, but on a mass basis. All Negroes, with white blood in them or not, in fact, everybody of whatever parentage, ought to have the right to vote, to live a decent life, and to have fair employment."

"Also to relate," said Simple.

"I keep telling you, race relations do not have anything to do with that kind of relating!"

"If they don't," said Simple, "they are not relations."

"Absurd," I said. "I simply will not argue with you any more. You're just as bad as those Southerners who are always bringing up intermarriage as a reason for *not* doing anything. What you say is entirely beside the point."

"The point must have moved then," said Simple.

"We are not talking about the same thing at all," I said patiently. "I am talking about fair employment, and you are talking about . . ."

"Race relations," said Simple.

THAT WORD *BLACK*

"This evening," said Simple. "I feel like talking about the word *black*."

"Nobody's stopping you, so go ahead. But what you really ought to have is a soap-box out on the corner of 126th and Lenox where the rest of the orators hang out."

"They expresses some good ideas on that corner," said Simple, "but for my ideas I do not need a crowd. Now, as I were saying, the word *black*, white folks have done used that word to mean something bad so often un-til now when the N.A.A.C.P. asks for civil rights for the black man, they think they must be bad. Looking back into history, I reckon it all started with a *black* cat meaning bad luck. Don't let one cross your path!

"Next, somebody got up a *black-list* on which you get if you don't vote right. Then when lodges come into being, the folks they didn't want in them got *black-balled.* If you kept a skeleton in your closet, you might get *black-mailed.* And everything bad was *black.* When it came down to the unlucky ball on the pool table, the eight-rock, they made it the *black* ball. So no wonder there ain't no equal rights for the *black* man."

"All you say is true about the odium attached to the word *black,*" I said. "You've even forgotten a few. For example, during the war if you bought something under the table, illegally, they said you were trading on the *black* market. In Chicago, if you're a gangster, the *Black Hand Society* may take you for a ride. And certainly if you don't behave yourself, your fam-ily will say you're a *black* sheep. Then if your mama burns a *black* candle to change the family luck, they call it *black* magic."

"My mama never did believe in voodoo so she did not burn no black candles," said Simple.

"If she had, that would have been a *black* mark against her."

"Stop talking about my mama. What I want to know is, where do white folks get off calling everything bad *black?* If it is a dark night, they say it's *black* as hell. If you are mean and evil, they say you got a *black* heart. I would like to change all that around and say that people who Jim Crow me have got a *white* heart. People who sell dope to children have got a *white* mark against them. And all the white gamblers who were behind the bas-ketball fix are the *white* sheep of the sports world. God knows there was few, if any, Negroes selling stuff on the black market during the war, so why didn't they call it the *white* market? No, they got to take me and my color and turn it into everything *bad.* According to white folks, black is bad.

"Wait till my day comes! In my language, bad will be *white.* Blackmail will be *white* mail. Black cats will be good luck, and *white* cats will be bad. If a *white* cat crosses your path, look out! I will take the black ball for the cue ball and let the *white* ball be unlucky eight-rock. And on my blacklist—which will be *white* list then—I will put everybody who Jim Crowed me from Rankin to Hitler, Talmadge to Malan, South Carolina to South Africa.

"I am black. When I look in the mirror, I see myself, daddy-o, but I am not ashamed. God made me. He also made F.D., dark as he is. He did not make us no badder than the rest of the folks. The earth is black and all kinds of good things comes out of the earth. Everything that grows comes up out of the earth. Trees and flowers and fruit and sweet potatoes and corn and all that keeps mens alive comes right out of the earth—good old black earth. Coal is black and it warms your house and cooks your food. The night is black, which has a moon, and a million stars, and is beautiful. Sleep is black which gives you rest, so you wake up feeling good. I am black. I feel very good this evening.

"What is wrong with black?"

DEAR DR. BUTTS

"Do you know what happened to me?" said Simple.

"No."

"I'm out of a job."

"That's tough. How did that come about?"

"Laid off—they're converting again. And right now, just when I am planning to get married this spring, they have to go changing from civilian production to war contracts, installing new machinery. Manager says it might take two months, might take three or four. They'll send us mens notices. If it takes four months, that's up to June, which is no good for my plans. To get married a man needs money. To stay married he needs more money. And where am I? As usual, behind the eight-ball."

"You can find another job in the meanwhile, no doubt."

"That ain't easy. And if I do, they liable not to pay much. Jobs that pay good money nowadays are scarce as hen's teeth. But Joyce says she do not care. She is going to marry me, come June, anyhow—even if she has to pay for it herself. Joyce says since I paid for the divorce, she can pay for the wedding. But I do not want her to do that."

"Naturally not, but maybe you can curtail your plans somewhat and not have so big a wedding. Wedlock does not require an elaborate ceremony."

"I do not care if we don't have none, just so we get locked. But you know how womens is. Joyce has waited an extra year for her great day. Now here I am broke as a busted bank."

"How're you keeping up with your expenses?"

"I ain't. And I don't drop by Joyce's every night like I did when I was working. I'm embarrassed. Then she didn't have to ask me to eat. Now she does. In fact, she insists. She says, 'You got to eat somewheres. I enjoy your company. Eat with me.' I do, if I'm there when she extends the invitation. But I don't go looking for it. I just sets home and broods, man, and looks at my four walls, which gives me plenty of time to think. And do you know what I been thinking about lately?"

"Finding work, I presume."

"Besides that?"

"No. I don't know what you've been thinking about."

"Negro leaders, and how they're talking about how great democracy is—and me out of a job. Also how there is so many leaders I don't know that white folks know about, because they are always in the white papers. Yet *I'm* the one they are supposed to be leading. Now, you take that little short leader named Dr. Butts, I do not know him, except in name only. If he ever made a speech in Harlem it were not well advertised. From what I reads, he teaches at a white college in Massachusetts, stays at the Commodore when he's in New York, and ain't lived in Harlem for ten years. Yet he's leading me. He's an article writer, but he does not write in colored papers. But lately the colored papers taken to reprinting parts of what he writes—otherwise I would have never seen it. Anyhow, with all this time on my hands these days, I writ him a letter last night. Here, read it."

Harlem, U.S.A.
One Cold February Day

Dear Mr. Butts,

I seen last week in the colored papers where you have writ an article for The New York Times *in which you say America is the greatest country in the world for the Negro race and Democracy the greatest kind of government for all, but it would be better if there was equal education for colored folks in the South, and if everybody could vote, and if there were not Jim Crow in the army, also if the churches was not divided up into white churches and colored churches, and if Negroes did not have to ride on the back seats of busses South of Washington.*

Now, all this later part of your article is hanging onto your but. You start off talking about how great American democracy is, then you but it all over the place. In fact, the but end of your see-saw is so far down on the ground I do not believe the other end can ever pull it up. So me myself, I would not write no article for no New York Times if I had to put in so many buts. I reckon maybe you come by it naturally, though, that being your name, dear Dr. Butts.

I hear tell that you are a race leader, but I do not know who you lead because I have not heard tell of you before and I have not laid eyes on you. But if you are leading me, make me know it, because I do not read the New York Times very often, less I happen to pick up a copy blowing around in the sub-

ways, so I did not know you were my leader. But since you are my leader, lead on, and see if I will follow behind your but—because there is more behind that but than there is in front of it.

Dr. Butts, I am glad to read that you writ an article in The New York Times, *but also sometime I wish you would write one in the colored papers and let me know how to get out from behind all these buts that are staring me in the face. I know America is a great country but—and it is that but that has been keeping me where I is all these years. I can't get over it, I can't get under it, and I can't get around it, so what am I supposed to do? If you are leading me, lemme see. Because we have too many colored leaders now that nobody knows until they get from the white papers to the colored papers and from the colored papers to me who has never seen hair nor hide of you. Dear Dr. Butts, are you hiding from me—and leading me, too?*

From the way you write, a man would think my race problem was made out of nothing but buts. But this, but that, and, yes, there is Jim Crow in Georgia but—. America admits they bomb folks in Florida—but Hitler gassed the Jews. Mississippi is bad—but Russia is worse. Detroit slums are awful—but compared to the slums in India, Detroit's Paradise Valley is Paradise.

Dear Dr. Butts, Hitler is dead. I don't live in Russia. India is across the Pacific Ocean. And I do not hope to see Paradise no time soon. I am nowhere near some of them foreign countries you are talking about being so bad. I am here! And you know as well as I do, Mississippi is hell. There ain't no but in the world can make it out different. They tell me when Nazis gas you, you die slow. But when they put a bomb under you like in Florida, you don't have time to say your prayers. As for Detroit, there is as much difference between Paradise Valley and Paradise as there is between heaven and Harlem. I don't know nothing about India, but I been in Washington, D.C. If you think there ain't slums there, just take your but up Seventh Street late some night, and see if you still got it by the time you get to Howard University.

I should not have to be telling you these things. You are colored just like me. To put a but after all this Jim Crow fly-papering around our feet is just like telling a hungry man, "But Mr. Rockefeller has got plenty to eat." It's just like telling a joker with no overcoat in the winter time, "But you will be hot next summer." The fellow is liable to haul off and say, "I am hot now!" And bop you over your head.

Are you in your right mind, dear Dr. Butts? Or are you just writing? Do you really think a new day is dawning? Do you really think Christians are having a change of heart? I can see you now taking your pen in hand to write, "But just last year the Southern Denominations of Hell-Fired Salvation re-

*solved to work toward Brotherhood." In fact, that is what you already writ. Do
you think Brotherhood means* colored *to them Southerners?*

*Do you reckon they will recognize you for a brother, Dr. Butts, since you
done had your picture taken in the Grand Ballroom of the Waldorf-Astoria
shaking hands at some kind of meeting with five hundred white big-shots
and* five *Negroes, all* five of them Negro leaders, *so it said underneath the
picture? I did not know any of them Negro leaders by sight, neither by name,
but since it says in the white papers that they are leaders, I reckon they are.
Anyhow, I take my pen in hand to write you this letter to ask you to make
yourself clear to me. When you answer me, do not write no "so-and-so-and-
so but—." I will not take* but *for an answer. Negroes have been looking at
Democracy's* but *too long. What we want to know is how to get rid of that*
but.

Do you dig me, dear Dr. Butts?

Sincerely very truly,
Jesse B. Semple

◎◎

AMOS 'N' ANDY

During its long stint on radio (1928–55), the Amos 'n' Andy Show *featured
white writers/actors Freeman F. Gosden and Charles J. Correll in the roles of
nearly all the characters. The television version of the show, however, was performed by an all-black cast, which included some of the funniest, most talented
comic actors then working. Standouts among them were Johnny Lee as the dis-
barred lawyer Algonquin J. Calhoun, Ernestine Wade as Kingfish's wife Sapphire, and Tim Moore as Kingfish, one of TV's most outlandish flimflam artists.
Its cast was one of the finest ever assembled on TV and offered a rare mainstream appearance of the comedy seen on the black theater circuit. Despite its
popularity, the show was canceled in 1953, after its third season, due to
protests from civil rights groups who objected to its portrayals of black profes-
sionals and black women. The following examples offer a glimpse of the principal characters in some typical situations.*

Andy:　　　I done told the clerk where I was goin', and he said he
　　　　　　ain't never heard a' nobody goin' to Arabia on vacation cause
　　　　　　it's too hot over there. Does he know what he's talkin' bout?

Kingfish:　Well, ahhh . . . yes, and no, Andy.

Andy: What'cha mean?

Kingfish: Well, I'll explain dat to you. At one time Arabia was the hottest country in de world. But dats all changed now in the past few years.

Andy: What'cha mean, done changed?

Kingfish: Well, Andy, they opened up the Suez Canal and let the breeze blow into Arabia . . .

Andy: How could it do dat?

Kingfish: Andy Brown, I'm surprised at you, a man a your intelligence asking a crazy question like dat. I'll explain dat to you. . . . Now on one end of Arabia, they got dah Suez Canal wit de gates open. And, den, on the other end, is dah Polish corridor.

Andy: Well, what about it?

Kingfish: Well, dere you is. Arabia is de only country in de world wit cross ventilation.

Andy: I don't guess dah clerk knowed nothin' bout dat.

*

Sapphire: Well, George, did'ya have any luck finding a job today?

Kingfish: No, honey, it just seem like dere ain't no employment around for mens. I hunted high and low, but I ain't give up. I gonna try again in three-four months.

Sapphire: Well, George, you don't have to look no more. I got some wonderful news for'ya.

Kingfish: Ahhh . . . what's that?

Sapphire: I got a job for'ya at Superfine Brush Company as a door-to-door salesman.

Kingfish: You done what! Now look here, Sapphire, you can't do that. It's a violation of the Atlantic Charter, the Constitution, the Monroe Doctrine, and not only dat, it's a violation of one of dah four freedoms, de freedom of speech!

Sapphire: Freedom of speech?

Kingfish: Yeah, you didn't give me a chance to say no.

*

[The following scene ensues when the obstreperous Calhoun arrives in court to defend Kingfish and Andy who have been mistakenly arrested and charged with theft.]

Calhoun: I'd like to enter a plea of not guilty for these two crooks.

Judge: On what grounds? According to the report these men were caught trying to break into a telephone coin box in the presence of a witness, who is also a police officer of this city.

Calhoun: Well, ahhh . . . Yes sir, your honor! But they done learned they lesson. They ain't never gone break into nothin' in front of a cop no mo'.

Judge: . . . This is an arraignment, not a trial. It's obvious from the evidence before me that these men should be bound over for trial.

Calhoun: Just a minute, yo' honor!

Judge: Do you have something further to say?

Calhoun: I'll say I is! This may be only an arraignment, but I demands justice for these two innocent mens. Yo' honor, let me tell you that you aaainnn' gone put these men behind bars! I happen to know mo' about . . . And another thing . . . I'm gonna see to it that you—

Judge: Wait a minute, counselor. Isn't your name Calhoun?

Calhoun: That's right, yo' honor, Algonquin J. Calhoun.

Judge: And didn't I disbar you three years ago!

Calhoun: Ahhh . . . so long, boys.

Kingfish: Excuse me, yo' honor, but how much ground did we lose while our lawyer was in defendin' us?

⊘⊘

SATCHEL PAIGE

Paige, one of the first black players in the American league, was also known for his laconic wit and was one of the most colorful baseball players of his era. His most quoted line was, "Don't look back, something might be gaining on you," *but Paige had a quip for nearly every occasion.*

ILLEGAL PITCHES

"I uses more psychiatry than I used to,"
Satch told a *Newsweek* reporter.
"I stares at them, slaps some rosin around and
by the time I lets go those batters'
legs starts to wobble. . . . I ain't never thrown
an illegal pitch. The trouble is once
in a while I tosses one that ain't been
seen by this generation."

IN DEMAND

Satch and all the Cleveland Indian
players were asked to fill out a
questionnaire and one question asked if they
were married. "Sometimes Satch answered yes,
sometimes no," the Indians' owner Bill Veeck said.
"Every day, though, he was leaving a
ticket at the box office for Mrs. Paige,
and every day a different woman
was picking it up."
Finally, the team confronted him
and tried to straighten out the records.
"Well, it's like this," Satch said.
"I'm not married but I'm in great demand."

SECOND BASE

"One time [Cool Papa Bell] hit a line drive past my ear.
I turned around and saw the ball hit his ass sliding into second base."

SECOND-CLASS IMMORTAL

After Satchel Paige was told that he had been elected
to the Negro League's Hall of Fame, he said,
"The only change is that baseball has turned
Paige from a second-class citizen
to a second-class immortal."

NIPSEY RUSSELL

AIN'T GHANA EAT

An African delegate was driving
along Highway One, between Baltimore and
Washington, D.C., and stopped at a restaurant to dine.
When he entered, they told him
they didn't serve blacks. The delegate,
flustered with embarrassment, pulled up
all his dignity and said in a loud voice,
"I'm the African delegate from Ghana."
The waitress looked him straight in the eye and
said, "Well, you ain't Ghana eat here!"

STILL A NIGGER

A guy sitting in bus station notices a scale
that tells your weight and your fortune.
He goes up to the scale, steps on,
and drops a coin into the slot.
A little card comes out. It reads,
"You weigh 150 pounds, you are a Negro,
and you're on your way to Chicago."
The man is surprised that he's been identified
as a Negro, so he tries it again.
And again the card comes and reads,
"You weigh 150 pounds, you are a Negro,
and you are on your way to Chicago."
The guy is amazed.
He sees an old Indian sitting all wrapped up in
a blanket, so he goes over, borrows the blanket
and wraps it around himself as disguise.
He sticks a feather in his hair,
goes back to the scale and deposits another coin.
Another card shoots out of the slot.
This time it reads, "You still weigh 150 pounds,
you're still a nigger, and by fucking
around, you've missed your bus to Chicago."

COMEUPPANCE

The diminutive Peewee Markham
was emcee at the famous jazz spot
Birdland during its heyday in the 1950s.
He was known for being as
irascible and verbally abusive as he was charismatic.
And one evening, after Peewee blasted
jazz musician Billy Mitchell
with a round of stinging sarcasm,
Mitchell walked over to him, peered down,
and stopped him in mid-sentence.
"Why don't you stand on a chair,"
Mitchell said, "So I can knock you down."
—Jazz pianist Junior Mance

TRAIN TO NEW YORK

Got on the train in Tampa, Florida, on the way to New York. Conductor came around, said, "Give me your ticket, boy." Gave him my ticket; he punched it and gave it back. Came around again in Richmond, Virginia, said, "Give me your ticket, boy." Gave him my ticket; he punched it and gave it back. In the Lincoln Tunnel on the way into New York City, conductor came around and said, "Give me your ticket, boy." Turned around to him and said, "Who the hell you callin' boy?"

—Two Tons of Fun

MY NIGGER

"My mother was working
for a wealthy doctor, who sent me to
the store on a hot Saturday afternoon,
one of the clerks asked,
'What do you want, nigger?'
He put so much venom into the word
that I ran, crying, to my mother.
She told the doctor, who went downstairs
and gave the clerk a beating
and said, in effect:
'Don't you call *my* nigger a nigger'"
—John H. Johnson,
from *Succeeding Against the Odds*

REDD FOXX

BOSS SPELLED BACKWARD

"Tote that barge and you lift that bale . . . [singing]" I ain't liftin' nothin' sucker. Don't write no number for me to work by. You know what I mean? See, blacks have had whites fooled for years with one word, *Boss.* "Good night boss, yes sir, *boss.*" You see boss spelled backwards is double S.O.B., and that's two of them. That's right, good night you son of a bitch you. Work me to death all week and ain't payin' me no decent salary. And then go to a big party and ask your friends, "Why do they steal?" 'Cause you wasn't payin' me nothin', that's why. That's why I rolled them tires out. And why I put that silverware down my pants leg and wrapped them steaks around my waist. Lotta ways to carry stuff out the job. Empty the garbage can eleven thirty at night—into your truck.

SNAKEBITE

Two cats was out hunting. During the night, one of the guys somehow got a rattlesnake in his sleeping bag and it bit him on the vital organ, right on the tip. His buddy jumped up and said, "Look, don't move. If you move that poison will go through your body. And if it goes through, you goin' to die." Said, "You lay still, and I'll run into town and get a doctor." So he ran into town—a mile across creeks, around bushes and trees, ducked cars, into the doctor's office.

Doctor was busy and said, "I can't leave, but I tell you what you do. Go back to your friend, take this knife and cut two slits where he was bitten and suck the poison out."

The guy ran all the way back to his camp—across creeks, and around trees and bushes, and over concrete fences. Got back to his buddy who was layin' there on the ground. His buddy looked up, he say, "What did the doctor say?"

He say, "The doctor say, you goin' to die!"

BLACK SCIENTISTS

We must utilize every black brain in America to make our country strong. We had great black scientists. One started a blood bank, one came up with blood plasma, another black scientist crossed some peanut butter with a mule. Got a sandwich with long ears and a piece of ass that sticks to the roof of your mouth. We need that black genius working in America. Let's open up our doors in our universities and whatever else you can open up.

SNEEZES

Hey, let me tell you about this chick. She had, ah, sneezes. You know, almost like, when you have hiccups, three or four, she had sneezes. Terrible. And, and every time she went to the doctor she say, "Doc, I have these sneezes. And every time I sneeze I have a climax."

He say, "Well what are you doing for it?"

She say, "Sniffin' pepper."

TOASTS

A toast. What's the difference between a Northern girl and a Southern girl? A Northern girl say you can, and a Southern girl say *y'all* can.

Another toast. What's the best way to cut off a cat's tail? Repossess his Cadillac.

I got more toasts, might as well have a couple a more while we're here. Toast. What's the difference between a goldfish and a mountain goat? A goldfish like to muck around the fountain.

Toast. Where do cousins come from? Aunt holes. . . . I ain't lied yet.

Okay, here's another one. Toast. What's the difference between a Peeping Tom and a pickpocket? A pickpocket snatches watches!

KNIVES

I was born in St. Louis, Missouri. Used to wake up buck naked and put my knife on. But that's a lie they tell about black people. Say all black people carry knives. I'm gonna tell the truth. It's a lie 'cause, in truth I've been carrying an ice pick for thirty-two years.

EAT WHAT YOU LOVE

Shucks, I don't like violence, that's why I don't join no groups and I'm gonna keep eating pork. I'm gonna keep eating beef and bananas. Whatever I like to eat, don't interfere with it. Eat what you love, don't mess with other folks. A hog ain't no uglier than a cow. . . . Let me get a fresh cigarette. I smoke and drink. A lot of you don't drink, don't smoke. Some people here tonight, they don't eat butter, no salt, no sugar, no lard, no biscuits, no gravy with onions in it. 'Cause they want to live, they give up that good stuff, neck bones, pig tails. You gonna feel like a damn fool layin' out in the hospital dyin' from nothin'.

I've been smoking forty years. If I don't have cancer now, I probably have something that will eat it up. Cancer better not fuck with my body. I mean that. It's a lot of things worse than cancer. A six-foot-six black nationalist in an alley with a hatchet, mad at you, is worse than cancer.

BACKING UP

I want to mention World War II, because a lot of you know that I was a hero. Wasn't easy though, backin' up. I backed up so far in one battle, I bumped into a general.

He said, "Why are you running?"

I said, "I'm running because I cannot fly!"

$240,000

Say, you remember about three years ago a guy out here found $240,000 on the street somewhere downtown here in Los Angeles? Remember him? You remember that fool, ah . . . fellow. Two hundred and forty thousand dollars cash, he found it in a bag. Was home free with the door locked— fives, tens, twenties, unmarked by human beings. No one knew he had it. He was in debt, coulda got straight. And he called the authorities up and told them, "I found this money that could of kept me cool for the rest of my life and I want y'all to have it back."

He lived next door to me. The reporters came out there, walked all across my grass and stuff and said, "Man, why?" Asked me, "Foxx, if you had found that money would you have turned it in?"

I said, "Yes, I would have turned it in. I would have turned it in to a pillowcase—and caught me a jet plane for the Congo, hired ten thousand Mau-Maus at a dollar a piece, sat down in the center of them while they were sharpening their poison darts and spears and blowguns and dared somebody to come and ask me something about $240,000.

OH, GEORGE!

Listen, I'm gonna show you how you can make a story out of a sentence by leaving one word off each time. Here's a sentence:

—Oh, George, let's not park here.
—Oh, George, let's not park.
—Oh, George, let's not.
—Oh, George, let's!
—Ooh, George!
—OOOHH!

SUGAR RAY

I know pain because I was a fighter. Like when I was younger. Fought Sugar Ray Robinson before he was champ. Could'a killed him, too, if he'd a slipped in my blood.

REVIVAL PREACHER

Shucks. It's too many different religions. Somebody's goin' to hell. It's goin' to be *crowded!* If you ain't got no reservation you might have to stand up.

There was a preacher was asked to come to a town. It was a small town, he was asked to come there for a revival, 'cause he was good—one of them good revival preachers. You know, he could get the thing on. He get the feelin' on in there, and people be puttin' some money in the collection plate. He could preach.

He got to town. Wasn't no hotels in town, so he had to sleep with one of the sisters—at her house. You know what I mean, have chicken and every-thing, you know them preachers. And after the revival meeting was over, he'd been there about three days, and Rev got ready to leave town. And he said to his hostess, he said, "Darling, never in my ecclesiastical career have I encountered such an abundant, satisfying, abiding manifestation of thor-ough, complete, and delightful exemplification of gratitude, graciousness, and hospitality."

Miss Wilson she smiled, she said, "Well Rev, I don't know what all them big words mean. But I want to say that you're a real world beater, a strong repeater, that you can you can do it neater and sweater and more com-pleter, with less peter than any preacher ever been here."

FM

Some people won't face the truth, but you might as well look at things your own way. You know what I mean? I was layin' up in the bed one night try-ing to get me some FM on the stereo. And by the way, FM was stolen from us . . . and they switched the initials. You know that belongs to us. You don't believe it, make one of us mad. Let one of us make one of us mad. See don't you be three of them before the fight starts.

PRESIDENT JOHNSON

President Johnson and Carl Stokes, you know, the brother, they were in the rest room in Washington and President Johnson looked over at Carl to speak to him. And being a little bit taller than Carl, he had to look down and he happened to glance into Carl's bowl. He said, "I'll be damned, Carl, how'd you get that?"

Carl say, "Well, just before I have sex I always beat it on the bedpost four times. Just take it and beat it on the bedpost four times. That's all I do."

President Johnson said, "Well, you know, I'm going to try that when I get home." He got home, took a shower, and walked in the bedroom and beat it on the bedpost four times.

Lady Bird woke up and said, "Is that you Carl?"

DEPRESSION TIME

During Depression time, we had it rough back there. Christmas of 1931 our landlady got put out. My grandmother was standing by the stove fixin' to cook in case anything came. My grandfather was in the backyard trying to catch a gopher with his crutch. And they called my grandmother and said, "HELEN, THE GARBAGE MAN IS HERE!"

She'd yell, "WELL, TELL HIM TO LEAVE THREE CANS!"

Maybe you haven't seen it rough, some of you folks. You're just young-sters. You know, you don't remember the Depression, some of you. But it make poverty look like a picnic. . . . Yeah, I helped poverty today. I ran over a tramp.

FIRST POLITICIAN

My great-great-grandfather Redd Foxx the 1st—don't laugh friends, I can trace my family back all the way back to Columbus—got a brother living in Cleveland. My great-great-grandfather was one of the first politicians in Mississippi. He ran for the border—and made it!

LOVE SONG

I've just composed a love song, it's called "I love you darling, if you never have any cash money in your pocket book during your entire life in this world. But I won't be with you, darling . . . If you never have any cash money in your pocket book during your entire life in this world or anywhere else you might go with nothing. 'Cause I don't need nobody to help me do bad. I can starve to death by myself, sugar. So try and forget me. But always remember, I love you more than any woman I've ever known in my life, 'cause that night I went up to your house and got drunk you didn't mess with none of the money that was left in my wallet 'cause you must have known, deep down in your heart, if I'd a come to and found some of my hard-earned money gone, I'd a went home and got a two-by-four that I been soaking in motor oil since 1953. And I'd a came back searching for you, and if I found you anywhere on earth with any of the money in your bag, I'd a took my greasy two-by-four, knowing that it would not break, bend, or splinter, and try to cave your skull in with it . . . cha-cha-cha."

PART FOUR

WHAT YOU SEE IS WHAT YOU GET . . .
CIVIL RIGHTS TO THE MILLENNIUM

This is the only country in the world where
a man can grow up in the ghetto,
go to the worst schools, be forced to
ride on the back of the bus,
then get paid $5,000 a week to tell about it.
                                        —Dick Gregory

America was embroiled in a full-scale social revolt by the early 1960s. In-spired by charismatic leaders like Martin Luther King, Jr., and Malcolm X, and organizations like the SCLC (Southern Christian Leadership Confer-ence), SNCC (Student Nonviolent Coordinating Committee), CORE (Con-gress of Racial Equality), and the NAACP, African Americans had taken to the street to protest and demonstrate in the fight for equal rights. The civil rights movement eventually broadened and led to demands for women's rights as well as gay rights, and black Americans assumed a more militant posture as their quest for equality moved from plea to demand. By the 1980s, America had experienced a radical facelift, and, as always, that change was emphatically echoed in the nation's humor. Nearly all taboos were chal-lenged, and little or nothing was considered too sacred. And nowhere was that shift more visibly reflected than in the outpouring of satirical, often brazenly risqué and critical, humor by black writers and comedians.

In literature, Ralph Ellison and even the usually grim social realist Richard Wright had begun gilding their fiction with folklore, satire, or candid depic-tions of black street humor. In the 1960s and '70s, they were followed by writers like Chester Himes, Charles Wright, Ishmael Reed, Cecil Brown, and others—many of whom made satire the central element in their fiction.

In general, street humor moved away from jokes about black deficien-

213

cies and turned decidedly toward politics, social injustice, and race. It also became less guarded—candidly citing whites and the government as the butt of jokes. It both prompted and reflected an overall acceptance of the profane, lurid, and sensational in popular American culture. The violence, bawdiness, and explicit language of so-called "Bad Nigger" tales and toasts were heightened and incorporated freely into not only the humor of streets but also stage, screen, and television comedy. By the 1990s, many Americans were expressing concern over the insistent vulgarity of the nation's comedy, and television shows like *Def Comedy Jam,* along with rap music lyrics, "shock jocks" like Howard Stern, and Hollywood's upsurge of "booty call" films were under fire. In general, subtly ironic or "polite" humor had been eclipsed and overshadowed by antiestablishment comedy that put a premium on grossness and shock.

The most dramatic shift in the evolution of African American comedy came with the upsurge in young, inventive standup comics who achieved mainstream success. Beginning with Dick Gregory's breakthrough in 1961, the last half of the century saw a stream of black comedians rise to fame and crossover popularity. Among them were Bill Cosby, a rediscovered Redd Foxx, Flip Wilson, Richard Pryor, Eddie Murphy, Whoopie Goldberg, Martin Lawrence, the Kings of Comedy, and Chris Rock. In some ways, the popularity of these performers muddied previous distinctions between black comedy and other ethnic forms. And by the twenty-first century, as America's pluralism and true multiethnic nature was more readily accepted, the once muted or silenced voices of black comedians had been unleashed to become a permanent, undeniable fixture in the nation's mainstream cultural expression. The selections that follow survey the best of the comedy that emerged during that explosive era.

@/@

FROM *NIGGER: AN AUTOBIOGRAPHY*

By Dick Gregory

As one of the first blacks to successfully work as standup comedians before white audiences, Dick Gregory took a calculated approach to the task. The following excerpt includes a description of the thought that went into that preparation and the opening to his monologue at the Playboy Club in 1961.

And then I began to figure it out. A white man will come to the Negro club, so hung up in this race problem, so nervous and afraid of the neighborhood and the people that anything the comic says to relieve his tension will absolutely knock him out. The harder that white man laughs, the harder he's saying, "I'm all right, boy, it's that Other Man downtown." That white customer in Negro club is filled with guilt and filled with fear. I've seen a white man in a Negro club jump up and say "Excuse me" to a Negro waitress who just spilled a drink in his lap. If that same thing happened in a white night club, that man would jump up, curse, and call his lawyer. . . .

This gave me something to think about, to work with. Some day I'm going to be performing where the bread is, in the big white night clubs. When I step up on the stage, in *their* neighborhood, some of them are going to feel sorry for me because I'm a Negro, and some of them are going to hate me because I'm a Negro. Those who feel sorry might laugh a little at first. But they can't respect someone they pity, and eventually they'll stop laughing. Those who hate me aren't going to laugh at all.

I've got to hit them fast, before they can think, just the way I hit kids back in St. Louis who picked on me because I was raggedy and had no Daddy. I've got to go up there as an individual first, a Negro second. I've got to be a colored funny man, not a funny colored man. I've got to act like a star who isn't sorry for himself—that way, they can't feel sorry for me. I've got to make jokes about myself, before I can make jokes about them and their society—that way, they can't hate me. Comedy is friendly relations.

"Just my luck, bought a suit with two pair of pants today . . . burnt a hole in the jacket."

That's making fun of yourself.

"They asked me to buy a lifetime membership in the NAACP, but I told them I'd pay a week at a time. Hell of a thing to buy a lifetime membership, wake up one morning and find the country's been integrated."

That makes fun of the whole situation.

Now they're listening to you, and you can blow a cloud of smoke at the audience and say:

"Wouldn't it be a hell of a thing if all this was burnt cork and you people were being tolerant for nothing?"

Now you've got them. No bitterness, no Uncle Tomming. We're all aware of what's going on here, aren't we, baby? Now you can settle down and talk about anything you want: Fall-out shelters, taxes, mothers-in-law, sit-ins, freedom riders, the Congo, H-bomb, the President, children. Stay away from sex, that's the big pitfall. If you use blue material only, you slip back into being that Negro stereotype comic. If you mix blue and topical satire that white customer, all hung up with the Negro sex mystique, is going to get uncomfortable.

In and out of Roberts [a black Chicago night club] in 1960, I had plenty of time to think. I realized that when I started working the white clubs, one of my big problems was going to be hecklers—especially in the beginning when I'd be in honky-tonk white clubs. Handling a heckler just right is very important to a comic. Unless you're well known as an insulting comedian you can't chop hecklers down too hard or the crowd will turn against you. Most hecklers are half drunk anyway, and you will lose a crowd if you get mean with a drunk. On the other hand, you have to put a heckler down. If a heckler gets the best of you, that crowd will start to feel sorry for you. I had worked it out pretty well in the Negro clubs. I'd put a drunken heckler down gently: "Man, I'd rather be your slave than your liver," and that would go even better in a white club. Whenever I got a vicious heckler, I could say something like: "Now how would you like it I came to *your* job and kicked the broom out of *your* hand?" That would work fine, too. But some day, somewhere, I'd be in a white club and somebody would get up and call me a nigger.

I worried about that. When that white man calls me nigger, every other white man in that club is going to feel embarrassed. The customers are going to tie in that uncomfortable feeling with that club—even after I'm gone—and the club owner knows this. He would rather keep me out of his club than take a chance on losing customers. It was the same thing when I got kicked in the mouth as a shoeshine boy—the bartender ran me out of the place, even though he felt sorry for me, because he couldn't afford to have the customers fight. But now I'm a man and I have to take care of myself. I need a fast comeback to that word. That split second is all the difference between going on with the show or letting the customers feel pity and a little resentment for the entertainer who got put down.

I used to make Lillian call me a nigger over the dining room table, and I'd practice the fast comeback. Somehow, I couldn't get it right. I'd always come back with something a little bitter, a little evil.

"Nigger."

"Maybe you'd feel more like a man if you lived down South and had a toilet with your name on it."

"No, Greg, that's not right at all."

I was lying around the house one night, watching television and feeling mad at the world. I'd been out of work for three weeks. The snow was so deep I hadn't even been outside the house for four days. Lil was sitting in a corner, so calm and peaceful, reading a book. There was no one else to pick on.

"Hey, Lil."

"Yes, Greg."

"What would you do if from here on in I started referring to you as a bitch?"

She jumped out of the chair. "I would simply ignore you."

I fell off the couch and started laughing so hard that old stomach of mine nearly burst. That was it. The quick sophisticated answer. Cool. No bitterness. The audience would never know I was mad and mean inside. And there would be no time to feel sorry for me. Now I'd get the come-back.

I got a chance a few weeks later, in a run-down neighborhood club on the outskirts of town. The customers were working-class white men, la-borers, factory hands, men whose only marks of dignity were the Negroes they bossed on the job and kept away from on weekends. It happened in the middle of the late show on the second night. Loud and clear.

"Nigger."

The audience froze, and I wheeled around without batting an eye. "You hear what that guy just called me? Roy Rogers' horse. He called me Trigger."

I had hit them so quick that they laughed, and they laughed hard be-cause that was what they really wanted to believe the guy had called me. But I had only bought myself a little time. There was an element in the house that really knew what he had called me. I had the crowd locked up with that fast comeback, so I took a few seconds to look them over and blow out some smoke.

"You know, my contract reads that every time I hear that word, I get fifty dollars more a night. I'm only making ten dollars a night, and I'd like to put the owner out of business. Will everybody in the room please stand up and yell nigger?"

They laughed and they clapped and I swung right back into my show. Afterwards, the owner came over and gave me twenty dollars and shook my hand and thanked me. I had made my test.

*

Good evening, ladies and gentleman. I understand there are a good many Southerners in the room tonight. I know the South very well. I spent twenty years there one night. . . .

It's dangerous for me to go back. You see, when I drink, I think I'm Pol-ish. One night I got so drunk I moved out of my own neighborhood. . . .

Last time I was down South I walked into this restaurant, and this white waitress came up to me and said: "We don't serve colored people here."

I said: "That's all right, I don't eat colored people. Bring me a whole fried chicken."

About this time these three cousins come in, you know the ones I mean, Klu, Kluck, and Klan, and they say: "Boy, we're givin' you fair warnin'. Anything you do to that chicken, we're gonna do to you." About then the waitress brought me my chicken. "Remember, boy, anything you do to that chicken, we're gonna do to you." So I put down my knife and fork, and I picked up that chicken, and I *kissed* it.

๛๛

THE BATTLE OF LITTLE ROCK

Folk

'Twas the first of September
   And all through the South,
Not a word could be heard
   From nobody's mouth.
The kiddies were ready
   For school the next day,
When all hell broke loose
   Down Arkansas way.
Ole Ike had give orders
   To mix up the schools,
But ole Faubus said, "Hold it!
   We ain't no fools.
If you know what's good
   You will stand back and listen,
'Cause we ain't gonna stand
   For no nigger mixin'."
He hollered an order
   Heard around the nation;
He called on the Guard
   To halt integration.
The Guard came runnin'
   And took up their stand,
To uphold up the right
   Of the good ol' Southland.
Ike didn't like this,
   So he ran to the phone

And called up ol' Faubus
　At his Arkansas home.
He said, "Meet me in Newport
　Tomorrow night,
'Cause the niggers and white
　Folks are fixin' to fight."
Faubus agreed
　And he hopped on his plane,
And left in a hurry
　In a drizzling rain.
Faubus returned home,
　But stuck to his rule:
"Ain't no nigger comin'
　To this here school."
So on come the troops
　In numbers yet bigger,
To make the white folks
　Go to school with a nigger.
Ol' Faubus was brave
　And made a gallant stand,
But he had to abide
　By the law of the land.

HEROES AIN'T BORN

"Lenny Bruce paved the way for all of us,"
Redd Foxx said at his comedy club during the sixties.
"Yeah," another comic said, "Lenny laid his
life down. He was a real hero."
"But you got to remember one thing," Foxx added.
"Heroes ain't born, they're cornered."

CADILLAC FLAMBÉ

By Ralph Ellison

It had been a fine spring day made even pleasanter by the lingering of the cherry blossoms and I had gone out before dawn with some married friends and their children on a bird-watching expedition. Afterwards we had sharpened our appetites for brunch with rounds of bloody marys and bull-shots. And after the beef bouillon ran out, our host, an ingenious man, had improvised a drink from chicken broth and vodka which he proclaimed the "chicken-shot." This was all very pleasant and after a few drinks my spirits were soaring. I was pleased with my friends, the brunch was excellent and varied—chili con carne, cornbread, and oysters Rockefeller, etc.—and I was pleased with my tally of birds. I had seen a bluebird, five rose-breasted grosbeaks, three painted buntings, seven gold-finches, and a rousing consort of mockingbirds. In fact, I had hated to leave.

Thus it was well into the afternoon when I found myself walking past the senator's estate. I still had my binoculars around my neck, and my tape recorder—which I had along to record bird songs—was slung over my shoulder. As I approached, the boulevard below the senator's estate was heavy with cars, with promenading lovers, dogs on leash, old men on canes, and laughing children, all enjoying the fine weather. I had paused to notice how the senator's lawn rises from the street level with a gradual and imperceptible elevation that makes the mansion, set far at the top, seem to float like a dream castle; an illusion intensified by the chicken-shots, but which the art editor of my paper informs me is the result of a trick copied from the landscape architects who designed the gardens of the Bellevedere Palace in Vienna. But be that as it may, I was about to pass on when a young couple blocked my path, and when I saw the young fellow point up the hill and say to his young blonde of a girl, "I bet you don't know who that is up there," I brought my binoculars into the play, and there, on the right-hand terrace of the mansion, I saw the senator.

Dressed in a chef's cap, apron, and huge asbestos gloves, he was armed with a long-tined fork which he flourished broadly as he entertained the notables for whom he was preparing a barbecue. These gentlemen and ladies were lounging in their chairs or standing about in groups sipping the tall iced drinks which two white-jacketed Filipino boys were serving. The senator was dividing his attention between the spareribs cooking in a large chrome grill-cart and displaying his great talent for mimicking his colleagues with such huge success that no one at the party was aware of what was swiftly approaching. And, in fact, neither was I.

I was about to pass on when a gleaming white Cadillac convertible, which had been moving slowly in the heavy traffic from the east, rolled abreast of me and suddenly blocked the path by climbing the curb and then continuing across the walk and onto the senator's lawn. The top was back and the driver, smiling as though in a parade, was a well dressed Negro man of about thirty-five, who sported the gleaming hair affected by their jazz musicians and prizefighters, and who sat behind the wheel with that engrossed, yet relaxed, almost ceremonial attention to form that was once to be observed only among the finest horsemen. So closely did the car brush past that I could have reached out with no effort and touched the rich ivory leather upholstery. A bull fiddle rested in the back of the car. I watched the man drive smoothly up the lawn until he was some seventy-five yards below the mansion, where he braked the machine and stepped out to stand waving toward the terrace, a gallant salutation grandly given.

At first, in my innocence, I placed the man as a musician, for there was, after all, the bull fiddle; then in swift succession I thought him a chauffeur for one of the guests, a driver for a news or fashion magazine or an advertising agency or television network. For I quickly realized that a musician wouldn't have been asked to perform at the spot where the car was stopped, and that since he was alone, it was unlikely that anyone, not even the senator, would have hired a musician to play serenades on a bull fiddle. So next I decided that the man had either been sent with equipment to be used in covering the festivities taking place on the terrace, or that he had driven the car over to be photographed against the luxurious background. The waving I interpreted as the expression of simple-minded high spirits aroused by the driver's pleasure in piloting such a luxurious automobile, the simple exuberance of a Negro allowed a role in what he considered an important public spectacle. At any rate, by now a small crowd had gathered and had begun to watch bemusedly.

Since it was widely known that the senator is a master of the new political technology, who ignores no medium and wastes no opportunity for keeping his image ever in the public's eye, I wasn't disturbed when I saw the driver walk to the trunk and begin to remove several red objects of a certain size and place them on the grass. I wasn't using my binoculars now and thought these were small equipment cases. Unfortunately, I was mistaken.

For now, having finished unpacking, the driver stepped back behind the wheel, and suddenly I could see the top rising from its place of concealment to soar into place like the wing of some great, slow, graceful bird. Stepping out again, he picked up one of the cases—now suddenly transformed into the type of can which during the war was sometimes used to transport high-octane gasoline in Liberty ships (a highly dangerous cargo for those round bottoms and the men who shipped them)—and leaning carefully forward, began emptying its contents upon the shining chariot.

And thus, I thought, *is gilded an eight-valved, three-hundred-and-fifty-horsepowered air-conditioned lily!*

For so accustomed have we Americans become to the tricks, the shenanigans, and frauds of advertising, so adjusted to the contrived fantasies of commerce—indeed, to pseudo-events of all kinds—that I thought that the car was being drenched with a special liquid which would make it more alluring for a series of commercial photographs.

Indeed, I looked up the crowded boulevard behind me, listening for the horn of a second car or station wagon which would bring the familiar load of pretty models, harassed editors, nervous wardrobe mistresses, and elegant fashion photographers who would convert the car, the clothes, and the senator's elegant home, into a photographic rite of spring.

And with the driver there to remind me, I even expected a few ragged colored street urchins to be brought along to form a poignant but realistic contrast to the luxurious costumes and high-fashion surroundings: an echo of the somber iconography in which the crucified Christ is flanked by a repentant and an unrepentant thief, or that in which the three Wise Eastern Kings bear their rich gifts before the humble stable of Bethlehem.

But now reality was moving too fast for the completion of this foray into the metamorphosis of religious symbolism. Using my binoculars for a closer view, I could see the driver take a small spherical object from the trunk of the car and a fuzzy tennis ball popped into focus against the dark smoothness of his fingers. This was joined by a long wooden object which he held like a conductor's baton and began forcing against the ball until it was pierced. This provided the ball with a slender handle which he tested delicately for balance, drenched with liquid, and placed carefully behind the left fin of the car.

Reaching into the back seat now, he came up with a bass fiddle bow upon which he accidently [sic] spilled the liquid, and I could see drops of fluid roping from the horsehairs and falling with an iridescent spray into the sunlight. Facing us now, he proceeded to tighten the horsehairs, working methodically, very slowly, with his head gleaming in the sunlight and beads of sweat standing over his brow.

As I watched, I became aware of the swift gathering of a crowd around me, people asking puzzled questions, and a certain tension, as during the start of a concert, was building. And I had just thought, *And now he'll bring out the fiddle,* when he opened the door and hauled it out, carrying it with the dripping bow swinging from his right hand, up the hill some thirty feet above the car, and placed it lovingly on the grass. A gentle wind started to blow now, and I swept my glasses past his gleaming head to the mansion, and as I screwed the focus to infinity, I could see several figures spring suddenly from the shadows on the shaded terrace of the mansion's far wing. They were looking on like the spectators of a minor disturbance at a dull baseball game. Then a large woman grasped that something was out of order and I could see her mouth come open and her eyes blaze as she called out soundlessly, "Hey, you down there!" Then the driver's head cut into my field of vision and I took down the glasses and watched him moving, broad-shouldered and jaunty, up the hill to where he'd left the fiddle. For a moment he stood with his head back, his white jacket taut across his shoulders, looking toward the terrace. He waved then, and shouted words that escaped me. Then, facing the machine, he took something from his pocket and I saw him touch the flame of a cigarette lighter to the tennis ball and begin blowing gently upon it; then, waving it about like a child twirling a Fourth of July sparkler, he watched it sputter into a small blue ball of flame.

I tried, indeed I anticipated what was coming next, but I simply could not accept it! The Negro was twirling the ball on that long, black tipped wooden needle—the kind used for knitting heavy sweaters—holding it between his thumb and fingers in the manner of a fire-eater at a circus, and I couldn't have been more surprised if he had thrown back his head and plunged the flame down his throat than by what came next. Through the glasses now I could see sweat beading out beneath his scalp line and on the flesh above the stiff hairs of his moustache as he grinned broadly and took up the fiddle bow, and before I could move he had shot his improvised, flame-tipped arrow onto the cloth top of the convertible.

"Why that black son of the devil!" someone shouted, and I had the impression of a wall of heat springing from the grass before me. Then the flames erupted with a stunning blue roar that sent the spectators scattering. People were shouting now, and through the blue flames before me I could see the senator and his guests running from the terrace to halt at the top of the lawn, looking down, while behind me there were screams, the grinding of brakes, the thunder of foot-falls as the promenaders broke in a great spontaneous wave up the grassy slope, then sensing the danger of exploding gasoline, receded hurriedly to a safer distance below, their screams and curses ringing above the roar of the flames.

How, oh, how, I wished for a cinema camera to synchronize with my tape recorder!—which automatically I now brought into the play as heavy fumes of alcohol and gasoline, those defining spirits of our age, filled the air. There before me unfolding in *tableau vivant* was surely the most unexpected picture in the year: in the foreground at the bottom of the slope, a rough semicircle of outraged faces; in the mid-foreground, up the gentle rise of the lawn, the white convertible shooting into the springtime air a radiance of intense blue flame like that of a welder's torch or perhaps of a huge fowl being flambéed in choice cognac; then on the rise above, distorted by heat and flame, the dark-skinned, white-suited driver, standing with his gleaming face expressive of high excitement as he watched the effect of his deed. Then, rising high in the background atop the grassy hill, the white-capped senator surrounded by his noble guests—all caught in postures eloquent of surprise, shock, or indignation.

The air was filled with an overpowering smell of wood alcohol, which, as the leaping red and blue flames took firm hold, mingled with the odor of burning paint and leather. I became aware of the fact that the screaming had suddenly faded now, and I could hear the swoosh-pop-crackle-and-hiss of the fire. And with the gaily dressed crowd become silent, it was as though I were alone, isolated, observing a conflagration produced by a stroke of lightening flashed out of a clear blue springtime sky. We watched with that sense of awe similar to that with which medieval crowds must have observed the burning of a great cathedral. We were stunned by the sacrificial act and, indeed, it was as though we had become the unwilling participants in a primitive ceremony requiring the sacrifice of a beautiful object in appeasement of some terrifying and long-dormant spirit, which the black man in the white suit was summoning from a long, black sleep. And as we watched, our faces strained as though in anticipation of the spirit's materialization from the fiery metamorphosis of the white machine, a spirit that I was afraid, whatever the form in which it appeared, would be powerfully good or powerfully evil, and absolutely out of place here and now in Washington. It was, as I say, uncanny. The whole afternoon seemed to float, and when I looked again to the top of the hill the people there appeared to move in slow motion through watery waves of heat. Then I saw the senator, with chef cap awry, raising his asbestos gloves above his head and beginning to shout. And it was then that the driver, the firebrand, went into action.

Till now, looking like the chief celebrant of an outlandish rite, he had held firmly to his middle-ground; too dangerously near the flaming convertible for anyone not protected by asbestos suiting to risk laying hands upon him, yet far enough away to highlight his human vulnerability to fire. But now as I watched him move to the left of the flames to a point allowing him an uncluttered view of the crowd, his white suit reflecting the flames, he was briefly obscured by a sudden swirl of smoke, and it was during this brief interval that I heard the voice.

Strong and hoarse and typically Negro in quality, it seemed to issue with eerie clarity from the fire itself. Then I was struggling within myself for the reporter's dedicated objectivity and holding my microphone forward as he raised both arms above his head, his long limber fingers widespread as he waved toward us.

"Ladies and gentlemen," he said, "please don't be disturbed! I don't mean you any harm, and if you'll just cool it a minute I'll tell you what this is all about . . . "

He paused and the senator's voice could be heard angrily in the background.

"Never mind that joker up there on top of the hill," the driver said. "You can listen to him when I get through. He's had too much free speech anyway. Now it's *my* turn."

And at this a man at the other end of the crowd shouted angrily and tried to break up the hill. He was grabbed by two men and an hysterical, dark-haired woman wearing a well-filled chemise-style dress, who slipped to the ground holding a leg, shouting, "No, Fleetwood. No! That crazy nigger will kill you!"

The arsonist watched with blank-faced calm as the man was dragged protesting back into the crowd. Then a shift in the breeze whipped smoke down upon us and gave rise to a flurry of coughing.

"Now believe me," the arsonist continued, "I know that it's very, very hard for you folks to look at what I'm doing and not be disturbed, because for you it's a crime and a sin"

He laughed, swinging his fiddle bow in a shining arc as the crowd watched him fixedly.

"That's because you know that most folks can't afford to own one of these Caddies. Not even good, hard-working folks, no matter what the pictures in the papers and magazines say. So deep down it makes you feel some larceny. You feel that it's unfair that everybody who's willing to work hard can't have one for himself. That's right! And you feel that in order to get one it's OK for a man to lie and cheat and steal—yeah, even swindle his own mother *if* she's got the cash. That's the difference between what you *say* you believe and the way you *act* if you get the chance. Oh yes, because words is words, but life is hard and earnest and these here Caddies is way, way out of this world!"

Pausing, he loosened the knot in his blue and white tie so that it hung down the front of his jacket in a large loop, then wiped his brow with a blue silk handkerchief.

"I don't mean to insult you," he said, bending toward us now, the fiddle bow resting across his knee, "I'm just reminding you of the facts. Because I can see in your eyes that it's going to cost me more to get *rid* of this Caddy the way I have to do it than it cost me to get it. I don't rightly know what the price will be, but I know that when you people get scaired [sic] and shook up, you get violent.—No, wait a minute . . ." He shook his head. "That's not how I meant to say it. I'm sorry. I apologize.

"Listen, here it is: This *morning,*" he shouted now, stabbing his bow toward the mansion with angry emphasis. "This morning that fellow Senator *Sunraider* up there, *he* started it when he shot off his mouth over the *radio.* That's what this is all about! I realized that things had gotten out of *control.* I realized all of a sudden that the man was *messing*... with ... my *Cadillac,* and ladies and gentlemen, that's serious as all *hell* ...

"Listen to me, y'all: A little while ago I was romping past *Richmond,* feeling fine. I had played myself three hundred and seventy-five dollars and thirty-three cents worth of gigs down in Chattanooga, and I was headed home to *Harlem* as straight as I could go. I wasn't bothering any *body.* I didn't even mean to stop by here, because this town has a way of making a man feel like he's living in a fool's *paradise.* When I'm *here* I never stop thinking about the difference between what it *is* and what it's *supposed* to be. In fact, I have the feeling that somebody put the *Indian* sign on this town a long, long time ago, and I don't want to be around when it takes effect. So, like I say, I wasn't even thinking about this town. I was rolling past Richmond and those whitewalls were slapping those concrete slabs and I was rolling and the wind was feeling fine on my face—and that's when I made my sad mistake. Ladies and gentlemen, I turned on the radio. I had nothing against anybody. I was just hoping to hear some Dinah, or Duke, or Hawk so that I could study their phrasing and improve my style and enjoy myself.—But what do I get? I'll tell you what I got—"

He dropped his shoulders with a sudden violent twist as his index finger jabbed toward the terrace behind him, bellowing, "I GOT THAT NO GOOD, NOWHERE SENATOR SUNRAIDER! THAT'S WHAT I GOT! AND WHAT WAS HE DOING? HE WAS TRYING TO GET THE UNITED STATES GOVERNMENT TO MESS WITH MY CADILLAC! AND WHAT'S MORE, HE WAS CALLING MY CADDY A 'COON CAGE.'

"Ladies and gentlemen, I couldn't believe my *ears.* I don't know that senator and I know he doesn't know me from old *Bodiddly.* But just the same, there he is, talking straight to me and there was no use of my trying to dodge. Because I do live in Harlem and I do lo-mo-sho drive a Cadillac. So I had to sit there and take it like a little man. There he was, a United States SENATOR, coming through my own radio telling me what I ought to be driving, and recommending to the United States Senate and the whole country that the name of my car be changed simply because *I,* me, LeeWillie Minifees, was driving it!

"It made me feel faint. It upset my mind like a midnight telegram!

"I said to myself, 'LeeWillie, what on earth is this man *talking* about? Here you been thinking you had it *made.* You been thinking you were as free as a bird—even though a black bird. That good-rolling Jersey Turnpike is up ahead to get you home.—And now here comes this senator putting you in a cage! What in the world is going on?'

"I got so nervous that all at once my foot weighed ninety-nine pounds, and before I knew it was doing *seventy-five.* I was breaking the law! I guess I was really trying to get away from that voice and what the man had said. But I was rolling and I was listening. I couldn't *help* myself. What I was hearing was going against my whole heart and soul, but I was listening *anyway.* And what I heard was beginning to make me see things in a new light. Yes, and that new light was making my eyeballs ache. And all the time Senator Sunraider up in the Senate was calling my car a 'coon cage.'

"So I looked around and I saw all that fine ivory leather there. I looked at the steel and at the chrome. I looked through the windshield and saw the road unfolding and the houses and the trees was flashing by. I looked at the top and I touched the button and let it go back to see if that awful feeling would leave me. But it wouldn't leave. The *air* was hitting my face and the *sun* was on my head and I was feeling that good old familiar feeling of *flying*—but ladies and gentlemen, it was no longer the same! Oh, no—because I could still hear that senator playing the *dozens* with my Cadillac!

"And just then, ladies and gentlemen, I found myself rolling toward an old man who reminded me of my granddaddy by the way he was walking beside the highway behind a plow hitched to an old, white-muzzled Missouri mule. And when that old man looked up and saw me he waved. And I looked back through the mirror as I shot past him and I could see him open his mouth and say something like, 'Go on, fool!' Then him and that mule was gone even from the mirror and I was rolling on.

"An then, ladies and gentlemen, in a twinkling of an eye it struck me. A voice said to me, 'LeeWillie, that old man is right: you are a fool. And that doggone Senator Sunraider is right, LeeWillie, you are a fool in a coon cage!'

"I tell you, ladies and gentlemen, that old man and his mule both were talking to me. I said, 'What do you mean about his being right?' And they said, 'LeeWillie, look who he *is,*' and I said, 'I *know* who he is,' and they said, 'Well, LeeWillie, if a man like that, in the position he's in, can think the way he doin, then LeeWillie, you have GOT to be wrong!'

"So I said, 'Thinking like that is why you've still got that mule in your lap,' man. 'I worked hard to get the money to buy this Caddy,' and he said, *'Money?* LeeWillie, can't you see that it ain't no longer a matter of money? Can't you see it's done gone way past the question of money? Now it's a question of whether you can afford it in terms *other than money.'*

"And I said, 'Man, what are you talking about, "terms other than money," '
and he said, 'LeeWillie, even this damn mule knows that if a man like that
feels the way he's talking and can say it right over the radio and the T.V., and
from the place where he's saying it—there's got to be something drastically
wrong with you for even wanting one. Son, the man's done made it mean
something different. All you wanted was to have a pretty automobile, but
fool, he done changed the Rules on you!'

"So against myself, ladies and gentlemen, I was forced to *agree* with the
old man and the mule. That senator up there wasn't simply degrading my
Caddy. That wasn't the *point.* It's that he would low-rate a thing so truly
fine as a *Cadillac* just in order to degrade *me* and my *people.* He was accusing *me* of lowering the value of the auto, when all I ever wanted was
the very best!

"Oh, it hurt me to the quick, and right then and there I had me a rolling
revelation. The *scales* dropped from my eyes. I had been BLIND, but the
Senator up there on that hill was making me SEE. He was making me see
some things I didn't *want* to see! I'd thought I was dressed real FINE, but I
was as naked as a jaybird sitting on a limb in the drifting snow. I THOUGHT
I was rolling past *Richmond,* but I was really trapped in a COON CAGE, running on one of those little TREADMILLS like a SQUIRREL or a HAMSTER.
So now my EYEBALLS were aching. My head was in such whirl that I shot
the car up to ninety, and all I could see up ahead was the road getting NAR-
ROW. It was getting as narrow as the eye of a NEEDLE, and the needle
looked like the Washington MONUMENT lying down. Yes, and I was trying to thread that Caddy straight through that eye and I didn't care if I
made it or not. But while I managed to get that Caddy through I just could-
n't thread that COON CAGE because it was like a two-ton knot tied in a
piece of fine silk thread. The sweat was pouring off me now, ladies and gentlemen, and my brain was on fire, so I pulled off the highway and asked
myself some questions, and I got myself some answers. It went this way:

"'LeeWillie, who put you in this cage?'

"'You put your own self in there,' a voice inside me said.

"'But I paid for it, it's mine. I own it . . .' I said.

"'Oh, no, LeeWillie,' the voice said, 'what you mean is that it owns *you,*
that's why you're *in* the cage. *Admit* it, daddy; you have been NAMED. Senator Sunraider has put the bad-mouth, the NASTY mouth on you and now
your Cadillac ain't no Caddy anymore! Let's face it; LeeWillie, from now on
everytime you sit behind this wheel you're going to feel those RINGS
shooting round and round your TAIL and one of those little black COON'S
masks is going to settle down over your FACE, and the folks standing on

the streets and hanging out the windows will sing out, "HEY! THERE GOES MISTER COON AND HIS COON CAGE!" That's right LeeWillie! And all those little husky-voiced colored CHILDREN playing in the gutters will point at you and say, "THERE GOES MISTAH GOON AND HIS GOON GAGE"—and that will be right in Harlem!'

"And that did it, ladies and gentlemen, that was the capper, and THAT'S why I'm here!

"Right then and there, beside the *highway,* I made my decision. I rolled that Caddy, I made a U-turn and I stopped only long enough to get some of that good white wood *alcohol* and good *white* gasoline, and then I headed straight here. So while some of you are upset, you can see that you don't have to be afraid because LeeWillie means nobody any harm.

"I am here, ladies and gentlemen, to make the senator a present. Yes, sir and yes, mam, and it's Sunday and I'm told that *confession* is good for the *soul.*—So Mister Senator," he said, turning toward the terrace above, "this is my public testimony to my coming over to your way of thinking. This is my surrender of the Coon Cage Eight! You have unconverted me from the convertible. In fact, I'm giving it to you, Senator Sunraider, and it is truly mine to give. I hope all my people will do likewise. Because after your speech they ought to run whenever they *look* at one of these. They ought to make for the bomb shelters whenever one comes close to the curb. So I, me, LeeWillie Minifees, am setting an example and here it is. You can HAVE it, Mister Senator. I don't WANT it. Thank you KINDLY and MUCH obliged . . ."

He paused, looking toward the terrace, and at this point I saw a great burst of flame which sent the crowd scurrying backward down the hill, and the white-suited firebrand went into an ecstatic chant, waving his violin bow, shaking his gleaming head and stamping his foot.

"Listen to me Senator: I don't want no JET! (stamp!) But thank you kindly.

"I don't want no FORD! (stamp!)

"Neither do I want a RAMBLER! (stamp!)

"I don't want no NINETY-EIGHT! (stamp!)

"Ditto the THUNDERBIRD! (stamp!)

"Yes, and keep those CHEVYS and CHRYSLERS away from me—do you (stamp!) *hear* me, Senator?

"YOU HAVE TAKEN THE BEST," he boomed, "SO, DAMMIT, TAKE ALL THE REST! Take ALL the rest!

"In fact, now I don't want anything you think is too good for me and my people. Because, just as that old man and the mule said, if a man in your position is against our having them, then there must be something

WRONG in our *wanting* them. So to keep you happy, I, me, LeeWillie
Minifees, am prepared to WALK. I'm ordering me some club-footed, pigeon-
toed SPACE SHOES. I'd rather crawl or FLY. I'd rather save my money and
wait until the A-RABS make a car. The Zulus even. Even the ESKIMOS! Oh,
I'll walk and wait. I'll grab me a GREYHOUND or a FREIGHT! So you can
have my Coon Cage, fare thee well!

"Take the TAIL FINS and the WHITEWALLS. Help yourself to the poor
raped RADIO. ENJOY the automatic dimmer and the power brakes. ROLL,
Mister Senator, with the fluid DRIVE. Breathe that air-conditioned AIR.
There's never been a Caddy like this one and I want you to HAVE IT. Take
my scientific dreamboat and enjoy that good ole GRACIOUS LIVING! The
key's in the ignition and the REGISTRATION'S in the GLOVE compart-
ment! And thank you KINDLY for freeing me from the Coon Cage. Because
before I'd be in a CAGE, I'll be buried in my GRAVE—Oh! Oh!"

He broke off, listening; and I became aware of the shrilling of approaching sirens. Then he was addressing the crowd again.

"I knew," he called down with a grin, "that THOSE would be coming soon.
Because they ALWAYS come when you don't NEED them. Therefore, I only
hope that the senator will beat it on down here and accept his gift before
they arrive. And in the meantime, I want ALL you ladies and gentlemen to
join LeeWillie in singing 'God Bless America' so that all this won't be in vain.

"I want you to understand that that was a damned GOOD Caddy and I
loved her DEARLY. That's why you don't have to worry about me. I'm doing fine. Everything is copacetic. Because, remember, nothing make a man
feel better than giving AWAY something, than SACRIFICING something,
that he dearly LOVES!"

And then, most outrageous of all, he threw back his head and actually sang
a few bars before the noise of the short-circuited horn set the flaming car to
wailing like some great prehistoric animal heard in the throes of its dying.

Behind him now, high on the terrace, the senator and his guests were
shouting, but on the arsonist sang, and the effect on the crowd was mad-
dening. Perhaps because from the pleasurable anticipation of watching the
beginning of a clever advertising stunt, they had been thrown into a panic
by the deliberate burning, the bizarre immolation of the automobile. And
now with a dawning of awareness they perceived that they had been
forced to witness (and who could turn away?) a crude and most portentous
political gesture.

So suddenly they broke past me, dashing up the hill in moblike fury, and
it was most fortunate for Minifees that his duet with the expiring Cadillac
was interrupted by members of the police and fire departments, who, ar-

riving at this moment, threw a flying wedge between the flaming machine and the mob. Through the noisy action I could see him there, looming prominently in his white suit, a mocking smile flickering on his sweaty face, as the action whirled toward where he imperturbably stood his ground, still singing against the doleful wailing of the car.

He was still singing, his wrists coolly extended now in anticipation of handcuffs—when struck by a veritable football squad of asbestos-garbed policemen and swept, tumbling, in a wild tangle of arms and legs, down the slope to where I stood. It was then I noted that he wore expensive black alligator shoes.

And now, while the crowd roared its approval, I watched as LeeWillie Minifees was pinned down, lashed into a straitjacket and led toward a police car. Up the hill two policemen were running laboredly toward where the senator stood, silently observing. About me there was much shouting and shoving as some of the crowd attempted to follow the trussed-up and still grinning arsonist but were beaten back by the police.

It was unbelievably wild. Some continued to shout threats in their outrage and frustration, while others, both men and women, filled the air with a strangely brokenhearted and forlorn sound of weeping, and the officers found it difficult to disperse them. In fact, they continued to mill angrily about even as firemen in asbestos suits broke through, dragging hoses from a roaring pumper truck and sprayed the flaming car with a foamy chemical, which left it looking like the offspring of some strange animal brought so traumatically and precipitantly to life that it wailed and sputtered in protest, both against the circumstances of its debut into the world and the foaming presence of its still-clinging afterbirth . . .

And what had triggered it? How had the senator sparked this weird conflagration? Why, with a joke! The day before, while demanding larger appropriations for certain scientific research projects that would be of great benefit to our electronics and communications industries, and of great importance to the nation as a whole, the senator had aroused the opposition of a liberal senator from New York who had complained, in passing, of what he termed the extreme vapidness of our recent automobile designs, their lack of adequate safety devices, and of the slackness of our quality-control standards and procedures. Well, it was in defending the automobile industry that the senator passed the remark that triggered LeeWillie Minifee's bizarre reply.

In his rebuttal—the committee session was televised and aired over radio networks—the Senator insisted that not only were our cars the best in the world, the most beautiful and efficiently designed, but that, in fact, his opponent's remarks were a gratuitous slander. Because, he asserted, the only ground which he could see for complaint lay in the circumstance that a certain make of luxury automobile had become so outrageously popular in the nation's Harlems—the archetype of which is included in his opponents district—that he found it embarrassing to own one. And then with a face most serious in its composure he went on to state:

"We have reached a sad state of affairs, gentlemen, wherein this fine product of American skill and initiative has become so common in Harlem that much of its initial value has been sorely compromised. Indeed, I am led to suggest, and quite seriously, that legislation be drawn up to rename it the 'Coon Cage Eight.' And not at all because of its eight, super-efficient cylinders, nor because of the lean, springing strength and beauty of its general outlines. Not at all, but because it has now become such a common sight to see eight or more of our darker brethren crowded together enjoying its power, its beauty, its neo-pagan comfort, while weaving recklessly through the streets of our great cities and along our super highways. In fact, gentlemen, I was run off the road, forced into a ditch by such a power-drunk group just the other day. It is enough to make a citizen feel alienated from his own times, from the abiding values and recent developments within his own beloved nation.

"And yet, we continue to hear complaints to the effect that these constituents of our worthy colleague are ill-housed, ill-clothed, ill-equipped and under-*treaded!* But, gentlemen, I say to you in all sincerity: Look into the streets! Look at the statistics for automobile sales! And I don't mean the economy cars, but our most expensive luxury machines. Look and see who is purchasing them! Give your attention to who it is that is creating the scarcity and removing these superb machines from the reach of those for whom they were intended! With so many of these good things, what, pray, do those people desire—is it a jet plane on every Harlem rooftop?"

Now for Senator Sunraider that had been mild and far short of his usual maliciousness. And while it aroused some slight amusement and brought replies of false indignation from some of his opponents, it was edited out, as is frequently the case, when the speech appeared in the *Congressional Record* and in the press. But who could have predicted that Senator Sunraider would have brought on LeeWillie Minifee's wild gesture? Perhaps he had been putting on an act, creating a happening, as they say, though I doubted it. There was something more personal behind it. Without question, the senator's remarks were in extremely bad taste, but to cap the joke by burning an expensive car seemed so extreme a reply as to be almost metaphysical.

And yet, I reminded myself, it might simply be a case of overreacting expressed in true Negro abandon, an extreme gesture springing from the frustration of having no adequate means of replying, or making himself heard above the majestic roar of a senator. There was, of course, the recent incident involving a black man suffering from an impacted wisdom tooth who had been so maddened by the blaring of a moisture-shorted automobile horn which had blasted his sleep about three o'clock of an icy morning, that he ran out into the street clothed only in an old-fashioned nightshirt and blasted the hood of the offending automobile with both barrels of a twelve-gauge over-and-under-shotgun.

But while toothaches often lead to such extreme acts—and once in a while to suicide—LeeWillie Minifees had apparently been in no pain—or at least not in any *physical* pain. And on the surface at least his speech had been projected clearly enough (allowing for the necessity to shout) and he had been smiling when they led him away. What would be his fate? I wondered; and where had they taken him? I would have to find him and question him, for his action had begun to sound in my mind with disturbing overtones which had hardly been meaningful. Rather they had been like the brief interruption one sometimes hears while listening to an F.M. broadcast of the musical *Oklahoma!*, say, with original cast, when the signals fades and a program of quite different mood from a different wave length breaks through. It had happened but then a blast of laughter had restored us automatically to our chosen frequency.

◎◎

FROM *THE WIG*

By Charles Wright

In The Wig, *Charles Wright depicted the comic exploits of a black man who, after transforming his appearance by straightening his hair, ventures into America's Great Society convinced that he would be accepted, that the "black clouds would soon recede," and he could now "shake his head triumphantly like any white boy."*

I took a handful of Silky Smooth and began massaging my scalp. Then, just to be on the safe side, I added Precautionary Oil, thick, odorless, indigenous to the Georgia swamps. Massaging deftly, I remembered that old-fashioned hair aids were mixed with yak dung and lye. They burned the scalp and if the stuff got in your eye you could go blind from it. One thing was certain: you combed out scabs of dried blood for a month. But a compassionate Northern Senator had the hair aids outlawed. Said he, in ringing historic words: "Mr. Chairman, I offer an amendment to this great Spade tragedy! These people are real Americans and we should outlaw all hair aids that makes them lose their vibrations and éclat." Silky Smooth (using a formula perfected by a Lapp tribe in Karasjok, Norway) posed no problems.

Yes indeed. A wild excitement engulfed me. My mirrored image reflected, in an occult fashion, a magnificent future. I hadn't felt so good since discovering last year that I actually disliked watermelon.

But the next step was the most difficult act of my life. I had to wait five minutes until the pomade penetrated, stiffened, evaporated. Five minutes of suffering. I stood tall like the great-great-grandson of slaves, sharecroppers, Old World royalty. Tall, like a storm trooper, like an Honor Scout. Yes! I'd stalk that druggist if the experiment failed. Lord—it couldn't fail! I'm Walter Mitty's target-colored stepson. Sweet dreams zipped through my mind. A politician had prophesied that it was extremely likely a Negro would be elected President of the United States in the year 2,000. Being realistic, I could just picture myself as Chairman of the Handyman's Union, addressing the Committee on Foreign Relations and then being castrated. At least I'd no longer have to phone Mr. Fishback, the necrophiliac funeral director, each time I went downtown. What a relief that would be. The dimes I'd save!

While the stuff dried I thought of Mr. Fishback. Sweet Daddy Fish, Nonnie I called him, but Nonnie liked to put the bad mouth on people. I owed Mr. Fishback for my latest (was it counterfeit?) Credit Card.

Beams of the morning sun danced through the ice-cube-size window as I began to wash the pomade out of my hair. I groaned powerfully. The texture of my hair *had* changed. Before reaching for a towel, I couldn't resist looking in the cracked mirror while milky-colored water ran down my flushed face.

Hail Caesar and all dead Cotton Queens! Who the hell ever said only a rake could get through those gossamer locks?

Indeed! I prayed. I laughed. I shook my head and watched each silky curl fall into place. I had only one regret: I wished there were a little wind blowing, one just strong enough to give me a wind-swept look; then I'd be able to toss a nonchalant lock from my forehead. I'd been practicing a week and had the bit down solid.

You could borrow an electric fan, I was telling myself, and just then I heard Nonnie Swift scream.

"Help! Won't somebody please help me?" The voice came from the hall.

Let the brandy bitch scream her head off, I thought. A Creole from New Orleans, indeed. If there's anyone in this building with Creole blood, it's me.

"I'm dying. Please help a dying widow . . ." the voice wailed from the hall.

I unwillingly turned from the mirror. The Wig was perfection. Four dollars and six cents' worth of sheer art. The sacrifice had been worth it. I was reborn, purified, anointed, beautified.

"I'm just a poor helpless widow . . ."

Would the bitch never shut up? With the majesty of a witch doctor, I went to Nonnie Swift's rescue.

*

Dammit! The doorbell buzzed, a desperate animal-like clawing, funny little noises, like a half-assed drummer trying to keep time.

Upset, I went and flung the open the door.

Little Jimmie Wishbone stood there. A dusty felt hat pulled down over his ears. Cracked dark glasses obscured his sultry eyes. The ragged army poncho was dashing and faintly sinister, like a CIA playboy.

"Brroudder! Ain't you cracked up yet?" Little Jimmie shouted. "I thought I'd see you over thar."

I stiffened but gestured warmly "Come in, man. When you get out?"

"Yestiddy, 'bout two o'clock."

"Good to see you, man."

Grunting like a hot detective, Little Jimmie surveyed the room. He flipped up the newspaper window shade and looked out on the twenty feet of rubbish in the backyard. He jerked open the closet curtains. Satisfied, he pulled a half gallon of Summertime wine and Mr. Charlie's *Lucky Dream Book* from under the poncho and put them on the orange-crate coffee table. "You're looking good," I said, hoping I didn't sound as if I were fishing for a compliment.

"Am I?" Little Jimmie wanted to know.

Sadly, I watched him ease down on the sofa bed, like a king in exile.

Aged twenty-eight, Little Wishbone was a has-been, a former movie star. *Adios* to fourteen Cadillacs, to an interest in a nationwide cathouse corporation. He had been the "fat" owner of seven narcotic nightclubs, had dined at The White House. Honored at a Blue Room homecoming reception after successfully touring the deep South *and* South Africa. At the cold cornbread and molasses breakfast, Congressmen had sung "He's a Jolly Good Nigger." Later, they had presented him with a medal, gold-plated, the size of a silver dollar, carved with the figure of a naked black man swinging from a pecan tree.

I had to hold back the tears. Could that have been only two years ago?

I wondered. I got a couple of goblets from under the dripping radiator. Mercy—depression multiplies like cockroaches.

I couldn't look at him, so I pretended to polish the goblets with a Kleenex, remembering.

The NAACP had accused Hollywood of deliberately presenting a false image of the American Negro. After the scandal subsided, Little Jimmie had the privilege of watching his own funeral. The government repossessed his assets. The Attorney General wanted him jailed for subversion but he pleaded insanity. Then his wife left him for a rock 'n' roll bass-baritone and that did send him crazy. Little Jimmie had spent the past year commuting between Kings County Hospital and Harlem, but he had endured. The famed lamb's-wool hair had turned white. Little Jimmie's gold teeth had turned purple. He was slowly dying. Time and time again the doctors had explained to him that Negroes did not have bleeding ulcers nor did they need sleeping pills. American Negroes, they explained, were free as birds and animals in a rich green forest. Childlike creatures, their minds ran the gamut from Yes Sir to No Sir. There was simply no occasion for ulcers.

I poured a goblet of Summertime, Little Jimmie drank straight from the bottle.

"What's wrong?" he growled.

"Nothing, man."

"Something must be wrong," he insisted.

"What makes you say that?"

"'Cause something is wrong. You ain't never drunk out of no glass like that before."

I blushed. "Oh, you mean . . ."

"No. I don't mean. Hell. I got eyes. What you trying to prove?"

"You don't understand," I said sharply.

"Whacha trying to prove?"

"Whacha see? What's the impression? Slice the tater, split the pea?"

In exactly one minute and three seconds, Little Jimmie had swallowed half of the wine. "Split the pea—I is with thee. What's the haps? Come clean. I is Little Jimmie Wishbone from Aukinsaw."

Brotherly love engulfed us. I drank from the bottle.

*

We had killed Summertime. Little Jimmie kept his eyes fastened on the empty wine bottle. He looked like an angelic little boy who had been kicked out of his orphanage for failing to take part in group masturbation.

"You look down," I said. "You need some nooky."

Little Jimmie signed. He looked very tired. "Nooky? Dem white folks messed wit yo boy. Shot all dem currents through me. Y'all took way my libin', I said. And they jest kept shooting electricity. It was even popping out of my ears. I took it like a champ. Kinda scared dem, too. I heard one of dem say: 'He's immune. It's the result of perpetual broilization. Nothing will ever kill a Nigger like this.' I did my buck dance and the doctor said, 'They got magic in their feet.' Man, I danced into the village. Now they can't figure out why those currents and saltpeter make me so restless. They puzzled. I'm amused. But it's not like my Hollywood days. All my fans and those lights and twenty-seven Cadillacs."

"Fourteen Cadillacs," I corrected.

"Fourteen," Little Jimmie agree. "But I traded them in every year. Les, I just don't feel right. I just ain't me."

"I know what you mean."

"What an I gonna do?"

"You need another drink."

"Yeah. Some juice. Out there . . ."

"You didn't escape, did you?"

"Where could I escape to?" Little Jimmie exclaimed.

"Nowhere, man," I said, averting my eyes.

"I can't even get unemployment, though I was honorary president of the Screen Guild."

"You could always pick cotton in Jersey," I said.

"Pick cotton?" Little Jimmie sneered. "What would my fans think? I think I'll appeal to the Supreme Court. I figure they owe me an apology. I worked for the government, man. I kept one hundred million colored people contented for years. And in turn, I made the white people happy. Safe. Now I'm no longer useful in the scheme of things. Nobody's got time for Little Jimmie Wishbone."

"What did you expect? Another medal? It's not profitable to have you *Tom* . . . It's a very different scene."

"Well, what are you gonna do? Why the hell don't *you* pick cotton?"

"What the hell do you think I was doing last summer? *Where* do you think I got the money for the fried chicken I brought you on Sundays?"

War between friends is deadly. I mustered up a breathless laugh. "I'm gonna try something I never tried before. Dig The Wig."

Little Jimmie grunted scornfully. "Look at all those curly-haired Mexicans they import to pick berries and cabbage."

"But I'm an American," I protested.

"And I've got a million dollars."

"I *am* an American. That's an established fact. America's the land of elbow grease and hard work. Then—you've got it made. Little Jimmie, I'm gonna work like a son of a bitch. Do you hear me?"

"Yeah, I heard you. Now let's make it to the streets. My throat's dry."

*

"Look at him," a small boy cried, pointing his hand at me. "I bet *he* ain't going to school!"

Smiling, I said, "No, Sonny, not today."

"But *he's* going to school," the boy's mother said to me, doubling a suede-gloved fist and slamming it against the boy's mouth.

"Jesus, he must be a very bad boy," I said.

"He is," the mother said vigorously.

I stared hard at the crying boy, "What did he do?"

"He doesn't want to go to a segregated school. I broke my broom handle on him a few minutes ago. That's what the NAACP and the Mayor and the Holy Peace-Making Brotherhood advised. You wouldn't have a pistol on you, would you?"

"No," I shuddered. A sudden pain hit me so hard that I felt faint. My throat was dry. "Isn't there some other way you can make the boy understand?"

"No," the mother replied.

"Maaa," the boy moaned. "Please take me to the hospital. I ache all over. I think I'm gonna die, Mama."

"Shut your trap."

Just then a soothsayer wearing a dark policeman's uniform walked up twirling his night stick.

"What's wrong, lady? Having trouble with your boys?"

"Only the little one," the mother laughed. "He doesn't want to go to a segregated school. I've got to beat some sense into the boy's head if it's the last thing I do."

"Wanna use my nightstick? I'm sorry I don't have my electric cow-prod with me because that does the trick every time. That always makes them fall in line."

"Oh, officer," the mother said, "you're so kind and understanding."

"Think nothing of it. Just doing my duty. I've got kids of my own. I certainly wouldn't want them to go to an integrated school."

"Now, wait a minute," I said angrily. "This isn't fair!"

"Buster," the policeman said, "do you want me to knock the grease out of your hair? I'll get you thirty days in the workhouse. You're trying to obstruct justice."

Silently, I watched the mother slam the night stick against the boy's head. The boy's mouth opened and he fell to the sidewalk. Blood flowed from his nostrils and lips. "Mama," he sighed, and closed his eyes.

"Get up from there, you nasty little thing," the mother cried. "Get up. Do you hear me? Just look at you, and I stayed up half the night getting your clothes clean and white for school."

"I think the boy's dead," I said.

"He ain't dead," the policeman said. "He's just pretending because he doesn't want to go to school."

The mother knelt down and shook the boy and then stood up. "He's dead," she commented in a clear voice. "I could never talk to him."

"It's not your fault," the policeman said. "Kids are getting out of hand these days."

I tottered off, knowing that I couldn't eat any free fried chicken even if it was my day. I hadn't been to a church in a very long time and I thought I might go to one, but then I remembered that all of the churches in Harlem were closed. The Minister's Union had declared April first to be a day of soul-searching, a day devoted to making money, a day of solitude for the ministers whose nerves had failed them.

So I veered on to Eighth Avenue and 116th Street, where all was quiet except for a rumble on the west side of the Avenue. Fourteen shoeshine boys were fighting savagely with a gleaming six-foot Negro man. The shoeshine boys were winning.

One ferocious shiner jumped me. "Are you a shiner?" he asked.

"Not today," I said.

"Where is it at?" the six-foot man asked. "I'll call the police on you little black bastards."

"Call'm," the shoeshine boys chorused. "We ain't done nothing against the Lily Law."

"That's right," the ferocious shiner said. "We ain't done nothing. We just invented this dust machine to help our business downtown. The dust shoeshine boy stands on the corner with the machine in a shopping bag from Macy's, rolling his white eyeballs and sucking a slice of candied watermelon. You know. Like he's waiting on his mama. Every time a likely customer walks by, the dust shiner pulls the magic string.

By the time the customer reaches the middle of the block he sure needs a shine. He our gravy. And now this mother-grabber is gonna call Lily Law. He wants to suck white ass. He ain't thinking 'bout us little black boys."

The gleaming tall man broke away and ran inside a diner. "I'll fix you little devils."

"I'll go inside and see what I can do," I told the shoeshine boys. "Now you boys run like crazy."

I wasn't a hero and I've never aspired to be one (except in a private, loverly sense—ah, The Deb), but I've always, always, tried to help people. It's a kind of perverse hobby with me. Opening the diner door, I offered a diplomatic grin. The gleaming man was on the telephone.

"Mr. Police. This is Jackson Sam Nothingham. Yes sir. The Black Disaster Diner. What do you mean . . . It's me, Mr. Police. Your sunny-side-up boy. That's right."

The diner owner hadn't noticed me. I eased over and deftly pulled the phone cord from the wall.

"What? I can't hear you. Say something, Mr. Police. I pays my dues . . . And what's more, I takes care of the Captain when he comes around . . ."

"Maybe they hung up on you, Mac," I said.

The bewildered owner swung around. "What you mean, boy? They hung up on me? Wait until the Captain gets a load of this. He knows I sell a little gin and whiskey in coffee cups after hours. All the Mister Polices on this beat says they don't know what they'd do without good old Jackson Sam Nothingham. My good down-home Southern cooking and nip on a cold rainy day. I'm keeping up the morale of the police force and you try to say they hung up on me?"

"That's the way the cookie crumbles," I philosophized. "It doesn't have to be a Chinese fortune cookie either."

The angry tall man looked hard at The Wig. "You curly-headed son-of-a-bitch. Git out of here. Git out of the Black Disaster Diner. I am the owner and I refuse to serve you. All you spicks and niggers are the cause of my troubles."

"If that's the way you feel about it," I said.

"Git out," the tall man shouted. His whole body trembled. "You people are ruining me. I've been in business twenty years and the white people have loved me and I've been happy."

He slumped down into a cane-backed chair like a wounded animal.

If that is how he feels, there's nothing for me to say, I thought, and, lowering my eyes, I walked briskly out of the Black Disaster Diner.

TEMPORARY JOB

"Now look, momma, you can't talk to me like that,
I'm the President of the United States."
"Yeah, another one of your temporary jobs," the
mother-in-law said. "In four years,
you'll be back on the street again."

— Timmie Rogers

STEAMIN'

"It's steamin' out here today," the old
dude said to his partner, as they sat out on
the stoop of their Harlem apartment.
"Yeah, it's sure 'nough warm," his partner said.
"But dis ain't nothin' like it was in Georgia."
"You mean it was hotter than this?"
"No doubt about it. So hot down there
one day I seen two pieces a ice
walkin' down the road fannin' they'selves."

— Folk

SLAPPY WHITE

CLOSER TO WELFARE

Mayor Daley did a nice thing to elevate the
dignity of a black family in Chicago. He
moved them from a $100 a month
apartment to one that rented for $300 so
they could be closer to the welfare office.

RUNNING FOR VICE PRESIDENT

*Slappy White once announced a mock run for the vice presidency and staged
a fake press conference that reflected his own special brand of social satire.
An excerpt follows.*

Q: Mr. White, I'm from NAACP, the black caucus of Capitol Hill.

A: You mind standing up, brother, so that I can see your black caucus?
     Oh, there you are. Do you mind dimming your teeth?

Q: Mr. White, you say that a black vice president will help the economy.
     Now how is that?

A: Right off the bat, I'll fire the chauffeur, I'll do the driving myself.

Q: Mr. White, you say that black is beautiful?

A: Yeah, but you got to turn the light on to appreciate it.

Q: Mr. White, what do you think it will be like when you become the first
     black vice president?

A: Well, I might not be black by the time I am elected.

Q: Oh, how is that?

A: Well, you know how a steak is good for a black eye? Well, I'm having
     a suit made out of meat.

Q: Mr. White, why was the black vote so low last election?

A: Well, it's hard to write with a ball-point pen . . . on wax paper . . . over
     butter.

Q: Mr. White, what's the biggest problem for you as a black man with the
     second spot on the ticket?

A: Tryin' to find a white man for the first spot on the ticket.

☺☺

A Fair Fight

A white mob caught a lone black civil rights
worker on a deserted road. They beat
him for a little while, then dug a hole,
buried him up to his neck in the ground and
sicked a vicious dog on him. The dog
attacked, but the man was shifting and moving
his head so fast that the mutt
couldn't touch him. Finally, frustrated and
exhausted, the dog crawled away. One of the
rednecks threw his beer aside and said,
"Nigger, stop all that damn duckin' and
dodgin' and fight my dog fair."

— Folk

A CARTOON

By Oliver W. Harrington

"An' the next time the gov'mint asks us if we have registered any niggras to vote we can look 'em right in the eye an' answer 'Yes'!"

ᘯᘯ

FROM *BLIND MAN WITH A PISTOL*

By Chester Himes

Chester Himes's satiric detective novels were often spiked with comic scenes derived from their Harlem setting. In addition to the exploits of the black detectives Coffin Ed Johnson and Grave Digger Jones, they featured outrageous characters like General Ham, the Messianic preacher-cum-commander who appears in the following excerpt.

INTERLUDE

Good people, your food is digested by various juices in the stomach. There is a stomach juice for everything you eat. There is a juice for meat and a juice for potatoes. There is a juice for chitterlings and a juice for sweet potato pie. There is a juice for buttermilk and a juice for hopping John. But sometimes it happens these juices get mixed up and the wrong juice is applied to the wrong food. Now you might eat corn on the cob which has just been taken out of the pot and it's so hot you burn your tongue. Well your mouth gets mixed up and sends the wrong signal to your stomach. And your stomach hauls off and lets go with the juice for cayenne pepper. Suddenly you got an upset stomach and the hot corn goes to your head. It causes a burning fever and your temperature rises. Your head gets so hot it causes the corn to begin popping. And the popped corn comes through your skull and gets mixed up with your hair. And that's how you get dandruff.

*Dusty Fletcher at the Apollo Theater on
125th Street in Harlem*

A man entered *The Temple of Black Jesus.* He was a short, fat, black man with a harelip. His face was running with sweat as though his skin was leaking. His short black hair grew so thick on his round inflated head it looked artificial, like drip-dry hair. His body looked blown up like that of a rubber man. The sky blue silk suit he wore on this hot night glinted with a blue light. He looked inflammable. But he was cool.

Black people milling along the sidewalk stared at him with a mixture of awe and deference. He was the latest. "Ham, baby," someone whispered . . . "Naw, dass Jesus baby," was the harsh rejoinder.

The black man walked forward down a urine-stinking hallway beneath the feet of a gigantic black plaster of paris image of Jesus Christ, hanging by his neck from the rotting white ceiling of a large square room. There was an expression of teeth-bared rage on Christ's black face. His arms were spread, his fists balled, his toes curled. Black blood dripped from red nail holes. The legend underneath read, THEY LYNCHED ME.

Soul brothers believed it.

The Temple of Black Jesus was on 116th Street, east of Lenox Avenue. It and all the hot dirty slum streets running parallel into Spanish Harlem were teeming with hot dirty slum dwellers, like cockroaches eating from a bowl of frijoles. Dirt rose from their shuffling feet. Fried hair melted in the hot dark air and ran like grease down sweating black necks. Half-naked people cursed, muttered, shouted, laughed, drank strong whiskey, ate greasy food, breathed rotten air, sweated, stank and celebrated.

This was *The Valley.* Gethsemane was a hill. It was cooler. These people celebrated hard. The heat scrambled their brains, came out their skulls, made dandruff. Normal life was so dark with fear and misery, a celebration went off like a skyrocket. *Nat Turner* day! Who knew who Nat Turner was? Some thought he was a jazz musician teaching the angels jazz; others thought he was a prizefighter teaching the devil to fight. Most agreed the best thing he ever did was die and give them a holiday.

A chickenshit pimp was pushing his two-dollar whore into a dilapidated convertible to drive her down to Central Park to work. Her black face was caked with white powder, her mascaraed eyes dull with stupidity, his thick lips shining like a red fire engine. Time to catch whitey as he slunk around the Lagoon looking to change his luck.

Eleven black nuns came out of a crumbling, dilapidated private house which had a sign in the window reading, FUNERALS PERFORMED. They were carrying a brass four-poster bed as though it were a coffin. The bed had a mattress. On the mattress was a nappy, unkempt head of an old man, sticking from beneath a dirty sheet. He lay so still he might have been dead. No one asked.

In the *Silver Moon* greasy spoon restaurant a whiskey-happy joker yelled at the short order cook behind the counter, "Gimme a cup of coffee as strong as Muhammad Ali and a Mittenburger."

"What kind of burger is that?" the cook asked, grinning.

"Baby, that's burger mit kraut."

To one side of the entrance to the movie theater an old man had a portable barbecue pit made out of a perforated washtub attached to the chassis of a baby carriage. The grill was covered with sizzling pork ribs. The scent of scorching meat rose from the greasy smoke, filled the hot thick air, made mouths water. Half-naked black people crowded about, buying red-hot slabs on pale white bread, crunching the half-cooked bones.

Another old man, clad in his undershirt, had crawled onto the marquee of the movie, equipped with a fishing pole, line, sinker and hook and was fishing for ribs as though they were fish. When the barbecue man's head was turned he would hook a slab of barbecue and haul it up out of sight. Everyone except the barbecue man saw what was happening, but no one gave him away. They grinned at one another, but when the barbecue man looked their way, the grins disappeared.

The barbecue man felt something was wrong. He became suspicious. Then he noticed some of his ribs were missing. He reached underneath his pit and took out a long iron poker.

"What one of you mother-rapers stole my ribs?" he asked, looking mean and dangerous.

No one replied.

"If I catch a mother-raper stealing my ribs, I'll knock out his brains," he threatened.

They were happy people. They liked a good joke. They believed in a prophet named Ham. They welcomed the Black Jesus to their neighborhood. The white Jesus hadn't done anything for them.

When prophet Ham entered the chapel, he found it filled with black preachers as he'd expected. Faces gleamed with sweat in the sweltering heat like black painted masks. The air was thick with the odors of bad breath, body sweat and deodorants. But no one smoked.

Prophet Ham took the empty seat on the rostrum and looked at the sea of black faces. His own face assumed as benign an expression as the harelip would permit. An expectant hush fell over the assemblage. The speaker, a portly man in a black suit, turned off his harangue like a tap and bowed toward Prophet Ham obsequiously.

"And now our Prophet has arrived," he said with his eyes popping expressively. "Our latterday Moses, who shall lead us out of the wilderness. I give you Prophet Ham."

The assembled preachers allowed themselves a lapse of dignity and shouted and amened like paid shills at a revival meeting. Prophet Ham received his acclaim with a frown of displeasure. He stepped to the dais and glared at his audience. He looked indignant.

"Don't call me a Prophet," he said. He had a sort of rumbling lisp and tendency to slobber when angry. He was angry now. "Do you know what a Prophet is? A Prophet is a misfit that has visions. All the Prophets in history were either epileptics, syphilitics, schizophrenics, sadists or just plain monsters. I just got this harelip. That doesn't make me eligible." His red eyes glowed, his silk suit glinted, his black face glistened, his split red gums bared from his big yellow teeth.

No one disputed him.

"Neither am I a latterday Moses," he went on. "First of all, Moses was white. I'm black. Second, Moses didn't lead his people out of the wilderness until they revolted. First he led them into the wilderness to starve and eat roots. Moses was a square. Instead of leading his people out of Egypt he should have taken over Egypt, then their problems would have been solved."

"But you're a race leader," a preacher shouted from the audience.

"I ain't a race leader neither," he denied. "Does I look like I can race? That's the trouble with you so-called Negroes. You're always looking for a race leader. The only place to race whitey is on the cinder track. We beats him there all right, but that's all. And it ain't you and me who's racing, it's our children. And what are we doing to reward them for winning? Talking all this foolishness about Prophets and race leaders."

"Well, if you ain't a Prophet and you ain't a race leader, what is you?" the preacher said.

"I'm a soldier," Prophet Ham said. "I'm a plain and simple soldier in this fight for right. Just call me General Ham. I'm your commander. We got to fight, not race."

Now they had got that point settled, his audience could relax. He wasn't a prophet, and he wasn't a race leader, but they were just as satisfied with him being a general.

"General Ham, baby," a young preacher cried enthusiastically, expressing the sentiment of all. "You command, we obey."

"First we're gonna draft Jesus." He held up his hand to forestall comment. "I know what you're gonna say. You're gonna say other black men, more famous and with a bigger following than me, are employing the Jesus pitch. You're gonna say it's been the custom and habit of our folks for years past to call on Jesus for everything, food, health, justice, mercy, or what have you. But there's two differences. They been calling on the white Jesus. And mostly they been praying for mercy. You know that's the truth. You are all men of the cloth. All black preachers. All guilty of the same sin. Asking the white Jesus for mercy. For to solve your problem. For to take your part against the white man. And all he tell you is to turn the other cheek. You think he gonna tell you to slap back? He's white too. Whitey is his brother. In fact whitey made him. You think he gonna take your part against his own creator? What kind of thinking is that?"

The preachers laughed with embarrassment. But they heard him.

"We hear you, General Ham, baby . . . You right, baby . . . We been praying to the wrong Jesus . . . Now we pray to the Black Jesus."

"Just like you so-called Negroes," General Ham lisped scornfully. "Always praying. Believing in the philosophy of forgiveness and love. Trying to overcome by love. That's the white Jesus's philosophy. It won't work for you. It only work for whitey. It's whitey's con. Whitey invented it, just like he invented the white Jesus. We're gonna drop praying altogether."

A shocked silence followed this pronouncement. After all they were preachers. They'd been praying even they started preaching. They didn't know what to say.

But the young preacher spoke out again. He was young enough to try anything. The old-fashioned praying hadn't done much good. "You command us, General," he said again. He wasn't afraid of change. "We'll give up the praying. Then what'll we do?"

"We ain't gonna ask the Black Jesus for no mercy," General Ham declared. "We ain't gonna ask him for nothing. We just gonna take him and feed him to whitey in the place of the other food we been putting on whitey's table since the first of us arrived as slaves. We been feeding whitey all these years. You know that's the truth. He grown fat and prosperous on the food we been feeding him. Now we're gonna feed him the flesh of the Black Jesus. I don't have to tell you the flesh of Jesus is indigestible. They ain't even digested the flesh of the white Jesus in these two thousand years. And they been eating him every Sunday. Now the flesh of the Black Jesus is even more indigestible. Everybody knows that black meat is harder to digest than white meat. And that, brothers, *IS OUR SECRET WEAPON!*" he shouted with a spray of spit. "That is how we're gonna keep feeding him the flesh of the Black Jesus until he perish of constipation if he don't choke to death first."

The elderly black preachers were scandalized.

"You don't mean the sacrament?" one asked.

"Is we gonna manufacture wafers?" another asked.

"We'll do it, but how?" the young preacher asked sensibly.

"We're gonna march with the statue of the Black Jesus until whitey pukes," General Ham said.

With the image of the lynched Jesus which hung in the entrance in their minds, the preachers saw what he meant.

"What you need for the march, General?" asked the young black preacher, who was practical.

General Ham appreciated this practicality. "Marchers," he replied. "Nothing takes the place of marchers for a march," he said, "but money. So if we can't find the marchers we get some money and buy them. I'm gonna make you my second in command, young man. What is your name?"

"I'm Reverend Duke, General."

"From now on you're a Colonel, Reverend Duke. I call you Colonel Duke. I want you to get these marchers lined up in front of this temple by ten o'clock."

"That don't give us much time, General. Folks is celebrating."

"Then make it a celebration, Colonel," General Ham said. "Get some banners reading 'Jesus baby.' Give a little sweet wine. Sing *Jesus Savior.* Get some of these gals from the streets. Tell 'em you want 'em for the dance. They ask what dance? You tell 'em *the* dance. Wherever gals go, mens follow. Remember that, Colonel. That's the first principle of the march. You dig me, Colonel?"

"We dig you, General," said Colonel Duke.

"Then I see you-all at the march," General Ham said and left.

Outside on 116th Street, a lavender Cadillac Coupe de Ville convertible, trimmed in yellow metal which the black people passing thought was gold, was parked at the curb. A buxom white woman with blue-dyed gray hair, green eyes and a broad flat nose, wearing a décolleté dress in orange chiffon, sat behind the wheel. Huge rose breasts popped from the orange dress as though expanded by the heat, and rested on the steering wheel. When General Ham approached and opened the door on his side, she looked around and gave him a smile that lit up the night. Her two upper incisors were crowned with shining gold with a diamond in between. "Daddy," she greeted. "What took you so long?"

"I been cooking with Jesus," he lisped, settling into the seat beside her.

She chuckled. It was a fat woman's chuckle. It sounded like hot fat bubbling. She pulled out in front of a bus and drove down the crowded street as though black people were invisible. They got the hell out of her way.

⊚⁄⊚

LEAN AND MEAN

Facing criticism from reporters and
fellow congressmen about his
extravagant lifestyle, the Harlem congressman
and pastor of the Abyssinian Baptist Church
Adam Clayton Powell Jr. told the press,
"If it's not illegal, immoral, or fattening, I'll do it."

And when his dedication to church affairs
was questioned by a congregation
member who challenged,
"I thought you were a man of the cloth,"
Powell replied, "I am—*silk!*"

BLACKFACE

Somebody has got to help me,
look at that, two white men put black cork
on their faces and went out as
Amos 'n' Andy and
made a million dollars. Here I am
born with the stuff, and I can't earn a dime.
—Ossie Davis, *Purlie Victorious*

TALL, TAN, YOUNG, AND FLY

By Frankie Crocker

Black radio deejays and announcers brought a more flamboyant, hipper style to the airways, and by the 1970s Frankie Crocker was one of the most popular radio personalities in New York. The following riff is an example of the kind of signature rap that set him apart.

This is the Frankie Crocker show. Stay with me, baby, 'cause it's bound to put more dips in your hips, more cut in your strut, more glide in your stride. If you don't dig it you know you got a hole in your soul—don't eat chicken on Sunday. Push, girl, push! While other cats be laughin' and jokin', Frankie's steady takin' care of bizness—cookin' and smokin'. For there is no other like this soul brother. Tall, tan, young, and fly . . . anytime you want me baby, I'm your guy! Young and single and love to mingle—can I mingle with you, baby? Closer than white's on rice; closer than cold's on ice; closer than the collar's on a hog; closer than a ham is on a country hog. Truly the eighth wonder of the world—before me there was no other, after me there shall be no more. Aren't you glad you live in this town—you can dig Frankie when the sun goes down. How can you lose with the stuff I use? Lemme rap to you, momma. If I'm all you got, I'm all you need. And remember, if your radio is not on the Frankie Crocker show, your radio is not on . . .

DICK GREGORY

BLACK RIOTERS

You know, I'd like you youngsters to do me a favor. One day this week or next week, first chance you get, go by the library and copy down the Declaration of Independence. Don't read it, just copy it. You know how to copy without reading, don't you? Sure you do. Here's what I want you to do for me after you copy down the Declaration of Independence. I want you to keep the Declaration with you twenty-four hours a day. Never be caught without that Declaration.

And here's the favor I want you to do for me. When the riot season open up again . . . Can you believe this old stinking system done programmed black folks into believing we got a riot season, July through August. Last year we didn't show up and the whole country got upset, "Where were they?" Yeah, we didn't show up last July and August and everybody got uptight, "Where were you all? We had the tanks waiting for you."

They asked George Wallace, "Why you think they didn't riot last season?"

He said, "Ah, you know them niggers is lazy and shiftless, they just got tired."

I tell you where we was last riot season. We got tired of stealing all them old bad, no good products. So last July through August, we decided to go underground and study the Consumer Report. So when the riot season open up again this year, we ain't stealin' no more [crap].

Now, here's the favor I'd like you to do for me. When riot season open up, I'd like for you to run home, get round your momma and daddy. And you black kids go home too 'cause you know you got some niggers living in those houses with you that think more degenerate and more corrupt than the Ku Klux Klan could ever think, and you do know what I'm talkin' about.

And get your television set and put it in the middle of the room. And then turn on the evening news cause their gonna show them niggers riotin', and lootin', and sockin' it to the town. After you get the news on, turn on Huntley and Brinkley 'cause they get close-ups. Yeah, them other two networks, they try to cover the riots in helicopters 'cause they scared, you know.

No, Huntley and Brinkley, they get such close-ups you can recognize your kinfolks. "Look at there, there go Uncle Dudley! I didn't know he was in Detroit. Hey, get it man! Get it!"

Now after you get Huntley and Brinkley on, and they be showing them niggers rioting, at that point run upstairs and get your Mom and Dad and bring 'em down and put 'em right in front of the television set. Just let them look, look at them niggers burn the town. Just listen to their reaction. You've heard it before. Then after you've heard enough of it, now the favor I want you to do me, I want you to go up and turn the sound off the television, pull out your Declaration of Independence and with the sound turned off so they can't hear nothin' just look at them black folks just loot and burn the town down. At that point, I want you to move way in back of your parents and while they're looking at them cats burn, I want you to read your Declaration of Independence as loud as you can read it. And maybe for the first time them fools will understand what they lookin' at.

WE HOLD THESE TRUTHS TO BE SELF EVIDENT. THAT ALL MEN ARE CREATED EQUAL AND ENDOWED BY THE CREATOR WITH CERTAIN INALIENABLE RIGHTS. THAT WHEN THESE RIGHTS ARE DESTROYED OVER LONG PERIODS OF TIME IT IS YOUR *DUTY* TO DESTROY OR ABOLISH THAT GOVERNMENT.

AMERICAN HISTORY

Now, I know at first them old fools is gonna assume that was some message Malcolm X left for Rap Brown. But I know with a minimum amount of persuasion you can teach them fools that was their beloved Declaration of Independence.

Yeah, that one with that mistake on it. The one where they forgot to write for white only. You know as funny as that may seem, you know we dumb enough that if you didn't put for white only on it, we dumb enough to read it and believe that the Declaration of Independence was written for all Americans.

But when we do what it says to do after long periods of injustice, you call us hoodlum and thugs, we realize, for the first time, that the Declaration of Independence was written for you. Why didn't you label it so we would know? And then get it out of my black ghetto.

I remember I was back in the ghetto, in grade school, happy, just being a good nigger singing my blues, "*I love my baby. Oh baby, Oh, baby . . . Old man river . . .*"

And the principal ran up to us one day and say, "Board of Education say you all can't graduate from grade school till you read and learn the Declaration of Independence."

I said, "What? The Decla-who? Man, we ain't gonna read that old white stuff."

Cat said, "You ain't gonna graduate."

I said, "Lay it on me then."

"After long years of injustices boys, you has a duty to destroy or abolish your government."

I said, "Hey baby, you'all got some more of this stuff layin' around?"

You white folks really sick enough to believe that you can put this stuff in our neighborhood and we're not gonna to read it and do what it says do? You white folks sick enough to believe you can still draft niggers into your army and send them down to Fort Benning, Georgia, and teach them how to be guerillas and send them to Vietnam, killing foreigners to liberate foreigners and think that they're not going to come back to America and kill you to liberate their mammy, then you sick and out your mind.

No, you ain't dealing with no World War II niggers no more, that you can just turn on and turn off.

And after you get that Declaration out of my community. Real quick run and get that, that filthy white boy American history book out my ghetto. 'Cause let me tell you something. There's no way in the world you can expect niggers to behave, you keep makin' us read your history.

Baby, your history tells me that from the time you landed on the Plymouth Rock, you shot and murdered your way all the way across to California. Are you serious, you really think you can give me that and think I'm gonna behave?

Have you ever read your history book? You think George Washington made the history book because he was a good preacher and he learned how to sing, "We Shall Overcome," and he went around preaching nonviolence? He made your history book because he kicked the hell out of the British. Killed every one of them he got his hands on.

You got to be joking with that history book of yours. You tell me that in that history book, you came to these shores and *discovered* a country that was already occupied. You think about that. And then got nerve enough to call a nigger "hoodlum." How do you discover something that is not only owned by someone else but it's being used at the time you discovered it?

That's like me and my old lady walkin' out of here tonight and you and your old lady sittin' in your brand new automobile and my lady say, "Gee honey, that sure is a beautiful automobile. I sure wish it was mine."

I say, "Well, Lillian, let's discover it."

I sure wish you white folks would read your history. Then maybe you'll understand me. "Give me liberty or give me death." Who said that? Rap Brown, didn't he?

What did Stokely Carmichael say, "Don't shoot till you see the whites of their eyes!"

Then you run around and tell me to have respect for the police and give me that old history book. You showed me in your history book, you didn't have no respect for the police. Yeah, it's in there. Said in the early days when the British was the police, a white boy by the name of Paul Revere, rode through the white community and said, "Get a gun, white folks. Police is comin'." You can understand the White Panthers, can't you? But the Black Panthers make you forget about your history, don't they?

And they got nerve enough to get upset over the riots when a nigger steal a television set and take it home with him. But you'll still give me that white boy history book telling me how your white folks got on that foreign ship and threw all that man's tea in the water.

What the hell you mad at, 'cause we got enough sense to take it home?

Let me tell you something. If you're gonna loot and take tea that don't belong to you and then tell me in your history book it was a Boston Tea Party, then every time a nigger take a television set, call that a Saturday Night Fish Fry.

◎∕◎

KITTENS AND BISCUITS

During a debate with a black academic,
Malcolm X argued that blacks were
not truly American citizens
since they were not accorded the rights
guaranteed by the Constitution.
"We didn't land on Plymouth Rock,
Plymouth Rock landed on us!" he said.
When his opponent insisted that despite
the way blacks had been treated he remained
a patriotic American, Malcolm asked,
"Why do you call yourself an American, Brother?"

"Because I was born in this country," the man shouted.
"Now, Brother," Malcolm calmly replied,
"If a cat has kittens in an oven,
does that make them biscuits?"
—James Farmer, from *Lay Bare the Heart*

FROM *YELLOW BACK RADIO BROKE-DOWN*

By Ishmael Reed

In this 1969 novel—touted as a "Hoodoo Western"—Ishmael Reed not only parodied a popular literary genre but also introduced a kind of "Bad Nigger" hero (the Loop Garoo Kid) who directly challenged the prevailing religious, social, and political order. Loop Garoo is also a conjure man ("born with a caul over his face and ghost lobes on his ears") and a deity in his own right. In the following selection the Pope has been called in to halt Loop's disruptive spree and bring him back into the fold.

At the celebration the Pope sat on a throne Drag had made for him. Drag sat next to him looking important. Whenever the Pope leaned over and whispered into his ear, he would look on to the proceedings knowingly, making a circle with his thumb and forefinger as if he had been privy to secret knowledge.

A commotion was caused in front of the door near the garden. Suddenly it opened. The preacher stood in its well. Iridescent wings annexed to his shoulders were flapping and his eyes were bugged. His tail was ignited with electricity. The preacher started across the floor towards the Pope. The Pope's aide brought a giant can of DDT and Pope started to squish. The preacher grabbed his neck and stumbled back. He keeled over with his feet up and wings oscillated until they were still. Never again would it oviposit eggs.

I'm-a sorry I had to do that to one of your dignitaries, Pope said to the Drag.

O that's all right Father. He tried his best but Protestantism was the heathen German's reaction to the glory of Rome. He was bound to go all atavistic sooner or later. Besides this was no costume party anyway. We is big time and serious.

Glad you understand Drag, the Pope said while people gathered around the Preacher on the floor.

Where can we talk about this Loop-a Garoo Kid?

Now you're talking there Father, Drag said, come on into my study.

The men went upstairs, the cowpokes stomping their boots so as to impress the hurdy gurdy girls they brought from Big Lizzy's on how they had access to high places.

Upstairs the Pope had an aide roll out a map while he held a pointer. It was a diagram of Yellow Back Radio.

Do you know where he's hiding out?

No, that's just it, the Drag said, there are so many caves around here he could be hiding out in who could tell. Why the night he came to our party there the men fearlessly rode after him and they couldn't find him. Right, men?

The foreman looked on as the other men lowered their heads. Right Drag, that's what we did. We almost had him but couldn't catch up.

Snow is the ticket, the Pope said, removing a cigar from his gown pocket and lighting up.

What happened to your final A's there Pope?

Shit, man! That's for suckers. Me and you cattlemen are in the same bag, always have been, moolas where it's at, look at that Sistine. Whatdaya think bilt that dump. Cheese? The mob loves final A's, them Protestants they never know, no ritual no class, so that when a generation of kids came along who could concentrate on more than one thing at a time they couldn't handle it.

The Pope's aide was handing out cigars and the men, leaning back in their chairs, laughed at one another while pulling forward their suspenders.

That was no threat for us. We hand out them wafers, and swing them censers, lot of loud singing, organs, processions. They like it that way.

That's the way I was running things Pope, till this nigger come in here and turned the place out.

Well we'll see about him—when we were threatened by the Albigenses, the Waldenses and other anarchists way back there when we couldn't absorb them we burned or hanged them. Where was I? the Pope continued.

You were talking about caves.

Look for the Peak of No Mo Snow, Drag. He hates snow.

Why I seed a naked mountain top just the other day, Skinny said. Let's go boys.

The men rose and were about to head for the hills when the Pope cautioned them:

Hold it, hold it, you don't go in there with your cowboy thing like that—shoot-em-ups won't work this time. He's got power stored in that mad dog's tooth hanging on that necklace he wears. The mad dog's tooth is the thing.

You have to find some way to remove it from his neck. Then he's powerless. In Haiti it's called an arret but here in America it's liable to be named anything. America is such a strange place that according to the new occult dictionary that just arrived at the Vatican Library there are more queer sects here than anywhere in the world. The religious turn out to be as ragtime a collage as the American Episcopalians who received their charter from a heretical Irish group.

Just for the record Father, Drag asked, what is he putting on us anyhow?

Well we've figured it to be the Hoo-Doo, an America version of the Ju-Ju religion that originated in Africa—you know, that strange continent which serves as the subconscious of our planet—where we've found the earliest remains of man. Ju-Ju originated in Dahomey and Angola. You'll find that wangol, one of the magic terms of the system, is a play on the country's name.

Who knows what lurks in the secret breast of that Continent, shaped so like the human skull? We've tried to hide the facts by ridiculing the history of Sub-Sahara Africa and claiming that of North Africa as our own. Notice how the term "blackamoor" was dropped from St. Augustine's name, and how our friends the German Aryan scholars faked the History of the Egyptians by claiming them to be white. Have you ever seen any example of their art? If you look at the pictures—the way they painted themselves black—and ignore the propaganda in our texts or Nefertiti which is a fraud, you will find that undoubtedly they are black people. The overwhelming majority of their art depicts black people.

Sometimes I suspect that if Eve had remained in that garden, probably located in Dahomey, because that's where the snakes are, Rome would be merely one of the centers of the Ju-Ju religion and I'd be nothing but a poor wretch, stomping grapes or directing traffic in New York City.

The men were falling asleep. Drag stood and fired into the ceiling. Wake up you guys, have a little respect for the Vatican.

Well anyway, the Pope continued, when African slaves were sent to Haiti, Santo Domingo and other Latin American countries, we Catholics attempted to change their pantheon, but the natives merely placed our art alongside theirs. Our insipid and uninspiring saints were no match for theirs: Damballah, Legba and other deities which are their Loa. This religion is so elastic that some to the women priests name Loa after their boyfriends. When Vodun arrived in America, the authorities became so paranoid they banned it for a dozen or so years, even to the extent of discontinuing the importation of slaves from Haiti and Santo Domingo.

Loop Garoo seems to be practicing a syncretistic American version. I'll bet you've found ugly matter in your pillows, dolls on the door steps, maybe a personal item of clothing and a portrait of yourself missing.

It's important that we wipe it out because it can always become a revolutionary force. Many of the Haitian revolutionaries were practicing priests, or houngans, as they are called. The present Prime Minister of Haiti Dr. François Duvalier was former head of the Haitian Bureau of Ethnology.

Loop seems to be scatting arbitrarily, using forms of this and adding his own. He's blowing like that celebrated musician Charles Yardbird Parker— improvising as he goes along. He's throwing clusters of demon chords at you and you don't know the changes, do you Mr. Drag?

Father, you let us handle this guy.

May I make a suggestion?

What is it Pope?

Does he have any close friends or companions?

Now that you mention it Pope, I think that I did see ride off from here last night and join two men who were waiting for him on the hill, said Skinny McCullough the foreman.

Then get 10 dollars and a bottle of wine plus two tickets to the East on the Black Swan Stagecoach. Those men will remove the mad dog's tooth from the necklace he wears around his neck, the source of his power. They're probably down and out artists. He always liked artists.

O Pope you don't believe in all the mumbo jumbo do you? I mean you're a swell conversationalist but come off of it Pope.

The Pope looked at Drag in disgust. One should always believe the other side is capable of doing anything it says—you're a young country and you don't know that but you'll learn—the hard way.

Just to placate the Pope, Drag gave the men a bottle of cheap dirty wine, 2 stagecoach tickets and a rolled-up 10 dollar bill. and they were off to find the Peak of No Mo Snow.

*

When they reached the Loop Garoo's hideout, the Peak of No Mo Snow, Skinny put his finger to his lips, a signal for the horsemen to shush and kneel behind the foliage some yards from the cave. The hours passed and the sun settled behind the hills.

The gang's patience was rewarded because it wasn't long before Alcibiades Wilson and Jeff Williams emerged from the cave's mouth.

Man, you know, Jeff, Alcibiades said, if a cat laid 10 dollars on me, a bottle of wine and a ticket on the Black Swan Stagecoach for the East I'd split in a jiffy. We can return to the cafes and just be throwing our mops against the walls and be boo-ga-looing until our heart's content.

You said it Alcibiades, I would do it too. The Kid really got the coo-coo fever. Having ceremonies with that snake, saying those curses and drawing funny scenes on the cave's wall; extinct creatures and cattle in a head-on collision. If we can get ot the East we'll be just in time to do some macking at the Washington Square Art Show.

Skinny McCullough walked out of the bush whistling with his hands behind his back. The two men, seated on a rock outside of the cave and smoking cigarettes, almost knocked each other over trying to run back into the hideout.

Hold on, hold on there men, you've nothing fear from me, why I'm nothing but a broken down hermit, given to such eccentricities as supporting artists and collecting roots. I live around these parts and just came over to comment on how much I like aquiline noses. You kids really look smart there, I mean those thin lips, you look like some of them Roman statoots.

You really think so? answered Alcibiades. Why I played Puck in the Central Park production of *Midsummer's Night Dream*

Me too!! Me too!! Jeff echoed. I've played Puck plenty of times.

You boys ought to go to New York and become artists and writers—I'll bet you'd be a hot hit right off.

That's what we were just saying, mister, we said if we had a bottle of wine, two tickets on the Black Swan Stagecoach, we'd be off for the East right away. We're being held captive by a mad man who wears a mad dog's tooth about his neck and talks crazy.

Is that so? Skinny answered. Why it just so happens I'm a collector of mad dogs' teeth. I need one more to round out my hobby. You think your friend there will give it to me?

Man, no good, Alcibiades answered, he plays with it all the time and never removes it from about his neck.

Skinny started to walk away but said over his shoulder, Gee that's too bad. I was going to give him a bottle of wine, two tickets back East and some fast finnifs.

Jeff and Alcibiades conferred rapidly as Skinny started down Peak's path.

Hey mister!! Wait a minute!! I don't think the Kid would mind if you borrowed it for a while. He's asleep right now but we'll go in and ask him.

Now you're talking, Skinny said, I'll wait right here.

The men lit torches and entered the cave. When they came upon the area where Loop Garoo was asleep they stole towards him and gently removed the necklace from around Loop's neck. The white python glared from his cage above the altar.

Alcibiades and Jeff crept away while Loop watched with one eye open. He chuckled to himself as the men headed out of the cave and into the night where Skinny was waiting. They extinguished the torches.

O.K., said Alcibiades panting like a puppy, suh, heah's yo mad dog's tooth.

Skinny examined the mad dog's tooth through a magnifying glass. Excellent!! Excellent!! Thank you gentlemen, and here is the filthy half-full bottle of muscatel wine in an ol beat up dirty sack, the tickets on the stagecoach and some finnifs for your trouble, Skinny said throwing the items at their feet.

Alcibiades started to fight with Jeff over the wine while Skinny leaned back and laughed heartily.

When they finished the bottle they picked up the tickets and money and ran down the hill towards Yellow Back Radio to fetch the coach.

They ran so hard that every few steps they leaped into the air like chickens.

Skinny walked to the bushes where the men were giggling over the scene they had just witnessed.

All right men, Skinny said, let's go get this black berserk who thinks he's a buckaroo. We'll show him a thing or two.

The men spat into their hands and, lighting torches, started into the cave.

The cowpokes descended, holding the flares in their hands until they came upon an opening where Loop Garoo lay, pretending to be asleep.

Gotcha now!! Gotcha now!! Raise your hands you frightening coon you!! Start grabbing the blue. You ain't so tough, cause you lost the mad dog's tooth from around your neck. Now we understand them dolls we found on the boss's doorstep every morning, making him sick, and the rooster with the top hat and tails. The goat without horns makes a lot of sense now, a lot of sense.

Them artists you've been holding captive, they took the thing and gave it to us and the Pope of the Romans—he snitched to us about what you were up to.

So the Pope told you of my connaissance huh? Loop asked sitting up from the cave floor.

Reach for the sky and don't be smart.

How's the Pope these days?

What, insolent nigger, you trying to question Rome or something? Skinny yelled, knocking the Loop Garoo to the ground. Get up and start marching.

They tied Loop's hands and began to shove him out of the cave.

He looked back to the altar. Then above to the cage. The cage was open and the snake was nowhere to be seen. Loop looked over to a dark pool on the other side of the cave and saw a white tail disappearing into the water.

I said move on Loop, keep movin, the foreman said, as he and the cow-pokes took their prisoner to Yellow Back Radio.

*

The hump-backed attendant was tormenting the Loop by dangling a grey mouse before him. He would rush forward with the dead rodent on a string and push it through the bars. As soon as Loop was about to knock the stick down the attendant would quickly retreat laughing.

Loop, impatient with the antics, was about to turn the little man into stone—having had it up to his ears with Yellow Back Radio—when he heard a commotion outside the cell block.

The Pope walked into the corridor of the prisoner's section. Other prisoners, when they saw the visitor, banged their coffee mugs against the bars.

Wow, the pin-headed attendant shouted when he saw the Pope. He ran up to the Pope and began kissing him all over his hands. Moof, moof, Pope, wait until I tell my mother about seeing you, moof, moof—let me hold your train.

The Pope stroked the attendant's back and it became straight. The attendant skipped about the room, then returned and kissed the Pope's hands with even greater passion.

O.K. little attendant, let's not get carried away now, take the rest of the day off—I want to be alone with the sinner.

You sure you don't need me Pope? He's a tough hombre, the attendant said, snarling at Loop.

I can handle him little attendant. Now you go off and fall into the first well you see.

Anything you say Father, the attendant said, running out of the block.

What do you want Innocent? Loop asked as soon as they were alone. Isn't it enough that you turned me in?

The Pope drew his skirts up around him and folded his hands glowing with huge rings.

Look Loop you know me, I wouldn't have done anything if it hadn't been for the woman. She wants you to come back Loop. Ever since her ascension she's been with the blues. T. S. Eliot, one of those trembling Anglicans, said "blue is her color." But now it's her song and her day. Those other two, they behave as if they had ice cubes up their asses.

The raunchy Pope, Loop grinned, you were always my favorite. What did they say to you?

> eight boys eight girls
> the Pope in sinful love begat
> Rome him "father" rightly calls

Cut it out Loop. Why don't you give up this nonsense and come back home?

Loop ignored the Pope's request and looked distantly out of his cell window.

How did you find me?

Wasn't hard—mass murder, sexual excess, drugs, dancing, music. It was quite simple. We used the Vatican dirigible and circled the Valley until we spotted the Peak of No Mo Snow. After all Loop, in these many years we have come to know you as well as the back of our left hands.

You've got your nerve. What about the Witches' Hammer that you and the ol man cooked up to crush my followers way back when? When you and your cronies finished it was so bad that in some villages only a few women could be found alive.

O Loop let sleeping dogs lie. Anyway I'm here to question you, not you me.

As always—Inquisition Inquisition. I would venture to guess that your Inquisition signaled the triumph of the clerk, the bureaucrat, and the West has been in the committee thing ever since.

Loop you know you could have leveled this town with a word. We were observing you. We looked it up in the Book of Mysteries and found what you were doing with the snake and the charms. We thought we'd play along with you. Of course the ol man wanted us to come blasting like before, you know how ill tempered he is—belligerent chariot fleets, thunder storms, earthquakes. But she overruled him, gave him a headache. At times it seems she's about to take over. Loop, we figured out your game, what's your point?

Horse opera. Clever don't you think? And the Hoo-Doo cult of North America. A much richer art form than preaching to fisherman and riding into a town on the back of an ass. And that apotheosis. How disgusting. He had such an ego. "I'm the Son of God." Publicity hound, he had to prolong it for three hours, just because the press turned out to witness. And his method had no style at all. Compare his cheap performance at the gravesight of Lot—sickening—and that parable of our friend Buddha and the mustard seed. One, just a grandstand exhibition, and the other, beautiful, artistic and profound.

Like Father like Son always, getting hang-ups in the way of craftsman-ship. Nails, driven into the wrist, hypocritical and maudlin women. Why she was screaming at his feet for three hours and the next night in my room I thought she would bite off my horns with the steel of her hungry teeth. Two weeks later I had her on the block and rolling bums. She even attracted two other tricks, and I had a family. It was groovy until that an-gel he sent—the impostor who spread the rumor of her ascension and be-fore you knew it—it became a Papal dogma.

She went uptown on me and left me holding the bag—and as soon as she left, Mighty Dike and Mustache Sal mustered enough courage to leave too.

You're his Son too, Loop.

Yes, the eldest according to what they call apocrypha. You know how his propagandists are—anything they disapprove of they ascribe to hearsay, apocrypha or superstition. But I've never cashed in on it like he did. I knew very early that he wasn't the only one, there were others—but his arrogance and selfishness finally got the best of him and he drove them all under-ground. Now they're making a strong comeback.

So you're through with this performance, huh Loop?

Yes, even martyrdom can be an art form, don't you think? Hoo-doo, which in America flowered in New Orleans, was an unorganized religion without ego-games or death worship. In the States, books like the *6th & 7th Books of Moses, The Art of Burning Candles, The Explanation of Voo-Dooism, Mystic Se-crets of Mind and Power, Egyptian Secrets of Albertus Magnus,* or *White and Black Art for Man & Beast,* are sold across the counter at drugstores. I even had a betrayal motif, giving one upmanship on his most obvious forms.

You always did dig artists Loop, in the old days passing the elixir to those writers and painters in the cafe, pretending to be a patron.

Loop reflected. Remember when he came home that day Innocent? The old man made love to him as if they were man and wife. He licked his punctures and fed him from the breast.

So you think by allowing yourself to be humiliated by mortals he'll respect you too, huh?

No I just wanted to show the world what they were really up to. I'm always with the avant-garde. Seems to me that people are getting sick of daddies. You know—"thou shalt have no other before me"—Tsars, Monarchs, and their deadly and insidious flunkies.

Loop, one last time before you get on your soap box. He wants you to come home too—she's driving them batty. O Loop she's so bitchy, you know how she is. He even put a curse on her but she found a way to absorb that. Matter of fact she's getting a following up there. Both of them are afraid she might start something that'll make your uprising look small.

There was never an uprising, Innocent, you know that. That was some of his propagandists in the late Middle Ages who came up with that idea. Just got sick of that set-up and left. The fool—vagabond with the rucksack on my shoulder—always on the road. That's me, the cosmic jester. Matter of fact, I've always been harmless—St. Nick coming down the chimney, children leaving soup for me—always made to appear foolish, the scapegoat of all history. You and your crowd are the devils. The way you massacred the Gnostics, not to mention the Bogomils, Albigenses, and Waldenses.

Loop, he sent me to do the interrogating . . . I ask you one more time Loop, end this foolishness and come on home. He built a special district for you, red lights, the works. He sent for some of your bohemian types to keep you and Diane company. You can start a commune if you want, get high, walk around nude, anything you want Loop, just so you satisfy the wench.

No dice, baby.

O.K., Loop, the worldly Pope said rising, I should know that when you have your mind made up on something, nothing can change it. When I get back he's really going to put me down.

How's that?

Makes me crawl on *my* belly toward him and kiss *his* feet. Some days Loop I can't stand the place. People singing the same old hymns and he sits there performing the familiar spectaculars—every day. I miss St. Peter's chug-a-lugging fine brandy with the gang and jamming some strumpets.

Sorry, can't help you out Innocent, I told the bitch to stay. I almost went out of my mind to suicide, but she went on. As they say, or as he use to say when he tried to con the farmers, pretending he was one of their own, "as ye sow so shall ye reap."

BEFORE GOD GETS THE NEWS

"I'm so fast," **Muhammad Ali** once bragged,
"I could hit you before God gets the news."

FROM *FOR COLORED GIRLS WHO HAVE CONSIDERED SUICIDE WHEN THE RAINBOW IS ENUF*

By Ntozake Shange

lady in blue
that niggah will be back tomorrow, sayin 'i'm sorry'

lady in yellow
get this, last week my ol man came in sayin, 'i don't know how she got yr number baby, i'm sorry'

lady in brown
no this one is it, 'o baby, ya know i waz high, i'm sorry'

lady in purple
'i'm, only human, and inadequacy is what makes us human, & if we was perfect we wdnt have nothin to strive for, so you might as well go on and forgive me pretty baby, cause i'm sorry'

lady in green
'shut up bitch, i told you i waz sorry'

lady in orange
no this one is it, 'i do ya like i do ya cause i thot ya could take it, now i'm sorry'

lady in red
'now i know that ya know i love ya, but i aint ever gonna love ya like ya want me to love ya, i'm sorry'

lady in blue
one thing i dont need
is any more apologies
i got sorry greetin me at my front door
you can keep yrs
i dont know what to do wit em
they dont open doors
or bring the sun back
they dont make me happy
or get a mornin paper
didnt nobody stop usin my tears to wash cars
cuz a sorry

i am simply tired
of collectin
          'i didnt know
          i was so important to you'
i'm gonna haveta throw some away
i cant get to the clothes in my closet
for alla the sorries
i'm gonna tack a sign to my door
leave a message by the phone
          'if you called
          to say yr sorry
          call somebody
          else
          i dont use em anymore'
i let sorry/didnt meanta/& how cd i know abt that
take a walk down a dark & musty street in brooklyn
i'm gonna do exactly what i want to
& i wont be sorry for none of it
letta sorry soothe yr soul/i'm gonna soothe mine

you were always inconsistent
doin somethin & then bein sorry
beatin my heart to death
talkin bout you sorry
well
i will not call

i'm not goin be nice
i will raise my voice
& scream & holler
& break things & race the engine
& tell all yr secrets bout yrself to yr face
& i will list in detail everyone of my wonderful lovers
& their ways
i will play oliver lake
loud
& i wont be sorry for none of it

i loved you on purpose
i was open on purpose
i still crave vulnerability & close talk
& i'm not even sorry bout you bein sorry
you can carry all the guilt & grime ya wanna
just dont give it to me
i can't use another sorry
next time
you should admit
you're mean/low-down/triflin/& no count straight out
steada bein sorry alla the time
enjoy bein yrself

⊚⁄⊚

GODFREY CAMBRIDGE

AFTER YOU

He was dressed just like I was, with an attaché case, too. You know they copy everything we do. After the doors of the elevator opened, we accidentally bumped into each other. He leaped aside and said, "After you. As a responsible member of the white community, I wouldn't want to set a spark to that smoldering resentment that's been harbored in the Negro community for over a hundred years." I leaped aside and said, "No, no, after you because as a responsible member of the Negro community, I recognize the danger of offending old friends in the white community and at the same time driving others into the waiting arms of extremists on both sides."

EATING TOO WELL

Right now, it's not a question
of getting served at the counter.
It's a matter of eating too much.
I never got served before, but now I have to eat
at all the restaurants. The food is so good and
I'm eating so well that I can't sing
'We Shall Overcome,' I have to burp it.

THE SUBURBS

If I really want to scare
the hell out of my white friends,
I drive out to the suburb
they live in and walk down their street
slowly, carrying the real estate
section of the *New York Times*.

JUST IN CASE

Now, at last I can get the kind of
job to which I can carry a briefcase—
with fried chicken and watermelon in it, of course.

⊚〰⊚

FROM *THE LOVES AND LIVES OF MR. JIVEASS NIGGER*

By Cecil Brown

Cassanova was also the only place in Copenhagen where Soul Music could
be heard; the Danish girls learned from the black soldiers how to do the
Monkey, the Boogalou, the Twist. And if you were walking along a street
(say, near the king's palace) and heard from the nurses' quarter of a hospital James Brown bellowing out, "Papa's Got a Brand New Bag," you knew
that someone up there is a "Cassanova girl."

Doc and George sat down, drinking from two mugs as they listened to
Otis Redding. A black soldier came up and asked them if they were in the
service and after they answered he then went on to say that he was never
going to return to the States. He got Doc's and George's support. After half
an hour with the soldier, George was getting bored.

Across from them another black soldier was telling his Danish girl a joke about a colored man. This colored man was in a multitude of people following Jesus across the desert, and they had been walking all morning and then when the sun was straight up (meaning it was lunchtime), Jesus turned to the multitude and said: Gather ye unto ye a rock. So everybody got a medium-sized rock, everybody except this colored dude; he got the tiniest pebble he could find. It was so small that he could hide it in the wrinkle in the palm of his hand. The reason he got such a little rock is, hell he figured they were going to have to carry the damn things and he didn't wanna be lugging all that dead weight.

But no, Jesus had another purpose in mind; he turned to the multitude and spoke these words: The rocks ye hold shall be turned to bread, so that ye may eat! Suddenly all the rocks were transformed into bread, and everybody had a fairly nice loaf because everybody had got a normal-sized rock. Everybody, that is, except this colored man. He had in the palm of his hand the tiniest crumb you ever seen in your life; I mean, it was just about the size of his pebble, and when he went to put it in his mouth he missed and dropped it in the sand, where, because the grains of sand was larger than the crumb, he lost it. Man, this dude was so mad with Jesus Christ that it was all he could do not to go up side Christ's head. And he was hungry. He was afraid to go over to Christ and tell him what happened—I mean, you know everybody's always accusing us colored people of shucking and jiving, so I mean, he didn't even have a chance. So he just went on holding the grudge.

Then around when the sun began to limp into sand (around dinnertime), Christ turned once again to the multitude and spoke thusly: Gather unto ye a rock. Three other black soldiers' ears had turned homewardly and were already cracking up behind the joke, the way the brother was telling it: taking his time, thoroughly enjoying his rap. And they were way ahead of the Danish girls who listened through rubber ears. Gather unto ya a rock. Man, when the brother heard this he broke for the biggest rock he could find, which was about ten feet tall and musta weighed five or six tons; he couldn't lift it, so he threw his arms around it and cried out: I got mines, Lord! And then the Lord turned and saw the huge rock and then he threw his finger out at the rock and say: Verily, verily, I say unto you, *upon this rock I shall build my church.* Then the brother said: The hell you is. You gonna make some bread outa this rock, now ain't you, Lord . . . I mean, I didn't get none the last time . . .

The brothers who had gathered around the table burst out laughing. Of course, it was an old one, but that only made it better. One of the brothers in uniform said y'all know the one about Efan the Bad Nigger and then he said during slavery times every plantation had a bad nigger, and the slave masters would be beefing about who had the baddest nigger, and so this particular slave master named Brian Coker had what he actually thought was the baddest nigger in South. The nigger's name was something like Ko-como, was about ten feet tall, had muscles like a mule and the general appearance of an ex-gorilla. Now the other slave master he had a nigger named Efan who used to go around bragging to his master and the other slaves or anybody he came in contact with about how bad he was. He was nothin' but a skinny, puny little-bitty fellow, but if you listen to him wolf about himself you'd think he was really bad. He was nothin' but a bullshit artist, see.

Another brother sat down at the table with a beer. He was round like a big, black rubber ball. He turned the chair backwards, straddled it, and threw his head back, laughing. He was wearing a red shirt with huge green and white palm leaves spread over it, and a pair of tan short pants. He said, What did you say that other bad nigger was, an ex-gorilla? Then he howled with laughter. Everybody else, the girls included, laughed too. Yeh, some-one said, an ex-gorilla. He sho' musta been bad. Hey, man, go on with the story, some G.I. in uniform said. Anyway, the red-haired storyteller con-tinued, this jiveass called Efan had his master going around thinking he was real bad, and so the master told Brian Coker the owner of that ex-gorilla that . . . The brother who came on like a big black rubber ball was bouncing on the floor . . . told him that he'd bet his plantations that Efan could beat his bad nigger. So the bet was on, 'cause Coker knew his nigger was really bad. They set the date, the place and time, and took care of all the formalities. Then the master went home and took Efan aside, and said, Efan, I have great confidence in you. I have just placed the destiny of not only the life and livelihood of my own family, but also that of your own people, in your hands. You're the baddest nigger in this section of the country, as you yourself have so many times stated, and so I have made it possible for you to use your talent, use it to further the cause of your peo-ple. If you beat Brain Coker's nigger next Monday, then we will win a whole plantation, and you'll be set up as overseer. I know you can do it, Efan. Do it for me, and more important—*do it for your people!!* Now, all the while the master was talking this way, Efan was shaking inside because he knew that his mouth had written a check his ass couldn't cash. He was scared but he didn't want the master to know it. He didn't want his master to think he wasn't as bad as he said he was. Efan had a lotta pride. And it was impos-sible for him to ever go back on his word, even though that *word* was straight from the mouth of Mr. Jiveass Nigger himself. Efan was a man who always backed up his bullshit with action, which explains why he was always getting himself in these impossible situations. So when the master said, I know you will skin the nigger alive, Efan, my man, when he said this, Efan said, Boss, go out there and dig a grave. What for, the master said. Efan said, 'Cause I'm gonna kill him, boss. Wait a minute, boss, you don't have to build no large grave, just a small hole like this. And he made a hole with his two open hands. Just a small hole what you use to bury guts in to keep 'em from the dogs will do, 'cause I'm going to crumble that nigger into little bits, I'm gonna pack him into a bucket, boss, like he was dirt. Man, if that master only knew that this skinny nigger was lying!

So for the next five days Efan lived like a king. He had the master working for him. Every morning he'd tell the boss, Boss, you go saddle up your best horse you got there. I'll be down as soon as I take a bath, shave, and get my shoes shined. Hitch the horse out there, comb the mane, and get them brand-new trace chains out. Efan told the master if he was gonna beat the nigger he had to eat well, and so he ate six meals a day in the Big House with Miss Ann and the white folks. He wore a white suit, a red handkerchief around his neck, got a haircut, had one of the slaves cleaning out his fingernails and everything. He got so particular that he made the boss get somebody to iron his drawers. "'Cause, boss, he said, I'm gonna beat that joker so he gonna look life a can of beef tripe when I get finish with his no 'count butt. . . . You sho' must be from down home, the way you talk about trace chains, man, a brother said; he had his fingers draped over the breasts of the young, cute girl sitting next to him. Whar' you from, man, the brother said. Let the man finish, someone said. . . . So when that Monday finally came, the poet continued, he took a big swig from the beer mug. When that Monday rolled around, everybody from all over the state, this was in Georgia, came to see the Big Fight. That bad nigger Kocomo was already there. He had ripped up some trees by their roots and throw'd them about a couple of miles to the side, and was at the time throwing a fifty-pound sledge hammer a mile or so up in the air and every time the hammer came down, it buried itself around five feet in the ground. And big Kocomo would reach down, snatch it up, and send dirt flying everywhichaway.

Thousands of people were standing around watching this and waiting for Efan. Efan was late. Then here come Efan and his master and Miss Ann in a fine golden coach driven by six fine black horses—not white horses, but *black* horses! When Efan saw that bad nigger Kocomo, he started tremblin' all over again. Great God! he thought to himself, if I don't think up somethin', that bad nigger gonna kick my ass and bury *me* in the ground like he doing that sledge hammer. He didn't know what to do, he was trembling so. The crowd was yelling. Efan looked at the bad nigger, and then spat in the dust. Then he climbed out of the coach, and as he stepped out, he flung off his cape. The crowd grew silent. Kocomo was about five times bigger than Efan, but the way Efan was carrying himself had everybody thinking he was bad too. The crowd watched Efan in silence and anticipation, watched Efan stroll calmly over to where this ex-gorilla was standing with the sledge hammer. Efan walked over to the sledge hammer that was lying at Kocomo's feet. He tried to lift it, but it wouldn't budge. But he didn't try too hard because he didn't want everybody to know exactly how weak he was. When he saw that he couldn't possibly lift the thing, he looked up to heaven, and with one hand on the handle of the hammer, he said: St. Peter, you hear me talking to you up there? Well, move over, and tell Sister Mary and them other sisters to move out of the way, okay? And move Baby Jesus too. When Kocomo heard this he start thinking, this sho' must be a bad nigger, to be talking like that. And so he got scared and start trembling a little bit himself. Then Efan reached down like he was gonna pick up the hammer again, but stopped and looked down at his hands. Then he looked over to the coach to where the master and Miss Ann sat, and he started walking over toward them. Everybody's eyes were glued on him as he took his time going over to the coach. Kocomo start to trembling, 'cause he didn't know what that nigger was gonna do next. He was fixin' to run, because he was sorta convinced already that there was something odd about this little-bitty nigger who think he can beat somebody five times his size. Efan finally got to the coach, climbed inside, and took Miss Ann's hand, and led her out so that were both in full view of the crowd. Then he slapped her across the face. You could hear the slap crack like a bullwhip. Efan said, Woman, didn't I tell you not to let me forget my white leather gloves. Where is my gloves at, huh? Now when Kocomo saw this, he jump up and start running. Lord have mercy, he said, any nigger slap a white woman in Georgia is too bad for me. And they never seen that bad Kocomo since.

◎◎

FLIP WILSON

COWBOYS AND COLORED PEOPLE

The Indians aren't ready yet. Now, quite often when I say that people feel that it's a harsh statement. But how harsh it is depends on how we look at it. Let's ask ourselves a question like, "Do you want to build a $50,000 home and have some guy put a wigwam next door?" I'm not against Indians! I don't want anyone to leave here feeling I'm against Indians! There have been Indians that I've admired, guys I've looked up to, fellows who in my opinion didn't let the fact that they were an Indian hold them back. They were aggressive, they went out and exerted that aggressiveness and made a name for themselves. Guys like Tonto . . . Little Beaver, those guys.

I tried to help an Indian once, he didn't appreciate it. He made a smart remark about colored people, and I got mad. I got mad because I like colored people. In fact, a colored lady raised me. Some of my best friends are colored people.

Let me tell you the way the entire situation came up. It was last year, beautiful day last year, I'm standing around, I didn't have anything to do. And I say to myself, "You ain't got nothin' to do." I'm walking down the street, there's a restaurant. I enter, I see an Indian sitting there in a booth. I say, "Damn, there's an Indian." I'm surprised because this looks like the guy off the nickel. That's who I thought it was, I say, "There's the guy off the nickel." And I want to get to meet him, be his friend, go places with him, let my friends see me with him. Then they'll say, "That's Flip Wilson, he hangs out with an Indian—the guy on the nickel." I'm gonna pick up the check, maybe we'll have a drink and go to a movie. Maybe we'll go see *How the West Was Won*. Indian should like that. So I approach him there at the table, and I say, "Good afternoon sir, you're an Indian, aren't you?"

He says, "Yeah, that's right, how'd you guess?"

I say, "Those feathers, baby. You're either an Indian or a chicken."

Then he said his name was Henry. I know the guy is lying because Indians don't have names like Henry. Who the hell ever heard of Henry Indian? But I'm gonna overlook this because I wanna help him. So I pull him aside, and I say, "Henry, come here."

I say, "Henry, look," I say, "Henry, you Indians have got to get organized and start making some progress, like the colored people are doin'. You know what I mean, Henry?" I said, "You Indians got a rough deal, Henry. You guys damn near got wiped out." Say, "There are only seven or eight Indians left, Henry. You're the second Indian I've seen in nine years."

Say, "Henry, the trouble with you guys is that pipe." Said, "I know what you got in that pipe. I'm not going to tell 'em because I don't want to see you go to jail. But I know what's in the pipe, Henry. If you guys had put the pipe down to stop and think for a minute you'd of realized what was happening when the Pilgrims ran that Thanksgiving game on you. Remember that come over to dinner thing, Henry? That was beautiful, "Come on over to dinner, come on." You guys come running over, they spread a little table out, give you little plates, some turkey, a little potato salad, slice of pie, glass of Kool-Aid. But that's all they gave you." Say, "They never invited you back though, did they?"

He say, "They never invited you people to dinner."

Now I'm mad. I'm mad because I don't have to take this from a damn Indian. I'm not going to let him get away with this. If I let him get away with this next he'll want to marry my sister. So I ask him, I say, "Henry, why should they invite us to dinner when we're doing the cooking?" Told him, I say, "The biggest thing that happened to you Indians is when they put you on the nickel. They put a buffalo on the other side, Henry." Say, "If you guys belonged to the NAACP we'd have you on the quarter. Maybe we'll change the name, Henry. Maybe we'll call it the National Association for the Advancement of Colored People Immediately and the Indians on a Gradual Basis.

"We're making progress, Henry. We got guys like Ralph Bunch, international mediator. That's all Ralph does, he goes all over the world looking for arguments." Say, "They pay Ralph for that. Jimmy Brown was playing football then, Jimmy got that ball [sound of running]. Willie Mays hits those home runs. Willie comes down that stadium in the afternoon. Willie's sharp. Willie don't come down there unless he's sharp. Got that lump in his pocket, that 100 G's from last year. When he come up to bat there's 20,000 girls in the stands screamin' at Willie, 'Hit that ball Willie, hit that ball honey. What you say.' Home run right out of that park." Said, "An Indian never hit a home run. Isn't that right?"

And he said, "Yeah, you're right, but I never heard of anyone playing Cowboys and Colored People."

KIDS

You meet a lot of nice people, you know, traveling from city to city. Like a few weeks ago, a lady came in, caught the show and after the show she spent a few minutes chatting with the entertainers. And then she says, "Come by the house. Let me fix a home cooked meal for you. You can get away from eating in the restaurants." Fine gesture. I accept.

I go by. The lady has a couple of kids. I get there a little late. She's already fed the kids, she's running their bath. She says generally she gives them their bath, they watch television, then into bed. The television doesn't work, the kids don't know. They sit there waiting for it to light up. When they fall asleep she puts them in bed. Three years the television hasn't worked.

What strikes me as unusual is she runs the water in the tub, and she puts the boy and the girl in the tub together. I'm watching this and I say,

"Damn, the boy and the girl in the tub together." I'm surprised. I was twenty-five before I got in on a set like this. They're standin' there in the tub lookin' at each other. She goes back in the kitchen, and I sneak behind the door, I'm going to watch. I'm watchin' through the crack in the door, and the girl says to her brother, "What's that?"

And he says, "Where?"

She says, "Right there."

He says, "I don't know."

She says, "Well what's it for?"

He says, "I told you I don't know."

She says, "Can I touch it?"

He says, "Heck no. You broke yours off already."

CHEAP HOTEL

I think it's a nice thing having fans, you know that. My uncle told me about that value of what it is to have fans. My uncle was an entertainer. He was a comic, too. My uncle was a part of a team. You know he was around during the days, the old days of the teams. You know, when the teams had the names like Off and On, Up and Down, Over and Under, and Stop and Go. My uncle belonged to a comedy team called Well Enough and Bad Enough. And, uh, they were doing all right. Then Bad Enough got married, my uncle started working alone. He was doing well enough.

He told me about an incident that took place. He was in Chicago for a one nighter. After the show he decided that instead of leaving out right then he'd spend the night and leave in the morning. That's a good time to leave if you're going to spend the night. No sense leaving before "in the morning." So he said he checked into a hotel, cheap hotel . . . cheap hotel. My uncle said, "That sure was a cheap hotel." That was the name of the hotel, Cheap Hotel. Had a big sign out front blinking on and off—CHEAP, CHEAP, CHEAP.

My uncle was afraid of risking spending the night in a room in a cheap hotel with four hundred dollars in his pocket. So, he says to the desk clerk, "Would you hold the four hundred dollars till in the morning. I'll pick it up when I come down."

The guy say, "*Yeah!*"

When my uncle comes down in the morning he says to the guy, "I'd like to get my four hundred dollars back."

The fellow says, "You didn't give me any money."

My uncle says, "You're the same guy who was here last night when I checked in right?"

Fellow says, "That's right. We only have one desk clerk. That's why this is such a cheap hotel." Said, "But you didn't give me any money."

My uncle tells him, "Look, you can't take my money like this and get away with it."

And the guy says, "You never know what you can do until you try."

So my uncle tells him, he says, "Look, if you don't give my money back, I'm going to hit you right in the mouth."

And the guy says, "Violence is the tool of the ignorant."

When he said that my uncle leaped at him . . . with the fury of a thousand jungle beasts. Just saw that in a picture yesterday, thought I'd throw that in. He leaped at him, the fellow stepped aside, he fell and the guy kicked him in the face. When the guy kicked him in the face, my uncle saw a baseball bat in the corner. So he ran, grabbed the bat, and he raised the bat like he was going to hit the guy with it and the fellow threw a cup of hot coffee in his face. And he grabbed his face. You'd grab your face somebody throw some hot coffee in it. He grabbed his face and the fellow grabbed the bat.

He said the guy beat him with the bat . . . about an hour, hour and a half. He said he didn't remember how long the guy beat him because when the fellow raised the bat he passed out. But he distinctly remembered that when he woke up the fellow was standing over him making some more coffee.

He ran out the door and found a policeman. He brought the officer back, they had the guy arrested. Now ironically, when the thing came up in court the judge had been at the show the night before and seen my uncle work. He was a fan of my uncle's.

The judge walks in and he says, "Well Enough, how you doin'?" They shook hands, you know. And the judge says, "What's the trouble?" He says, "Look, while I'm taking care of the case you sign a couple of autographed pictures for my wife and my kid, they loved you. They loved you. Now, what's the problem here?"

And the judge listened to the entire case. And when it reached the time for a decision the judge told the defendant, he said, "Look, I don't want you to think that the fact that I admire this great man here is going to influence my giving a just decision here. But it is the decision of this court that you return to this man the four hundred dollars that you took and you give him an extra two hundred dollars for damages and that for the next ten years he'll get to stay in your hotel for free room and board, for *nothin'.* In addition to which the court sentences you to ninety days in jail."

And the guy says, "Your honor, how come you're being so hard on me?"

And the judge says, "Because I'm trying to teach you to leave Well Enough alone."

CHURCH ON SUNDAY

Can't wait till Sunday. I go to church every Sunday. I have a very strong religious background. I go to church. I go. I'm in different cities I go to different churches. Last week I went to a beautiful little church uptown. It was nice . . . they charge you a dollar to get in. You know . . . you pay their dollar, they give you a sandwich, something like that. Then they have a little group there that plays. The group does a forty minute set, then the Rev comes on and does twenty minutes.

And, well like, Rev opened the service by passing the plate. Plate shot around the room, came back, nothing in it. Rev said, "Y'all there's nothing in the plate." Said, "I lost money coming down here." Said, "I'm going to send the plate back out there again and give y'all a chance to clean this up." Plate shot around the room, came back, nothing again. Rev said, "Now brothers and sisters we can't make it like this." Said, "Now I'm sure that everybody wants this church to PROGRESS! AND IF THIS CHURCH IS GOING TO PROGRESS, FIRST IT'S GOTTA CRAWL! THIS CHURCH HAS GOTTA CRAWL!"

And the congregation yelled, "LET IT CRAWL, REV, LET IT CRAWL!"

Rev said, "And after this church has crawled its gotta stand up and WALK!"

And the members yelled, "MAKE IT WALK, REV, MAKE IT WALK!"

Rev said, "And after this church has walked its gotta RUN! This church has gotta RUN!"

And the members yelled, "MAKE IT RUN, REV, MAKE IT RUN!"

Rev said, "For this church to RUN, its gonna take MONEY!"

And the members yelled, "LET IT CRAWL, REV, LET IT CRAWL!"

UGLY BABY

In traveling, lots of unusual things happen. A few weeks ago I'm riding the train between New York and Washington. When I boarded the train the first thought is to find my seat, get settled, and relax. Once I'd gotten settled, I glanced across the aisle and I noticed the woman occupying the seat there had a baby with her . . . ugly baby—bad looking baby. And I want to make it clear that, generally, I'd be reluctant to express an opinion of someone's kid. But I know an ugly baby when I see one, and I only had a glimpse, a quick look.

Then this fellow enters the coach, he's half smashed. When he gets to the section where the woman is with the baby, he stops and he's staring. And the lady is watching. She heard him when he said to himself, "Damn."

And the lady said, "What are you looking at?"

Guy said, "I'm looking at that ugly baby—that's a bad looking baby, lady." Said, "That's a hell of a kid you got there." Said, "I bet you save a lot of money with that baby. You don't have to hire a baby sitter. No one's going to bother that kid."

The woman took this as an offense. She pulls the emergency cord, the train stops, there's a big scene, the conductor comes running in, "What's going on in here? What's going on in here?"

And the lady says, "This fellow just insulted me. I don't have to spend my money to ride this railroad and be insulted."

Conductor says, "Now, calm down." Say, "Madam, the railroad will go to any extent to avoid having differences between the passengers." Said, "Perhaps, it would be more to your convenience if we were to rearrange your seating and, as a small compensation from the railroad, if you'll accompany me to the dining car we'll give you a free meal and—maybe we'll find a banana for your monkey."

CHRISTOPHER COLUMBUS

Everyone has idols, right? People who inspired them and drove them on to greater horizons. As a kid my idol, and he's still my idol, of all the great American heroes my idol was Chistopher Columbus. What a great thing that was, discovering America. I wouldn't a found it. I don't know where you people would have been, I wouldn't have found it. You know, discovering America wasn't a thing that Christopher Columbus got wrapped up in after getting older. As a kid this was all he talked about.

He lived in a little town with his mother and father. Their names were Mr. and Mrs. Columbus. Everybody thought Chris was off his cookie. Like the neighbors would tease him, they'd come by and lean over the fence. He'd be there in the yard, and they'd say, "Chistopher Columbus, what are you going to do when you grow up?" And he'd say, "I'm going to discover America." They'd say, "You'd better cut that out. You know there isn't any America. You know the world is square." Chris would say, "They sure are."

At thirty-five he'd gotten out of grammar school. He arranged an audience with the Queen, Queen Isabelle . . . Isabelle Johnson. That was the Queen's name. And she asked him about this America project, and Chris tells her that "if I don't discover America there's not going to be a Benjamin Franklin or a Star Spangled Banner and a land of the free and the home of the brave. And no Ray Charles." When the Queen heard no Ray Charles, she panicked. The Queen say, "Ray Charles? You goin' find Ray Charles?

He in America?" Chris say, "Damn right! That's where all those records come from."

So the Queen's running through the halls of the castle screamin', "Chris gonna find Ray Charles, honey. He goin' to America on that boat. What you say." She wrote him out a traveler's check. Chris ran to the local Army–Navy store. He bought three used ships, two pairs of fatigues, some shades. Then he got his supplies for the ship. He got two chicken sandwiches, three cans of Vienna sausages, five cases of scotch, and a small 7-Up. Then he got a new rag to tie his head with too. He was ready to leave!

All the photographers and reporters are at the pier to see him off. All the girls are there. They're all screamin', "Good-bye Columbus. He goin' on that boat. He goin' to America." Isabelle was there, and she'd had a few. Isabelle say, "Chris goin' find Ray Charles, honey [sound of fingers snapping]."

Chris said, "Be cool Isabelle, be cool." Then he turned to the first mate and he said, "Weigh the anchor." About ten minutes later the guy says, "7,482 pounds." Chris says, "Put that anchor in the boat. Don't weigh it. Just put it—you all don't even know how to weigh the anchor."

When they'd gotten out of the harbor the first mate asked, "Chris, which way is America?" Chris say, "I don't know. We're gonna have to sail around and we'll bump into it." Say, "We better go this way. If we go that way we'll sail off the edge like them other guys."

A hundred days later, the men are ready to mutiny. Chris has been goofing. He's been goin' though a bit like, "BACK UP! MAKE A RIGHT! WATCH OUT FOR THE EDGE!"

First mate say, "Come here Chris." Say, "Come here." Say, "Chris, the men are ready to mutiny. The cabin boy said that if you don't find America in two days he's gonna smack you in the mouth." Right then a piece of wood floats by the ship.

Chris said, "There's a piece of wood." Said, "We're not far from America. That's American wood." Said, "I know American wood when I see it."

First mate said, "Why don't you cut that out. It's a piece of the ship. They're breaking up on us."

Right then the guy on the mast yells, "LAND HO!"

Chris says, "What does that mean?"

Fellow says, "That means that he sees land."

Chris says, "Well pull over! Maybe that's America. You're goin' to pass right by it. You guys don't even know America when you see it." Said, "That is America." Said, "Look at all those spacious skies. Those amber waves of grain." Said, "Dig that purple mountain's majesty. I bet there's fruit out there on the plain."

It's a big holiday in America that day. Big holiday called Not Having Been Discovered Yet Day. All the Indians are on the beach there celebratin'. They got sandwiches, six packs, three or four bags of whatever it is they're puttin' in the pipe. Chris leans over the rail of the ship, he says, "HEY Y'ALL, Y'ALL, WHERE IS THIS?"

Fine little Indian girl [whistle], fine little Indian, fine little West Indian girl standin' there on the beach, say, "Why, what's your name? What the hell you want? Comin' round here in those ships."

He said, "My name is Christopher Columbus. I'm a discoverer." Said, "I'm gonna discover America. I'm gonna discover y'all."

Little girl say, "We don't want to be discovered. You can't discover nobody if they don't want to be discovered. You better discover your ass away from here."

First mate say, "Chris, they're hostile."

Chris say, "Yeah, and they mad too." Said, "But we're goin' in there anyway. That's America. They can't keep us out of there. America belongs to everybody. LET DOWN THE LONG BOAT!"

And they let down the long boat, which was really a short boat on the side of the big boat. They called it the long boat because they had a peewee boat but they weren't goin' to use that. They piled ashore, and they're heading in, and the men are laying down because the Indians are throwin' rocks and spears, flamin' arrows, and tree trunks. Yellin' out a bunch of profanity about Chris's mother and everything.

First mate say, "Chris, we better not go in there. Those Indians are crazy."

Chris said, "Turn the boat around. We'll leave. We'll make a map and give it to the Pilgrims. Pilgrims will fix their ass."

◎◎

PAUL MOONEY

PAUL REVERE/BETSY ROSS

Thank God Paul Revere was white, 'cause we wouldn't be sittin' here now. 'Cause if he'd a been black, somebody would have shot that nigger, "Oh that nigger stole that horse." They'd a shot Paul Revere.

Hey, who do the white people say sewed the flag? Who's this white woman supposed to have sewed the flag? Betsy Ross . . . ain't that a bitch. Now come on, they had slaves. That bitch was asleep at six. You know some big black fat Aunt Jemima was up all night sewing that flag.

BLAME-A-NIGGER

They don't want to give us any credit. They just want to blame everything on niggers. Didn't some white man in Boston shoot his pregnant wife and then shot hisself, talkin' about, "Oh, niggers did it." Always trying to blame some niggers. . . . That's why I'm gonna start a new ad, 1–900-Blame-a-Nigger. So when white folks get in trouble, just call my agency.

"Hello, Blame-a-Nigger? I just pushed my mother down the stairs. I don't want to go to jail. Send a nigger over here!"

"All right, I got one on parole. I'll send him right over ma'am."

NIGGER RAISINS

White folks favorite TV commercial is that little, wrinkled, black, shriveled-up raisin. Little nigger raisin with a hat, they think that shit is cute, singin', "*Heard it through the grapevine.*" They think that shit is cute.

"Oh, look at the cute nigger raisin."

"*Heard it through the grapevine.*"

They've gone nigger fuckin' raisin crazy. They made Ray Charles a raisin. Oh fuck him, he's blind. [singing] "*What I say?*" Then I looked up one morning and Michael Jackson was a goddamn raisin.

I said, "They've gone nigger fuckin' raisin crazy." And the shit ain't cute. I bet if I get me some marshmallows and put some arms and legs on them goddamn marshmallows and let 'em sing *Surfin' USA,* they won't think that shit's so goddamn cute.

❦

FROM *SOUTH STREET*

By David Bradley

In his 1975 first novel, David Bradley focused on Philadelphia's South Street and the denizens of Lightnin' Ed's Bar and Grill. A tragicomic tale of a neighborhood in transition, South Street *was highlighted by its vivid depictions of the area's colorful characters and their unconventional attitudes. Comedy reigns in the following set piece involving the bartender Leo, the resident prostitute Big Betsy, and a wayward cleric.*

"A *what?*" roared Big Betsy the whore.

"You heard me," Leo said.

"Well, what the hell is a goddamn preacher doin' in a goddamn bar?"

"Most likely he's drinkin' a little beer an' watchin' the ballgame an' not botherin' nobody with a lot of bullshit, which is a lot moren I can say for some folks."

"Drinkin' *beer?* Damn, Leo, everybody knows preachers don't drink beer."

"Now, how'd you find out so much about preachers? I'd say you been tryin' to whore your way into heaven, but even preachers don't got that much charity."

"I learned 'bout preachers the same way you learned 'bout women," Big Betsy informed him. "Somebody told me. Damn, Leo, you can't start havin' a bunch a preachers hangin' out in here. The place'll go to the damn dogs."

Leo regarded her sourly. "There's a rumor goin' round that I'm already runnin' a kennel, 'cause you spend so much time in here."

"Kiss ma ass," Big Betsy said. "You ain't got no respect for your old customers. You gonna have a bunch of preachers in here eatin' fried chicken an' scarin' the tricks away."

"Betsy," Leo told her, "you wouldn't have no more customers if they was to line up every damn preacher in South Philly an' blow his damfool head off. Only way you gonna get more business is if they make it illegal to screw a woman that ain't got a senior citizen's card."

Big Betsy's sagging jowls sagged further. "That Leo, was cold."

"Well if you don't wanna get froze," Leo said, "then you get up offa ma case. The man is a preacher, just like I'm a bartender an' you're a whore. Everybody's got to get along the best they can doin' the best they knows how. Preacher's got a right to have a quiet drink if he wants one without everybody forkin' shit on him just 'cause he peddles Bibles instead a peddlin' his ass or somebody else's. He's a nice dude, an' he knows more about the Phillies than Dizzy Dean an' the damn TV computer put together, an' he don't try to tell me who I can have in ma bar an' who I can't, so you can just shut your goddamn mouth an' fuck off."

Big Betsy stared at Leo, her mouth open. "Damn, Leo. You queer for the dude or somethin'?"

Leo gave her a long, hard look, then he leaned over and whispered in her ear. "You cool it, fat stuff, or I'ma tell everybody 'bout the time you tried to make it with the beer bottle."

"That was along time ago," Big Betsy protested.

"It had to be," Leo snapped, " 'cause even a beer bottle couldn't keep it up over you any more."

"Damn, Leo," said Big Betsy.

"You just let him be if he comes in. You hear?"

"I hear you talkin'," Big Betsy said.

"You best quit hearin' me talkin' an' commence to listenin' to what I'm sayin'."

"I am, I am," Big Betsy said. "You say he's okay, then he's okay. After all, it's your bar, Leo. You got a right to have anybody in it you wants. You wants a preacher, you gets a preacher. You wants a honky, you can get one a them, too."

"Ain't nobody said nothin' 'bout no honkies," Leo snapped.

"Well, it's the next step, Leo," Big Betsy said. "You get a couple preachers, the next step is to have a bunch a honky social workers. Next thing you know they done fixed the street, put in new sewers, built a new school, an' raised the taxes. There goes the damn neighborhood."

Leo uneasily examined her logic for a moment, then gave up and stuck to his guns. "All I got, an' all I'm gonna have, is one damn preacher. I ain't no preacher-lover, but he's a nice fella. There's gotta be some nice preachers somewheres."

"I ain't never met one," said Big Betsy.

"Well, you oughta meet this one."

"What the hell . . ." Big Betsy stopped suddenly and her face assumed an expression that screamed of calculation. "Well, now," she said slowly, "maybe I should. I mean, if the man drinks beer maybe he's up for a little action." Leo put down the glass he had been polishing and stared at her. "W'hell," said Big Betsy defensively, "maybe I'm just what he's been lookin' for."

"I doubt it," Leo said. "He sure musta seen you by now. You're too damn big t'overlook."

"Maybe he's shy," snapped Big Betsy. "We ain't been introduced. You gotta introduce us, Leo."

"Oh, God," Leo muttered. "Betsy, I got better things to do than play pimp to a preacher."

"Humph," said Big Betsy. "Trouble with you, Leo, is you don't change your Kotex real reglar."

"You remember what them things is for, do you?" Leo said. "You not only look like one, you got a mem'ry like one." He grinned at Big Betsy, who ignored him pointedly for a few moments, then sighed.

"All right, Leo. Like what?"

"A snaggle-toothed elephant," Leo said.

"Fuck off," said Big Betsy, and marched off toward the ladies' room. Leo grinned and went back to polishing glasses.

It was shaping up to be a quiet night, one of the nights when Leo loved his job, a night free from drawn knives, squabbling couples, sick drunks, maudlin whores, irate wives, henpecked husbands, and idiots who insisted on playing Russian roulette with Leroy Briggs. Such nights had been rare of late—the hot summer seemed to be drawing the sweat and blood and ornery out of everybody. Leo had felt the change in himself as the August heat had taken its toll. He had begun to notice the hard edges of things, instead of sensing the softer interiors: when he looked at Big Betsy he saw her bitchiness before he saw her loneliness, he saw Rayburn Wallace as weak rather than meek, as powerless more than as gentle. Leo realized suddenly that over the long hot weeks he had been withdrawing into himself, spending more time with the TV. Leo drew himself a long, cold beer and took a thoughtful swallow. Then he leaned over and unplugged the set. Tonight, Leo decided, the bar would get his full attention. He would dedicate the evening to breaking out of the crust that the summer had baked onto him. He stretched, expanding his beer-and-sweat-stained shirt past all reasonable expectation. He slurped his beer and trundled down to make amends with Big Betsy, who was now sitting and smoldering at the far end of the bar. Impulsively, Leo poured a shot glass full of gin and placed it before her. Big Betsy eyed it with suspicion.

"What the hell's that?" Big Betsy demanded.

"It's a slug a gin," Leo said. "Beefeater."

"I can see that, Leo," Big Betsy snarled. "What the hell's it doin' there?"

Leo regarded the shot glass appraisingly. "Not much," he admitted.

"Well what the hell's it *for,* Leo?" said Big Betsy with exaggerated patience.

"It's for you."

"For me?"

"That's right," Leo said. "That there gin is a peace offerin.'"

Big Betsy stared at him for a moment, and then her face burst into a jack-o'-lantern grin. "Damn, Leo, I knowed you'd come around. You might almost be human." Big Betsy reached out and grasped the glass. She leered at Leo, but in an instant the leer turned into a scowl, and she flung the gin straight into Leo's face. "Only trouble with your thinkin,'" she continued without noticeable rancor, "is that I ain't hardly desperate enough to be givin' no pieces away for one lousy slug a gin."

Leo stood with gin running out of his sparse hair and onto his face, dripping off his nose and onto his thick lips, off his chin and onto his broad chest. He made no motion. Leo appeared to be in shock.

"Haw, haw, haw," laughed Big Betsy. "You sure do look like a goddamn fool, Leo. Shame to waste good gin, but it's worth it. Haw, haw, haw." Leo remained catatonic. His tongue flicked out and, ever so gently, absorbed the liquid that had dripped down to within its range. His eyes blinked as a few drops of gin trickled into them, then closed. Big Betsy stopped laughing. "Leo?" said Big Betsy. Leo did not move. "Leo!" Leo remained motionless, like a lumpy carving in dark wood. "Omigod," said Big Betsy. "Omigod."

Brother Fletcher entered Lightnin' Ed's just as Big Betsy reached out a crooked forefinger and jabbed her long fingernail into Leo's protruding paunch. Leo rocked back on his heels, nearly toppling over backward before the counterweight of his pot belly swung him back into balance. Big Betsy emitted an anguished choke and tried to back away from Leo's rigid form while still perched on the bar stool. As a direct result, Betsy and bar stool became a tangled mass on the floor, which Brother Fletcher eyed with some astonishment. Big Betsy bounced up like an overinflated volleyball, while the stool, two of its legs snapped neatly by the sudden application of Big Betsy's weight, remained on the floor. "Omigod," whispered Big Betsy, her eyes on motionless Leo.

"What's the matter?" asked Brother Fletcher.

Big Betsy pointed her finger at Leo, looked down at it, and quickly hid her hand behind her back. "Omigod," said Big Betsy, "I done made poor Leo bust a goddamn blood vessel. I done give poor Leo a stroke, or he's havin' a fuckin' fit, an' it's all ma fault. Omigod."

To Brother Fletcher it appeared that it was Big Betsy who was having the fit. She jabbed Leo in the solar plexus with her forefinger; breath escaped burbling through Leo's pursed lips, but his face remained immobile and his body rigid. "Omigod." She tore her eyes away from Leo and focused them on Brother Fletcher. "I threw a whole glass a Beefeater in his face, an' now he's havin' a fit. Poor Leo, I done him in. I didn't mean it."

"Of course not," soothed Brother Fletcher. "But I really don't think a glass of gin . . ." Brother Fletcher stopped suddenly, realizing that he had not the slightest notion as to the possible effects of a glass of gin administered externally, or internally, for that matter.

"It wasn't the goddamn gin," Big Betsy wailed. "I shot Leo down. Shot him cold."

"You *what?*"

Big Betsy nodded. "In flames. I burned him clean. You see"—she turned her wistful gaze on Leo—"me an' Leo, we ain't exactly in *love* or nothin', but, well, we been together a long time, you know? An' I guess Leo just couldn't take it when he fin'ly got around to astin' for some an' I turned him down." She turned back to Brother Fletcher. "Some men's like that, you know. A girl says no, an' they got to be takin' it all personal."

"I'm sure he'll . . . recover," Brother Fletcher said.

"I don't know," Big Betsy said doubtfully. "I shouldn'ta done like that t'old Leo." She wiped a tear from her eye. "I mean, always figured me an' Leo'd, well, you know, sooner of later. Right now I got ma career, but . . ." Her voice trailed off. She regarded Leo sadly.

Brother Fletcher looked down at Big Betsy's plumb-bob breasts and congested face and repressed a shudder. He reached out and removed the side towel from Leo's lax fingers. "Here," he said, handing it to Big Betsy. "Why don't you go run some cold water on this?"

"What for?"

"We'll put it on his head."

"Oh." Big Betsy looked pityingly at Leo for a moment, then waddled off to the rest room. As soon as the door had closed behind her Leo stuffed both hands in his mouth and fell across the bar, his big body shaking.

"You all right?" asked Brother Fletcher.

"No, no," moaned Leo. "No, the damn bitch is killin' me. I'm dyin', Rev, I'm dyin'." Leo wiped tears from his eyes and tried to push himself off the bar, which was creaking ominously from his weight.

Big Betsy burst from the ladies' room holding a soggy side towel in both hands. The water ran down her fat arms and dripped off her elbows. She stopped and stared. "He ain't dead!"

"You keep breathing in ma damn face an' I will be dead," growled Leo. He stopped laughing and managed to push himself off the bar.

"I thought you was gone, Leo," Betsy said.

Leo looked at her calmly, snorted, picked up a fresh side towel and started polishing glasses.

"I thought sure he was a gonner," Big Betsy said to Brother Fletcher. She laid the wet side towel down on the bar.

"I, ah, think you can stop worrying," Brother Fletcher said.

"Worrying?" snapped Big Betsy. "Me? 'Bout Leo? Why the hell would I wanta worry about Leo? He ain't good for nothin' 'cept pourin' gin. An' beer," Big Betsy added as Leo place a frosty mug in front of Brother Fletcher. "An'," Big Betsy continued, "there's plenty bartenders can do that better. Leo can't even pour a lady a glass a gin without gettin' it all over his ugly face."

"But—" Brother Fletcher began.

"What lady?" Leo cut in. "I don't see no damn lady."

"He's blind, too," Big Betsy confided.

"But you—" began Brother Fletcher.

"If I wasn't," Leo said, "I sure as hell wouldn't be able to stay in the same damn room as you. Every time you goes to take a piss I gotta buy a new mirror."

"What . . ." began Brother Fletcher. Then he closed his eyes, shook his head, and took a long swallow of his beer.

"Don't pay no attention to Leo, Cutie-pie," Big Betsy said, patting Brother Fletcher's arm. "Leo don't know if his mother was Lassie or Rin-Tin-Tin." She turned to Leo and glowered. "You know somethin', Leo? You think you're hot shit an' you go around puttin' down your old friends. But hot shit don't end up to be nothin' but cold turd, Leo. You remember that." She sneered at Leo and whirled on a mystified Brother Fletcher. "You know what Leo done?" she asked accusingly.

"No," said Brother Fletcher quickly.

"Well, I'll tell you," Big Betsy said. "You oughta hear it. You oughta know what kinda fool you been buyin' beer from. Leo's tryin' to turn this place into a fuckin' Sunday School. How do you like that?"

"Uh, Betsy," Leo said quickly, "I do believe it's gettin' to be time you shut your mouth or your ass or whatever you been makin' noise with."

"You don't know shit, Leo," Big Betsy said. "You don't even know the difference between your mouth an' your asshole."

Leo looked up at the ceiling, his tongue jammed into his cheek. "Betsy, now, I know *ma* mouth from *ma* asshole, but in your case there just ain't that much difference. Now why don't you just close whichever—"

"This here conversation," Big Betsy said with frosty dignity, "is *strictly* between me and Cutie-pie here. Now quit bein' jealous an' go piss."

"Yes ma'am," said Leo obediently, his eyes still on the ceiling, "but I still think—"

"I doubt it," Big Betsy snapped. Leo shrugged, made a motion of washing his hands and moved away, being careful to stay within earshot. "Don't you mind *him,* Cutie-pie," Big Betsy said, settling herself on the stool next to Brother Fletcher like a hen on a nest. "He just doesn't want nobody to know he's turnin' this place into a damn church social. You ain't gonna believe this, but he started lettin' *preachers* in here."

Brother Fletcher choked convulsively and half-swallowed beer sprayed across the bar top. His features under rigid control, Leo moved in with his side towel and mopped up the mess, wordlessly refilled Brother Fletcher's glass. Big Betsy was pounding Brother Fletcher on the back. Brother Fletcher clapped a hand over his mouth to hold his plate in. "You gonna be sick, Cutie-pie?" gasped Big Betsy between pounds. "Leo, what you done with your damn foolishness? Cutie-pie's fixin' to heave."

"Maybe I made him sick," Leo said, "but you're the one beatin' him to death. Let up on him, for God's sake."

Big Betsy stopped pounding, permitting Brother Fletcher to reposition himself on the stool and his dentures in his mouth. "You all right, Cutie-pie?" Big Betsy asked urgently.

"F-f-f-fine," sputtered Brother Fletcher.

"See, Leo?" accused Big Betsy. "The thought a havin' preachers in here messes folks all up."

"Uh huh," said Leo.

Brother Fletcher reached out a shaking hand, picked up his beer glass, and drained it to the dregs.

"You oughta pay more attention to the way folks feels, Leo," Big Betsy said.

"Uh huh," Leo said. He drew Brother Fletcher another beer. Brother Fletcher looked at him gratefully.

"Preachers is all right," Big Betsy continued, "But only where they be-longs. Same as everybody. Now a preacher ain't got no more business in a bar than I does in a damn monastery. Ain't that right, Cutie-pie?"

Brother Fletcher reached for his glass.

"It ain't like I got nothin' against preachers," Big Betsy went on. "I *like* preachers. I even know a few can hold their end up in bed. Matter a fact, I knowed quite a few. But they didn't hang around in no bars scarin' the johns away. Hell, no. They stayed at home an' ate fried chicken an' fucked widders like preachers is supposed to."

Leo grinned wolfishly and set another beer in front of Brother Fletcher, who this time did not bother to look up.

"Course now," Big Betsy ruminated, "I did know a preacher one time that wasn't satisfied with fuckin' widders. He useta go over to this woman's house in the afternoon an' tear off a piece, an' then he'd go on downstairs an' eat up whatever was in the icebox 'fore her man come home. That sorry fool be comin' home 'bout six o'clock after bustin' his nuts all damn day an' he say, 'Hey, baby, what's for dinner?' an' she say, 'Well, we was gonna have fried chicken, but the preacher was over an' he done ate everythin'.' Well, after this fool went hungry for about a week in a row he decides to come home early an' see can he get in some greasin' 'fore the preacher ate everythin' up. Only when he comes in the kitchen door there ain't no preacher. Ain't no preacher in the dinin' room neither. So he tiptoes on upstairs an' there's the preacher with his head down there 'tween that woman's legs just chewin' away. Well the dude hauls off an' pulls the preacher outa there an' knocks him over in the corner an' says, 'Damn, Rev, ain't it bad enough you gotta be fuckin' up ma eatin', now you gotta be eatin' up ma fuckin', too? "Haw, haw, haw."

Leo hugged himself, a formidable task. Brother Fletcher made a grab for his glass and downed the contents like a shot. "Haw, haw, haw," roared Big Betsy. "Ain't that a blowjob? Ain't that a fuckin' blowjob?" She slapped Brother Fletcher soundly on the back. Brother Fletcher felt his upper body accelerate rapidly in the direction of the wall until it was arrested sharply by his spine. Brother Fletcher choked. Leo slapped another glass of beer into Brother Fletcher's feebly clutching fingers, and Brother Fletcher poured it down his throat. "Damn," said Big Betsy in admiration, "you sure can put it away. That must be five you had since you got here, an' that wasn't but a minute ago."

"Is that all?" moaned Brother Fletcher. "It felt longer."

"You got it backwards, Cutie-pie," Big Betsy informed him. "First you feel it, an' *then* it gets longer. Haw, haw, haw."

"Sweet Jesus," breathed Brother Fletcher. He hauled himself off the stool just in time to avoid the slap that Big Betsy had launched at his back, and tottered off to the men's room.

"Nice fella," Big Betsy commented. "He ain't no powerhouse, but he sure can soak up some suds."

"Uh huh," said Leo.

"I ain't seen him before. He's new, huh, Leo?"

"Uh huh," Leo said.

"Can't you say nothin' but 'uh huh'?" demanded Big Betsy. "You sound like a fuckin' cow."

"I sound like a fuckin' bull," Leo said. "A fuckin' bull goes 'uh huh.' A fuckin' cow goes 'uh.'"

Big Betsy gave Leo a look of complete disgust. "That," she said, "is foul."

"Sorry," Leo said meekly.

Brother Fletcher returned from the men's room, his face a trifle ashy. He walked carefully, like a septuagenarian strolling over hot eggs, and slid gingerly onto his stool. "Do you think I could have another beer, Leo?" he said softly.

"Why sure, Re—ah, Cutie-pie," Leo said.

"Whatsa matter, Leo, can't you remember the man's name?" snapped Big Betsy. She turned and smiled seductively at Brother Fletcher. "Leo may look like a chocolate-covered elephant, but he's got the mem'ry of a two-year-old M&M." She turned her glare on Leo. "Only he ain't gonna be meltin' in ma mouth *or* in ma hand."

"Could I have another beer, Leo?" Brother Fletcher said.

"You got one," Leo said.

"Oh," said Brother Fletcher. He picked up the glass and emptied it. Leo refilled it wordlessly.

"Don't pay no attention to Leo, Cutie-pie," Big Betsy said. "Leo just don't know what to do with hisself when there's a real man around. All Leo knows is to talk some dirty fuckin' shit an' the rest of the time he hangs around with preachers. Next thing you know, it'll be choirboys, an' Leo gonna sprout ten pairs a wings." Big Betsy grinned and made flipping motions with her hands.

Leo grinned at her. "Now, Betsy, I do seem to recall you was talkin' about how you was gonna be slingin' some action the preacher's way soon as he showed up. Ain't that right?"

"That is true, baby," said Big Betsy soothingly, while shooting thirty-eight caliber glares at Leo. "I did say that, but that was 'fore *you* got here. I mean, 'fore you come in onliest thing in sight even comin' close to bein' a man was Leo, an' next to Leo any damn thing would look good. Small, but good. Even a preacher. But that don't make no difference now I got you."

"Leo," said Brother Fletcher, "another beer." Leo complied, grinning happily. Brother Fletcher downed the whole thing.

"Preachers ain't nothin' when you get right down to it," Big Betsy said. "I'd rather be with you, Cutie-pie, than any damn preacher." Big Betsy reached out and stroked the back of Brother Fletcher's neck.

"Leo," croaked Brother Fletcher. Leo filled the glass. Brother Fletcher took a swallow, turned to Big Betsy. "I wish you wouldn't do that."

"Aw, now Cutie-pie, don't be that way," whined Big Betsy. "I tell you, that preacher ain't nothin' to me. The last time I made it with a preacher he wasn't even no good. Couldn't get it up until I got him thinkin' I was a plate a fried chicken an' his pecker was a fork. An' then he wanted to use his fingers. So then I told him it was ham an' red-eye gravy, an' then he ate for *hours*. Haw, haw, haw."

Brother Fletcher looked distinctly uncomfortable, and even Leo turned slightly gray. "You want another beer?" Leo asked.

"You haven't got anything stronger?" Brother Fletcher asked weakly. Leo nodded and poured out two glasses of scotch. He gave one to Brother Fletcher and lifted the other to his own lips. As he set the glass down Jake shuffled in.

"You an' me, Cutie-pie, we gonna have a time no preacher ain't even thought about," Big Betsy said.

"Evenin', Betsy. Evenin', Leo. Evenin', Reverend," Jake said.

"Evenin', Jake," Leo said.

"Whad you say?" asked Big Betsy.

"I said 'Evenin',' " Leo said blandly.

"Not you. *You!*"

"I said evenin', too," Jake said. "What the hell?"

"You said, 'Evenin' Reverend,' " Big Betsy accused.

"That's right," Jake said. "That's what I said. Good evenin', Reverend."

"Good evening," said Brother Fletcher solemnly.

"Omigod," said Big Betsy.

"What the hell's goin' on?" demanded Jake.

"Oh, nothin'," said Leo. "We just been tryin' to figure out which is bigger, Betsy's foot or her mouth. Mouth won."

"Omigod," said Big Betsy. "Omigod. I didn't mean—lookahere, Cutie—I mean, Reverend, I'm sorry—"

"It's all right," Brother Fletcher said gently. "No one could take offense from a lady as lovely as you." He smiled. His eyes were a little glassy

"Wahuh?" said Big Betsy.

Leo looked at Jake, held up eight fingers. Jake held up eight fingers with a questioning look on his face that quickly changed to an expression of disbelief. Leo nodded slowly. Jake shook his head. Leo shrugged. Brother Fletcher smiled happily and began to slide off the stool. Leo grabbed him by the collar, and Jake held him erect while Leo came around the bar. They deposited him gently in one of the booths along the wall. Brother Fletcher opened his eyes, smiled, said thank you, and went into a sound sleep. Big Betsy regarded him with a horrified look on her fat face. "Omigod," said Big Betsy. "Omigod."

☉╱☉

MAGID AND MUDBONE

THE HIGH WIRE SATIRE OF LENNY BRUCE AND RICHARD PRYOR

By Mel Watkins

Lenny Bruce and Richard Pryor were the most innovative and influential comedians to emerge in mid-twentieth-century America. Not coincidentally, they approached the comedy stage in an unmistakably distinct, yet remarkably similar manner. Their social concerns and their emphatic personal identification with the alienated voices they echoed—as well as the targets of their stinging satire—reveal an affinity that cuts far deeper than the obvious semblance between their highly publicized drug excesses and frequently outrageous public displays.

Both couched their observations in the gritty, imaginative language of the street. They reveled in the exploration of its double-edged meanings, rich allusions, and profane possibilities. Bruce's act, observed Jonathan Miller in a *Partisan Review* article, was "like reading *Finnegans Wake* over and over," his improvisational, jazz-influenced delivery, with its "hesitant, mumbling, slipped-geared technique, full of breaks and riffs, untunes the ear of the conventional night-club audience." After the release of his 1979 *Live in Concert* film, Richard Pryor would be hailed by the *New Yorker* critic Pauline Kael as a "the only great poet satirist among our comics . . . a master of lyrical obscenity."

Interweaving the satiric styles of their own ethnic traditions with the voices of characters from the nation's hybrid cultural heritage, Bruce and Pryor fashioned comic personas that reflected what the novelist and social critic Albert Murray has called America's "composite" or "mulatto culture." Humorist Tony Scherman credited their improvising impulse to those who had "mastered the high-wire act of affirming his existence, of celebrating himself, in the face of adversity." Such "extemporizing," as Albert Murray once argued, "is a way of confronting, acknowledging, and contending with the infernal absurdities and ever-expanding frustrations inherent in the nature of all existence."

Few comic artists have navigated that treacherous high wire or contended with those absurdities with as much resolve, originality, or passion as Lenny Bruce and Richard Pryor.

*

Bruce combined an intellectual disposition and facile delivery groomed in New York's secular Jewish community with the zeal of a crafty Jewish preacher (or *magid*). His satire was inspired by the hip iconoclasm of the jazz clubs he haunted, the raucous impiety of the Jewish entertainment world he encountered in New York City, and the ambiance of the down-and-dirty nightclubs in which he honed his act. It had no precedent on the American stage. Temperamentally out of step with the 1950s American ethos of conformity, he defiantly attacked it—alluding to a more contentious, Rabelaisian alternative. His approach to comedy disturbed middle-class America more than any they had previously witnessed.

In 1964, however, just as he was making inroads on the mainstream comedy circuit, Bruce was busted on an obscenity charge. That arrest, during a two-week engagement at New York's Café au Go Go, and the subsequent conviction apparently broke his spirit; the constant harassment had taken its toll. Afterward, he became more legist than comedian, substituting earnest recitation of courtroom proceedings for the rowdy, penetrating satire that had previously marked his work. Obsessed with his defense, still hounded by authorities, and unable to find work in clubs outside the San Francisco strip, he hit rock bottom. In 1966, Bruce was found dead in his Hollywood home—the apparent victim of a drug overdose.

No one immediately emerged to equal or even challenge the intensity of Bruce's no-holds-barred assault on mainstream hypocrisy. Despite political pundits such as Sahl; racial and political ironists such as Cambridge, Mabley, and Gregory; social critics such as Carlin; and comedians like Cosby, Woody Allen, and Bob Newhart who turned their wit back onto themselves; an only occasionally disrupted veneer of polite respectability once again settled over the American comedy scene. More than a decade would pass before Richard Pryor emerged to dramatically and recklessly explore and expand the terrain Bruce had pioneered.

*

Pryor was born on December 1, 1940, in Peoria, Illinois. His upbringing, by most standards, was unusual. His family ran a string of brothels in which his mother sometimes worked. Even so, his mother and grandmother insisted that he attend church and tried to instill a sense of dignity and middle-class values. At an early age, however, the clash between the reality of his home life and outside estimates of the family business became apparent; as importantly, when he began public school and was confronted with the term "nigger," he realized that to many he was a member of a despised minority.

The youthful submersion in the underground world of hustlers, pimps, johns, and prostitutes, as well as brushes with heartland racial bigotry, would clearly influence his life view and comedy. In a late 1960s routine, he recalled the "nice white dudes" who visited his neighborhood: " 'Hey, little boy, is your mother home? I'd like a blow job!' I wonder what would happen if some niggers go through white neighborhoods doin' that. 'Hey, man, is yo' momma home? Tell the bitch we wanna fuck.' "

Pryor, whose antics regularly disrupted his classes, quit school after the eighth grade. Following odd jobs as a laborer and a stint in the Army, he began his comedy career. After cutting his teeth in black Midwestern clubs, he arrived in New York City in 1963. Between 1964 and 1966, his career soared. *Variety* critics lathered over his "healthy instinct for irreverence." Hailed as the new Bill Cosby, Pryor moved from Greenwich Village cafes and coffeehouses to midtown clubs and glitzy Las Vegas showrooms. Unlike Bruce, who seldom saw the lights of a network television studio, Pryor was a frequent guest on Johnny Carson's "Tonight Show" as well as the Ed Sullivan and Merv Griffith variety shows.

Relying on innocuous, "white bread humor" that was perfectly suited for television during the early 1960s, Pryor had become a successful, well-respected, if noncontroversial, comedy star. His advisers strove to perpetuate that image. One agent urged, "Don't mention the fact that you're a 'nigger.' . . . Be the kind of colored guy we'd like to have over to our house. Now, I'd introduce Bill [Cosby] to my mother, but a guy like you . . ." They "were gonna help me be nothing as best they could," Pryor recalled.

Haunted by that darker comic vision, he became increasingly dissatisfied with his success and the content of his act. "I made a lot of money being Bill Cosby," he said later, "but I was hiding my personality. . . . I was being a robot comic . . . repeating the same lines, getting the same laughs for the same jokes." In his autobiography, *Pryor Convictions,* he wrote: "There was a world of junkies and winos, pool hustlers and prostitutes, women and family screaming inside my head, trying to be heard. The longer I kept them bottled up, the harder they tried to escape. The pressure built till I went nuts."

Something like that occurred in 1967 at the Aladdin Hotel in Las Vegas. Depending on whose version is to be believed, Pryor either stopped in the middle of his act, asked himself, "What the fuck am I doing here?" then walked off the stage or, after questioning himself, stripped, ran into the casino, jumped on a table, and yelled, "Blackjack!"

Pryor moved to Los Angeles, and began hanging out at the Redd Foxx comedy club with Foxx and the young black comic Paul Mooney, who would later collaborate in writing some of his best routines. Among the initial fruits of his revamped approach was a parody of Superman, which reflected Pryor's more aggressive racial perspective.

"I always thought—why they never have a black hero? I always wanted to go to the movies and see a black hero. I figured, maybe someday on television they'll have it. . . . 'Look! Up in the sky! It's a crow. It's a bat. No, it's Super Nigger! Able to leap tall buildings with a single bound; faster than a bowl of chitlins. . . . We find Super Nigger with his x-ray vision that enables him to see through everything, except whitey. . . . disguised as Clark Washington, mild-mannered custodian of the *Daily Planet*, shuffling into Perry White's office. . . . '

" 'Talk to me, Jack, 'cause I'm ready to quit. I've had it up to here, you dig? Tired of doin' them halls, every time I finish, Lois Lane and them come slippin' and slidin' down through here and I have to do it over again. You dig it, baby? I'm through . . . *fire me!* "

In 1970, Pryor moved to Berkeley, California, where he met a group of young black intellectuals and writers that included Ishmael Reed, Claude Brown, and Cecil Brown. Inspired by his new friends, Pryor began reading the speeches of Malcolm X, whom he came to regard as "someone who thinks like I do." With his return from self-imposed exile in 1971, it was apparent that a new, rejuvenated Richard Pryor had surfaced. He prowled the stage effortlessly, shifting chameleon-like from one vivid characterization to another. The nod toward middle-class approval that had constrained his act in mainstream venues had vanished. Even the titles of his albums, such as *That Nigger's Crazy*, would announce his bad-ass irreverence.

Pryor's revised comic approach was as radical as Bruce's. Now, he quipped to hip, integrated crowds, "It's amazing, we can all sit here in the same room together . . . and not understand each other. It could only happen in America." If still raw, his humor had taken on the qualities that would lead the playwright Neil Simon to call him "the most brilliant comic in America."

Pryor had begun using the intricate interplay between his own narrative voice and his characters that *Rolling Stone* magazine called "a new type of realistic theater," and comedy club impresario Budd Friedman deemed the comedy of "story theater." His routines included a chorus of "blacker," grittier ghetto types and others that he had previously stifled.

In one bit about a police lineup, the suspects included a belligerent Black Panther arrested for handing out antigovernment literature. (He threatens, "That's right, gonna hand out ass-whippings as soon as I git these handcuffs off"); a middle-class black child molester (who pleads, "This is obscene in itself. I have some friends on the city counsel and you *will* hear from them"); and a teenage car thief who defends himself with, "Ah, I thought that was my mother's car, man. . . . Yeah, I took the car. I was about two blocks from home, and dug this white lady sitting next to me screaming and shit—I didn't know what was happening. I thought it was a stickup."

If Bruce had used multiple voices to drive home philosophical points, Pryor used them to create dramatic vignettes that impressionistically conveyed both satire and pathos. Pryor's acting talent and uncanny knack for mimicry and mime added another dimension to his humor. "The Wino and the Junkie" (a routine as eloquently structured as a well-crafted short story), for example, winds through a hilarious encounter between a pompous, older wino and a down-and-out young junkie (at one point, the wino quips, "Better lay off that narcotic, nigger . . . shit done made you null and void") to conclude with the following exchange.

Junkie: I'm sick, pops. Can you help me? My mind thinkin' about shit I don't wanna think about. I can't stop the motherfucker, baby. Movin' too fast for the kid. Tell me some ah them ole lies ah yours and make me stop thinkin' 'bout the truth . . . could you help me?

Wino: Yeah, I'm goin' help you, boy. 'Cause I think you got potential. That's right! You don't know how to deal with the white man, that's yo' problem. See, I know how to deal with 'em. That's right. That's why I'm in the position I'm in today.

Lenny Bruce was a pioneer in uncloaking aspects of a hip Jewish sensibility during the 1950s. And, during the 1970s, Pryor disclosed to white society the elements of a closely guarded black world, especially racial anger and cultural eccentricities that were "embarrassments to the black middle class and stereotypes in the minds of most whites." But while Bruce most often satirized the lower-middle class and the authorities they respected from the perspective of the hipster world, Pryor's barbs derived from the viewpoint of black street people who were most affected by racism and were usually aimed at the white middle class, its representatives, and those Negroes who accommodated its views.

He lampooned the nation's skepticism about police brutality with a comic reenactment of the anxiety and tension that often accompanies African Americans' confrontations with police officers: "See, white folks get a ticket they pull over . . . 'Hey, officer. Yes, glad to be of help . . . cheerio!' Niggers got to be talkin' 'bout, 'I am reaching into my pocket for my license, 'cause I don't want to be no motherfuckin' accident.' " From there he moved up the jurisprudential ladder to mock bias in the courts: "I went to jail for income tax evasion, right. . . . I told the judge, said, 'Your honor, I forgot, you know.' He said, 'You remember next year, nigger!' . . . They give niggers time like it's lunch down there. You go down there looking for justice, that's what you find—just us!"

Much of Pryor's humor issued from the stark contrast of the more uninhibited, earthy behavior of the black lower-middle class with the tightly restrained and sometimes fatuous conduct of the white middle class.

He parodied the views of both on sex with a story of a young, lower-class black who, after his date offers only a good-night kiss at the door, explodes with, "Nigger spend thirty dollars—somebody goin' fuck," and a suburbanite who, when his wife responds to an inquiry about sex that night with a curt, "No," says, "Oh, what the heck." He ridiculed white middle-class pretense and reserve with a contrast of marital feuds: "White men and women, they seldom ever have fistfights. They be goin' intellectual, hurtin' each other . . . so they say. White woman say some funny shit to her man, 'Your dick is short and can't even screw.' And the white dude go, 'Uh, we'll discuss it tomorrow.' You say that shit to a nigger, you got a fight. 'Bitch, is you crazy?'"

He mocked religious piety with: "White Protestant churches scared me. They have that weird music going, 'woo-oh, ah-ahh-ohh.' I expected Dracula to come jumping out any second. If he had, I'd a held up the cross . . . 'cause he's allergic to bullshit." And, suggesting a more earthbound and skeptical view of religion, he parodied a black preacher's encounter with God:

"I never will forget this. You see, I was walkin' down the street. . . . And I heard the voice of God call out onto me. And I knew it was the voice of God. For it came from without a dark alleyway, as only the voice of God can come. However, my brothers and sisters, I did not venture down that dark alleyway. For it might not have been the voice of God . . . but two or three niggers with a baseball bat. God only knows! He wasn't talkin' . . . and I wasn't walkin'."

Neither did Pryor spare political figures or their policies, such as the welcome mat extended to Vietnamese refugees. "We the motherfuckers got to give up the jobs for 'em. Didn't ask us shit. . . . Got all the Vietnamese in Army camps . . . learnin' how to say 'nigger'—so they can be good citizens."

Pryor's satire was story based; it flowed in roundabout fashion from the dramatic scenarios he created. Although blunt, it could be as indirect as the tall tales and lies of the underclass people whose voices he echoed. Even more alienated than Bruce's hipsters and hustlers, they lacked the cachet of those supercool, upper-echelon outcasts who rubbed shoulders with jazz and show business people. Pryor's street people were often country folk who prided themselves on the slippery, double-edged currency of their raps.

Not surprisingly, Mudbone, Pryor's sly, down-home raconteur, was among his most popular and vividly drawn characters. Through him, Pryor was able to reflect the rural wit that still informed much of the urban, street-corner humor that dominated his routines. A Mudbone monologue that recounts mistreatment at the hands of a Southern landowner concludes: "So I sawed the bottom outta the outhouse. . . . Then I sat in the bushes and waited for this big collard-green eatin' bitch to go to the bathroom, see. . . . She wobbled out to the outside, opened the door, went in and shut the door. Then I heard a big splash, you know. That's when I got in the tractor and drove up here—I wasn't mad no mo' either."

Much of Pryor's social commentary and many of his disclosures of blacks' disparaging views of mainstream authority were aired in a similarly circuitous manner. At the end of his uproariously vivid but seemingly innocuous re-creation of the much publicized New Year's Eve confrontation with his wife, during which he fired on his own car, Pryor recalled: "Then the police came . . . I went into the house. 'Cause they got magnums, too. And they don't just shoot cars, they shoot *nig-gars*."

And the conclusion of the dramatic reenactment of his own heart attack is at once a slap at popular "whitewashed" culture and an affirmation of black pride. "I woke up in an ambulance, right? And there wasn't nothin' but white people staring at me. I say, 'Ain't this a bitch! I done died and wound up in the wrong motherfuckin' heaven. Now I gotta listen to Lawrence Welk for the rest of my days.'"

Pryor did not always aim his satire at the foibles of the white middle class or demand that his humor always reflect positive race consciousness. He also directed his scathing wit at the foibles of black life. He moved perilously close to the edge when mocking the attitudes of his core audience. A quip about interracial relationships, for example, was greeted by boos and catcalls and nearly prompted the audience to turn on him: "Don't ever marry a white woman in California. A lot of you sisters probably sayin', 'Don't marry a white woman anywhere, nigger. Shit! Why should you be happy?' . . . Sisters look at you like you killed your momma when you go out with a white woman. And you can't laugh that shit off, either." On other occasions, his humor was directed at his own limitations. After describing how blacks routinely boast of their sexual exploits, he added: "You some lyin' motherfuckers . . . I can make love for about three minutes. I do about three minutes of serious fuckin', then I need eight hours sleep and a bowl of Wheaties."

Despite the comical deflation of blacks–himself included–Pryor rarely succumbed to the pitfall of stereotypical depiction that had marked mainstream presentations of black humor prior to the 1960s and would ensnare many of his imitators in the 1980s and '90s. "I think there's a thin line between being a Tom . . . and seeing [blacks] as human beings," he said. "I have to do it true. If I can't do it [true], I'll stop right in the middle rather than pervert it and turn it into Tomism." He had devised a tactic that allowed him to both express the satirical thrust of black street humor and expose the frailties that lay beneath it.

More than any comedian before him, Pryor humanized characters that were outlaws even in the ghetto. With his skill at caricature and intimate knowledge of lower-class blacks, he transformed one-dimensional outcasts into resonant human beings. By displaying their vulnerability as well as his own, he transcended race, permitting nearly everyone to identify with him.

Pryor's ability to appeal to both a hard-core black and a crossover audience was an indications of the success of his approach. His nonconcert films, in which he was often teamed with the Jewish comedian Gene Wilder, were box office hits even though many were critically dismissed. And behind the scenes, he not only wrote for such black comics as Redd Foxx and Flip Wilson but also worked with Lily Tomlin and collaborated with Mel Brooks on the script for *Blazing Saddles.*

Although Pryor was not the first comedian to drawn upon black America's presumed "low" street humor–with its vulgarity, profanity, explicit sexuality, blunt satirical outlook–he was the first to present it to mixed audiences in an undiluted black voice that candidly exposed the way black people joked among themselves when most critical of America. "It was human humor, too," Pryor said. "And human beings were liking it. I'd get confused to see more and more whites in the audience. What was happening was that they were saying, 'Hey, we're people. We enjoy something good.'" As Pryor insisted, his humor transcended simple ethnic categorization. He had taken the humor of the streets and, without losing any of its intensity, turned it into high art.

*

"I'm not sick," Lenny Bruce insisted, when labeled a "sick comedian" by some critics. "The world is sick and I'm the doctor . . . I'm a surgeon with a scalpel for false values." On another occasion, he said, "When I'm interested in a truth, it's a *truth* truth. And that's a terrible truth to be interested in."

Pryor, too, was obsessed with honesty. "Art is the ability to tell the truth, especially about yourself," he told one interviewer. While insinuating a more authentic and humane vision of the outcast inhabitants of the black underclass, he also indicted the duplicity of a mainstream culture that isolated and stigmatized nearly everything that did not conform to its narrowly defined vision of reality.

Mudbone, in his own folksy, streetwise manner, perhaps best captures the inherent risks of the brand of comedy Bruce and Pryor were pursuing: "See, I was honest with this motherfucker. I told him comedy—real comedy—wasn't only tellin' jokes. It was about telling the truth. Talking about life. Makin' light of the hard times . . . Definitely not as funny as it look . . . You start telling the truth to people and people gonna look at you like you tryin' to fuck their mama or somethin'. The truth is gonna be funny, but it's gonna scare the shit outta folks.

"And maybe you, too."

☺☺

BASEBALL JOKES

Does Pete Rose hustle? Before the All-Star Game
he came into the clubhouse and took off
his shoes, and they ran another mile without him.
—Hank Aaron

It took me seventeen years to get
three thousand hits. I did it in one
afternoon on the golf course.
—Hank Aaron

Sometimes I hit [Steve Carlton] like I
used to hit Koufax, and that's
like drinking coffee with a fork.
—Willie Stargell

Asked what he thought of artificial turf,
baseball slugger **Richie Allen** said,
"If horses don't eat it, I don't want to play on it."

I'd rather hit than have sex.
                                    —Reggie Jackson

The only reason I don't like playing in the
World Series is I can't watch myself play.
                                    —Reggie Jackson

The only thing Reggie can do better
than me on the field is talk.
                                    —Rod Carew

"In Cleveland, pennant fever usually ends up
being just a forty-eight-hour virus," Cleveland Indians
manager **Frank Robinson** told a reporter.

Baseball is very big with my people.
It figures. It's the only time we can get to
shake a bat at a white man without starting a riot.
                                    Dick Gregory

NIGGER LOOK JUST LIKE YOU

By Richard Pryor

Police degrade you, I don't know, it's often you wonder why a nigger don't go completely mad. No, you do. You get your shit together, you work all week, right. Then you get dressed, you make, say a cat make $125. He get $80 if he lucky, right, and go out get clean, be drivin' with his old lady going out to a club. Then the police pull over. "GET OUT OF THE CAR! THERE WAS A ROBBERY, NIGGER LOOK JUST LIKE YOU. ALL RIGHT PUT YOUR HANDS UP, TAKE YOUR PANTS DOWN, SPREAD YOUR CHEEKS."
     Now, what nigger feel like havin' fun after that?
     "Oh, let's just go home, baby." You go home and beat your kids and shit. You goin' take that shit out on somebody.

DON'T LET ME DOWN

By Eddie Murphy

I was yo' one and only
Until I read the news.

Now, I'm sad and lonely,
Since I put down the Jews.
We have so much in common,
'Cause we both been so oppressed.
We both have big noses,
And gold chains on our chests.

Don't let me down
(I'm begging you, please).
Don't let me down
(I'm down on my knees).
Don't let me down, Hymie Town.

⊙⁄⊚

O. J. SIMPSON JOKES

GOING TO CANCUN

When detectives went to arrest O. J., he came to his front gate
carrying an overnight bag and tennis racket; he was dressed
in white linen slacks and shirt, and had a sweater tied around his
shoulders. "Why you dressed like that, boy?" one detective asked.
"You said I was going to Cancun, right?" he said. "Naw," the other
detective said, "We said 'You going to the can, Coon.'"

—Folk

THE BEST DEFENSE

"They ain't never goin' to convict O. J.—don't matter if he did it
or not," the old man said to his friend. "See, the way I figures it,
it's all about money. If it was you or me or some other nigger, we'd a
had one a dem public defenders rep-a-sentin' us and we be guilty
as sin. It's all 'bout defense, and dat boy done bought the best
defense in de world." "Maybe so," the friend said, "but seem to me
de fence what got him in trouble from the get-go. If de fence 'round
his house hadn't a been so high, he wouldn't a drop dat glove tryin'
to climb over it—wouldn't a needed no high-priced lawyers and such."

—Folk

BAD FIT

"If it don't fit, we must acquit!"
—Johnny Cochran

THE DOZENS—CAPS AND SNAPS

SMELL AND LOOKS CAPS

- Your hair so nappy, yo' momma broke three pairs of wire cutters trying to give you a fade.
- You so fat, every time you step out the house in broad daylight, there's a solar eclipse.
- If ugly was octane, you'd be high test.
- You so fat, you need a tow boat to get into the swimming pool.
- If ugliness was contagious, you'd be quarantined.
- Your sister so fat, before she go out to eat, she got to call for an estimate.
- You so ugly, when you were born the doctor tried to circumcise your nose.
- Your hair so nappy, Brer Rabbit jumped in there to get away from Brer Wolf.
- Your sister so fat, I took her to 7-Eleven and she didn't come out until 12:15.
- You so black, you can cast a shadow on coal.
- You so fat, your blood type is Crisco.
- If ugly was gold, you'd be Fort Knox.
- Your sister so ugly, even the tide won't take her out.
- Your breathe smell so bad, you got to put a gas mask on your toothbrush.
- You so ugly, Kodak warns its customers not to focus on you.
- You so black, bats come out at noon to follow you around.
- You ugly enough to be the racial profile for the Abominable Snowman.
- Your nose so big, you can smell perfume over the telephone.
- Your sister so cross-eyed, she can look at the Hudson River and the East River at the same time.
- Your teeth so bad, instead of a filling the cavities the dentist put a "condemned" sign in your mouth.

- You so ugly, after the doctor delivered you he slapped himself.
- Your feet so stinky, when you go to Foot Locker the shoes run out.
- Your sister so ugly, she went into a haunted house and came out with a job application.

                                                        —George Wallace

- You so filthy, lice boycott yo' ass.
- Your daddy so fat, when he has to haul ass he got to make two trips.

DUMB AND POOR CAPS

- You so stupid, you thought sickle cell was a tool shed at Attica.
- You're so dumb, it takes you an hour and a half to watch *60 Minutes.*
- Your brother so lame, he thinks a slam dunk is throwin' a donut into a cup of coffee.
- You so stupid, you thought showing up in timely fashion was wearing a Rolex.
- Your momma so poor and dumb, when I told her she was "down and out" she got on her knees and crawled out the door.
- You so dumb, when you got to New York and saw a sign say, "DETOUR," you tried to buy a bus ticket for a sight-seeing trip around the city.
- Your daddy so dumb, he thought they only served Quaker Oats at religious services.
- You so poor, you got rejected for a credit card at the Ninety-Nine Cent store.
- If money was air, you'd have to borrow an oxygen tank to breathe.
- Your daddy so dumb, when the president declared a state of emergency he drew another star on the flag.
- You're so stupid, it takes you an hour to cook Minute Rice.

                                                        — Heavy D

- You so stupid, if you was a duck, you'd be flying north every winter.
- You sister so dumb, you thought a "drive-by" was the car lane at Mickey-D's.
- You so stupid, you got locked up for turnstile jumping on the way out of the subway.

- You so dumb, when the judge said he was gonna throw the book at you, you ducked.
- Your sister is so stupid, she thought Tiger Woods was part of the Bronx Zoo.
- Your sister is so dumb, when I took her to a restaurant and she saw the sign on our table saying RESERVED she wouldn't eat cause she didn't want no leftovers.
- You so dumb, you thought a foot stool was a big piece of shit.
- You so dumb, you thought the Supreme Court was where Diana Ross played tennis.
- Your daddy so lame, he thought a serial killer was somebody who finished off the last of the Wheaties.
- Your sister so stupid, when she found out she had a cold sore she stuck her head in the oven and kept it there for a week.
- You so dumb, when I gave you a Ice T album, you stuck a straw in it and tried to drink it.
- You so dumb, you thought Social Security was a breath mint.
- You so dumb, when the doctor said you had high blood pressure, you pulled out a dime bag and said, "Damn, this shit is better than I thought."
- Your sister so dumb, she thought "sour grapes" was bad wine.
- You so stupid, you thought Roto-Rooter was a letter from a cheerleader.
- Your sister so dumb, she thought a head hunter was a nigga looking for a blow job.

THE DOZENS—YO' MOMMA CAPS

- The bags under your momma's eyes so big, when she go to the airport they make her check 'em at the luggage counter.
- Your momma is like a drawbridge, every time a big dinghy come by her legs go up.
- Your momma so fat, her mouth got stretch marks.
- I fucked your mama
  For a solid hour.
  Baby came out
  Screaming, Black Power.
  —H. Rap Brown
- If ugliness was rain, your momma would be treading water and your daddy would be building an ark.

- Your momma so stupid, she thought Jim Crow was an Indian chief.
- Your momma so fat, she come from both sides of the family.

                                        —Damon Wayans

- Your momma so fat, your daddy got to hug her on the installment plan.
- Your momma so stupid, she thought a shell steak was seafood.
- Your momma givin' up so much ass, she started handed out E-Z passes to speed the line up.
- His momma so bald, when she go to sleep at night her head keep slippin' off the pillow.

                                        —Will Smith

- Fucked yo' momma on the refrigerator,
  Copped some ice, say, see you later.
  Seen you sister at the picture show,
  She ain't too smart, but she sho' can blow.
- Your mamma so ugly, she went into a haunted house and the ghosts ran out.
- Your momma a stone freak, when she went to *Ripley's Believe It or Not* they took down all the exhibits and made her the star attraction.
- Your momma so fat, she got to buy a round-trip ticket to go one way.
- Your momma so dumb, she thought a rain check was the bill you got at an outdoor restaurant.
- Your momma so fat, she got her own area code.
- Your momma so full of shit, I wouldn't believe her if she had her tongue notarized.
- Your momma like a doorknob, everybody gets a turn.
- Your momma so dumb, she thought a layaway plan was kicking it with a stranger on vacation.
- Your momma so fat, when she step on a scale it say, "Overload."
- Your momma like a road map, brothers pick her up looking to get the lay of the land.
- Your momma so fat, when she broke her leg gravy ran out.
- Your momma so stupid, she thought Frankenstein was a two-man comedy team.
- I saw his momma at Super Cuts, and when she sat down to get a haircut she opened her shirt.

                                        —Arsenio Hall

- Your momma so black, she must've been born during an eclipse.
- Your mamma so fat, she use a paint brush to apply makeup.
- Your momma so stupid, she thought an IRA was the Jewish guy who run the pawnshop down the street.
- Your momma like a railroad track, everywhere she go, brothers pull a train* on her.

* In African American slang, to "pull a train" on someone is to persuade her to have sex with multiple partners.

WOMEN AND MEN

MARITAL COUNSELING

"We need to go to therapy,"
a distressed housewife told her husband.
"No," the husband said
"I'm not going to therapy. This
whole therapy thing is just an excuse for
women to do the two things they love most—
talk and spend money!"

—Folk

EQUAL RIGHTS

I'm all for equal rights
for women, honey, and it's about time!
But some women got to be told,
equal rights ain't got nothin' to do
with your neighbor's husband.

—LaWanda Page

A PRAYER AND A PROMISE

Now I lay me down to sleep;
I pray the Lord that John don't creep.
If he should stray before I wake;
I promise God his soul to take.

—Folk

DIFFERENT STROKES

White folks do things a lot different
than niggers. They eat quiet and shit. They be,
"Pass the potatoes—thank you, darling.
Could I have a bit of that sauce?
How are the kids coming along
with their studies? Think we'll be having
sexual intercourse this evening?
We're not? Oh well, what the heck."
                                    —Richard Pryor

OLD MAN AND YOUNG MAN

You know how I said a old man couldn't do
nothin' for me but bring me a message
from a young man? Well, he brought it—
he brought the message.
He say, "Stay with the old man."
But I ain't goin' do it
because I found out when he said, "I do,"
he couldn't. And I'm not going
through this world lookin' for memories.
Oh, that old man was too old for Mom at that time.
He was older than white bread.
And you know that's gettin' old.
                                    — Moms Mabley

PERFECT HEALTH

Returning from her annual checkup,
the 40-year-old woman rushed into
her living room with a big smile
on her face. Her balding husband
sat in front of the TV set.
"My doctor said I'm in perfect health,"
she shouted. "Say, I've got the
body of a 20-year-old, the breasts
of 25-year-old, and the legs of a 30-year-old."
The husband said, "What about your ass?"
She say, "I don't know about that, honey.
I didn't have time to ask about you."
                                    —Folk

WOMEN VS. WOMEN

Women are very strange creatures.
Most don't like to see other women happy.
Whether it's envy or jealousy, I don't
know, but I'd be hanging out with a woman and if a
pretty woman walks by, the first thing that comes out of
her mouth is, "That bitch thinks she's cute."
Men don't trip like that.
You'll never see a man look at another man and say,
"He thinks he's got a nice ass."
A man knows he shouldn't be looking at
this guy's ass in the first place.

                                        —Damon Wayans

PAYBACK IS A BITCH

A few days after Hillary Clinton was elected senator,
she said to Bill, "Now that I'm an elected
official, I think I'll get me a young intern
to add to my list of daily activities."
"Ah—what? Why, Hillary?" the ex-President said.
"Two wrongs don't make a right."
"Oh, don't worry, Bill, honey," she said.
"You taught me well. I'm not stupid.
I won't buy him any gifts. I've got a better plan.
I'll buy myself a pair of licorice panties,
and I'll make sure he eats the evidence."

                                        —Michelle Youngblood

LOST LUGGAGE

Overheard at the baggage counter:
Airport Clerk—We're sorry ma'am, but your bags
didn't arrive on the plane. We don't know what happened.
Passenger—If you can fly this airplane 600 miles an hour,
in a thunderstorm, in the middle of the night
and find New York City—
then you can *find* my luggage!

                                        —Folk

CURB YOUR DOG

"All men are dogs,"
the sexy rap star **Eve** asserted,
"but I can train a dog."

HUNTERS

Men have nice cars, not because
they like nice cars, but because they know
women like nice cars. That's how it goes.
'Cause men are hunters and
the car is the bait. Women come up
and say, "Nice Porsche!"—
"Gotcha bitch!"

    —Dave Chappelle

OVEREATING

I've got a liberal white co-worker
who has recently cozied up to me—
probably because I'm the only black person she knows.
Anyway, the other day while I was
having ice cream for lunch,
she gave me an article on black women overeating.
I straightened her out right there—
told her black women don't overeat,
that's a white girl thing.
We're in training, bulking up for the battle
against racism—every damn day!

    —Janet Cormier

ⓔⓔ

RANDOM QUIPS FROM FAMOUS WITS

GETTIN' IT

Collectors were always calling me.
They call so much,
I developed routines. They say,

"When can we expect payment?" I say,
"You can *expect* it anytime you want
—*gettin'* it is gonna be your problem."
—Steve Harvey

SENILITY

Don't worry about senility.
When it hits you,
you won't know it!
—Bill Cosby

NEW TRICKS

You can teach an old dog new tricks.
You just don't want
to see the dog doing them.
—Bill Cosby

ON MY FEET

"You fool, you thirty cents
away from having a quarter.
How the fuck you goin' get a boat?"
"Don't worry about it."
"You goddamn right, don't worry about it.
Look at you! You raggedy as a roach,
eat the hole out a donut—"
"I'll be on my feet, soon enough."
"Not in them raggedy-ass shoes.
Look at you! Shoes so run over,
you got to lay down to put 'em on."
—Spike Lee, *Do the Right Thing*

NOT ALL BLACK

All niggers ain't black, you know.
If you don't believe it,
watch *Hee-Haw.*
—Redd Foxx

JUST US

We go down there [to court]
lookin' for justice,
and that's what we find—
Just Us!
                    —Richard Pryor

BEING FAMOUS

You know, all Monica Lewinsky ever
wanted to do was suck the dick of a powerful,
famous man. . . . And until then I never
understood how famous the President was.
I had dreamt of being famous, but I never dreamt of
being that famous. Imagine if somebody could suck
your dick and then they're famous—that's crazy!
What a pickup line!
"Hey, suck my dick—there's a future in it.
Ah, that's it, yeah—now get out there and be somebody.
Go write a book!"
                    —Dave Chappelle

THE AMERICAN DREAM

Clarence Thomas is *the* nigger!
He got the nigger dream in America.
He had a big dick, a white woman,
and a life-time job.
That's the nigger American dream.
                    —Paul Mooney

PASS THE MILK

There were thirteen kids in my family.
We were so poor we had to eat
cereal with a fork, so we could pass
the milk to the next kid.
                    —Bernie Mac

FROM *YOU SO CRAZY*

By Martin Lawrence

Now that's my sport, boxing. A lotta people don't know that. That's my motherfuckin' sport. I used to box. And I was good, yeah, I was a motherfucker here, like ba-bam. And I used to move all the time 'cause I didn't wanna get hit, you know. I thought I was gonna grow up and look finer than a motherfucker so I didn't want nobody busting that up. But I used to move, boy, all the time, like jazz. I was like Ali with my shit. You know, just dancing, moving. My coach had a good saying about me, "One thing about Martin, he ain't gonna get hit. And he ain't gonna hit nobody." 'Cause I dance all motherfuckin' night. Ding.

"Good round, motherfucker, good round." 'Cause my thing was, I didn't wanna get knocked out, man. That's too motherfuckin' embarrassing. Pow, to get knocked out and shit. You know, you brothers get knocked, bam, don't even know where they at. Now, bam, "Give me a Caesar salad, a bag o' Twizzlers, all that shit, man. Two bus passes." Motherfuckers don't know where they are and need two bus passes, man. You know, and what do you say to the motherfucker if he's a friend that got knocked out? You driving home with this motherfucker and you like, "Shew, damn. Did he hit you as hard as it fuckin' looked, man? No, I ain't found your teeth. I don't know where them motherfuckers are at."

See, that's why I thought like if you're a fighter, you should be humbler than a motherfucker, man. When you walk to the ring, shut the fuck up, don't say nothing when you go in the fight. Just walk in the ring and fight. And if you get knocked out, you know, you tell the media, "Fuck y'all. I ain't telling you motherfuckers I wasn't gonna get knocked out. I ain't said shit."

See, you got brothers that walk in and talk a good game and get knocked out, then they're embarrassed afterward. 'Cause before the fight, they—you can ask 'em, "What is your strategy for the fight?" And those motherfuckers, "Well, as you well know, I have the best jab in the business. Uh, I feel better than I've ever felt in my life. I'm in the best condition of my life. What I plan on doing is coming out the first couple of rounds, throwing the jab which is the best jab in the business, I'm gonna hit him a couple of times, soften up the face. I'm probably going to the body on him. See, I'm a people's choice. People like me. I'm the champ, you understand? I can't see the fight going any other way. I'm gonna hurt the boy. I'm gonna hurt him bad. I can't see it going any other way."

Then the nigger get in the ring, it's some different shit, right. Bam. Motherfucker's different shit. His speech is like this. "What happened?" "Uh, okay, well, I came out and tried to use the jab that I had told you that was supposed to be the best jab in the business, I put it out there, he came over with a right hand. I went to my right leg but see, I had hurt that in practice. I was abused as a child and a lotta people don't know this shit." Fuck that shit; don't say nothing, man.

And boxers kill me 'cause everybody has a motherfuckin' shout-out. You know, when they win or whatever. They wanna get in front of the camera and say hello to everybody. Black people especially. We got shout-outs for your ass. "Just won the belt this year. Ray. Irv. Cha-cha. A-a-a—all the motherfuckers that down at se'en-eleven, you know, bringing the belt home. Yeah, well, I told you boys."

White people don't do all that shit, man. They get right to the fuckin' point: "Tucson, Arizona, coming home." They don't do all that shit, man. Y'all want a white heavyweight champion bad, don't ya? That's all right, say it, sir. It's all right. You want a white, heavyweight champion, don't ya? Say it, goddamnit, say what you—There you go, man. See, it's coming out, isn't it? "Goddamnit, Martin, I want one." That's what I wanna hear you say, man. This is America. You can say what you want. It's all right to feel you wanna white heavyweight champion. Shit ain't gonna happen. Shit just ain't gonna motherfuckin' happen. Long as a brother outta work, this shit just not gonna happen. You got some brothers that will beat your ass for two dollars and a biscuit, motherfucker.

Boxin' is rough. You know what I'm saying? 'Cause see women love fighters; ladies feel protected by fighters. You motherfuckers felt like, oh, if somebody hits you, pow, "Baby, hit the motherfucker, hey, man." You know a fighter: "Don't you ever put your motherfuckin' hand on my lady." If Mike Tyson smacked my lady, shit, I'd fight Mike Tyson. For smacking my lady. Let's think about this shit now, you all. You know, 'cause this is Mike Tyson. You know what I'm saying? I know, I wanna jump on him, but I got to think before I go jumping on Mike. I gotta think, How good has my girl been to me? And is this bitch worth dying for? Fuck all that.

I try to get outta fight quicker than a motherfuck. Mike Tyson can smack my lady right in front of me, pow. I'm like, "Hey, hey, man, Mike, Mike, hold on, man. Hold on. What happened? What'd she do? What's the problem? Uh-uhh. Well, she does that shit a lot. She does that a lot. Well, look, go on about your business, man, you're in enough trouble. Stop that shit, man. Girl, get the fuck outta here and leave Mike alone. You know he's got some shit on his mind."

I ain't fighting no Mike, man, for nobody. Well, if Mike hit my mother, I guess I have to fight, huh? I don't know though, man. 'Cause I—you know, man, that's Mike Tyson, I got to think. I know that's my mom but I got to think first. You know? How good had my mom been to me coming up? I never did get them Nikes I wanted, you know . . .

◎◎

THE OLD SCHOOL

ALL TURNED AROUND

Folk

Two elderly black men sitting in Harlem's Morningside Park saw a group of teenagers entering the park dressed back in the latest hip-hop fashion. One man looked at the other and winked. "I don't know what the world comin' to," one said. "That's a cryin' shame. Look at that boy, pants 'bout to fall off his behind, ain't got sense enough to tie his shoes, and wearing a jacket look like it was made for King Kong's daddy."

"Yeah, and look at that other one," his friend said. "Cap all turned 'round on his head. Fool done forgot where his face is!"

COCKEYED JUNIOR

By Richard Pryor

I worked for this white man, his name was Budd Jenning. . . . He was all right to work for, see. He was all right, for a white man he wasn't bad, see. But he had a son named Junior, he was cockeyed. We called him Cockeyed Junior. And he was hard to work for, man, 'cause the eyes went every which'a way. He say, "Nigger, pick that up." You know, and four, five niggers bend down, see.

OLD BULL AND YOUNG BULL

Folk

Two bulls was standing up on top of the hill, and they saw a whole bunch of cows down in the pasture. The young bull was real anxious, you know. He say, "Why don't we run down there and fuck one of 'em?"

Old bull looked at him and smiled, say, "Why don't we walk down there and fuck all of 'em."

RUNNING MACHINERY

Folk

A teenager working as busboy in a little bar and grill in Harlem was finishing up his work one evening. He was down to his last chore, sweeping the floor, and he was rushing, trying to get off as early as he could. Just as he was about ready to finish, he passed by an old gentleman all slumped down at a table and accidentally brushed his feet with the broom.

The old man happened to be one of them real superstitious Negroes from the South and knowed that touching your feet with a broom was serious bad luck. When the broom hit his foot, he jumped up from his seat, mad as hell. He was stammering and hopping up and down on one foot trying to wipe his shoe against the back of his pant leg. Finally, he yelled, "Boy, what you doin'? Why don't you put that damn broom down—you know you don't know nothin' 'bout running no sophisticated machinery!"

I AIN'T LOSS!

Folk

The young black man was getting more and more frustrated. He had pulled off Route 95 in Virginia to gas up his Lexus and couldn't find his way back to the highway. Finally, he saw an old black dude dressed in overalls walking down one of the back roads. He stopped, rolled down the window, and waved the man over.

"Say, Pops, I don't see no signs around here. You know how to get back to the main highway?"

The old man looked in at the snappily dressed driver, then stepped back to admire his brand new car. Finally, he stuck his head back in the window and said, "Naw, caint say that I does."

"Well, maybe you can tell me where I am. I got a map; maybe I can figure it out."

"I be mighty pleased to he'p you," the man said, "but I ain't sure about dat neither. 'Round here we just calls it 'The Bottoms.'"

"Damn, nigger," the driver blurted, "you don't know shit."

The old man smiled and turned to walk away. "Now that may be so, Junior," he said, "but least I know one thing—I ain't loss."

TRIFOCALS

From *Time Flies*
By Bill Cosby

"These will be perfect for you," the ophthalmologist said when he fitted me. "In the top band of the glasses, you can see things far away. In the middle band, you can see things about fifty yards away. And in the bottom one, you can read your medicine."

HARD TO FOOL

Folk

When he was governor, President Bush was asked to act as a ceremonial Texas state trooper for a day. He was operating a speed trap when an elderly black man passed, driving ten miles over the limit. Bush pulled him over. He lectured the man about obeying laws made by his superiors and was generally condescending. Finally, he started writing the ticket, but he was continually interrupted by some flies that kept buzzing around his head.

"Having some problems with them circle flies, sir?" the driver asked.

"Well, yes," Bush said, "but I never heard of circle flies."

"Ah, they're common out here in the country, sir. They call 'em that cause they's almost always found circling around the back end of a mule."

Bush stared at the man for a second, then went back to writing the ticket. Then he looked up and said, "Hey, wait a minute, are you trying to call me a jackass?"

"No, 'course not, Governor. I got way too much respect for you to even think about calling you a jackass."

"I didn't think so," Bush said, grinning broadly, as he finished writing up the ticket. When he was done, he handed the driver the summons.

"Hard to fool them flies, though," the man said as he drove away.

PENNIES FROM HEAVEN

Folk

The preacher pass the plate around after the sermon and it come back empty for the third Sunday in a row. He was mighty disappointed, since he had fallen on hard times and didn't know how he was goin' make it through the week. So when he got home, he went to his room, got down on his knees and he started to pray.

He say, "Lawd, how long is a million years to you?"

The Lawd say, "My million years is like a second to you."

"Well, Lawd, how much is a million dollars to you?'

The Lawd say, "A million dollars ain't nothing but a penny to me."

The old preacher stood up with a big smile on his face and say, "If that's so, could you spare one of them pennies for me?"

The Lawd say, "Sure I can—wait a second."

TOP THAT

Folk

A young man decked out in his best Nike sweats and Air Jordan kicks raced across the field, then pulled up to look at his stopwatch, timing hisself, you know. Satisfied with his time, he sat down on a bench next to the old fellow who'd been watching him.

"You pretty quick there, son. What—you a runner or somethin'?"

"Yeah, pops, getting ready for the relays. What you think?"

"You quick all right, but did you ever hear tell a Jesse Owens, the 'lympic champ? Remember one time he beat a race horse, running backward. Boy was so fast, say he could turn off the switch at one end a the room and be in bed 'fore the lights went out."

"Ah, man, you old timers always talking about some shit back in the day. What about now? You heard of Allen Iverson? That nigga's so fast he can grab a rebound at one end of the court, throw a alley-oop pass toward his own basket, then run it down, catch it, and dunk it before the defense get back."

"Yeah, that's sho nuf fast—but that don't beat the fastest man I ever seed. Boy from Mississippi name Mercury—yeah, that's what they call him—made his rep'atation when he outrun a pickup truck fulla rednecks. Say, after they gived up, had to rebuild the engine in that machine. Boy was so fast he run down lightnin' and hobble thunder. Dat quick enuf for you, junior?"

⊘⊘

THE NEW SCHOOL

WORSE THAN THAT

Folk

Your honor, I was married to that man for sixteen years and he cheated on me with twenty-eight different women. I went through the alphabet, and I found a name for every letter. He's a dog, your honor—a dog!"

"There doesn't seem to be any doubt about that," the judge said.

"Then I found out he was takin' money from them women!"

"You mean you married a gigolo."

"Worse than that, your honor, that man is a *gigo-ho!*"

ONE WHITE GUY

I try to tell brothers,
every group of brothers should have
at least one white guy in it.
I'm serious—for safety!
'Cause when the shit goes down,
somebody goin' need to talk to the police!
—Dave Chappelle

HYDE PARK

Folk

This young black stockbroker had a great year. Made more money than he thought he ever would. He had never been out of the country, so he decided to spend his vacation in England. He checked into a posh hotel and went out for a walk. He was strolling along in London, enjoying the sights and congratulating himself on his success, when he got to Hyde Park. He sat down on a bench, and a few minutes later a pretty English girl came along and sat on the same bench.

They started talking, and she was telling him about the city and stuff, you know—where to go, what to see. They were getting along pretty good, and he thought he was getting over. But since he didn't know anything about the customs over there, he decided to chill.

Then, she smiled innocently and asked, "Would you like to stroke my pussy?"

"Yeah!" he said, "That's just what I was thinking, but first you got to move that cat off your lap."

FOOL ME ONCE

Folk

Two young women, barely in their twenties, were sitting on the stoop of their Brooklyn apartment building when one turned to the other and said, "What's up with you, girlfriend? I don't mean to get in your business, but seem like you pregnant again."

The pregnant woman reluctantly nodded her head.

"Girl, I don't understand you. You already got four kids and you ain't married. They was all by different men, and I bet this one is by somebody else."

"Yeah, honey, you right. I ain't goin' let no man make a fool of me twice."

UNFORGETTABLE

Folk

"Yo, homeboy, what's up with you?" the Buppy said to his partner. "Since that ho got hat, you ain't been yourself—walkin' around here all dazed and down on yourself. She wasn't into shit, bro, had attitude big as her behind— why don't you forget her?"

"Yeah, I know, my man, but it ain't easy to forget a woman when Master Charge keep remindin' you how much you owe on the gifts you bought."

RAPPERS

I can't believe that rappers
are killing each other. Over what, lyrics?
How ignorant can that be? I can just see some
angry rapper saying, "Hey, man, that's
my shit! I rhymed 'now' with 'cow.'
Don't even think about using it!"
I hope this kind of ignorant shit
doesn't start happening in the comedy world.
"Man, did you hear that
Eddie Murphy shot Chris Rock
because Rock stole his doo-doo joke?
Yeah, man, Eddie shot him dead.
Eddie says he wants his doo-doo joke back."
—Damon Wayans

FORMAL INTRODUCTION

Folk

An attractive young woman approached a well-to-do matron at a chi-chi Harlem cocktail party and introduced herself. She then asked, "Where are you from?" The haughty matron glanced at her and said, "Don't you know you should never end a sentence with a preposition," and turned away with her nose in the air.

The young woman paused, took a sip of her cocktail and said, "Okay, then, where are you from—bitch!"

DON'T BLAME ME

Folk

A young black lawyer met one of his former buddies from the hood in downtown Miami. "Hey, bro," he said, "what's up? You still trying to break into show biz?"

"Yeah, man, I'm still workin' at it."

"So, what did you think about that election—wasn't that a bitch."

"I passed, man—ain't got nothin' to do with it," the friend laughed. "I always say, 'If God had meant for us to vote, he would have given us candidates.' Maybe I should have though, this is some shit we in, ain't it? Last time somebody listened to a Bush, folks wandered in the desert for forty years."

"Hey, don't blame me," the lawyer. "I voted for Gore . . . *I think.*"

YARDWORK

Folk

A youthful-looking black stockbroker had recently bought a home in a posh Connecticut suburb. One Sunday afternoon, he was strolling across his front lawn, admiring the estate and occasionally stopping to putter with his wife's flower garden. As he stooped to pick up a piece of paper that had been blown onto the lawn, one of his new neighbors pulled up in a flashy Mercedes and shouted from the window, "Hey, boy, we need a little help over at our place. How much do they pay you for yardwork?"

"Well, suh," the stockbroker said in exaggerated dialect, "I gets to kick it with the mistress of the house whenever I wants to. I sho would be glad to come over and oblige you."

@/@

FROM *OXHERDING TALE*

By Charles Johnson

The following excerpt is from Charles Johnson's second novel, Oxherding Tale *(1982), which parodied not only slave–master relationships but also the florid style of the bildungsroman form in the nineteenth-century English novel. The*

opening chapter, reprinted below, sets the stage for the hero's exploits and mis-
adventures in the curious world of antebellum America.

Long ago my father and I were servants at Cripplegate, a cotton plantation
in South Carolina. That distant place, the world of my childhood, is ruin now,
mere parable, but what history I have begins there in an unrecorded accident before the Civil War, late one evening when my father, George
Hawkins, still worked in the Big House, watched over the owner's interests,
and often drank with his Master—this was Jonathan Polkinghorne—on the
front porch after a heavy meal. It was a warm night. An autumn night of fine-
spun moonlight blurred first by Madeira, then home-brewed beer as they
played Rummy, their feet propped on the knife-whittled porch rail, the dark
two-story house behind them, creaking sometimes in the wind. My father
had finished his chores early, for he was (he says) the best butler in the country, and took great pride in his position, but he wasn't eager to go home. He
stayed clear of his cabin when my stepmother played host for the Ladies
Prayer Circle. They were strange, George thought. Those women were harmless enough by themselves, when sewing or cleaning, but together their col-
lective prayers had a mysterious power that filled his whitewashed cabin
with presences—Shades, he called them, because they moved furniture in
the cabin, destroying the laws of physics, which George swore by, and drove
him outside to sleep in the shed. (Not that my father knew a whole lot about
physics, being a slave, but George knew sorcery when he saw it, and kept
his distance.) He was, as all Hodges knew, a practical, God-fearing man who
liked to keep things simple so he could enjoy them. He was overly cautious
and unnerved by little things. So he avoided his cabin and talked about
commonsense things like politics and the price of potatoes on his Master's
porch long after the last pine-knot candles winked out in the quarters.
Whiskey burned, then exploded like gas in his belly. He felt his face expand.
His eyes slid slowly out of focus. Hard old leaves on magnolias overhanging
the porch clacked, like shells, in a September wing sprinkled with rain.

Twelve o'clock. A typical Saturday night.

"George," said Jonathan, his voice harsh after consuming forty-eight
ounces of Madeira in what my father figured to be half an hour, "if I go to
bed at this advanced hour, smelling of spirits, my Anna will brain me with
a milkstool." Low and deep, George laughed, then hiccoughed. He rubbed
his legs to start blood circulating again. "And your wife, Mattie," Jonathan
added, passing his bottle to my father, "she'll chew your fat good, won't
she, George?"

Because he had not thought of this, my father stopped laughing, then breathing for a second. My stepmother frowned on drinking—she frowned, in fact, on most things about George. She was no famous beauty, fat as she was, with brown freckles, a rich spangled voice, and more chins (lately) than a Chinese social register, but my stepmother had—or so George believed when Jonathan arranged their wedding—beautiful ways. Her previous owners, friends of the Polkinghornes, were an old New England family that landed with the Pilgrims at Cape Cod Bay. Mattie, their servant, was sure some days that she had married below herself. She was spiritual, high-strung, respected books, and above all else was dedicated to developing George into a real gentleman, even if it killed him—she selected his clothes for him, corrected his speech, and watched him narrowly for the slightest lapse into Negroness, as she called it. Added to which, and most of all, George liked his women big and smart (you could have cut two good-sized maids out of Mattie and still had leftovers). As he uncorked a bottle of gin, poured a glass for Jonathan, then toasted his Master's health, he could not bear the thought of disappointing her by stumbling into their cabin reeking of liquor—it would destroy her faith that he was not, after all, a common nigger with no appreciation for the finer things; she would be waiting, he knew, turning the tissue-thin pages of her Bible, holding her finger on some flight of poetry in Psalms, which she planned to read to George for his "general improvement." She made him bend his knees beside her each night, their heads tipped and thighs brushing, praying that neither jealousy nor evil temper, boredom nor temptation, poverty nor padderolls, would destroy their devotion to each other. "You have me, I have you," Mattie whispered, "and we both have Jesus." It made George shudder. Why were black women so mystical? Religion was fine, but if you carried on too much about it, people were liable to think something was wrong with you. "No," he said, shaking his head, glancing left at Jonathan, "I'd best not go home tonight."

"Nor I." Jonathan sat back heavily on his cane-seat chair, crossing his knees, and lit a cigar. "But there must be *some* alternative."

My father raised his shoulders in a shrug.

They drank on in the darkness, grinning more and more now under the influence of gin-and-water. The porch fogged with smoke. At length, Jonathan lifted his head and touched my father's knee.

"George, I have it."

"Yessir?"

"*I* can't go upstairs to face my Anna. And *you* can't return to the quarters." Thoughtful, he picked at his lip. "Are these premises correct so far?'

"Yessir," George rocked his head. "I think so."

"But there's no harm in switching places for one night, is there, with me sleeping in the quarters, and you upstairs?"

George gave him a look. He was sure it was the gin, not Jonathan, talking.

"George, when*ever* I advance an idea you have a most annoying way of looking at me as if I'd just suggested that we strangle a child and sell its body to science. No good will come of this. Goodnight," Jonathan said, steadying himself with one had on the porch rail as he stood. He rocked off for George's cabin. "I'll see you at breakfast."

How long George waited on the front porch, sweating from the soles of his feet upward, is impossible to tell—my father seldom speaks of this night, but the great Swiss clock in Jonathan's parlor chimed twice and, in perfect submission to his Master's will, he turned inside and walked like a man waistdeep in weeds down a hallway where every surface, every shape was warped by frail lamplight from Jonathan's study. His Master's house was solid and rich; it was established, quiet, and so different from the squalid quarters, with vases, a vast library, and great rooms of imported furniture that had cost the Polkinghornes dearly—a house of such heavily upholstered luxuriance and antiques that George now took small, mincing steps for fear of breaking something. In the kitchen, he uncovered a pot of beef on the table, prepared a plate for Mattie (he always brought my stepmother something when he worked in the house), wrapped it in paper, drained his bottle of gin, then lit a candle. Now he was ready.

My father negotiated the wide, straight staircase to Anna's bedchamber, but stopped in the doorway. In candlelight like this, on her high bed with its pewterized nickel headboard, Anna Polkinghorne was a whole landscape of flesh, white as the moon, with rolling hills, mounds, and bottomless gorges. He sat down on a chair by the bed. He stood up. He sat down again—George had never seen the old woman so beautiful. Blurred by the violence of his feelings, or the gin, his eyes clamped shut and he swallowed. Wouldn't a man rise new-made and cured of all his troubles after a night in this immense bed? And the Prayer Circle? Didn't his wife say whatever happened was, in the end, the Lord's will? George put his plate on the chair. He stared—and stared—as Anna turned in her sleep. He yanked off his shirt—wooden buttons flew everywhere, then his coarse Lowell breeches and, like a man listening to the voice of a mesmerist, slipped himself under the bedsheets. What happened next, he had not expected. Sleepily, Anna turned and soldered herself to George. She crushed him in a clinch so strong his spine cracked. Now he had fallen too far to stop. She talked to George, a wild stream of gibberish, which scared him plenty, but he was not a man to leave his chores half-finished, and plowed on. Springs in the mattress snapped, and Anna, gripping the headboards, groaned, "Oh *gawd,* Jonathan!"

"No, ma'am. It ain't Jonathan."

"*Geo-o-o-orge?*" Her voice pulled at the vowel like taffy. She yanked her sheet to her chin. "Is this *George?*"

"Yo husband's in the quarters." George was on his feet. "He's, uh, with my wife." None of it made sense now. How in God's name had he gotten himself into this? He went down on all fours, holding the plate for Mattie over his head, groping around the furniture for his trousers. "Mrs. Polkinghorne, I kin explain, I think. You know how a li'l corn kin confuse yo thinkin'? Well, we was downstairs on the porch, you know, drinkin', Master Polkinghorne and me. . . ."

Anna let fly a scream.

She was still howling, so he says, when George, hauling hips outside, fell, splattering himself from head to foot with mud deltaed in the yard, whooping too when he arrived flushed, naked, and fighting for breath at his own place, the plate of beef still miraculously covered. He heard from inside yet another scream, higher, and then Jonathan came flying like a chicken fleeing a hawk through the cabin door, carrying his boots, his shirt, his suspenders. For an instant, both men paused as they churned past each other in the night and shouted (stretto):

"George, whose fat idea was this?"

"Suh, it was *you* who told *me.* . . ."

*

This, I have been told, was my origin.

It is, at least, my father's version of the story; I would tell you Anna Polkinghorne's, but I was never privileged to hear it. While Jonathan survived this incident, his reputation unblemished, George Hawkins was to be changed forever. Anna, of course, was never quite herself again. All this may seem comic to some, but from it we may date the end of tranquility at Cripplegate. Predictably, my birth played hob with George's marriage (it didn't help Master Polkinghorne's much either) and, just as predictably, for twenty years whenever George or Jonathan entered the same room as Mattie, my stepmother found something to do elsewhere. She never forgave George, who never forgave Jonathan, who blamed Anna for letting things go too far, and *she* demanded a divorce but settled, finally, on living in a separate wing of the house. George, who looked astonished for the rest of his life, even when sleeping, was sent to work in the fields. This Fall, he decided, was the wage of false pride—he had long hours to ponder such things as Providence and Destiny now that he was a shepherd of oxen and sheep. It was God's will, for hitherto he and Mattie—especially Mattie—had been sadditty and felt superior to the fieldhands who, George decided, had a world-historical mission. He had been a traitor. A tool. He refused Jonathan's apologies and joked bleakly of shooting him or, late at night when he had me clean his eyes with cloth after a day of sacking wool, even more bleakly of spiritual and physical bondage, arguing his beliefs loudly, if ineffectively, on the ridiculously tangled subject Race. My father had a talent for ridiculing slaveholders in general and the Polkinghornes in particular—who knew them better than their butler?—that ultimately went over big in Cripplegate's quarters. When I look back on my life, it seems that I belonged by error or accident—call it what you will—to both house and field, but I was popular in neither, because the war between these two families focused, as it were, on me, and I found myself caught from my fifth year forward in their crossfire.

It started in 1843 when Jonathan realized he would have no children, what with Anna holed up with flintlock and twenty-five rounds of ammunition in one half of the house. What had been a comfortable, cushiony marriage with only minor flare-ups, easily fixed by flowers or Anna's favorite chocolates, was now a truce with his wife denying him access to the common room, top floors, and dining area (he slept in his study); what was once a beautiful woman whose voice sang as lovely as any in this world when she sat at the black, boatlike piano in the parlor, one foot gently vibrating on the sostenuto pedal, was now an irascible old woman who haunted the place like a dead man demanding justice, who left terrible notes on the kitchen table, under Jonathan's cup, who, locked in her bedchamber like a prisoner, finished the plates the housemaid left outside her door, but would not throw the latch: a rotten business, in Jonathan's opinion. He came half-asleep to her door night after night, night after night, night after night, and asked helplessly, "Can we talk about it?"

She sat up and shouted, "No!"

"We *all* make mistakes, Anna. For God's sake, George and I meant no harm. . . ." He paused. The inevitable question still nagged him. "Anna, you *wanted* George, not me, to be there, didn't you?"

Silence. After a second: "Is that boy still here?"

"In the quarters," he said. "He's living with George, and he's beautiful, Anna. He had your hair, your—"

"You send him away!"

The old man gulped. "He's your son as much as George's, isn't he?" He rubbed the floor with the toe of his slipper. "We should do for him, you know, like he was ours. . . ."

"I know no such thing!" Her voice became flat and tired. "Go away."

"This is *my* house!" he barked, trembling with fury. "I live here, too!"

"Go *away!*"

Exactly five years to the day George sprang from Anna's bedsheets, Jonathan sat in his study until dawn, writing advertisements for a tutor, which he sent to the best schools. So September, October, and November passed; and on a cold morning in December a gloomy but gifted teacher—a graduate of William and Mary—arrived unannounced on foot from Hodges. By a riverboat, by a stagecoach, by a wagon, by a horse, by a rail—by traveling for five weeks he came with a stupendous headcold to Cripplegate, bearing letters of reference from Amos Bronson Alcott, Caleb Sprague Henry, and Noah Porter, who wrote, "This candidate knows as much about metaphysics as any man alive, and has traveled in India, but you must never leave him alone for long in a room a little girl."

Porter wrote:

"He is, let us say, born to Transcendentalism by virtue of a peculiar quirk of cognition that, like the Tibetan mystic, lets him perceive the interior of objects, why no one knows; whatever his faults, he is perhaps the only man in North America who truly understands the *Mahàbhárata,* and has a splendid future as an Orientalist ordained for him, provided he isn't hanged, say, for high treason, or heresy. He is well suited for the tutorial position you advertise if, and only if, you do not set him off. Never," wrote Porter, "mention his mother."

That winter, the worst in South Carolina's history, five men froze to their horses. Up in the hills, they weren't found until March thaw, their bodies white pap and bloated fingers inside the horses' bellies for the blood-warmth. In this bitter season, snow sat on the rooftops, where its weight cracked wooden beams like kindling; snow brought a silence like sleep to the quarters, where it frosted the great family house and, like a glacial spell, sealed off the hills, the forests, and the fields in blue ice. This drowse of winter released a figure who evolved in pieces from the snowdrifts, first a patch of bloodless fingers and a prayerbook, then a black coat, a hatbrim dusted with ice crystals. Snow lay like a cloak on his shoulders and like spats on the tops of his boots. He sloshed, coughing, up a path made by the wagons to the paddocks—it was eight-thirty—and there he stamped his feet. Jonathan bounded outside in his housecoat, he picked up the stranger's portmanteau, then pushed a tumbler of claret at him. My tutor brushed it aside. "I never drink before noon."

"Nor I," chuckled Jonathan. "But it must be noon *some*where." He threw down the tumbler, then took the stranger's arm:

"How are you called?"

Dropping his gloves into his hat, he pulled back, did a heelclick in the hallway, and bowed. "My Christian name is Ezekiel William Sykes-Withers."

"Of course," Jonathan said, blinking—he couldn't stand people with two last names. "I wouldn't have it any other way."

They sat, these two, on straw chairs by the windows in the study. As Jonathan served hot cups of milk tea with honey, dickered over Ezekiel's wages, and spelled out his chores, Anna must have whiffed trouble, because the slumbrous feel of the morning was broken by a crash from her bedchamber upstairs, then a groan; the plank-ribbed ceiling buckled, Jonathan spilled boiling tea on his lap, and yelped, "Pay no attention—we're having some work done upstairs." In the doorway, I listened; the interview did not seem to be edited for my benefit.

"You're welcome to the guestroom," said Jonathan. "It's right below my wife's bedroom, so you can look in when she rings her bell."

"By your leave," sniffed Ezekiel—he blew his nose into his handkerchief, looked inside to see what he'd got, and said, "I will sleep closer to the boy."

"My thought exactly." Jonathan finished his tea, then placed his cup and saucer on a candlestand. Unconsciously, he swung his left foot. What he thought we shall never know, but this was clear: my tutor, he learned, was, as Porter hinted, an Anarchist and member of George Ripley's Transcendental Club— a brilliant man, a mystic whose pockets bulged with letters, scraps of paper, news clippings, notes scribbled on his handkerchiefs, his shirtcuffs, and stuffed inside his hat. He looked in the study's weak light like engravings I'd seen of Thomas Paine, or a Medieval scholar peering up from his scrolls, and at other times reminded me of a storybook preacher (Calvinist), and was , we learned, one of the two or three authorities on the Rhineland sermons of Meister Eckart. He was thin as a line in Zeno, with a craglike face, wild goatish eyes, and blood pressure so staggeringly high that twice during the interview he ran outside to rub his wrists with snow. His tight, pale lips were the whole Jeffersonian idea of Insurrection. Whenever he pronounced the words "perceiver" and "perceived," which he referred to often that morning, he smothered them in his long nose into "per-r-receiver" and "per-r-rceived" with a kind of solemn quiver as he rolled them out. He smelled of laudanum. He smoked while he was eating, disdained comfort, and died, ten years later, under circumstances that left the exact cause of death a mystery. "You don't drink heavily, do you, Ezekiel?" asked Jonathan. "No," he said. "Or take opium?" "No." "And you have no wife, no relations?" Ezekiel's brow wrinkled and he shook his head violently. "I've stayed to myself since the death of my parents, Mr. Polkinghorne."

"I'm sorry." Jonathan tapped the end of his broad, bell-shaped nose. "I lost my father not long ago, too—I know how you must feel."

"*My* father," said Ezekiel, "deeply loved the things of this world, he held his family and work in the highest esteem. He was piously religious to his Creator, loyal to his country, faithful to his wife, a kind relation, a lasting friend, and charitable to the poor." He sat stiffly on his chair, fists clenched tight. "He shot my mother and sister, and would have blown me to Kingdom Come, too, I assure you, had I not been away that evening. When I arrived home, they were all dead, over their *apéritif,* at the dinner table. Have you," Ezekiel asked, "ever considered suicide?"

"Why no!" Jonathan rubbed his nose, "Never!"

Ezekiel said, "You should."

"And what is *that* supposed to mean?"

"I only mean," said Ezekiel, "that we do not think of death until we are well within her jaws." What he meant by this, he did not say. From his pocket he withdrew a tobacco pouch and a big Nuremberg pipe, thumbed down a pinch of Latakia, and said, "This boy, you say, is a mulatto?"

Jonathan nodded yes.

"In his horoscope Mars confronts Mercury at three angles, and this is promising," said Ezekiel. "It signifies the birth of a philosopher. Is he yours?"

Witheringly, Jonathan glanced toward the door, wagged his head, and said, "No." The reply and gesture nihilated each other. "What I mean to say is that Andrew is my property and that his value will increase with proper training." He looked away, quickly, from the door, then sighed. And what was I thinking? What did I feel? Try as I might, I could not have told you what my body rested on, or what was under my feet—the hallway had the feel of pasteboard and papier-mâché. A new train of thoughts were made to live in my mind. Jonathan hung his head a little. He said to Ezekiel, without looking up from the floor, "Five dollars monthly, and board, are all I can offer. Are you still interested?"

Ezekiel's face wrinkled into an infernal, Faustian leer. "He *isn't* your son?"

"Are you," Jonathan asked, crossly, "interested?"

"I will teach the boy, yes, using a program modeled on that of James Mill for his son John Stuart, but I am never to be disturbed on Sundays, or during the evening. I never eat meat. Or eggs. I would like one wall of my room covered with mirrors. Don't ask why—I live a bit to one side of things. Do you," he asked, stretching out a hand soft and white as raw dough toward Jonathan, "agree to these conditions?"

"Yes." My Master blinked and pushed back his chair. "Agreed."

By the age of eight I began, with Ezekiel, learning Greek; by the time I was twelve I had read Xenophon and Plato. Next came Voice, Elocution, and Piano lessons. He gave George and Mattie orders that I was not to touch silver, gold, or paper currency; nor was I allowed to listen to the Mixed Lydian and Hyperlydian Modes in music, lest these melancholy strains foul Ezekiel's plans for what was—in his view—a perfect moral education. By the age of fifteen I began to fare badly. I could ask to use the silver chamber pot in George's cabin, where I slept curled up on a pallet, in Latin more perfect than native tongue; I received lectures on monadology, classical philology, and Oriental thought—the better to fathom Schopenhauer, a favorite of Ezekiel, who often spent days in his cabin, reading Hegel and Thoreau, with whom he'd corresponded earlier, and Marx, who paid him a visit at Cripplegate in 1850. (Of Karl Marx's social call more will be said later.) He taught me the 165 Considerations, Four Noble Truths, the Eight-Fold Path, the 3,000 Good Manners, the 80,000 Graceful Conducts; but I must confess that reading Chinese thought was a little like eating Chinese food: the more one read Lao tzu and Chaung tzu, or ate subgum chop suey, the emptier one's head and stomach felt hours later. Too, I could never remember if it was ▽ before ⊥ except after 盒 , or 网 before 呆 except after 爲 , and always got the meanings confused. And there is also this to say:

Soon all life left my studies—why I couldn't say, but I had, at least, this theory: these vain studies of things moral, things transcendental, things metaphysical were, all in all, rich food for the soul, but in Cripplegate quarters all that was considered as making life worth living was utterly wanting. And so I became restless and unquiet. So restless, in fact, that on the eve of my twentieth birthday, a rainy Sunday evening, I rose from my pallet in George's dreary, two-room cabin, and carried all my confusions to Master Polkinghorne.

May 6 of the year of grace 1858.

My clothes were soaking, my frock bunched up like a woman's bustle in the back as I scaled a hillslope between the quarters and house. The yard, as wide as a playing field, was wet and slippery to my feet. Farther on, around the lee side and behind long chintz draperies, a chandelier glowed faintly with fumes of golden light like luminous gas in one ground-floor window. For an instant, I paused beside the broad bay window, watching an old woman, all wrinkled, nothing but pleats and folds, almost bedridden now, burnt down to eighty pounds, dying faster than Dr. Horace Crimshaw in Hodges could feed her pills for migraines, pills for stomach cramps, and potions (Veronal and chloral hydrate) for the rest. Jonathan loved his old woman, I knew, and me as well, but could not live with us both. He would slip away some evenings, yes, riding his one-horse chaise off on the remains of old plank roads to tumble, it was rumored, the wives of farmers gone to market in Greenwood. He became, in fact, a hunter of women—a broken-down old man, perfumed, who wore powdered wigs and ribbons in his hair like a Creole dandy. The sort of a man who told women, "My wife and I live like brother and sister," or, "Older men make, of course, the best lovers." So it was for years with my Master before sickness brought his wife back downstairs. His chest shrank, his stomach filled, and duty replaced his desire for Anna. But he never thought—he was too loyal to think—of abandoning her, although now she could only stare back at him through burnt-out eyes, coughing blood into her brass thunderpot, crepitations like the dry induviae of brittle leaves in the folds of her nightgown: a fragile mass of living jelly, and no more wife to Jonathan now than a stump of firewood.

A thousand drubbing fingers of rain flew against my face as I leaned forward from my hips and climbed the six wooden steps of the dry-rotted porch. The nerves of my teeth reacted to the cold. Shivering, I lifted, then let fall once—twice—the long brass knocker on the door, waited, then stepped back quickly. For now the latch was thrown, and the huge door opened with a splinter of milkblue candlelight and a dragging sound. It opened, old hinges grating for want of oil. And in the doorway stood my Master, his back hooped like a horseshoe, breathing as if he'd been running for hours. His eyelids were puffy. He scuffed in his stiff, sliding walk onto the porch, lifted his candle higher, oblivious to hot wax trickling down his forearm into his sleeve, and winced when he saw me. A tic twitched in one of his eyes. He saddled his nose with wide spectacles, and asked, full of affection (for the old quop did, indeed, love me like a son), "Is this Andrew?"

"It is, Master Polkinghorne." He pressed his cold lips in a moist kiss against my forehead, and I, in return, affectionately squeezed his arm. "May I come in, sir?"

"You can't stay," he said. "My wife is up and about, you see."

"This won't take too long." I coughed into my hand to clear my throat. "You'll not be troubled by me again."

"You're not in trouble, are you? You haven't murdered someone, have you?" Jonathan sighed. "If so, I hope it wasn't anybody white, Andrew."

"No sir, nothing like that." At that moment I decided to tell him nothing, and confide only in you of my brief but unsettling encounter earlier that afternoon. Near the southern hills, close to the backroad, just where the plantation approaches a dark stretch of woods, I had been herding my father's Brown Swiss calves, his Leicester sheep, when the girl—this was Minty—appeared in an osnaburg skirt and white blouse, beneath an old Leghorn hat, with a blue satin ribbon, toting a washtub of clothes. I had known her since childhood—whenever she saw me, her lips made a kissing-sound and she called me away. To Master Polkinghorne's big twelve-stanchion barn. There, beside bins of old oats going bad, in a loft of straw and musty hay, I think I saw her—*really* saw her for the first time. Not, I say, as the wild daughter of Jonathan's maid, who teased me when I traipsed off for my sessions with Ezekiel, hid my books, and mocked my speech, but as all the highbreasted women in calico and taffeta, in lace-trimmed gingham poke bonnets and black net hose, that I had ever wanted and secretly, hopelessly loved. What seemed physical shortcomings, defects in her childhood—eyes too heavy for a child's small head, a shower of sienna hair always entangling itself in farm machinery—seemed (to me) that afternoon to be purified features in a Whole, where no particular facet was striking because all fused together to offer a flawed, haunting beauty the likes of which you have never seen. Do not laugh, sir: I was stung sorely, riveted to the spot, relieved, Lord knows, of my reason. How much of her beauty lay in the Minty, and how much in my head, was a mystery to me. What beauty truly *in* things? Was touch in me or in the things I touched? These things so ensorceled me and baffled my wits that I prayed mightily, *Give me Minty.* And, God's own truth, I promised in that evanescent instant that she and I, George and Mattie—all the bondsmen in Cripplegate's quarters and abroad—would grow old in the skins of free man. (Perhaps I was not too clear in the head at that moment.) But how long would this take? Forty years? Fifty years? My heart knocked

violently for manumission. Especially when, as we straightened our gar-
ments, I saw her eyes—eyes green as icy mountain meltwater, with a hint of
blue shadow and a drowse of sensuality that made her seem voluptuously
sleepy, distant, as though she had been lifted long ago from a melancholy
African landscape overrich with the colors and warm smells of autumn—a
sad, out-of-season beauty suddenly precious to me because it was imperfect
and perhaps illusory like moonlight on pond water, sensuously alive, but delivering itself over, as if in sacrifice, to inevitable slow death in the fields. Her
name, now that I think on it, might have been Zeudi—Ethiopian, ancient, as
remote and strange, now that something in me had awoken, as Inca ruins or
shards of pottery from the long-buried cities of Mu. But this is not what I
said to Master Polkinghorne. I said:

"She has never liked me, has she?"

"Perhaps you will find forgiveness in your heart for her, Andrew." Now we
entered his study. "Our relations are somewhat on the stiff side." There was
a bureau with swinging brass handles, a diamond-paned bookcase, and a
soft calf-bound set of Hawthorne. On an elbow-chair near the fireplace my
Master lowered his weight, then looked up. "Would you rub me along the
shoulders, Andrew the pain is there again." As I did so, Jonathan talked on,
as if to himself. "My Anna is mad, gloriously mad, and it's all my doing." He
forced a laugh, full of gloom. "And I'll tell you true, I hate her sometimes.
Many a night I stand by her door, listening to Anna breathe—it's horrible.
Just *horrible!*" His voice began to shake. "I pray that her lungs will fail, and
when they *do* stop, faltering sometimes in a hideous rattle, I pray just as
desperately for her to breathe again, and when this happens . . . ah, Andrew,
I'm sorry once again." He rubbed his face with both hands as I crossed to
the fireplace and stood with my back to the flames, facing him, opening my
palms to catch the heat, closing them. The next time he looked at up there
were tears in his eyes. "What business brings you here tonight?"

"With your permission," I said, "I have come to tell you that Minty, your
seamstress, and I plan to be married. That, however, is not all, sir."

"Oh?" He squinted suspiciously.

"Meaning no disrespect to you, sir, I want to draw up my deed of manumission."

My Master was silent for so long I could hear rain patter, lightly, against
the windowpanes. Make no mistake. That night I trembled. A pulse began
to throb in my temple. Beneath the sausage-tight skin of slavery I could
be, depending on the roll of the dice, the swerve of the indifferent atom,
forever poised between two worlds, or—with a little luck—a wealthy man

who had made his way in the world and married the woman he loved. All right—be realistic, I thought. Consider the facts: Like a man who had fallen or been rudely flung into the world, I owned nothing. My knowledge, my clothes, my language, even, were shamefully second-hand, made by, and perhaps for, other men. I was a living lie, that was the heart of it. My argument was: Whatever my origin, I would be wholly responsible for the shape I gave myself in the future, for shirting myself handsomely with a new life that called me like a siren to possibilities that were real but forever out of reach. My Master sat, blinking into the fire, then up at me, the corners of his mouth, tucked in, his expression exactly that of a man who has come suddenly across cat fur in a bowl of soup. I walked to the study window. Air outside still smelled of rain. Breezes flew over the grass like shadows or grandfather spirits—so I imagined—in search of their graves. Clearly, I remember the night sky as applegreen, the chirring of grasshoppers in a crazy sort of chorus. Abruptly, Jonathan Polkinghorne brought out:

"You haven't been smoking rabbit tobacco again, have you, Andrew?"

"No, sir."

His eyebrows drew inward.

"Touch your thumb to your nose."

I did so.

"Now say, 'The rain in Spain falls mainly on the plain.'"

I assured him I was sober.

"Then, Andrew," he said, "you will understand that you are too young for these freedom papers. All our bondsmen will be released after Anna and I close our eyes. This is in our will. You haven't long, I suppose, to wait." His face was pale and strained and vague—Jonathan rather hated all discussions of death, especially his own. Moving toward the door, his shoe knocked a chair, and he swore irritably. Massaging his toe, he turned to ask, "Is there anything else?"

"Sir," I said, struggling, the reflections of the balls of my eyes so utterly without depth in the window that even I could not tell what I was thinking. "Long ago, you would not have me, and you turned me out to the quarters, then over to a teacher. . . ."

"Ezekiel Sykes-Withers." He drew his mouth down. "That was a mistake. The man was crazy as a mouse in a milkcan. Should've been a monk. He was hired to teach you useful *skills,* Andrew—things like book-keeping, and market research, and furniture repair, and what have we to show for his time here?"

"He taught me to read," I said.

"Well, that's some consolation."

"He taught me to control my heart and, when I walk, leave no footprints."

"Are these what they call *metaphors* Andrew?" As always when facing figurative language, my Master was a little flummoxed. "I think I'm a pretty clear-witted man," he said, "but this outdoes me, Andrew." It's only about once in a lifetime that you stumble upon a first-rate philosophical metaphor, and when you do, people are bound to say, "Huh?" and take all the starch out of it. "You got out of bed to tell me all this?" He scratched his head. "Manumission and marriage?"

"Yes, sir."

"And what shall you do if I sign these papers?"

"Work for myself," I said, too loudly. "Within a year I'll be back to buy Minty, then George and Mattie from you." Our eyes met—mine squinted, small as sewing needles, like a murderer's; my Master's cold and critical, the eyes of an eagle, infinitely wise.

Softly, the clock in the corner chimed twice.

"I see."

He did not, I knew, see it at all.

"Then I tell you what, you *will* have an opportunity to work for yourself—or at least work this foolishness out of your system." He went to his bureau, taking out paper, ink, and a quill, but his jaw was set—that meant something. "However, as I say, I will sign no freedom papers until you return, as promised, with the money for the others."

"You will have it," I said. "every penny."

Glasses clamped on his nose, he wrote quietly while I paced, and in a cramped, arthritic script that made his letter resemble a cross between cuneiform, Arabic, and Morse code. When he finished this tortured message, he folded the paper, and pressed it into my hand.

"This letter will see you get work with one of my old acquaintances in Abbeville. We have not corresponded in years, but I believe she will put you to work." He said this woman—Flo Hatfield—would see to all my needs (he didn't say what needs), and would keep me busy (he didn't say how). Standing, he rumpled my hair, which I hated, and said, "Now go and tell George and Mattie where you're off to."

I started to hug him, then thought better of it, and ran down the hallway, though I had no reason, and leaped from the porch. The beauty of the night made me shout a cry that set sleeping dogs to barking and hummed for minutes afterwards in my ears. A fine rain fell. I sang out, now to trees that nodded respectfully in return, now to invisible blackbirds that called back from the bushes. Then I hurried on through foamy mud to the quarters, the letter tucked inside my shirt, sank slowly to sleep, and, dreaming, saw myself counting coins at the end of the week.

But first I had to work for Flo Hatfield.

◉◉

LEIGHANN LORD

ACNE CURE

Next time you go to the doctor, please be very careful because I promise, the side effects of what he prescribes may be worse than the original problem. Yeah, there's this prescription acne medicine . . . it clears up acne but it also causes birth defects. Very bizarre!

It's like, "Hey, girl, how you doing? You're looking good. How's the baby?"

"Oh, little Quasimodo is fine. Hey! Stop trying to stand up straight, child! That'll hurt your back."

BIG WORDS

Some people don't know how to take it when I use big words. I was talking to this guy once, and, well, I don't want to say he was a racist, but he stopped me in mid-sentence and said, "Leighann, I know you're black . . . "

I have no idea what tipped him off.

Anyway, he said, "Leighann, I know you're black, but how come you don't talk like you're from the ghetto?"

And I said, "Because a ghetto is where the Nazis forced the Polish Jews to live during World War II. And, quite frankly, the only Yiddish word that comes to mind right now is *schmuck*."

THIRD WORLD PERFUME

Have you noticed how a lot of companies think that if they use black actors in their advertising, black people will be more inclined to buy the product? Like Revlon . . . they came out with a new perfume targeted to black women. The ad said that this perfume is the essence of Africa and the power of women. What does that mean? You put it on and European countries can't resist the urge to colonize you?

WRONG WAR

Did you know America ranks the lowest in education but the highest in drug use? It's nice to be number one, but we can fix that. All we need to do is start the war on education. If it's anywhere near as successful as our war on drugs, in no time we'll all be hooked on phonics.

◎/◎

FROM *ROCK THIS!*

By Chris Rock

REVERSE RACISM

The country's in an uproar. Everybody's mad at each other.
  It's sad.
  Black people are mad. White people are mad.
  Black people yell racism.
  White people yell reverse racism.
  Chinese people yell sideways racism.
  Just what is reverse racism? Is there something white people are *not* getting? Is there a job a white man didn't get yesterday? Reverse racism is like Mike Tyson saying, "It's not fair; me always having to fight the heavy guys. From now on, I only want to fight lightweights."

*

Whenever the white man's got me down, I turn on the TV and watch boxing. White guys cannot box. Black guys fight better than white guys, Puerto Rican guys box better than black guys, and so on. I guess the lower you are on the socioeconomic ladder, the better you fight. I bet for every Puerto Rican fighter, there's an American Indian waiting to kick his ass.

I feel bad about the American Indians. We took—wait a minute, *white* people took—their land. Now they have very little left. And everything exploits the Indians. There was "F-Troop," the Mazola commercial, the Atlanta Braves, and the Cleveland Indians. And during football season, they have to hear about the Washington Redskins. That's like having a team named the Newark Niggers.

Remember the Indian chief with the tear in his eye, supposedly crying for the environment? He wasn't crying for the environment; he was crying because somebody took his land, then fucked and killed his wife.

The ozone was the least of his worries.

Since the Indians got swindled over some beads, nobody in America has been too excited about newcomers. Every racial and ethnic group gets treated like shit when they get here—by the racial and ethnic group that got treated like shit when they came in on the earlier flight. Nobody says, "Hey, here are the new guys. Let's welcome them. Let's bake a cake for the Irish."

A COUNTRY DIVIDED

People act as if there's the possibility of a real race war. They say the country's divided over race. Split in half.

Bullshit.

Black people are only 12 percent of this country's population. Twelve percent isn't half! You can't have a race war when it's 88 percent versus 12 percent.

We'd lose!

We're in New York, L.A., D.C., Chicago, Atlanta. Maybe ten places altogether. Have you ever been to Montana? Not a lot of brothers there. Not too many black people in Minnesota, aside from Prince and Kirby Puckett.

In New York, sure. We're half the city. But upstate, the only place you'll find more blacks than whites is in Attica.

I've been to every state in the union. There's *a lot* of white people out there. But some militant black people still make noises like, "Hey, we should just take over."

Forget it. Malcolm X counted up them and us. Then he said, "Oh, shit. We could try, but I think we might get *fucked* up."

Unless the race war takes place in a boxing ring, one guy at a time.

THE BLACK EXPERIENCE

Sometimes I hate life because I was born a suspect. All black men are born suspects. When I came out of my mother, right away, if anything happened within a three-block radius, I was a suspect. As a matter of fact, the day I was born, somebody's car got stolen from the hospital parking lot. They made me stand in a lineup. That was pretty tough, considering I wasn't even a day old and couldn't crawl, much less walk. Good thing I had a couple black nurses to help hold me up. I got lucky. They were in the lineup, too.

If you're born a suspect, everybody's scared of you. I can walk down the street anywhere in America and women will clutch their purses tighter, hold on to their Mace, and lock their car doors. If I look up into the windows of the apartments I pass by I can see old ladies on the phone. They've already dialed 9–1 . . . and are just waiting for me to do something wrong.

*

Most black people I know have felt the consequences of racism: bad neighborhoods, bad services, crime. But in the black community they're just part of life. We notice, but we don't really notice.

To feel real in-your-face racism—to be called a nigger and be treated bad, bad, bad—we have to go to where white people live and vacation. Like the Hamptons. The only black people around are those working for white people. Walk into a store and if you're black, no one says hello. They say, "What do you want?" as in "What the hell are you doing here and how soon are you leaving?"

If you're black and have money—if you buy the house and live in the white neighborhood—you feel it even more.

I had a white friend who used to go to downtown Brooklyn with his brother. They'd go into a store and wait until a group of black kids came in. Immediately, security started following the black group. That's when my white friend and his brother just started taking whatever they wanted. They didn't even have to hide it. They'd walk out wearing coats with price tags hanging down.

A message to store owners: "That's right. Better keep watching those black kids."

I'm always afraid of those stores where they have to buzz you in. I'm concerned that they won't buzz me in. Then I'll just have to stand there feeling like shit. My fantasy is to go up to one of these fancy boutiques on Fifth Avenue, take a brick out of my coat, and throw it through the fucking window.

And then I'll write them a big fat check that not only covers it but also pays for everybody's lunch.

Of course, I won't ever *really* do that because I avoid those stores. Black people stay away from a lot of stuff where white people are in charge. A lot of us don't vote. We go to the doctor less. We're intimidated by institutions.

Hmm. I think it started with the institution of **slavery.**

WE ALL LOOK THE SAME IN THE DARK

White people don't know how to tell the difference between one black man and another. If they could, we'd all get along. It would solve everything. But to the white man, we're all the same.

Trouble.

They see two black men together and it's a crowd. A dangerous mob. To white people, even Ed Bradley and Bryant Gumbel hanging out, waiting to cross the street together, is potentially scary. Clarence Thomas in an Adidas warm-up suit will *not* get a cab in Washington, D.C. He *will* get followed around in the mall while he tries to check out athletic footwear.

White people are so blind that they can't even tell the difference between me and a larger-than-life character like Suge Knight. But my friends, there's a **BIG FUCKING DIFFERENCE.** You can tell just by looking that one of us is not to be fucked with.

Blacks, however, can immediately distinguish between white guys. For instance: Pauly Shore and J.F.K., Jr.

See what I mean? You know immediately.

Why is this so? Because blacks have *had* to learn to differentiate. We're confronted by white faces on TV. We pay our rent to a white guy. We work for white guys. White people don't have to know anything about black people to survive. They can go their whole lives and never even know a black person.

*

Black people have gone to the Olympics for years, representing America. Not black people, but America. That's the problem with black people. We want to be down. We want to be cool. When other ethnic groups get dissed they form their *own* communities.

Chinese people came over here. They got dissed. They said, "Fuck you! We got Chinatown. All right? Our own thing."

Italian people came over here. They got dissed. They said, "Yo man, fuck you! Little Italy. All right? We got our own thing."

You ever heard of Little Africa?

Didn't think so.

Little Africa is the GHETTO.

Let's see: I don't think we created the ghetto on purpose.

Black people have it bad. At least the Chinese and Italians have their own restaurants.

That's right. We don't even have our own food. Soul food is *not* black food. It's just some nasty shit they fed to the slaves. You think a ham hock tasted good the first time the white man shoved it in our faces? No. We had to cover it in seasoning to make it work. Black people don't even have salad dressing—and *everybody* has salad dressing, even Paul Newman. Our salad dressing is hot sauce.

HELP WANTED: ONE LEADER. PLEASE APPLY WITHIN.

Things would get better for black people if we could just get a leader. We need a leader. We need one bad. We need someone who is recognized by everyone. Someone undisputed and unanimous. We need a man we can point to and say, "He's the guy."

But it's a very hard position to fill. Everybody who had the job before got shot in the head.

POTENTIAL LEADER: Oh, how'd the last guy do? Why did he leave? Did he get another job?

US: Kinda . . . you could say that.

It's hard to fill that vacancy. Harder than selling Nicole Brown's condo. It doesn't matter how many benefits you give.

US: We got dental.

POTENTIAL LEADER: That's all right. I'll pass.

But we still need a black leader. Someone qualified. Someone who won't just beg for money from white people. But even if the job weren't dangerous, every candidate has something wrong with him. There's always a catch. I'm talking about major flaws. Let's break it down:

Al Sharpton: I'm sure he's done a lot of good things for the community, but when you bring up his name people act as if he's a comedic punch line.

"Why'd the chicken cross the road?"

"Al Sharpton!"

He looks like Bookman from "Good Times," with a damn perm. How can you take anyone seriously with that hair? No matter what he says, you can't take your eyes off the hair. If Al Sharpton said he could cure AIDS, you'd say, "Right. Look at that hair."

Jesse Jackson: We can't question his credentials: marched with Dr. King, a leader in the Civil Rights movement. But what happened to Jesse? Jesse was real *for a minute.* He ran for President, had some influence. Then it got out of hand. He'd run, then not run. Run, then not run. He couldn't make up his mind. Next, he started rhyming just a little too much. Just got silly.

"Education. Procreation. Be a man. I like ham."

I thought maybe he was making an album with Puffy.

Then he stopped preaching. Jesse used to be a reverend, right? But when was the last time you saw Jesse in church? The man's *never* in church. He's on TV.

I went to a Tyson fight one Saturday night. You know what fights are like in Vegas? Nothing but pimps, prostitutes, drug dealers, and naked ring girls holding up the round placards. The most sleazy thing. Not a godly atmosphere. And there was Jesse sitting next to me. I turned to him and said, "It's Saturday night. Ain't church tomorrow?"

Louis Farrakhan: Good organizational skills. The man who brought us the Million Man March. But Farrakhan has a problem with the Jews. Can this help us?

It's not really constructive. Besides, I don't get it. The only way you can get over is to hate *nobody*.

I'm around brothers every day, all the time, and I've *never ever* heard a bunch of black people talking about Jews. Never.

Black people don't hate **Jews.**

Black people hate white people.

Just because we can tell the difference between one white guy and another doesn't mean we have time to dice them up into little groups.

"The Jews are fucked, but Irish are cool."

You're *all* white to us.

The problem with all our black leaders is that their consciousness is defined by their views of white people.

If white people didn't exist, most black leaders would be out of work.

A lot of people ask me why I don't include Colin Powell when I mention black leaders. To be a true black leader, you have to be self-made. The fact that he was chairman of the Joint Chiefs of Staff makes him the equivalent of a sitcom in a good time slot. Is "Suddenly Susan" any good? We don't know. It's on after "Seinfeld."

No matter how you feel about Louis Farrakhan, Al Sharpton, or Jesse Jackson, they stand on their own. Nobody gave them what they have.

*

If there's any disagreement between blacks and Jews it's over which was worse: the Holocaust or slavery.

I'll tell you which was worse: It's a tie. Except for one thing. The Holocaust was illegal. Afterward, the Allies got to arrest people, lay blame, hold trials, and have a sense of closure.

Slavery was legal. No closure. Just over. As far as America is concerned, slavery and segregation were fads, just like pet rocks and disco.

Was there ever an apology?

I'd like one.

Reparations?

That's okay now, but at the time it would have been justice.

The Civil War was nice, but in the real history books it wasn't about slavery. It was about taxes.

Slavery affected the black psyche. Now, we're like Ron Goldman's father without a criminal "guilty" verdict. We're like battered wives ordered to stay with their husbands.

No wonder we're fucked up.

A Creative Solution

We still need a black leader. What are we going to do?

They import basketball players from Africa. How about bringing in one of those kings? They ran a country. We need a leader who already ran something. But we never get that guy. We get the *next* guy. Martin Luther King got shot—Jesse was standing right next to him.

"Let's use him."

As far as I'm concerned our leader doesn't even have to be black. Let's get Pat Riley. He's led a lot of black men to championships. Maybe he can take us to the promised land.

Having no leader has taken its toll. Now we're preoccupied with entertainers.

"You're role models. You have to act right."

Why does the public expect entertainers to behave better than everybody else?

It's ridiculous.

No one gave a fuck that Babe Ruth was an alcoholic. That was his problem. When Dwight Gooden got hooked on coke, that was his problem. It fucked with their teams, but it's not like they let the *community* down. They let themselves down. They're not thinking about you. They shouldn't be thinking about you. They should be thinking about getting off that shit.

Of course, this is just for *black* entertainers. You don't see anyone telling Jerry Seinfeld he's a good role model. Why? Because everyone *expects* whites to behave themselves. Goes with being white, I guess. But blacks . . .

In the old days, a black entertainer was just that: a black entertainer. He sang his song and that was it. No one cared about what he was doing off-stage. It was his business. In the old days Sammy Davis, Jr., could fuck a white girl, snort some cocaine, get his eye knocked out, and it was cool. It was no reflection on black people. It was *his* business.

Nowadays, you've got to be an entertainer *and* a leader. It's too much. Rappers get shot and the people are overcome. I loved Tupac and Biggie, but don't act like it's bigger than it is. Let's not blow it out of proportion.

"Biggie Smalls was *assassinated.* Tupac Shakur was *assassinated*."

They weren't assassinated.

Martin Luther King was assassinated.

Malcolm X was assassinated.

The *Kennedys* were assassinated.

Those brothers just **got shot!** They had some beefs. They're not here anymore. But don't make it bigger than it is.

I love Tupac and Biggie, but school is still going to be open on their birthdays. There won't be any pictures of the two hanging in Grandma's kitchen.

"Gramma, is that . . . Biggie? What was he like?"

WHO YOU CALLING RACIST?

Who's more racist: black people or white people?

Black people.

You know why? Because black people hate black people, too. Everything *white* people don't like about black people, *black* people don't like about black people. It's like our own personal civil war.

On one side, there's black people.

On the other, you've got niggers.

The niggers have got to go. Everytime black people want to have a good time, niggers mess it up. You can't do anything without some ignorant-ass niggers fucking it up.

Can't keep a disco open more than three weeks. Grand opening? Grand closing.

Can't go to a movie the first week it opens. Why? Because niggers are shooting at the screen.

"This movie is so good I gotta bust a cap in here."

I love black people, but I hate niggers. I am tired of niggers. I wish they would let me join the Ku Klux Klan. I'd do a drive-by from L.A. to Brooklyn.

You can't have anything valuable when you're around niggers. You can't have a big-screen TV. Well, you can have it, but you better move it in at three o'clock in the morning, paint it white, and hope niggers think it's a bassinet.

You can't have anything in your house. Why? Because the niggers who live next door will break in, take it all, and then come over the next day and go, "We heard ya got robbed."

"You know because *you* robbed me. You weren't hearing shit because you were *doing* shit."

I'm tired of niggers. Tired, tired, tired.

Niggers always want credit for some shit they're *supposed* to do. They'll brag about some stuff a normal man *just does*. They'll say something like, "Yeah? Well, I take care of my kids."

You're supposed to, you dumb motherfucker.

"I ain't never been to jail."

Whaddya want? A cookie? You're not supposed to go to jail, you low-expectation-having motherfucker.

The worst thing about niggers is that they love to *not know*. Nothing makes a nigger happier than not knowing the answer to your question.

YOU: What's the capital of Zaire?

NIGGER: I don't know that shit.

YOU: Why the hell not?

NIGGER: Don't know.

YOU: Don't know?

NIGGER: Just keep'n it real.

Niggers love to keep it real. Real dumb. Next time niggers break into your house, if you want to save your money, put it in your books. Niggers don't read. Books are like kryptonite to a nigger.

YOU: Here. Read this book.

NIGGER: NOOOOOOOOO!

I'm tired of their shit. Our kids can't play anywhere. Every year the space gets smaller.

"Okay, you can go between that corner and corner. Okay, that's too far. Now you can go between that gate and that gate."

By the time the kid's ten she's just hopping in circles.

I'm tired, tired, tired. Fee-fie-foe-figure, boy do I hate a nigger.

Now the politicians are trying to get rid of welfare. Every time you see a welfare story on the news, you always see black people. Hey! Black people don't give a fuck about welfare. But niggers are shaking in their boots.

"They gonna take our shit!"

A black man who works two jobs, every day, hates a nigger on welfare.

"Nigger, get a job. I got two, you can't get one? I would give your lazy ass one of mine, but then you'd get fucked up, laid off, and they wouldn't hire another nigger for ten years."

A black woman, with two kids, going to work every day, busting her ass, hates a bitch with nine kids collecting welfare. All she thinks is: "Bitch, stop fucking. Stop fucking! Stop it. Put the dick down. Get a job. Yes, you can get a job. Get a job holding dicks. But whatever you do, *get paid to do it.*"

*

I know what all you black readers think.

"Man, why you got to say that? Why you got to say that? It isn't us, it's the *media.* The media has distorted our image to make us look bad. Why must you come down on us like that, brother? It's not us, it's the media."

Please cut the shit. When I go to the money machine at night, I'm not looking over my shoulder for the media.

I'm looking for niggers.

Ted Koppel never took anything from me. Niggers have. Do you think I've got three guns in my house because the media's outside my door trying to bust in?

"Oh shit. It's Mike Wallace, Run!"

MOMMY? CAN I SAY "NIGGER"?

I just said "nigger" a whole lot. You probably think I shouldn't use the N-word, but that rule is just for white folks. Any black person can say "nigger" and get away with it. It's true. It's like calling your kid an idiot. Only *you* can call your kid that. Someone else calls your kid an idiot, there's a fight.

Yet some white people still wonder why black people can say "nigger" and they can't. Believe it or not, it's a very common question. I hear it all the time.

WHITE PERSON: Chris, can I say "nigger"?

ME: Why would you even *want* to?

WHITE PERSON: I don't mean anything *bad* by it. I've traveled the world.
I got a yacht. I fucked Raquel Welch. Now, if I could just
say "nigger," everything would be complete.

ME: No. After I smack you upside the head everything will
be complete.

"Nigger" is one of those words, like "fuck," that means different things
depending on how you use it.

"I love you, nigger." Good.

"You're my nigger." That's nice.

"Shut up, nigger!" Not so good.

"I'm going to kill you, nigger." You better run.

Of course, "nigger" is just a word. White people could call us anything,
like "butter."

"Hey, you fucking butter! Pick that cotton, butter!"

The problem is that then they wouldn't be able to use the word "butter"
for anything else. But they've got to use *something*. Next thing you know,
white folks are sitting around the breakfast table with their eggs and toast,
saying, "You're kidding. I can't believe it's *not* nigger."

THE MOST RACIST GUY IN THE WORLD

Who are the most racist people in the world?

Old black men.

A brother in his sixties hates everybody.

He can't stand white people. Why? Because old black men went through
real racism. He didn't go through that "I can't get a cab" shit. He *was* the
cab. The white man would jump on his back and say, "Main Street."

An old black man also hates young black people. To him, they've fucked
up everything he's worked for.

But when an old black man sees an old white man, the old black man
always kisses the old white man's ass.

"How you doing, sir? Pleased to meet you. Whatever I can getcha, you
let me know."

But as soon as the white man walks out of sight, the black man starts
up:

"Crack-ass cracker . . . put my foot in his cracker ass, crack-ass cracker.
I wish that cracker would have said some shit to me. Lick my ass, fat-ass
cracker, motherfucker, saltine cracker."

But when the white man comes back, it's, "Howdy, sir."

I have a 55-year-old uncle who *hates* white people. But he's married to a white lady. Can you believe it? He sits around going, "These crackers ain't shit . . . 'cept for Susie." He tried to explain the whole thing to me: "I got a white wife. So what? I love her, she loves me, that's all that matters. But I tell you this, if the revolution ever comes, I'll kill her first—just to show everybody I mean business."

He really said that.

I guess that's what O.J. was up to. He thought the revolution had already come.

COLOR CODING

No matter where I go, I always see signs of racism and racial imbalance.

For instance, white guys have quality dirty magazines like *Playboy, Penthouse,* and *Club*. What do black guys have? *Players* magazine, the lowest, nastiest publication on the face of the earth. The pictures aren't even in focus. They show a bunch of black girls getting off the toilet, trying to shield their faces. It's like the women are saying, "Hey, what are you doing in here? Are you crazy? What's wrong with you, you pervert?" I guess they don't even bother to ask permission to take the picture in the first place.

In *Playboy,* the women are posed sensually, like they're happy and getting paid. In *Players,* the women look mad, like they're only getting ten dollars and their pimp is taking eight.

In *Playboy,* the women don't have a blemish on their bodies. In *Players,* the model's got stretch marks from the eight kids she's had, plus the bullet wound from that time she got shot in the ass.

It's the same when you look at a white porno flick and compare it to a black porno flick. The white one's got actors, actresses, a plot, and even some extras who keep their clothes on—people who walk through, or hang around, who aren't even having sex.

A black porno flick is the sorriest thing on earth. No actors, no actresses, just a bunch of people siting in a hotel room waiting for somebody to yell, "Action."

When somebody does, there's an argument.

"ACTRESS": Where's my money? Where's my money? Yeah, I'll fuck him when I get paid.

Sometimes you'll pick up a black porno flick and with luck get a *real* actor—some out-of-work brother that you used to see on TV. You'll be watching and you'll say, "Hey, wait a minute, isn't that Sticks from 'Happy Days'?"

*

Before I moved out of my parents' house and got my own place, my mother would sometimes clean up my room. Whenever she did, she used to take away all my dirty magazines.

When your mother takes your magazines, you can't say anything about it. You have to play it off like they were never there in the first place. She doesn't say anything, you don't say anything.

But you know it's happened because you're sitting around eating breakfast with your mother there's this tension at the table. You both know you're not her little baby anymore.

You're like some pervert she's given birth to.

So you try to break the silence by asking a question:

"Mom, have you seen my baseball glove?"

And your mother goes, "No. Maybe you left it in the *Penthouse.*"

Sometimes you don't realize your mother has taken your stuff until it's too late. It's three o'clock in the morning, and your sexually explicit material is gone, just when you need it most. So you have to search the whole house for *anything* with a picture of a woman on it.

Pretty soon you're at the pantry, staring at a box of Aunt Jemima.

Get the box down. Look at her. Now she's looking at you. Your imagination kicks into gear and Aunt Jemima starts looking real good. She's young now. She takes that rag off her head, her hair touches the ground. Her big buttermilk breasts are hanging; she's got a big fat ass. And she starts talking to you in a real sexy voice.

"Come on, baby, let your auntie suck it. Come on, baby, put some syrup on that bad boy."

But right when you're ready to explode, Uncle Ben jumps off his box and says, "Leave her alone. That's my woman."

SUPERMARKET SWEEPSTAKES

I see inequality everywhere. For instance, ever notice how every city has two malls? The white mall, and the mall the white people *used* to go to. *That* mall must be something awful to actually *keep* white people from going.

"It's too black in here."

White people like black people the way the way they like their seasoning: Just a dash.

I hate the black mall. There is nothing in the black mall but sneakers and baby clothes. I guess that's all they think we're doing: running and fucking. Fifteen sneaker stores: Footlocker, Athlete's Foot, Foot in Your Ass. In the white mall they have big-ass stores. Valet parking. Personal shoppers.

In the black mall, there's no Macy's, no Saks. Just an eight-story Woolworth with personal shoppers who say, "Can I help you with your *cheap shit?*

Yet these days all you hear is, "Gotta shop black. Keep it in the community." It's easy to shop black if all you want is a pack of potato chips.

The only thing worse than the black mall is the black market. Forget the word "super." Hell, I don't even know why they've got the word "market" in there. When I was a kid my mother used to drive an hour to get food and I never knew why, until I grew up.

White people have nice supermarkets. Inviting supermarkets. In the white supermarket, the nice doors slide open, you step in, and a cool breeze hits your face. It's lovely. The whole place says, "Come on in."

All the white people reading this book: next time you go to the market, kiss your grocer.

In the black supermarket the doors are always fucked up. You have to jump on the electric pad two or three times to get them open. Now and then the doors will hit back and smack you in the head. It's almost as if they know you're broke. When you get in, a hot, hot breeze hits you in the face and the place is dark. Half the lights don't work. Some markets don't even have lights—only skylights. When the sun goes down, the supermarket is closed.

There's nothing fresh in a black supermarket, unless you count "fresh from the can." There's no red meat. The meat is brown. And if you do get some red meat, you better cook it *that* day because it's gonna be spoiled tomorrow. You'll wake up and locusts will be having a convention on the meat—and all because you wanted to shop black.

All the fruits are nasty, too. Flies circle around the fruit and even the flies aren't new. Sometimes the grocer sticks in plastic fruit to try and fool you— and the flies. If you can get an apple, it's got a worm in it.

And the worm is dead.

WHY DO YOU THINK THEY CALL IT "SCHOOL"?

Sometimes I think I need to go back to school. But the problem is that if you're black, you get more respect for going to jail than for going to school. You come out of jail and you're the fucking *man.* You come out of school, nobody cares.

"Hey, I just graduated from high school."

"So what, ya punk-ass bitch. Don't come around with all that reading and shit. Don't come around with all that counting and shit. I can count too: one, two, four, five, nine . . . so what?"

You could have a master's degree. Niggers don't care.

"I got my master's."

"What? You my master now? I'm supposed to listen to your punk ass? Fuck you, nigger. So what if you got your master's degree? You the smarty-ass nigger? So, let me ask you this: Can you kick *my* ass?"

I dropped out of school. Sorry. I guess I'm not the best role model. Later, I got a G.E.D. You know what G.E.D. stands for? Good-Enough Diploma. A G.E.D. is bullshit, I don't get it. You mean I can make up four years in six hours? When you get a G.E.D., someone always has the nerve to say, "*Now you can go to college.*"

Hey, you can't go to a *real* college with a G.E.D. The only place that will take you is a community college. You know why they call it community college? Because it's like a disco with books. Anybody in the community can go: Crackheads, prostitutes, drug dealers. "Come on in!"

*

I once took a black history class. I figured since I'm black I already knew everything. I figured I'd pass just by showing up.

Failed it.

Isn't that sad, a black man failing black history? But I didn't know anything about Africa. When you go to white schools you learn about Europe up the ass, but you don't learn that much about Africa. The only thing I know about Africa is that it's far, far away. A 35-hour flight. Imagine the boat ride. The boat ride's so long there's still slaves on their way here.

All I learned in school about being black was Martin Luther King. That's all they ever teach. Martin Luther King. He was the answer to everything.

TEACHER: What's the capital of Zaire?

ME: Martin Luther King.

TEACHER: Tell us the name of the woman who would not give up her seat on the bus.

ME: Oh, that's hard. Are ya sure it was a woman? Okay, I got it, Mar*tina* Luther King.

You know what's sad? Martin Luther King stood for nonviolence. Now that he's dead he stands for a holiday and a street. Martin Luther King Boulevard. No matter where you are in America, you'll find one. And you can be certain that if you're on Martin Luther King Boulevard, there's some violence going down. It isn't the safest place to be. You can't call anybody and say you're lost on MLK.

"I'm lost on Martin Luther King."

"Run! Run! Run! The media's out there!"

Sad, sad, sad!

*

A few states still don't celebrate MLK's birthday. Others celebrate but don't let you get off work. But federal employees get off—*including prisoners*. Even James Earl Ray, the man we convicted of killing MLK, gets the day off. Of course, he's so crazy he probably walks around prison thinking, "Hey, everybody's off today and nobody even bothered to thank me."

One way you can tell MLK's birthday is now a real holiday is that it's become a good reason for stores to have sales: furniture sales, clothing sales, white sales. They're even using his speeches in advertisements.

"I had a dream I could get an ice-cold Coca-Cola."

"Here at Bay Ridge Toyota, Toyotas are almost free . . . at last. Free at last."

MONEY MONEY MONEY MONEY

You know what racism is *really* about?

Money.

Everybody thinks the next man's got more than they do.

"They got too much shit."

"No, they got *all* the shit!"

"Wait! They got *our* shit!"

White people are mad because they think they're losing everything. Blacks just think everyone else has too much shit.

BLACK MAN: Y'all ain't losing shit. You all still own everything. Just go check. See?

WHITE MAN: Oh, wow. You're right. We *still* own everything.

If there's one thing that scares white people more than black people, it's *poor* white people.

I've seen white people living in the projects. They've been there so long that their white friends don't even visit them anymore. You can tell because their little white kids have black nicknames, like Mookie. But it's all right when white people live in a black neighborhood. It's no big thing. We don't mind. We'll call you a name for about two days, but about the third day, you're cool. We'll give you love.

"Hey, White Bob. You want to play some ball?"

The trouble is that there are lots of broke white people now. I've seen white people so poor that they don't live in a trailer home—they live under it. The people who live *in* the trailer look down and say, "How you doing? Here's your mail." These people aren't white trash, they're white toxic waste. They're a bunch of Shaggy-looking people from *Scooby-Doo*—eating mayonnaise sandwiches, fucking their sisters, listening to John Cougar Mellencamp records.

And they're mad. They think they're broke because the black people took it all away. Not true. They're broke because they have a third-grade education and a tooth coming out of their ear. But if they see a black man who's a lawyer, they go, "How'd that nigger get that job?"

He went to school, Toothy.

If people want to get their due, they have to work for it. But there are white people who think they should get theirs just because they're white.

"White? That's twenty-five thousand a year, right? At the very least. What's happened to this country?"

White people aren't used to being broke. White people go broke and it's scary. They start crying. They call the news. Next thing they're on "60 Minutes" and "20/20."

WHITE PERSON: I can't believe what's happening to us. We're Americans and we want a congressional investigation to get down to the bottom of this. My father came here on the fucking *Mayflower* and we want justice!

What do we have to do—hold a telethon for broke white people?

There's nothing scarier than a broke white man. The broker they are, the madder they are. That's when white people start forming groups and blowing up shit. Freemen. Aryan Nation. Klan. Poor, pissed-off white people are the biggest threat to the security of this country. Look at what happened in Waco, Texas. Look at the Freemen of Montana, and the Unabomber. Look at the Oklahoma City bombing. Who did it? Some broke white man so poor he had to make his bomb out of cow shit.

As a black man—as someone who's been poor—let me offer you hate group guys a few sincere words of guidance.

Things can get better. So cut out the shit!

*

Broke-ass white people have it bad. I'll bet you a set of black satin sheets that 80 percent of the Ku Klux Klan makes less than $13,000 a year. No wonder they hate black people, especially those who have any money. There's nothing a white guy with a penny hates more than a nigger with a nickel.

But to watch the news or read the paper, you might think the welfare rolls are crammed only with black folks. This whole welfare controversy makes it sound like black people just don't want to work.

If I'm not mistaken, didn't black people work 200 years **for free?** They worked really hard, too. No breaks, no time off. Slaves didn't get vacations. Where could they possibly go?

SLAVE #1:   Massa gave me a vacation.

SLAVE #2:   Massa gave me one, too. Where you gonna go?

SLAVE #1:   'Round back. Where you gonna go?

SLAVE #2:   To the well. You should bring your kids. It's nice over there.

Forget vacations. In all those slave movies, I'll bet you never saw a couple slaves kick back and one say to the other, "Hey, how's the cotton treating you?"

*

Slavery *had* an up side, though.

In the old days, even if they were poor, at least white people had slavery to make them feel exalted.

If there was one person in your life whose ass you could beat when you felt like shit, do you know how happy you would be? You could keep them locked in a room. Then, when you got frustrated, you could stick your head in and say, "Fuck you!" When you were mad, you could go in there and kick them. Horny? That's right, you could mosey in there and fuck them.

Then you could be nice to everybody else.

It was the same with segregation. It made things cool for white people.

No matter how fucked up your life was, no matter how broke and dirty your house was, no matter how ignorant you were, couldn't read, couldn't count, fucking your sister, no matter how sorry and pathetic your future looked—you could rest your head on the pillow every night thinking, "I'm living better than a nigger."

White people had that.

White people lost that.

Yes, yes. Times have changed.

Segregation kept the white man in check. But black people have some money now. We have as much money as broke white people. We're coming up. Now broke black people live right next door to broke white people, and the white people don't know what the hell's going on.

They're wondering, "Oh shit. There's a lot of niggers out here. Am I becoming a nigger?"

*

What's really sad now is that *everybody's* broke. Black people *and* white people. Of course, black people are used to being broke.

"You broke. I'm broke. Fuck it, let's hang out."

I don't want to be broke, even though in some ways it's cool because you know who your friends are. If you're broke and someone wants to hang out with you, they *really* want to hang out with you. If you're broke and in a relationship and somebody loves you, that person *loves* you.

Anybody can love you when you're rich.

Yeah, it's tough being a white person these days.

But not that tough. I am absolutely certain.

Why? Because there's not a white person reading this book who would change places with me.

And I'm rich!

Come on. Change places with me.

See? Even you white guys making minimum wage are going, "Uh uh. I'm going to roll these white dice and ride this white thing out a *little* longer. See where it takes me."

ME: But you get a big house.

WHITE GUY: Oh, that's okay. I'll stay in my shoe box.

And that's all you need to know about the racial divide.

AUTHORS AND COMEDIANS

Eddie "Rochester" Anderson (1906–1977)—Anderson was one of the most successful black comic actors in the mid-twentieth century. His parents were minstrel performers, and he began his stage career as a song and dance man in small-time vaudeville theaters during his teens. In 1937, he was featured as Noah in the Hollywood black-cast film *Green Pastures,* and later rocketed to fame as Jack Benny's irreverent gravel-voiced valet on the Jack Benny radio show. He co-starred with Lena Horne in another big-budget black-cast film, *Cabin in the Sky* (1943), and had supporting roles in numerous Hollywood features, including three with Jack Benny. He also appeared on Benny's television show in the 1950s.

Willie Best (1915–1962)—Recruited on the streets of Watts by a Hollywood studio agent who noticed his resemblance to Stepin Fetchit, Best, often billed as "Sleep 'n' Eat," appeared in a series of comic films during the 1930s and '40s. His movies credits included *The Littlest Rebel* (1935), *Thank You Jeeves* (1936), *The Smiling Ghost* (1941), *Cabin in the Sky* (1943), and *Suddenly It's Spring* (1947). The actor later had continuing supporting TV roles on *The Stu Erwin Show* and *My Little Margie.*

David Bradley (1950–   )—Bradley was born in Bedford, Pennsylvania, and was for many years an English professor at Temple University in Philadelphia. *South Street* (1975), his first novel, was a tragicomic tale of a neighborhood in transition set on the streets of Philly and highlighted by vivid depictions of the area's colorful characters and their unconventional attitudes. He won the Pen/Faulkner Award for his second novel, *The Chaneysville Incident,* in 1981.

Cecil Brown (1943–   )–*The Loves and Lives of Mr. Jiveass Nigger* (1969), Brown's first novel, was a picaresque bildungsroman that charted the lustful exploits of the trickster hero George Washington in America and Europe. The author is also a screenwriter whose credits include *Which Way Is Up?* (1977)–co-written with Richard Pryor–and has taught at Berkeley University. Born in Bolton, North Carolina, Brown's books include a second novel, *Days Without Weather* (1983), and *Coming Up Down Home: A Memoir of a Southern Childhood* (1993).

Butterbeans and Susie [Jodie (1895–1967) and Susie Edwards (1896–1963)]– Butterbeans and Susie began their show business careers in a pickaninny act in the Moss Brothers Carnival in 1910. By the 1920s, they were the hottest husband and wife team on the black theatrical circuit. They carried on the tradition of dance, song, signifying, heckling, suggestive banter, and mock anger established by predecessors who had originated lines like, "When I start after you, you'll run so fast you'll cut out a new street." As with most husband-wife teams, the insults and heckling were all in fun; married in 1916, they remained together until Susie's death and were among the most beloved acts on the black circuit.

Godfrey Cambridge (1933–1978)–In 1956, Cambridge left college to pursue an acting career on the Broadway stage. His early credits included *Detective Story, The Blacks* (for which he won an Obie), and *Purlie Victorious.* He also established himself as a fine screen actor, appearing in the film version of *Purlie* as well as Melvin Van Peebles's *Watermelon Man* and Ossie Davis's *Cotton Comes to Harlem.* His standup comedy career took off after his first comedy album, *Ready Or Not, Here's Godfrey Cambridge,* was released and reached the top-five on the charts in 1965. He was one of the most popular comics in America during the late 1960s and early '70s. His career was cut short when he died of a heart attack while filming *Victory at Entebbe* in 1978.

Charles Waddell Chesnutt (1858–1932)–Born in Cleveland, Ohio, of free parents, Chesnutt was exposed to the dialect speech and characters that were central to his fiction after his family moved to Fayetteville, North Carolina, in 1866. In his early twenties as a self-taught scholar, he returned to Cleveland and, after passing the bar, established a practice in legal stenography and law. He also had stories accepted by *Atlantic Monthly* in the late 1800s and, in 1899, two volumes of his stories–*The Conjure Woman* and

The Wife of His Youth—were published by Houghton Mifflin. Chesnutt went on to write several novels, but his short stories are generally considered his best work. He was one of the few black writers of his era to make humor a prominent part of his fiction and was particularly effective at reversing the popular use of black dialect to demonstrate characters' ingenuity rather than confirming their ignorance.

James David Corrothers (1869–1919)—A minister and poet, Corrothers was born in Cass County, Michigan, and published many of his poems in *The Century Magazine.*

Paul Laurence Dunbar (1872–1906)—The precocious son of former slaves, Dunbar was one of America's most popular poets at the beginning of the twentieth century. After graduating from high school in his native Dayton, Ohio, he worked as an elevator operator while writing his first volume of poetry, *Oak and Ivy.* It was published in 1895 and, before his untimely death, Dunbar produced five more poetry collections, four novels, and four collections of short stories. *The Strength of Gideon,* from which the selection in this anthology appeared, is generally considered his best fictional work.

Ralph Ellison (1914–1994)—The 1952 National Book Award winning author of *Invisible Man* was born in Oklahoma City, Oklahoma, and studied music at Tuskegee Institute before moving to New York City in 1936. In 1965, in a poll of writers and critics, his acclaimed first novel was selected as "the most distinguished single work" written in the United States. Ellison's books include the essay collections *Shadow and Act* and *Going to the Territory,* and the posthumously published second novel *Juneteenth.* The selection appearing in this collection was edited out of the latter before its publication in 1999.

Stepin Fetchit (1902–1985)—Born with the unlikely name Lincoln Theodore Monroe Andrew Perry in Key West, Florida, Stepin Fetchit began his entertainment career in a traveling plantation show and became part of a comedy-dance duo called Step 'n' Fetchit. The actor kept the name when he appeared in the 1927 silent film *In Old Kentucky.* He received rave reviews and, after his appearance in the early talkie *Hearts in Dixie* in 1929, was signed to a long-term contract with Fox. As the self-proclaimed "first black movie star," he went on to appear in dozens of films during the 1930s, nearly always portraying the shuffling, mumbling, shiftless darky. His popularity waned in the 1940s, and by the 1960s he had become a virtual outcast. Still, he resurfaced as a friend of Flip Wilson and part of Muhammad Ali's entourage. He appeared in *Amazing Grace* in 1974, several years before the stroke that ended his career.

Rudolph Fisher (1897–1934)—As a graduate student, Fisher came to New York in 1927 to study medicine at Columbia University and pursue a career as a doctor, but became one of the Harlem Renaissance's finest satirical writers. In his short fiction and two novels—*The Walls of Jericho* (1928) and *The Conjure-Man Dies* (1932), the first published detective novel by an African American writer—he humorously explored many of the contradictions that arose in a Harlem community which, although rife with poverty, had become the Mecca of the New Negro and black cultural revolution. His first novel offered a panorama of Harlem life, from street folks to community leaders and the literati ("The Litter Rats"). He is widely recognized as the "first Negro to write social comedy."

Clinton "Dusty" Fletcher (c. 1900–1954)—The Des Moines, Iowa, native began his show business career in tent shows and carnivals as a teenager. He claimed to have originated the famous "Open the Door, Richard" routine in the mid-1920s and it was his signature act throughout his career. Fletcher appeared in dozens of so-called "race movies" with legendary comics like Moms Mabley, and was a regular on the Theater Owners Booking Association (TOBA) tour as well as a member of the ensemble cast that performed comedy sketches at the Apollo Theater.

Redd Foxx (1922–1991)—Born John Elroy Sanford in St. Louis, Missouri, Foxx was known as the king of blue comedy before the hit TV series *Sanford and Son* (1972–1977) made him a national celebrity. The actor and comedian changed his name in the early 1940s after moving to New York, where he sang with a small band. He turned to comedy in the late 1940s and for a time teamed with Slappy White. They parted in the 1950s, and Foxx began to develop the provocative single act that inspired his blue party records. He reportedly sold more than fifteen million copies of his fifty-four albums. Guest spots on TV and regular appearances in Las Vegas brought mainstream recognition and the attention of producer Norman Lear, who cast him as Fred Sanford, the crafty Watts junk dealer who took America by storm. After *Sanford,* Foxx starred in several other TV projects and remained a huge draw in Las Vegas. His movie credits included *Cotton*

Comes to Harlem (1970) and *Harlem Nights* (1989). He died of a heart attack on the set while taping *The Royal Family,* a new sitcom.

Dick Gregory (1932–   )–As one of the pioneer black standup comics who brought racial and social commentary to mainstream integrated clubs, Gregory helped transform the image of African American comedians in show business. Born in St. Louis, Missouri, Gregory attended college for two years before joining the U.S. Army in 1954. He moved to Chicago after leaving the service and began performing in small clubs as a comic. His break came when he was called as a last minute replacement for another act at the Playboy Club in 1961. He received rave reviews and, within a year, became a national celebrity. A 1962 *Newsweek* article proclaimed: "From the moment he was booked into the Playboy Club . . . Jim Crow was dead in the joke world." He left the night club circuit in 1967, but continued lecturing on the college circuit and is a frequent guest and moderator on TV and radio talk shows. He is also the author of over a dozen books, including the 1965 autobiography, *Nigger.*

Oliver W. Harrington (1912–1995)–Born in Valhalla, New York, Harrington graduated from the Yale School of Fine Arts and began publishing cartoons in black newspapers during the 1920s. He gained national recognition after the cartoon panel "Dark Laughter," which featured the popular character Bootsie, appeared in *The Amsterdam News* in 1935. Langston Hughes called him "America's greatest black cartoonist." An outspoken critic of America's racial policies, he came under fire during the McCarthy era. He moved to Paris in 1951, then to Germany, where he continued publishing his work in European newspapers and magazines until his death.

Joel Chandler Harris (1848–1908)–Harris was born in Eatonton, Georgia, and at age thirteen became an apprentice printer on a local newspaper. He later worked for *The Savannah Morning News* as a printer and began dabbling with writing. In his late twenties, he moved to Atlanta and began writing for *The Atlanta Constitution,* where the tales he had gleaned from Georgia slaves in his youth were first published. When they appeared in book form in 1881, Harris quickly became a national celebrity.

Chester Himes (1909–1984)–Himes was a prisoner in the Ohio State Penitentiary when he published his first story in *Esquire* in 1932. After his release, he moved to Los Angeles and, in 1945, published the novel *If He*

Hollers Let Him Go. A second novel, *Lonely Crusade,* followed in 1947. Angered by the lukewarm mainstream critical response to those "serious" naturalistic works, he moved to Europe in the late 1940s and spent most of his remaining years in France and Spain. He continued writing, but turned to the detective story genre, which he had explored while imprisoned, and produced a series of satiric novels set in Harlem and laced with comedy and vivid descriptions of ghetto life. *Pinktoes* (1961), *Cotton Comes to Harlem* (1966), and *Blind Man with a Pistol* (1969), a selection from which appears in this collection, are among his novels.

Langston Hughes (1902–1967)—A poet, playwright, novelist, and one of America's most accomplished humorists, Hughes grew up in Cleveland, Ohio, and, after graduating from Lincoln University, published the first of his ten volumes of poetry, *The Weary Blues,* in 1926. It was in his novel *Not Without Laughter* (1930), one critic claimed, "that the comedy of the [Harlem] Renaissance reached its apogee." But the Jesse B. Simple stories (first published in his *Chicago Defender* column in 1943) represented his "finest works of humor." Hughes was also the author of the short story collection, *The Ways of White Folks* (1934), and two autobiographies, *The Big Sea* (1940) and *I Wonder as I Wander* (1956). In 1960 he received the Spingarn Medal as "Poet Laureate of the Negro Race."

Zora Neale Hurston (1907–1960)—Born in Eatonville, Florida, Hurston moved to New York City in 1927 and received a B.A. from Barnard College before studying folklore with Franz Boas at Columbia University. She was among the most versatile and vocal of the Harlem Renaissance writers. In addition to her folklore classic *Mules and Men* (1935), she was the author of four novels—including *Jonah's Gourd Vine* (1934) and *Their Eyes Were Watching God* (1937)—the autobiography, *Dust Tracks on a Road* (1942), and four plays, including *Mule Bone* (1930), which was written with Langston Hughes and staged at Lincoln Center in the 1990s. Hurston was also a credible comic stage performer whose credits included an off-Broadway play that starred Moms Mabley.

Charles Johnson (1948–   )—Johnson, the Pollock Professor of Humanities at the University of Washington, is among the most influential contemporary African American novelists. He turned to writing after beginning a career in the visual arts and publishing two collections of editorial cartoons, *Black Humor* (1970) and *Half-Past Nation Time* (1971). *Faith and* *the Good Thing,* his first novel, was published in 1974 and he has subsequently published five other books. They include the 1990 National Book Award winning novel *Middle Passage* and the 1998 historical novel *Dreamer,* which explored the life of Martin Luther King, Jr. Johnson was also a recipient of the prestigious MacArthur Foundation award in 1998.

Martin Lawrence (1965–   )—Lawrence grew up in Landover, Maryland, and began performing at local comedy clubs as a teenager. An appearance on *Star Search* in 1987 caught the eye of Columbia Pictures executives, and he was offered a role in the sitcom *What's Happening Now!* He appeared in Spike Lee's *Do the Right Thing* in 1989 and starred in an HBO comedy special in 1990. His hit TV sitcom, *Martin,* debuted in 1992, and he hosted Russell Simmons' *Def Comedy Jam* on HBO from 1992 to 1993. With release of the concert film *You So Crazy* in 1994, Lawrence not only established himself at the forefront of the nineties' new breed of brash, uncensored comics but also became one of Hollywood's biggest box-office draws. His film credits include *Bad Boys* (1995), *A Thin Line Between Love and Hate* (1996), *Blue Streak* (1999), and *What's the Worst That Can Happen?* (2001).

Leighann Lord (1967–   )—A native New Yorker, Ms. Lord is a stand-up comedian, writer, and actress. She graduated magna cum laude from Baruch College, City University of New York, with a B.A. degree in Journalism and Creative Writing. She performs throughout the country at colleges and universities, and has appeared on many television shows (including Lifetime's *Girls Night Out,* HBO's *Def Comedy All-Star Jam,* and Comedy Central's *Premium Blend 2*). She was named the official comedian for Harlem Week in 1993 and 1994, and won the New York City Black Comedy Award for "The Most Thought-Provoking Female Comic" in 1994. Her one-woman show, *The Full Swanky,* earned her a Best Actress award from The Riant Theater Women's Play Festival and an AUDELCO award nomination for Best Solo Performance.

Thelma "Butterfly" McQueen (1911–1995)—McQueen joined an amateur stage company when she and her mother moved from Tampa, Florida, to New York City around 1930. She began her career as a stage actress in the mid-1930s and gained national recognition in her first film role as Prissy in *Gone With the Wind* (1939). Her high-pitched voice and quirky, childlike demeanor on camera made her an instant favorite. During the 1940s she had supporting roles in such Hollywood films as *Affectionately Yours*

(1941), *Cabin in the Sky* (1943), and *Duel in the Sun* (1947), and appeared later in *The Phynx* (1970) and *Amazing Grace* (1974). She also appeared in independently produced "race" films like *Killer Diller* (1948) and, as Oriole, was a regular on television's short-lived *Beulah* during the early 1950s.

Jackie "Moms" Mabley (1897–1975)–"Moms" was born in Brevard, North Carolina, as Loretta Mary Aiken and moved to Cleveland as a teenager. By age sixteen, she had begun a show business career. She started as a dancer and singer on the TOBA circuit, and, with the support and assistance of Butterbeans and Susie, began appearing in blackface comedy skits. In the late 1920s, she adopted the stage guise of an older woman and began wearing the baggy gingham dresses, oversized clodhoppers, and oddball hats that remained her signature costume. She occasionally abandoned the guise and appeared in off-Broadway stage productions and had a small part in the film *The Emperor Jones* (1933). But comedy was her mainstay. Billing herself as "Moms," she became one of the first black comics to use monologue humor. Like Dick Gregory, a 1960s appearance at the Playboy Club provided mainstream recognition. "Moms" recorded over twenty albums and, by the end of her career, had become a frequent guest on TV talk shows and a headliner at night clubs and theaters like the Apollo.

Dewey "Pigmeat" Markham (1906–1981)–In 1917, Markham joined a minstrel company, performing at tent shows, carnivals, and TOBA theaters for two decades before becoming a headliner and legend at the Apollo Theater. The name "Pigmeat" came from a character in a black circuit comedy skit (Sweet Papa Pigmeat) in which the comic was featured while with the Gonzelle White vaudeville troop in the 1920s. His Broadway stage credits included *Hot Rhythm* (1930) and *Cocktails* (1932). During the 1940s and early 1950s, Markham was featured in a series of independent black films—including *Shut My Big Mouth, One Big Mistake,* and *Fight That Ghost.* He appeared on Ed Sullivan's TV variety show on numerous occasions and had guest spots on *The Tonight Show* and *The Merv Griffin Show.* In the 1960s, after Sammy Davis, Jr., and Flip Wilson reprised his "Here Come the Judge" routine on *Rowan and Martin's Laugh-In,* his career was briefly revitalized.

Miller and Lyles–Flournoy Miller (1887–1971) and Aubrey Lyles (1885–1932) began their careers as playwrights in Chicago around 1912, and would later write *Shuffle Along,* which in 1922 became the first all-black musical to appear on Broadway. They also starred in two early movies, *Jimtown Speakeasy* and *The Mayor of Jimtown* (both 1929) that were loosely based on that musical. Their writing and performances were extremely influential in the transition of African American stage humor in the early twentieth century. Two black characters that they created—a fast-talking city slicker and a naïve, bumbling underdog—according to some, were prototypes for Amos and Andy on radio and television. On stage, their act was highlighted by what they called "mutilatin' the language" ("You gotta be repaired for dat" or "I'se regusted") and classic comic routines like their "Multiplyin' and Mulsifyin'" and "Indefinite Talk" bits, which were popular favorites on the black theater circuit until the 1950s. After Lyles died, Miller continued as a performer and writer. On stage he often appeared with Mantan Moreland and Johnny Lee (who played Calhoun on the *Amos 'n' Andy* TV show) and was featured with the latter in the black cast film *Stormy Weather* (1943). Miller was also a writer for the *Amos 'n' Andy Show.*

Paul Mooney (19??–   )—The West Coast-based writer and comic has written for Redd Foxx, Richard Pryor, and Eddie Murphy, as well as for TV shows including *Sanford and Son, The Flip Wilson Show, In Living Color,* and *Saturday Night Live.* In the 1980s, he emerged as an scathing satiric standup comedian. A headline act at comedy clubs nationwide, he has appeared on HBO's *Def Comedy Jam* and BET's *ComicView* and has released two comedy albums, *Race* (1993) and *Master Piece* (1997).

Tim Moore (1888–1958)—At age twelve Moore left his Rock Island, Illinois, home to join Dr. Mick's Traveling Medicine Show and soon won a part as one of the original "Gold Dust Twins." After less than a decade, he left show business to become a boxer and jockey. He returned to the stage in the mid-1920s with a one-man version of *Uncle Tom's Cabin,* playing the roles of both Simon Legree and Tom. A featured comic role in Lew Leslie's *Blackbirds of 1928* was followed by parts in other Broadway shows in the 1930s and '40s. Moore also worked the black theater circuit and appeared in a dozen or so independently produced "race" films (including Oscar Micheaux's *Darktown Revue*) during that time. Moore received some national exposure as a guest on Ed Sullivan's *Toast of the Town* in the late 1940s, but it was his role as Kingfish in the controversial sitcom *Amos 'n' Andy* (1951–53) that cemented his status as a comic superstar.

Mantan Moreland (1901–1973)—Perhaps best known for his role as the chauffeur, Birmingham Brown, in the Charlie Chan film series, Moreland was a ubiquitous presence on screen from the 1930s to the '50s. He joined a circus in 1915 and toured with a minstrel troupe before appearing in such shows as *Connie's Inn Follies of 1927* and *Blackbirds of 1928, 1930,* and *1932.* After his film debut in *That's the Spirit* (1932), Moreland went on to appear in over three hundred Hollywood and all-black race movies. His wide bubble eyes, quick double takes, seemingly elastic face, and superb timing made him one of the era's most durable and arresting screen comics. Moreland was also a favorite on the TOBA circuit, appearing as a single or teaming with comics like Flournoy Miller, Tim Moore, Redd Foxx, Moms Mabley, and Nipsey Russell. Near the end of his career, he was a guest on numerous sitcoms, including *Love, American Style* and *The Bill Cosby Show.* His last appearance in films was Melvin Van Peebles's *Watermelon Man* (1970).

Leroy "Satchel" Paige (1904–1982)—The colorful Negro League and Major League baseball pitcher was noted nearly as much for his wry comments, eccentric behavior, and celebrity status off the field as he was for his amazing career as a professional baseball player. Paige, who is said to have pitched over 2,500 games during his nearly thirty-year career, left the Negro League to sign with the Cleveland Indians in 1948. He was inducted into the Baseball Hall of Fame in 1971.

Richard Pryor (1940–   )—Born in Peoria, Illinois, Pryor had spent two years in the army and bounced around the black night club circuit in the Midwest for a few years before arriving in New York, determined to make it as a comedy star, in 1963. Doing what he called "white bread humor," his career quickly took off, and, by the mid-1960s, he was being touted as a "rising young star." In the late '60s, however, Pryor shifted his comic approach, turning to characters and stories that reflected unique aspects of black culture, including street types (hustlers, prostitutes, con men, etc.) who authentically mirrored the bottom rung of ghetto life. After a short hiatus in Berkeley, California, his comedy act was totally revamped. His revised approach (called "reality theater" by *Rolling Stone*) was revolutionary. His work in films and on stage and records during the 1970s led to critical acclaim as a comic genius and, after the release of the 1979 concert film, *Richard Pryor Live in Concert,* he was recognized as the nation's premier funnyman. He is "the most brilliant comic in America," the playwright Neil

Simon said. "There's no one funnier or more perceptive." Pryor's recordings include, *Craps (After Hours)* (1971), *That Nigger's Crazy* (1974), *Bicentennial Nigger* (1976), and *Wanted* (1978)—all of which are now included in a boxed CD set. His film credits include *Lady Sings the Blues* (1972), *Silver Streak* (1976), *Which Way Is Up* (1977), *Blue Collar* and *The Wiz* (1978), *Some Kind of Hero* (1982), *Richard Pryor . . . Here and Now* (1983), and *Critical Condition* (1987).

Ishmael Reed (1938–   )—The Chattanooga, Tennessee, born author emerged on the literary scene in the late 1960s at the height of a Black Arts Movement that advocated realistic, social protest fiction and a narrowly defined black aesthetic. His unconventional narrative approach, freewheeling satiric and comedic style, and brash lampooning of Western culture established him as a maverick and innovator from the start. "Let the social realists go after the flatfoots out there on the beat," he announced, "we'll go after the Pope and see which action causes a revolution." Reed's novels include *The Free-Lance Pallbearer* (1967), *Yellow Back Radio Broke-Down* (1969), *Mumbo Jumbo* (1973), and *Reckless Eyeballing* (1989). Other books include the essay collections *Writin' Is Fightin'* (1990) and *Airing Dirty Laundry* (1993) and the poetry collections *Conjure: Selected Poems* (1972) and *Chattanooga* (1974). *Conjure* was nominated for both the Pulitzer Prize and the National Book Award.

Chris Rock (1966–   )—Rock, who was born in South Carolina and reared in Brooklyn, New York, began his standup comedy career as a teenager in the mid-1980s. In 1987, he appeared in *Uptown Comedy Express* with a group of more seasoned comedians and, in 1990, joined the *Saturday Night Live* cast. He left *SNL* in 1993, appearing briefly on *In Living Color* and producing *CD4,* a cinema parody of gangsta rap. During the mid-1990s, he attracted national attention as the voice of "Little Penny" Hardaway on Nike's sneaker commercials and as a Comedy Central political correspondent at the Republican National Convention. The release of his 1996 HBO comedy special *Bring the Pain* cemented his place as one of America's top comedians. He won an Emmy in 1997 for *Bring the Pain* and a Grammy for the CD, *Roll With the New.* His HBO comedy show, *The Chris Rock Show* (1997–2000) won a Cable Ace Award in 1997 as well. That same year, a Los Angeles Times critic hailed him as the "smartest, most dangerous, most fearless comic working in America." Rock's film credits include *New Jack City* (1991), *Boomerang* (1992), *Lethal Weapon 4* (1998), and *Pootie Tang* (2001).

Nipsey Russell (1924–   )–Russell began in show business at age 6, singing, dancing, and acting as emcee for a children's troupe in his home-town, Atlanta, Georgia. He attended the University of Cincinnati and, after serving in the army during World War II, returned to earn a B.A. in English in 1946. During the late 1940s and early '50s, he worked black circuit clubs in the Midwest and East Coast and was eventually booked at the Apollo Theater and Catskills' resort hotels like the Concorde. A 1959 appearance on Jack Paar's *Tonight Show* led to a supporting role on the 1961 sitcom *Car 54, Where Are You?,* and regular guest spots on TV talk and game shows, where his witty one-liners and impromptu limericks earned him the title of "Poet Laureate of Comedy." His movie credits include *The Wiz* (1978), in which he played the Tin Man and received rave reviews.

George Schuyler (1895–1977)–Born in Providence, Rhode Island, Schuyler spent eight years in the army and worked as a civil service clerk before turn-ing to writing in the early 1920s. He began as a staff writer for *The Messen-ger* in 1923 and was a columnist for the black newspaper *The Pittsburgh Courier* from 1924 until the mid-1940s. He was also a frequent contributor to the H. L. Mencken–edited *American Mercury* magazine. Although better known as a journalist and critic, Schuyler was the author of two novels, *Slaves Today* and *Black No More,* both published in 1931. The selection ex-cerpted in this collection was taken from the latter, a social satire that lam-pooned racial bigotry, greed, the myth of the color line, and false race pride.

Ntozake Shange (1948–   )–The poet, playwright, and novelist was swept into the national spotlight after the opening of the off-Broadway produc-tion of *for colored girls who have considered suicide when the rainbow is enuf,* which won an Obie Award in 1976. She also won an Obie for *Mother Courage and Her Children* in 1980. Shange was born Paulette Williams in Trenton, New Jersey, and while living in St. Louis was among the first black students to attend integrated schools in Missouri. She returned to New Jer-sey to finish high school and graduated from Barnard College before re-ceiving an M.A. at the University of Southern California. Her fiction and poetry includes *Nappy Edges* (1978), *Sassafrass, Cypress, and Indigo* (1982), *Betsy Brown* (1985), and *Ridin the Moon in Texas: Word Paintings* (1987).

Mel Watkins (1940–   ) is a former editor and writer for *The New York Times Book Review.* He is the author of *Dancing with Strangers,* a recollec-tion of growing up in Youngstown, Ohio, and attending Colgate University during the 1950s and '60s at the dawn of the civil rights movement. He is also author of *On the Real Side: A History of African American Comedy,* an analytical study of black humor. He frequently writes for major newspapers and magazines and has often appeared as a commentator on television documentaries about comedy and show business personalities.

Williams and Walker—Bert Williams (1876–1922) and George Walker (1873–1911) met in San Francisco in 1893 and began performing as a team in traveling shows. In 1896, they opened on Broadway as the "Two Real Coons" and soon became one of the most sought-after blackface specialty acts on the vaudeville circuit. Typically, in their stage act, Williams assumed the role of the shiftless darky and Walker played the fast-talking trickster or dandy. By the end of the decade, they also began producing and starring in their own musical comedies, which included *A Lucky Coon* (1898), *The Policy Players* (1900), *In Dahomey* (1902), and *Bandana Land* (1908). Walker became ill during the latter's run and retired to a convalescent home, where he died at the age of thirty-seven. At the end of the nineteenth and early twentieth centuries they were among America's most influential comedy/dance teams.

Bert Williams (1876–1922)—Born in the Bahamas, Williams grew up in Riverside, California, where he finished high school before starting in show business. After the death of his partner George Walker in 1911, Williams worked as a single act but maintained the stage guise of the shiftless darky. He added mime to his monologue humor, and from 1912 to his death was recognized as one of America's foremost comedians. His pioneer work as the nation's first black superstar entertainer broke barriers and eased the way for all who followed. His 1901 recordings with Walker were the first documented instance of blacks on phonograph records. He was the first black performer to star in a motion picture (*Fish* and *A Natural Born Gambler,* both in 1916), and when he died he was the highest paid performer in the Ziegfeld Follies. Booker T. Washington asserted that Williams did more for the Negro race than any other contemporary black, and Flo Ziegfeld wrote that he "was one the greatest comedians I ever employed. In fact, one of the greatest in the world."

Flip Wilson (1933–1998)—Born in Jersey City, New Jersey, Wilson grew up in foster homes before falsifying his age and joining the Air Force at sixteen. When discharged in 1954, he set out to become a comedian. After nearly a decade performing in small black clubs and theaters, he arrived in New York, where he frequently appeared at the Apollo as a comic and emcee. An appearance on *The Tonight Show* in 1965 accelerated his career, and in 1970, when his hit TV variety show debuted on NBC, he emerged as one of nation's most popular comedians. Wilson's comedy albums include *Cowboys and Colored People* (1967) and *Flip Wilson—You Devil You* (1968). He appeared in the 1974 film *Uptown Saturday Night* and, and after leaving TV with his variety show at the height of its popularity that same year, returned briefly in the short-lived 1985 sitcom *Charlie & Company*.

Charles Wright (1932–　　)—Born in New Franklin, Missouri, Charles Wright is the author of *The Messenger* (1963) and *The Wig* (1966), two of the most highly acclaimed satiric novels written in the 1960s. He was among the authors included in Langston Hughes's *Best Short Stories by Negro Writers* (1967) and, in 1973, published *Absolutely Nothing to Get Alarmed About,* an avant-garde work that combined fiction and personal journalism. "Of young black fictionists," one critic wrote, "Wright was one of the first to shatter old conventions, presenting the usual 'search for meaning' theme in a radical new form: imaginative literature and ultimately fantasy."

CREDITS

Adams, E.C.L.–"A Roost on the Rim of the Moon" from *Nigger to Nigger* (1928). Public domain.

Bradley, David–Selection from the novel *South Street* by David Bradley. Copyright © 1975 by David Bradley, Jr. Reprinted by permission of the Wendy Weil Agency, Inc.

Brown, Cecil–Selection from *The Loves and Lives of Mr. Jiveass Nigger* by Cecil Brown. Published by Farrar, Straus & Giroux and The Ecco Press. Copyright © 1969 by Cecil Brown. Reprinted by permission of Cecil Brown.

Chesnutt, Charles Waddell–"The Passing of Grandison" from *The Wife of His Youth and Other Stories* (1899). "The Conjurer's Revenge" from *The Conjure Woman* (1899). Public domain.

Corrothers, James David–"An Indignation Dinner" from *The Century Magazine,* circa 1900, reprinted in *The Book of American Negro Poetry* by James Weldon Johnson (1913). Public domain.

Courlander, Harold–"The Champion," "Old Master and Okra," "The Ducks Get the Cotton," "John Sharecrops for Old Boss," "John in Jail," "The Horsefly," and "John and the Blacksnake" from *A Treasury of Afro-American Folklore* by Harold Courlander. Copyright © 1976, 1996 by Harold Courlander. Appears by permission of the publisher, Marlowe & Company.

Dorson, Richard M.–"Baby in the Crib," "The Mojo," "The Yearling," "Old Marster Eats Crow," "The Fight," "Old Boss and John at the Praying Tree," "Talking Turtle," and "John Praying" from *American Negro Folktales* by Richard M. Dorson. Reprinted by permission of Susan Titus, Trustee of the Richard M. Dorson Trust.

Dunbar, Paul Laurence–"When Malindy Sings" from *The Complete Poems of Paul Laurence Dunbar* (1913). "The Fruitful Sleeping of the Rev. Elisha Edwards" from *The Strength of Gideon and Other Stories* (1900). Public domain.

Ellison, Ralph–"Cadillac Flambé" by Ralph Ellison Copyright © 1999 by Fanny Ellison. Reprinted by permission of William Morris Agency, Inc. on behalf of the author.

Fisher, Rudolph–Selection from *The Walls of Jericho* copyright © 1994 by the University of Michigan Press. Reprinted by permission of the University of Michigan Press. "The Conjure-Man Dies," public domain.

Foxx, Redd–Selections from the routines of Redd Foxx from recordings and notes taken at live performances. TM The Estate of Redd Foxx by CMG Worldwide Inc., Indianapolis, Indiana, 46256, www.cmgww.com; reprinted by permission.

Gordon, A. C.–"De Ole 'oman An' Me," circa 1900, public domain.

Gregory, Dick–"Black Rioters" and "American History" from the album *Dick Gregory: The Light Side; The Dark Side.* Copyright © 1969 by Dick Gregory. Reprinted by permission of Dick Gregory. Selection from *Nigger: An Autobiography* by Dick Gregory with Robert Lipsyte. Copyright © 1964 by Dick Gregory. Reprinted with the permission of Simon & Schuster.

Watkins, Mel—Selection from "The High-Wire Satire of Lenny Bruce and Richard Pryor" from *Common Quest Magazine,* Winter 1998. Copyright © 1998 by Mel Watkins. Reprinted with permission of the author.

Wepman, Dennis, Ronald B. Newman, and Murray B. Binderman—"Mexicano Rose" from *The Life: The Lore and Folk Poetry of the Black Hustler* by Dennis Wepman, Ronald B. Newman, Murray B. Binderman. Copyright © 1976 University of Pennsylvania Press. Reprinted with permission.

Williams, Bert—Selections from Bert Williams songs, jokes, and sayings from "Anecdotes, Jokes, Axioms, Proverbs, Funs and Puns compiled, some constructed, some re-constructed. All 'spade footed' for Bert Williams by Alex Rogers" (1918) at Schomburg Center for Research in Black Culture and "Bert Williams: Philosophical Tidbits Gleaned from His Songs and Stories," an unpublished Works Project Administration Research Paper by Lawrence Gellert, n.d. Public domain.

Wilson, Flip—"Cowboys & Colored People," "Kids," "Cheap Hotel," "Church on Sunday" and "Christopher Columbus" from the album *Cowboys & Colored People,* Copyright © 1967 Atlantic Recording Corp., and "Ugly Baby" from the album *Flip Wilson—You Devil You,* Copyright © 1968 Atlantic Recording Corp. reprinted by permission of the Flip Wilson Living Trust.

Wright, Charles—Selections from *The Wig,* copyright © 1966 by Charles Wright. We have made every effort to find the copyright holder for this material. If you have information regarding the copyright holder please contact Lawrence Hill Books, 814 N. Franklin St., Chicago, IL 60610.

INDEX